NATHAN SÖDERBLOM

Nathan Söderblom

Called to Serve

Jonas Jonson

Translated from Swedish by Norman A. Hjelm

William B. Eerdmans Publishing Company
Grand Rapids, Michigan

Wm. B. Eerdmans Publishing Co.
2140 Oak Industrial Drive N.E., Grand Rapids, Michigan 49505
www.eerdmans.com

Originally published in Swedish as *"Jag är bara Nathan Söderblom satt till tjänst": En biografi* by Verbum AB, Stockholm. © 2014 Verbum and Jonas Jonson.

Printed in the United States of America
22 21 20 19 18 17 16 1 2 3 4 5 6 7

Library of Congress Cataloging-in-Publication Data

Names: Jonson, Jonas, 1939-
Title: Nathan Söderblom: called to serve / Jonas Jonson;
translated from Swedish by Norman A. Hjelm.
Other titles: Jag är bara. English
Description: Grand Rapids, Michigan: Eerdmans Publishing Company, 2016. |
Includes bibliographical references and index.
Identifiers: LCCN 2015048560 | ISBN 9780802873088 (pbk.: alk. paper)
Subjects: LCSH: Söderblom, Nathan, 1866-1931. | Svenska kyrkan—Bishops—Biography.
Classification: LCC BX8080.S6 J6613 2016 | DDC 230/.41092—dc23
LC record available at http://lccn.loc.gov/2015048560

Literary Credits

Erik Gustaf Geijer, "Alone in a fragile vessel . . . ," quoted in chapter 8: Reproduced from *A History of Swedish Literature* edited by Lars G. Warme by permission of the University of Nebraska Press. Copyright 1996 by the University of Nebraska Press.

Translation by Jonas Jonson of a hymn by Siri Dahlquist, quoted in chapter 27: MAY OTHER PEOPLES LEARN THE LAW OF CHRIST (LÅT NYA TANKAR TOLKA KRISTI BUD) Music: David Wikander. Lyrics: Sigrid Dahlquist. English translation: Jonas Jonson. © Nordiska Musikförlaget/2007 Gehrmans Musikförlag AB. Printed with permission.

Translation by Erik J. Sharpe of Nathan Söderblom's poem "The vessel burst and fragrant oil is pouring!" in chapter 32: From Ion Bria and Dagmar Heller, eds., *Ecumenical Pilgrims: Profiles of Pioneers in Christian Reconciliation* (Geneva: World Council of Churches, 1995), p. 225. Used with permission.

Photo Credits

Photos in chapters 1, 5, 16, 17, 22, 27, and 33: Uppsala University Library.
Photo in chapter 2: Photo: Heinrich Osti. Uppsala University Library.
Photo in chapter 6: Courtesy Zornmuseet.
Photo in chapter 27: Photo: Emil L: son Finn. Uppsala University Library.
Photo in chapter 33: Photo: Olof Östling. Uppsala University Library.
Photo in chapter 33: Photo: Axel Malmström. Nordiska museet.

Publication of this book has been made possible in part by the Augustana Heritage Association and with the endorsements of the Christian Council of Sweden and the Nathan Söderblom Memorial Fund

Contents

Foreword ix

Introduction 1

1. A Son of a Pastor in Lower Norrland 5

Childhood in Trönö • Family in Hälsingland and Denmark • Revivalist Atmosphere • School in Hudiksvall • Graduation

2. Student Life in Uppsala 16

Uppsala in Transition • Memories of Boström, Geijer, and Wikner • The Student Missionary Association • The Theological Faculty

3. Afflicted and Born Again 30

The Theological Association • "Free from the Heart" • Wellhausen and Ritschl • A Struggle for Faith and Clarity

4. With Moody and Mott in America 39

First Long Journey • New England's Cultivated Protestantism • Students in an Age of Energy • Legends of Revivals and an Apprenticeship in Ecumenism

5. With Words at His Command 49

The Neo-Protestant Way • The Young Luther • Encounter with the Holiness of God • Anna Forsell • President of the Student Body • Master of Rhetoric • Ordination

6. The Pastor in Paris 64

Choosing the History of Religion • Zarathustra • The Persian Language • Dreams of Paris • Marriage • La ville lumière • Swedish Artists

7. Social Christianity and Christian Socialism 79

Auguste Sabatier • Christian Social Movements • "The Sermon on the Mount" • Stockholm Congress on the Study of Religion • Dissertation

8. The Young Professor 94

Trial Lectures in Uppsala • "Doves of Peace with Blood on their Wings" • A Nordic Festival • Address to the Theological Students • Instruction • Torgny Segerstedt

9. God Speaks Many Languages 105
Religion of Revelation and Religion of Culture • Religious Experience as Fundamental • Mysticism of Infinity and Mysticism of Personality

10. The Professor as Priest 116
Stabby Parsonage • Holy Trinity Church • The Prepared Improviser • Theology Translated into Church Art • Dissolution of the Union • A New National Romanticism

11. First Steps in Ecumenism 128
Illness and Aid toward Recovery • The Olaus Petri Foundation • First Meeting with the Archbishop of Canterbury • Meetings with Anglicans, Uppsala, 1909

12. The Student Awakening 142
Literary Essays • The Rise of the Young Church Movement • "The Church's Body and Soul"

13. Institutional Coercion or Spiritual Freedom? 154
Modernism in the Catholic Church • "The Problem of Religion" • A Journey to Rome and Constantinople

14. With the Saints as Models 167
Heroes, Geniuses, and Saints • "For All Thy Saints" • The Church of Revelation

15. An Interval in Leipzig on the Way to the Archbishop's Palace 176
Professor in Leipzig • "The Origin of Belief in God" • Election of the Archbishop in Uppsala

16. Archbishop of Sweden 189
The World Situation • The Consecration • Gustavus Adolphus and Martin Luther • Episcopal Letter

17. Will and Sincerity 199
The Realization of a Dream • Primus inter pares • Service Is What One Makes of It • A Communicating Bishop and the Joy of Responsibility • Music and Prayer

18. The Diplomat of Faith 212
Sweden, 1914 • The Appeal for Peace • Colleagues • Aid to Prisoners of War • A Neutral Peace Conference

19. Bishop of the Diocese of Uppsala 225
The Archdiocese • Visitations and Clergy Convocations • The Place of the Sermon in the Feast of the Liturgy

20. The Freedom of the Church 239
The Bishops Conference and the General Synod • Arthur Engberg's Struggle over Culture • Church and State • The Labor Movement

21. Practical Christianity 255
Canceled Conferences • The Olaus Petri Foundation as an Ecumenical Instrument • Starving Children • A Manifesto for Peace

22. The Love of God Unites Enemies 265
Failures in Convening Conferences • Faith and Order Comes to Uppsala • Oud Wassenaar • Evangelical Catholicity • English Participation in the Consecration of Swedish Bishops

23. Luther and Lutheranism 277
Reformation Jubilee, 1917 • "Humor and Melancholy in Luther" • The Skeptical Lutherans

24. The Swedish Academy 289
Coup at the General Synod, 1920 • Friend of Authors • Election to the Swedish Academy

25. Mission Is Dialogue 299
The Church of Sweden Mission • India • Plans for a University in China • Karl Ludvig Reichelt

26. Mare Lutheranum 310
Nordic Bishops' Meeting, 1920 • Finland • Estonia • Latvia • Poland

27. Tagore, Heiler, Schweitzer, Sundar Singh, and Ras Teferi 322
Nobel Prize Winner Rabindranath Tagore • Theologian Friedrich Heiler • Sadhu Sundar Singh • Missionary Doctor Albert Schweitzer • Ethiopia's Crown Prince Ras Teferi

28. The Road to Stockholm 336
Geneva, 1920 • The Orthodox Presence • Faith and Order • Helsingborg, 1922 • Bishops Protest against the French Occupation of the Ruhr

29. A Detour to America 349
United States, 1923 • The Augustana Synod • Before Stockholm: An Ecumenical Hymnal and a Cope

30. Christianity's Conference 363
Organization • Patriarch Photios • Meal • Worship • Kingdom of God • Conclusion

31. The Difficult Way Forward 375
Sixtieth Birthday • Bern, 1926 • League of Nations • Lausanne, 1927

32. The Pope in Conflict with the Swedish Archbishop 389
The Encyclical "Mortalium Animos" • Söderblom's Response • Max Pribilla • "The History of Christ's Suffering" • The Canceled Journey to Jerusalem

33. In Weakness, Strong 399
Bishops' Motion for the Freedom of the Church • The Eisenach Resolution • The Nobel Prize, 1930 • Alone at the Barricades

34. The Death of a Saint 414

The Gifford Lectures • The Last Days • Söderblom's Death and Burial • Legacy • A Heritage to Preserve

Afterword 427

Sources and Literature 431

Index of Selected Names 440

Foreword

ALMOST EVERY DAY I look into the face of Nathan Söderblom.

A bust of him was long ago placed in front of the General Secretary's office in the Ecumenical Centre of the World Council of Churches in Geneva. I think it is a proper place for it. After all, Söderblom's leadership was important to the international cooperation for peace after World War I, a legacy that remains manifest in the activities and buildings of this Swiss city. But his image is also an asset in the house built for the World Council of Churches and its sister organizations. He can almost be called the founder of the organized ecumenical movement, with his attempt to bring the churches together in the great meeting in Stockholm in 1925.

Nathan Söderblom reminds those who work in the Ecumenical Centre that we serve the efforts of Christian churches to find one another, calling one another to common witness and service for the good of humanity, and that peace is a value of the reign of God. We are not an institution that lives our own life in our own world. Söderblom assures the visitors that we are working with a broad perspective, historically and theologically, taking new initiatives to realize the potential of religion as a contributor to peace and justice, offering new perspectives in the realm of religion, and nurturing true spirituality. He reminds me that leading this movement requires creative engagement, building relations, commitment, resilience, vision, and the ability to convey this commitment through many forms of communication.

In this light, Bishop Emeritus Jonas Jonson's brilliant presentation of Nathan Söderblom in this biography has some very special qualities:

Jonas Jonson writes from inside the story. He is Swedish, he knows the language, the culture, the churches, the places and houses where Söderblom lived and displayed his talents and ideas. He knows the effect of Söderblom's work and merits in the life of the Church of Sweden. As the sources and literature listed at the back of the book give evidence, the author has studied an enormous range of texts, letters, protocols, books, hymns, articles in periodicals and newspapers, and much more.

Furthermore, Bishop Jonson writes from within the circles of family, successors, friends, and opponents in Sweden that lived together with and mostly after Archbishop Söderblom. He knows of what is written and not written about Söderblom and his unique personality, his relationships, and his effect on others.

Even more relevant for me, Jonson writes from within the ecumenical movement. He knows the ecumenical movement as his own calling in life, as a passion, as a source of theological reflection, as networks and relations that are challenging and always offering a lot more than you invest yourself.

My enthusiasm for this biography increased as I read and found that Jonas Jonson offers an academically strong yet engaging and literary text. He is a brilliant story teller. All the dimensions of the life and work of Söderblom so well presented here are relevant. Though the volume is long, sometimes I even wished Jonson could have written more.

For the Swedish audience Jonson's biography was a significant contribution to the centennial celebrations in 2014, yet it also sheds light on the broader Scandinavian and European contexts in which Söderblom operated. He played as much in an international and ecumenical arena as he did at home in the Uppsala Diocese. He became a figure in the history of the worldwide church that we all need to know better to understand, for example, the ecumenical movement.

Söderblom's visits to other countries, and particularly to the United States, receive attention here. The life of the Lutheran churches in America is also shaped by the impulses from him.

Beyond the historical and biographical qualities of the book, I find several theological impulses from Söderblom (and I think some from his biographer, as well) that are of significance in reflection about the way forward in the ecumenical movement today. One is the strong connection to spirituality and liturgy as expressions of the theology of the ecumenical movement. I particularly appreciate that some of the hymns of Söderblom are presented in their context and in his life. The author, himself a hymn writer, shows how much theology and life are concentrated in the hymns. Another relevant feature is the reflection on the call to the churches to contribute to peace as a dimension of being church, almost a criterion for being church. A third is the contextual approach to theology. In this book we see that contextuality is not about geography but at heart is a matter of discerning the features of the time in which we live and the challenges that theology and the churches together must confront.

I hope that this volume finds many readers within and outside the church. The combination of all these aspects, woven together in a story of his life, makes this book fascinating and exciting to read.

Standing in front of the bust of Nathan Söderblom, I once asked my colleagues in the WCC when the ecumenical movement had received the Nobel Peace Prize. When we read why Söderblom received the prize in 1930, we can claim a connection to our life as the WCC. Today we are still challenged by his example to show that peace and unity are mutually interrelated.

Olav Fykse Tveit
General Secretary,
World Council of Churches

Introduction

> How beautiful upon the mountains are the feet of the messenger who announces peace, who brings good news, who announces salvation, who says to Zion, "Your God reigns."
>
> *Isaiah 52:7*

SWEDISH LIFE AT THE BEGINNING of the twentieth century was notable for the influence of strong personalities — Harald Hjärne, August Strindberg, Selma Lagerlöf, Anders Zorn, Hjalmar Branting, Sven Hedin, and many others. Nathan Söderblom was among them. For three decades he stood in the Swedish public eye. Moreover, his influence was felt far beyond his country's borders and long after his death.

On November 8, 1914 — now more than a century ago — he was consecrated Archbishop of the Church of Sweden. Several months had passed since Archduke Frans Ferdinand and his young wife Sophie were assassinated in Sarajevo, leading to the outbreak of World War I. Everything had taken a new direction. *La belle époque* was over. Faith in the superiority of Western civilization, which legitimized colonialism and gave brightness to the years around the turn of the century, had sunk from sight.

Christendom was in deep crisis. Its picture of the world was seen as obsolete, its great words empty of meaning. Its claim to be a religion of peace lost credibility as one after another "Christian" nation went to war and hundreds of thousands of young men were slaughtered in the trenches. Even as Nathan Söderblom was being vested in a golden cope in the Uppsala Cathedral, French and English troops were struggling to prevent Calais and Dunkirk from falling into German hands. He had been a seamen's pastor there and had seen his own children playing on the beaches. Now he could visualize how the Atlantic coast's airy light transformed into the dense fog that accompanies fire and death. He loved the French, German, and English cultures and had friends on both sides of the battle lines. He himself had already initiated efforts for peace, efforts that were to become his life's work.

This, like ecumenism in general, was Söderblom's self-assumed responsibility, even though such works had not been among the previous expectations for a Swedish archbishop. He was to use his position to realize his ecumenical vision. In this he received less support from other bishops, priests, and church leaders than he did from academics, artists, and members of the aristocracy. The latter hoped that he would be able to modernize Christendom. With his international contacts, his broad theological vision, and his personal piety, they thought that he, if anyone, could lead the church through the present devastating catastrophe and formulate new tasks for a new time. But not one of them could imagine the role he would play on the European scene. He had wanted to become archbishop and he believed he could fulfill the task. His father's last words sounded in his ears, "Not as lords over the congregation; rather, we are workers with you for your joy" (cf. 2 Cor. 1:24). Those words would hold his egotism and presumption in check.

Nathan Söderblom was convinced that uniquely chosen people determine the choice of paths for humanity. Now the responsibility was laid upon him. He understood himself to be called by God, his life's purpose being to write history. He had pursued a course of thought that led to an abyss where everything is dissolved in doubt and relativism, but he nevertheless remained convinced that God lives. He had encountered God's consuming holiness and his boundless mercy and had given himself over to him. Trust was his source of freedom. God is greater than theologians dare to think and he does not let himself be ensnared in dogma or locked up in prayer houses or cathedrals. The gospel belongs to everyone. God has an ally in every human person. The church knows no boundaries.

For thirteen years Söderblom had been a professor; for nearly seventeen years he would be archbishop. He led the aged Swedish state church into modernity and gave it pride and self-confidence, but its structures prevailed. He afforded European Christendom a new feeling of togetherness and gave it a large dose of ecumenical energy.

After World War I, he assumed a leading role among the world's evangelical church leaders, constructive and controversial, prophetic and forceful. He was hailed as a scholar, a person of culture, and a proponent of peace. Fourteen honorary doctorates and membership in the Swedish Academy as well as the royal academies of science and music contributed to the aura around him. He received numerous honors including Knight of the Royal Norwegian Order of St. Olaf, the French Legion of Honor, and Knight of the Royal Order of the Seraphim in his native Sweden. In 1930 he received the Nobel Prize for Peace. He died in 1931 at the age of sixty-five. As long as he lived, he met with opposition. After his death he was accounted among the saints, who by his own definition were people who by their lives showed that God lives.

Anyone who studies Nathan Söderblom can see how his goals, strategies, and tactics gradually developed. Nothing was clear from the beginning. He adjusted himself to rapidly changing outer realities, but he never lost focus. His theological presuppositions remained largely constant. The first was that God is a living God who reveals himself through prophets, historical events, and in all authentic religion, acting through humans who place themselves at his disposal. The second was that the church as an organization assumes different expressions, but that Christendom has a "soul" that is common, enduring, and centered around the atoning cross. The third was that all churches — Roman Catholic, Orthodox, and those of the Reformation — share equally in "evangelical catholicity" and that the office of the bishop is a visible expression of their solidarity and connection to common origins. Added to this was his conviction that Sweden, through historical circumstances, had received a special commission to bring the churches together and to contribute to peace in the world.

Söderblom took it as a personal vocation to unify the churches for common action and to strengthen international law as a way to peace. His strategy was first to gather the churches that already stood close to one another through their evangelical confession and the historic episcopacy, and ultimately to approach even Orthodox churches. He realized early on that it was futile to include the Roman Catholic Church so long as it was controlled by reactionary forces that held modernity, science, and democracy at a distance. His tactic was, with Uppsala at the center, to create a network of leading Christians, to bring them together in worship and deliberation, and finally, to create an ecumenical council that could provide Christians with a unified voice to the world. In order to accomplish this goal, he would have to use his considerable diplomatic talents to the utmost and mobilize both moral and financial support.

All of Western civilization was at stake. The map of Europe had been redrawn and its empires were falling. The Peace of Versailles had proven illusory. When Söderblom's time came to an end, the stock market had crashed and the Great Depression was in full force. Hitler and Mussolini were already marching in the streets.

* * *

This is an account of Nathan Söderblom's life. Its emphasis is on his international ecumenical activity. The biography builds largely on the research of others, as I acknowledge at the end of the book, but also on Söderblom's own writings and correspondence, original documents, and newspaper clippings. Söderblom was determined to separate his family life from his public life. This book, accordingly, does not reflect much on his private situation. Its intention is to set the Church of Sweden's most significant twentieth-century leader in context, thus making him known to a new generation.

The early twentieth century was stunningly different from the early twenty-first century. Every generation must write its own history to avoid being stricken with a collective dementia. Memory fades quickly, even with respect to people and events that continue to influence us. In order to understand who Nathan Söderblom was, how he thought, and what he did, I have gathered material from both old and new sources. In spite of all that I have read and heard, I have only caught a glimpse of him, jogging along with his clerical coat unbuttoned, his gold bishop's cross bouncing on his chest, his watch in his vest pocket, his hat in hand, his arms outstretched as though he would take everyone he met into his embrace.

1

A Son of a Pastor in Lower Norrland

> Things are going well in school and I have gotten an A or A- every time on my German lessons.
>
> *Nathan Söderblom, 1876*

NATHAN IS THIRTEEN YEARS OLD. *He climbs to the top of the church steeple in Hudiksvall. From the ground below, his brother Svante watches with a pounding heart as he creeps out through an opening at the very top. There are little notches on the steep roof up to the top of the spire. A round sphere holds up the golden cross. Nathan climbs up the notches and sits on the sphere with his arms around the cross. Far below small people move about in the clutter of gray wooden houses. In the harbor he sees freighters from foreign lands. On the horizon, the sea and the sky merge into each other. He looks out over the world. Even fifty years later, Svante felt ill at ease when he recounted his brother's foolhardy adventure.*

* * *

It was a boy again. The first had died the year before, just nine months old. Papa Jonas Söderblom was forty-three, a pietistic pastor of the Church of Sweden who was worn by the demands of service and conscience. He uttered a prayer of wonderment and thanksgiving when he saw the newborn baby lying in the crib at the side of his young wife Sophia's bed. Ten days later the boy was baptized and given the name Lauritz Olaus Jonathan: Lars after his mother's father, Olof after his father's grandfather, and Jonathan — "gift of God" — taken from the Old Testament, which Jonas regularly read in Hebrew. The boy, however, came to be known as Nathan.

Nathan Söderblom was born to Jonas and Sophia Söderblom on January 15, 1866 in the parsonage of Trönö, not far from Söderhamn in the province of Hälsingland in northern Sweden. Snow covered the landscape. Winter days were short. In spite of layers of rag rugs there were drafts in the crevices of the floor. The cleaning girls worked in the fluttering light that came from fireplaces and suet candles. When darkness came, at about four in the afternoon, they could barely see the little gray thirteenth-century stone church through the frosty windows.

The vicar's rectory, on a steep hillside a few hundred meters north of the church, was large and tall, built around a stall, a barn, and a shed for a carriage. The priest lived, like all others in the area, from what the earth provided. As the son of a farmer, Jonas tended to the land along with his farmhands. They plowed the fields, gathered in the hay, harvested the rye, and dug up the potatoes before the frost set in. The work possessed its own rhythm, determined by the time of year and the weather: chopping wood, washing and baking, sowing, harvesting, and slaughtering. For everyone in the area, baptisms, confirmations, weddings, and funerals marked the changes of life. Sundays and feast days reminded people of the church's year. Farms on the hillsides were covered in silence, even more so the gray timbered cottages near the edge of the forests. The silence was broken when the bell in the towering steeple rang, but also by noisy sheep, mooing cows, rolling carts, and creaking sleighs. The roads were often impassable. There was no electricity, and not even kerosene lamps. Seven of ten Swedes lived in rural areas and lived off the land. Behind striped curtains, many shared bedstraw and skin rugs.

In the area there were self-sufficient farmers in newly built manor houses marked by magnificent entryways and biblical scenes painted on the walls of the grand halls. Some of these were trusted jurymen and church wardens. Artists, actors, and storytellers wandered between the villages. In the manor houses, many gathered to study well-worn Bibles and to sing revivalist songs. The population grew, but the farms were too small to be passed on to new generations. Social mobility for many was downwards. People who possessed no land formed a kind of proletariat. Sons of farmers became day laborers, looking for work at the small sawmills along the streams, moving to the cities where industrialization had begun, or emigrating to America. Growing numbers lived from hand to mouth. Rural society in Sweden, which had been relatively stable for hundreds of years, creaked at the joints.

Winters were cold during the nineteenth century. Everyone had experienced autumns when the frost cut short the harvest, but never had it been so severe as when Nathan was small. After several difficult years, 1867 became the worst "lean year" in memory, bringing the last famine in Swedish history. The lakes did not thaw before late in June and the frost came back when things had just begun to grow. Shiploads of grain, which sold at costly sums, did not reach the harbors on the Norrland coast before they were iced in. From Hälsingland and northward large numbers of starving children went from village to village begging for bread. For those who had nothing to store in their barns it was a terrible decade. Clergy and wealthy farmers fared well, but hundreds of others went under, in spite of relief aid. Small landowners and their helpers packed their "America suitcases" in order to seek better things on the other side of the Atlantic.

Jonas Söderblom wandered between the villages in order to preach; he regularly visited homes to console the members of his congregation. Sometimes he harnessed up his horse and traveled to the village of Orsta in the neighboring parish of Söderala. There was the home of his birth, which had been in his family for at least ten generations. His parents, the church warden and accountant Jon Olsson and Margta Olofsdotter, had seen that Jonas, as the eldest son, received an education and was ordained. His brother Sven took over the farm. Jonas became a student at Uppsala in 1844. Like many other students who came from a rural background, he took a new family name. The name Söderblom would always remind him of Söderala's incredibly beautiful meadows and summer flowers. Apart from his student years, Jonas never left Hälsingland. He lived his whole life within a radius of sixty miles.

One of Nathan's forefathers had been a member of the peasants estate and had sat in the old Parliament. A new time, however, was on its way. A consitutional reform, which took place half a year after Nathan's birth, gave Sweden a two-chamber Parliament. The law was construed so that conservative and careful politics continued comfortably. The priests were the great losers since the ecclesiastical estate was eliminated and their political influence diminished dramatically. Political life took on new shapes, but disruptive or revolutionary movements remained at a distance. In the small villages of Hälsingland there were few with an income or inheritance large enough to secure election to the new Parliament. The political arrangements in Stockholm did not arouse much interest among the people who lived several days' travel away.

In the small towns along the coast there were only a few tradesmen or people of means. One exception was the bearded physician Laurentius Blume. A Dane, he had come to Sweden to assist during the cholera epidemic of 1834 and had remained, becoming a Swedish citizen. After twenty years he had moved to Hudiksvall with his family. He was well-to-do, socially respected, approachable, and admired for his Danish geniality. His wife, Johanne, was the daughter of a clergyman from the well-known Koefoed family in Denmark. Her mother's father had been mayor of Copenhagen and further back in her family tree one could find a Bishop of Oslo. Blume's three sons had careers on the sea. The oldest emigrated to America and became a harbormaster in San Francisco. One of the daughters married a Norwegian who established himself as a ship owner in Stockholm. The Blume family was cultivated and intellectually alert. There was empathy, optimism, and a love of adventure.

Johanne Blume died in 1861. That year Blume's daughter Sophia, whose sorrow at her mother's death was deepened by her melancholy and introverted temperament, first came into contact with Jonas Söderblom. There had been a spiritual revival that centered on him in Hudiksvall, and Sophia found consolation in his message. He took a liking to the religiously sensitive girl, who accepted his proposal of marriage. Her father, the Danish doctor, did not care much for pietists, especially those of the rigid type found in Norrland. He had no liking for the fanatic clergyman and feared that life as a pastor's wife would demand all too much of his daughter. Nevertheless, he reluctantly gave his assent to the marriage, perhaps because Sophia, who was going deaf, otherwise might have had no family. She had, in spite of everything, a great deal to gain by entering Jonas's world and chose to take the bad with the good. They were married in 1863. She was twenty-three years old; he was thirty-nine. The next year they moved to Trönö.

Doctor Blume was right. Jonas Söderblom's horizon was narrow and his religion inflexible. He had been formed by the strict legalistic revival that swept through Hälsingland during the first half of the nineteenth century. That movement was led by clergymen who constantly admonished their listeners concerning that most perilous condition for the human soul: certainty. Their Lutheran pietism was permeated by a consciousness of sin and they lived in terror of "the old serpent's craftiness and cunning." That led to puzzlement and doubt, anxiety and remorse. Nathan's father's father Jon Olsson and his wife Margta had been converted in 1818. He had a reputation as a quiet and saintly person. She was more lively. They lived a God-fearing life. Fiddles and alcohol were not allowed in their home; rather, groups gathered there to seek guidance from God's Word and to be strengthened in common prayer.

The awakening took place in differing ways. The tradesman Erik Jansson from Biskopskulla in the province of Uppland also came to Söderala preaching a more radical Christianity that included collective property as well as holy living. With hypnotic power, he gathered followers and bound them to himself, at times seeming to identify himself as the Savior. Toward the end of the 1840s, when the Swedish authorities had issued a warrant for his arrest, he fled to America with fifteen hundred disciples. Those who survived the hardships of the voyage founded Bishop's Hill in western Illinois, named after the town in Uppland. From the village of Alfta in Hälsingland alone three hundred people made the journey. They sold their farms and put the money in a common fund. Some people from Söderala were also among Jansson's followers, one of them being Sven Svenson, Jonas Söderblom's cousin. Svenson became a leader of the sect after Erik Jansson was murdered in 1850.

As a teenager, Jonas had a deep religious experience and adopted his parents' style of life. He could well have gone the way of Sven Svenson, his cousin, but after his school years in Hudiksvall and Gävle and his university studies at Uppsala, he was ordained in 1847 and returned home. A legalistic piety that demanded everything of him led to a crisis in the young pastor's life. The crisis did not deal, as for many in the next generation, with the infallibility of Scripture in a scientific age, but rather with justification and grace, as in Luther's time. Jonas stood at the brink of a psychological breakdown and his physical body suffered from extreme asceticism before he finally dared to trust in unconditional grace. The creed he had affirmed at his ordination included the article, I believe "in the forgiveness of sin," but it was a long time before he could make that confession his own. He never left legalism completely behind, but a milder tone began to mark his preaching. He knew both P. P. Waldenström and Anders Wiberg, founders of the Swedish Mission Covenant Church and the Swedish Baptist Union, but he was more deeply influenced by the confident teaching of C. O. Rosenius. In 1895, he became provincial deputy of the Evangeliska Fosterlandsstiftelsen (later, the Swedish Evangelical Mission).

Many priests in Hälsingland participated in the evangelical revival and lived serious, abstinent, and pious lives, but few could match Jonas Söderblom. He was not a noteworthy speaker, yet he knew his Hebrew Old Testament so well that he could have been named to the Uppsala faculty. But for him there was only one task that mattered: to reach as many as possible with the message of salvation through the blood of Christ. He had no doubt about the destiny of humanity: God wished to liberate humans from the emptiness and bondage of the world and give them eternal life.

At times Jonas was called the barefoot priest. He scurried between the villages of his parish with his boots on his back, both in order to move quickly and to prevent wearing out the soles of his boots. In his zeal he could not be hindered by family responsibilities, so he waited a long time for marriage. He did not seek a regular post but served in various places, here and there. Many viewed him as awkward and odd and he elicited both offense and contempt. He was somewhat credulous, impulsive, and a bit suspicious, but he was a good singer and a biblically knowledgeable preacher. In his radicalism he conveyed a kind of Franciscan spirit. His exalted spirituality and his gift of speaking brought large crowds of people who wanted to hear him. He did not like either administrative tasks or rules and regulations, but no one could question his care for souls or his devotion. He possessed a kind of early Christian enthusiasm, marked by a wild, unbridled eagerness. For fifteen years he was, as Nathan wrote of his childhood memories, an ascetical, singing, preaching pastor with flaming blue eyes and a burning heart who went from community to community, awakening sleeping souls with his message.

He disciplined his worldly desires and held his dreams for the future at a distance. When at long last it came time for marriage, Sophia came into his life. The doctor's daughter and the country priest were an unlikely pair. As he continued untiringly to preach the depravity of sin and justification by the precious blood of Jesus, she withdrew to her rooms, increasingly hard of hearing. The singular center in their home was their religion. The couple shared their faith and held daily prayers, but they did not always share mealtimes with each other. Jonas sat in his cold room and studied the Bible while his distance from Sophia grew. As long as the children were small, she filled the parsonage with warmth, song, and music, but when they left home for school in Hudiksvall she shut herself off almost totally from the outer world. She confined herself to a silent solitude, reading and rereading the letters from her children. At times she would write in her diary about Jonas's strictness.

His self-sacrifice and strong will made an impression on people in his congregation. Nathan wrote in his Episcopal Letter of 1914 that whenever he even mentioned his father's name, people would begin to speak of him. They remembered his passionate restlessness, his changeable disposition, and his credulity. When, after a difficult inner struggle, he came to faith in Christ's atonement, he had no other choice than to proclaim the gospel as long as his well-disciplined body would allow. No hour was too early or too late for him, no road too long or too difficult. Neither fatigue nor illness prevented him from consoling the sick and dying, from helping the poor, and from expounding the words of Scripture. Nathan recalled how those in need of spiritual care sought out his father. Letters came and letters were sent. They began with "Brother in Christ" and ended with the salutation "Grace and Peace." When the children of grace came together, they had other things to speak of than the weather, the harvest, cattle, politics, business, joys, and misfortunes. They spoke of the power of sin and joy in God, the promises of Scripture, and the well-being of brothers and sisters in the faith. Such were the things that preoccupied them.

Jonas Söderblom was clearly an original — stern in his speech and strict in his lifestyle. He had an intractable will and exercised ruthless self-discipline. These traits influenced his children. He tolerated neither easy convenience nor idleness. The children were not to feel sorry for themselves, and it was best that they not even cough when suffering from colds. They were admonished not to be fearful when they walked through the pitch-dark cemetery at night. At an early age they were required to fetch wood and water and do such things as they were capable of. Even as a five-year-old Nathan began to plow through Latin word lists. His excellent grades in school never satisfied his father. But behind Jonas's hard exterior were a hidden tenderness and even some humor. He had great hopes for his children, especially for Nathan who had a special place among them, a fact that also contributed to his son's strong self-confidence later on in life. Jonas once wrote in a letter to Nathan: "I have built my future hope on you and expect good things at school, church, and even the state from you." Nathan answered with deep and lifelong affection. The children received a strict Christian upbringing: morning and evening prayers, long sermons on Sunday, and many prohibitions. Parlor games, dancing, and alcohol were never allowed at home.

Sophia was very unlike Jonas, much younger, and a city child with sisters and brothers spread around the world. She gave birth to seven children, although two died early. When the youngest child was born, Sophia was forty-five and Jonas sixty. During their first years, the children were educated at home. Sophia was a clever teacher who brought out the best in them. Nathan described her warmly as a kind-hearted, pious, and quiet person who silently and deeply thought things through in order to gain theoretical clarity. She was one who, as people used to say, had never fallen from baptismal grace. She never fully recovered from an illness contracted when her youngest daughter was born and was often confined to bed. But while they lived in Trönö and Nathan was small, she was young and strong. She would willingly sing and play salon music on a square piano. The children had a good time sitting on the floor near the piano, but when their parents took out *Tunes of Zion* or the *Songs of Ahnfelt* in the evening, they sat the children on their chairs for evening prayer. Sophia's quiet clarity made her a fine teacher. "I have during my life had many teachers, but none were better than she," wrote Nathan when he was himself nearly sixty. With great interest, she followed his theological development in a totally different way than his father. In her later years, up to her death in 1913, Sophia lived in one of the houses on the grounds of the Stabby rectory in Uppsala. But in spite of her gifts, she is not much of a factor in Nathan's reports on his own life. The patriarchal father remained his model for the Christian life and dominated his memories of childhood.

It is not difficult to understand why Dr. Blume disliked his son-in-law, who possessed none of the Danish folk church's warm generosity and joy in creation. Nathan's brother Svante, who had problems in high school and was not thought of as conscientious, was more or less forced to emigrate to America when he was nineteen. There he became a military musician who always longed for home. His other brother, Johan, studied agriculture and became a consultant to farmers in northern Sweden. His sister, Elsa — "the best of us" — became a nurse and a farmer's wife in Darlecarlia, while his other sister, Hanna — artistic and somewhat mentally unstable — cared for their mother. Nathan's home milieu was not only pious. It was also demanding and lacking in harmony, at times filled with discord to the brink of destruction.

Certain elements in Nathan's personality can easily be traced to his parents. From his father he received his deep religious conviction, his capacity for persevering at demanding work, his ability to concentrate, and perhaps even a kind of bipolarity, the dark side of which he hid well from those around him. From his mother he inherited the "Danish" element in

The Söderblom family travels by horse and wagon to Norrbo near Bjuråker. Nathan is holding the bridle. Circa 1880.

his personality — his extroverted character, his ease in social situations, his musical and artistic interests, and his humor and delight in human contact.

When the towheaded Nathan was seven years old, his father became vicar in Bjuråker, near Delsbo. And when he turned nine, it was time to begin secondary school in Hudiksvall, more than twenty miles away. There he would remain until he graduated eight years later. His father, who had inherited some forest, purchased a cottage just below the Hudiksvall church for the children. There what amounted to a dormitory was set up. Karin Gisselsson-Tadda was hired to take care of the children. She came from a family of musical craftsmen and school teachers in Trönö and had been a babysitter for the children since they were small. She remained with the family even to the time when Nathan became archbishop.

A fisherman delivered herring and potatoes to the cottage. Meat and cheese were sent from the rectory, but in order to get fresh milk, the children had their own cow. They fed the cow and milked it, which made Nathan nervous. "The cow is giving much less milk than before and she digs around so much that we think she is not happy," he wrote to his mother. He was a conscientious and practical boy who took care of his younger siblings and slept head-to-foot with his brother on a sofa bed with a hay mattress and a sheepskin cover. After a few years, his restless father moved to Hälsingtuna just outside Hudiksvall and in 1886 he became vicar in Norrala and Trönö. That same year Nathan began his studies at Uppsala.

Hudiksvall was a small town oriented toward the larger world. Here, sailboats with destinations like Helsinki, Hamburg, and Hull were loaded and unloaded. Nathan and his comrades had good times at the harbor. With seamen in his family, he wanted to learn about ships and the sea. He had begun school a year before the others and later skipped a grade. During one of many snowball fights, he grew close to Herman Palmgren from Forssa who became his lifelong friend and a high-ranking civil servant. One time, he also encountered an archbishop, Anton Niklas Sundberg, installing a new vicar. When Sundberg knelt at the altar in his golden cope, Nathan, seated in the balcony, could not help thinking of a large, magnificent beetle. He did not suspect that some thirty years later he would himself be garbed in such a cope. He not only climbed the church steeple in Hudiksvall, but in 1880, he also carved his name on a gold button on the tower of the church in Järvsö. He took piano lessons, sometimes playing the organ at services in the church, and also playing the cornet in his school's orchestra. Athletics and sports did not interest him, but he became part of a student association in which members practiced writing essays, holding lectures, and performing music. Secondary school, the gymnasium, presented no difficulties for Nathan. He was gifted in languages and studied Latin and Greek, Swedish, French, and German, but he did little more than poke his nose into English. In biblical studies and church history he did especially well.

When Nathan was fifteen, he was confirmed by his father. This involved deep instruction in Luther's *Small Catechism* and an introduction to "right teaching" as Jonas Söderblom with his pietistic presuppositions and his puritanical tendencies interpreted it. Memories of the fanciful zealot Erik Jansson lived on, the influence of P. P. Waldenström was starting to take shape, and the Swedish Baptist Union had begun to spread in Hälsingland. Consequently, Jonas Söderblom in his catechetical instruction, which brought Nathan to Holy Communion for the first time, placed special emphasis on baptismal grace and the doctrine of objective atonement. The sacrament of Holy Communion was celebrated very seldom; the custom had been broken and it was observed almost solely in connection with the confirmation of young people. Legalistic preaching kept "unworthy" people from the Communion Table. Nathan had no sacramental tradition from his home and all sacramentalism was thus foreign to him. The whole of his youth was marked by a strict, individualistic, and other-worldly piety encompassed within general Lutheran customs.

He graduated in 1883 when he was seventeen years old. His grades were mediocre, no more than average. That could have been an accident. He was, in any case, ready to move on to Uppsala. That he was to become a priest was not self-evident, but his father applied pressure and was glad that at least one of his sons was considering following in his footsteps. At the same time, Jonas Söderblom was uneasy. What delusions might capture Nathan in Uppsala where both Charles Darwin and Karl Marx were beginning to get hearings? Hälsingland had more than enough spiritual fanaticism, drunkenness, and knife brawling, but what might await a pure-hearted youth in the academic halls, student societies, and bordello streets of Uppsala? There were more dangerous temptations there than the dark, violent, and wild tones that musicians brought forth from their fiddles.

From his home Nathan brought the *Tunes of Zion*, a sense of duty, and total abstinence from alcohol. In Hälsingland low-church life was the rule as much in medieval churches as in newly built prayer houses. He did not give these things up. Throughout the changes in his life he would often return to his childhood, his rural roots, and the evangelical revival. He had been raised by simple, good-hearted, and conscientious people who possessed an inner confidence and abiding care for their fellow humans. An awareness of genuine, experiential religion would guide him in his studies and personal relations and he would always remember the blue mountains that watched over the valleys with their villages and endless pine forests.

Yet in spite of his background, he was drawn irresistibly into modernity. Awakenings, emigration, industrialization, and the natural sciences all pointed in the same direction. The encounter with the future had begun. He must find a new language for faith. Thus, Nathan's inner journey was different from that of his parents. He became a supplicant and intellectual seeker who tested not only the content of his inherited faith but also his relation to music, literature, and art, to society, and to politics. His father had journeyed between social classes, but for him that was not a long journey. His spiritual horizon was narrow; up to his death he was ill at ease with everything that threatened his faith. Nathan, who was soon to learn the language of Søren Kierkegaard, let loose and plunged in.

2

Student Life in Uppsala

Whoever grew up in the eighties, will afterwards retain the impression that that was the driest period in world history.

Nathan Söderblom, 1926

THE MELANCHOLY PROFESSOR of theoretical philosophy Pontus Wikner is holding his final lecture in Uppsala. He will be moving to Oslo. With a sad smile he reports that the hall used to be fully occupied. Now eight students are sitting there. Time has passed him by, but still, educated people study his thinking, beautifully expressed in books bound in velvet. Regardless of the weather, Wikner walks with umbrella and galoshes alone and absent-mindedly through the city. He takes his meals at a restaurant as his eyes wander among the young male students. He is leaving Uppsala with his heavy secret. Nathan feels the subsiding vibrations of romanticism and idealism.

* * *

Nathan Söderblom was a teenager when he came to Uppsala in the fall of 1883. There he would remain, with a couple of interruptions, for the rest of his life. The university became his alma mater, the city his home. It had seventeen thousand inhabitants, less than one-tenth of them being students. In Uppsala there was much building going on. After the great city fire in 1702, which turned most everything to ashes, development had slowed down, but during the nineteenth century there was construction as never before. In 1807, when Carl von Linné would have been one hundred, the botanical institution and the botanical gardens were dedicated in the park of the Renaissance castle. The university library, Carolina Rediviva, was ready to be occupied in 1841. Institutions for natural sciences and medicine were erected on the edges of the old university quarter. Fraternities, "student nations," built pompous houses in the style of the times. Soon the cathedral with Carl Hårleman's clumpy towers was covered by scaffolding and under the direction of Helgo Zettervall, the heavy red brick church was changed to a tasteful Gothic cathedral with graceful upwardly pointing spires. The main building of the university, which the government had promised to underwrite in connection with the university's four hundredth anniversary in 1877, was being built.

On the other side of the Fyris river, massive stone buildings were being built on all four sides of the Great Square. The city came to an end at the railroad station that had been completed in 1866. At Luthagen, where cows had grazed not long ago, stood two-story wooden houses in tight rows. That part of the city, which later became the most attractive quarter in Uppsala, had the sad atmosphere of being temporary, nearly a community of barracks. Poor students, among them many theologians, could get cheap living quarters there. Nathan found a room not far away but he soon moved into ramshackle quarters appropriately named by students "Imperfectum." After a couple of years there he found a double room on Svartmangatan, which for several years he shared with his schoolmate Herman Palmgren. People often saw the young light-haired student, who was becoming well known, going up the hill. They noticed two things: he was always in a hurry, but he also stopped willingly to talk a bit with the children who were playing on the street.

It was not only in external respects that Uppsala was changing. When Methodist, Mission Covenant, and Baptist churches were built near the railroad station and when the Salvation Army appeared on the streets with bands and banners, the church divisions of the 1870s became visible to everyone. Staunchly conservative and royalist romanticism had had its time. Student festivals, nations, and songs survived, but not much more. Scandinavian demonstrations, drenched in arrack punch, were things of the past; only the white student caps remained. The once influential historian Erik Gustaf Geijer was memorialized in a statue in front of the university. The leading philosopher of idealism, Jacob Boström, had been dead for many years. The dominance of the humanities in the university was diminishing as the natural sciences elbowed their way forward and took on more and more prominence. Uppsala had its first woman doctor of philosophy, Ellen Fries, but she was an exception that proved the rule. The academic society was masculine and would remain so for decades. Women students were so few that no one could have dreamed that a century later they would dominate the student body and occupy one after another professor's chair as the men moved to the rear. Perpetual students continued to live bohemian lives in cheap student rooms, but their number became smaller as academic life took on a more structured shape. Students formed professional interest groups and some began to challenge the unquestioned authority of the professors.

The number of students who were sons of clergymen had decreased and both farm boys and the sons of nobility became fewer. More than half of the students now belonged to the new bourgeois middle class. But instruction was carried on in the same old sleep-inducing way. What was offered were public lectures and some private classes. Certain professors would still attract large numbers of students, but in general, the lecture halls became empty. This was especially true for the humanities and for theology. More up-to-date methods of instruction were required. In line with German practice, professors began to organize seminars in which students could discuss texts, methodological questions, and academic problems.

The seventeen-year-old Söderblom was short and blond, with his hair slicked down like a confirmand when on September 19, 1883 he approached the newly built house of the Gästrike-Hälsinge nation to enroll in the university. The same fall, the future bishop of Karlstad, J. A. Eklund, came to Uppsala. The two were destined to compete with each other for attention, for a professor's chair, and for the archbishop's position, but that lay far in the future. Natanael Beskow also enrolled at the same time. He had grown up in the upper class of the evangelical revival, a dreamer and visionary who was to unite his intellectual freedom with radical social activism. Broad-minded and artistically gifted, he had much more in common with Söderblom than with the awkward tailor's son from Skara, Eklund. All three were convinced low churchmen, although in somewhat different ways. They stood for something wholly other than the high church movement that dominated the theological faculty in Lund. In Uppsala, that movement was championed by the archbishop, Anton Niklas Sundberg.

They came to a city and a university where a new era had begun. The splendid jubilee of 1877, when Uppsala University observed its four hundredth anniversary, had been the dividing line. The Rector Magnificus of the university, Carl Yngve Sahlin — a philosopher in the succession of Boström and a guardian of morals — together with the deeply conservative archbishop, who was Pro Chancellor of the university, led the celebration.

Nathan Söderblom as a seventeen-year-old student

Many people received doctorates *honoris causa*. Viktor Rydberg, who set the tone for the cultural life of the time, composed a cantata full of implicit faith to provide consolation for those who were anxious concerning the upheavals of the time. It was often quoted, especially the words:

> Thy noble thoughts, thy acts of love. Thy dreams
> Of beauty — these Time can never devour;
> Eternity like some great storehouse teems
> With sheaves safe-garnered from destruction's power.

The university was on the way toward its greatest time. That time would be notable more for the empirical natural sciences than for the classical humanities. When the university's main building was dedicated with the still-debated inscription over its entrance, "To think freely is great, to think correctly is greater," a new orientation was a fact.

For over twenty years C. J. Boström had trained Uppsala students in platonic idealism. That philosophy drew a distinction between the material world and the world of ideas. Only ideas possessed reality and independent existence; only ideas provided enduring knowledge. What humans believed to exist around them actually was to be found only in their imaginations. The supreme idea, God, alone possessed perfection; from him emanated all ideas in the hierarchy of existence. Nearest to God was the king who was called to administer the state. He did not receive his power from the people, but from God. Ministers and civil officials were to help him preserve the state and its enduring laws and values. The primary duty of such officials was, according to Boström, to obey authority, not to defend the interests of citizens. The people, however, were to be represented in practical politics and Boström was convinced that a parliament formed on the basis of the traditional "estates" best served that goal. He did not live to see history destroy his construction; he died a few months after the constitutional reforms of 1866. However, his views concerning the unity of knowledge seemed increasingly illusory and they were overthrown for good in 1876 when the university went the way of specialization and differentiation. His idealistic description of reality, however, was not completely spent. C. J. Boström's shadow stretched even into the twentieth century, some theologians and legal scholars holding on to the view of church and state that he developed on the basis of platonic philosophy.

Söderblom was not unaffected by the idealism of C. J. Boström, but for him, Erik Gustaf Geijer meant a great deal more. He had been the university's most prominent professor during the early decades of the nineteenth century. Early on he gave up romanticism and idealism and chose to move toward liberalism. For that decision he paid a high price. For New Year's Day 1838, he wrote a few lines that caused tremors in Uppsala and that students learned by heart:

> Alone in a fragile vessel the sailor
> Ventures in the wide sea;
> The starry sky flames above him,
> Below, his grave roars horribly.
> Forward! — That is the commandment of his fate;
> And God dwells in the depths as well as in the heavens.

Geijer was a many-sided figure: a musician, poet, and intellectual who held faith and natural science together. He began his academic career in philosophy, but he became Sweden's most important historian who, by describing the nation's gathering around the king and the church, gave Swedes a common identity and memory. He rejected the Enlightenment's cold adherence to reason and utility, emphasizing instead the function of history to teach humans what is good and evil, right and wrong. He saw the path of history as the struggle toward freedom. Great personalities brought about humanity's advance and their responsibility to improve the world was supported by faith in a personal God. In Hudiksvall, Nathan had written his graduation essay on Geijer and thus knew of him before he came to Uppsala. Geijer, dead since 1817, became his intellectual companion and conversation partner for life. Söderblom's well-worn copies of Geijer's collected writings are full of underlining and notations, a witness to how intensively he studied those works. In a forty-page essay on Geijer, written in 1906, Söderblom painted a picture that contained much of himself: many-sidedness, discernment of essential matters, musicality united with religiosity, love for homeland, and a developed sense of history. Söderblom must also have recognized himself in Geijer's outward life: a demanding father, foreign travels, and a remarkable academic career.

Disciplined and with determination, Söderblom took his first degree, a bachelor's degree that served as the foundation for solid classical studies.

He was gifted in languages and studied Latin, Greek, and Hebrew so that he could read and understand original texts. He also studied Arabic, Nordic linguistics, philosophy, and history. In order to complete the requirements in at least one area of natural science, he took a brief course in geology, a popular subject demonstrating the truth of evolution. It took three years for him to take this basic degree. He spent his vacations in Norrala, where his siblings welcomed him. He helped out on the farm and hauled in timber from the woods. Since childhood he had known how to harness a horse, cut with a scythe, and thresh in rhythm. Through his own work he learned something of the conditions of laborers. During vacations he also fulfilled his military obligation at the Royal Helsinge Regement. He formed a choir of soldiers, received permission to hold evening lectures on abstinence, led chapel services, and served as a stretcher bearer. He was, however, most eager to devote himself to his books and — like his father — preach whenever the occasion arose.

The first time Nathan Söderblom ever entered the pulpit was in the Hälsingtuna church on Midsummer Day in 1883. He was seventeen and had just finished secondary school but had not yet gone to Uppsala. His long sermon on John the Baptist was vetted by all the rules of homiletics. He gave a "trial sermon" before his father. The sermon revealed a wide-ranging knowledge of the Bible and showed insights concerning the "order of grace." When he spoke of John the Baptist's ascetic life, abstinence, and lifelong call to preach, one could catch a glimpse of his father, Jonas Söderblom. Those who heard him must have understood that here was a student who would not only be ordained but would go far in life.

Preaching by laity was greatly valued among adherents of the revival movement. They were often to hear Nathan preach in the area. Before he was ordained, according to preserved records, he had preached at least seventy-seven times, mostly during his vacations in Hälsingland. As priest, professor, and archbishop he continued this steady stream of proclamation week after week to the time of his death. He had taken after his father who continually worked with biblical texts in order to expound on them wherever people gathered to hear. In every kind of worship service the sermon was the central element. Hymns and prayers served largely as framework; the eucharist was seldom celebrated.

It was 1883. Söderblom had not been in Uppsala long. The Norwegian missionary Lars Skrefsrud, who was well known for his work in India, delivered a lecture on paganism and Christianity in Uppsala's Trinity Church. His own life story captured his listeners. As a youth he had been sentenced to a long imprisonment for theft. In prison he was converted and experienced a call to become a missionary. The Norwegian Mission refused to send out someone with a criminal record, but with German and Danish assistance he was able to begin work in India, among the Santals, a discriminated minority group in Bihar, Odisha (formerly Orissa), and West Bengal. He was linguistically gifted and learned one language after another: Hindi, Bengali, Sanskrit, and Santali. Skrefsrud visited villages and studied local customs, music, and culture. With the assistance of the British colonial authorities, the Norwegian missionaries protected the Santals against unfair treatment by Hindus. This created trust and after a cautious start many thousands of people were baptized. When Skrefsrud described this, a wave of warmth went through the audience and some felt a call to be missionaries, among them Ernst Heuman who, after many years in the Norwegian Santal Mission, became a bishop in South India and Erik Folke, who became one of the most well-known Swedish missionaries in China.

Nathan Söderblom had mission in his blood. In Hälsingland there had long been wide support for the work of the Evangeliska Fosterlandsstiftelse in Ethiopia and Eritrea. Few parishes could match Norrala and Trönö when it came to collections for missionaries. At baptisms, weddings, and funerals money was collected for those who sat in "heathendom's midnight darkness." As a child Nathan had gone with his father to mission prayer meetings in small cabins and was along at gift auctions when woolen stockings, potatoes, cereals, and birchwood for fires were called in. When he came to Uppsala, it was natural that he sought out people who shared his interest in mission.

He sat in the balcony and listened as hours went by, the candles burned, and fresh air seemed to disappear from the crowded church. Skrefsrud was experienced, level-headed, and learned. He had given the Santali a written language and helped them preserve their culture. According to him, one must require of missionaries that they "not have a head stuffed full of porridge." That appealed to Söderblom. Christian missions were not for simple-minded and opinionated fanatics. On the contrary, mission required the greatest of talents. The encounter with Skrefsrud determined much of his views on mission. He returned often to his experience of that evening.

The same fall, a handful of students started the Student Missionary Association. Söderblom soon became a member. This was the beginning of his life's international and ecumenical commitment. The Association created a small library that concentrated on the burgeoning research regarding mission. Members studied, formed a choir, exchanged correspondence with missionaries and students in other countries, and heard lectures that often dealt with other world religions. This introduced Söderblom to the idea of studying other religions, but many years passed before that could be realized.

The membership of the Student Missionary Association was not large, but they were the first in Uppsala to follow developments in Africa and Asia. One of the most active members was Natanael Beskow. He wrote a number of hymns for the Association and they were spread throughout the country. The most well known, "Oh, Jubilee Day of the world's expectation when earth is God's Kingdom of blessed accord," was set to music by Waldemar Rudin. Another driving personality was the good-humored and practical Karl Fries, who gave up a promising career as an Orientalist in order to become involved in the YMCA and later to play a leading role in the ecumenical movement. He was the one who sent Nathan Söderblom out into the world.

Nathan was chosen to be deputy auditor of the Association. That was his first formal position, but others awaited him. In 1888, he became editor for the Association's *Messenger*, an ambitious little publication that came out about three times a year in an edition of 450 copies. Söderblom edited this paper from his student room for four years, distributed it himself, and also collected the subscription fees. At times there were hard discussions about what should be printed, but articles on both the China Inland Mission and the Ethiopian Orthodox Church were given space since the Association openly encouraged differing views. That there was an ecumenical problem in connection with mission did not escape him. The Protestant missionary movement had is roots in the neo-evangelical revival. The Student Missionary Association mainly supported the work of the Church of Sweden Mission, which, in comparison to other missionary societies, was anchored in the church, academically oriented, and institutionalized. It was not an issue if the students were also sympathetic toward other mission organizations. The expansive American Student Volunteer Movement in 1886 set "the evangelization of the world in this generation" as its ambitious goal. Students in Uppsala also wished to contribute to those efforts.

Söderblom published an essay on "Sweden's First Christian Teachers" in the *Messenger* in 1889. This was a suggestive account concerning the missionary bishops, Ansgar (801–865) and Sigfrid (eleventh century). He posed the question, "Was Ansgar a great man?" Was he a genius who should be counted among the great? Naturally the answer was affirmative. Such a pivotal, courageous, and pious person could not be denied a place among the church's most outstanding personages. Söderblom's question was more interesting than his answer since it was a question to which he would steadily return. He was captivated by those who were uncommonly gifted, having already learned from Professor Harald Hjärne, whom he admired greatly, about the role of great personalities in human history. He was drawn toward people who mastered a specific field, were artistically endowed, and spoke well. Early on in his career he had become convinced that the fate of the world lay in the hands of bold heroes and trailblazing scholars. He was a kind of "elitist" who in his very first sermon spoke of the necessity of "noble competition." He elevated genius to the sky even though he also had a warm heart for the poor and uneducated. Toward such people he could be as indulgent as anyone, but he would never accept anyone being lazy. He had greater tolerance toward energetic and gifted people, even if they used their talents in bizarre and useless ways.

The beloved Professor of Nordic Languages, Adolf Noreen, had developed a new phonetic way of Swedish spelling that attracted Söderblom. Toward the end of his time as editor of the *Messenger*, he began to use the new spellings. This was an eccentricity he soon abandoned, but he was fully aware of the nuances and possibilities of language and he often paid minute attention to his own texts. Even if the academic content was complicated, he carefully examined the form of his writing, including his choice of metaphors. This did not mean, as we shall see, that the content of his writing was always comprehensible.

The Student Missionary Association shaped Söderblom and opened him to the world. Critical questions concerning racism, Eurocentricity, and cultural imperialism were seldom raised during this period when colonialism, evolutionary theory, and optimism about the future were on the rise. Most people held that it was clear that the Christian West must take responsibility for "civilizing" other people. Among the religions, Christianity was the most superior. Time would show that Christ was the crown of the religions. The West was taken with itself and with its desire for conquest. The future of the world lay, politically, above all in the hands of Great Britain, but in respect to religion, American Protestantism had the initiative. This would determine much of Söderblom's understanding of the international role of Christianity.

He began theological studies in 1886. Not content with the qualifying examination required of all who would be ordained, he elected to move toward a theological candidate (*teol. cand.*) examination, which could lead to further studies. He was twenty — conscientious, intelligent, and charming, at home in university social life, and interested in everything. However, he remained fixated in the view of biblical infallibility that he had inherited from home and that the Uppsala faculty largely affirmed. The first theological course he enrolled in was taught by Professor Martin Johansson. Its subject was "the last things," and the professor began by saying that the theologians of the early church had definitively answered the questions of the Trinity and Christology. The Reformation, he further held, had solved the question of salvation. What remained were the issues of resurrection and eternal life. The professor was confident, moreover, that theology would soon come up with clear and definitive answers even to these questions. Theology at Uppsala was practiced in a world of self-evident dogma. Everything was settled; most matters of doctrine had been dealt with.

When Söderblom years later spoke of the 1880s as "the driest period in world history," that description was largely shaped by the general conservatism of the theological faculty and his own feelings of confinement. He was a brilliant speaker and everyone paid attention to him. He began to read the Nobel laureates Verner von Heidenstam and Selma Lagerlöf, and the poet Gustaf Fröding; he sang in the men's chorus, Orphei Drängar, the Servants of Orpheus; and he devoured modern German theology. But it was only after a severe crisis of faith that occurred around Christmas 1889 that he began to rebel in a struggle to be free. But before that, much would happen.

The university, as we have pointed out, was in the midst of thoroughgoing changes. New professors in the natural sciences had been installed and the student body organized itself. Karl Staaff, who would become Prime Minister in 1905, had been among the founders of "Verdandi" in 1882. That group set the tone for radical students and with its small publications had an influence far beyond its own membership. Long and hot-tempered discussions marked student life. Well-established positions were often challenged and changed. At Nathan Söderblom's nation, Gästrike-Hälsinge, there was a discussion forum that stirred up the students with conflicting viewpoints and also presented well-seasoned debaters such as the theologian Knut Henning Gezelius von Schéele; the well-traveled professor of Semitic languages Herman Almkvist; and the controversial mathematician Knut Wicksell. Verdandi became a forum for the most provocative positions. The whole country reverberated when Wicksell became involved in a debate on sexuality. Ultimately, he was convicted of blasphemy and sentenced to prison. Even though these debates were governed by rules and were strictly controlled, they often became fiercely bitter. If Christianity was on the agenda, the professors of theology excused themselves; it was the historian Harald Hjärne who came to the defense of the faith.

In this milieu, where faith and morality were subject to intellectual scorn and naturalists and opponents of Christian faith trampled everything that was regarded as holy under their feet, Nathan Söderblom learned to stand up for his views. In the crosswinds of obsolete idealism, newly awakened liberalism, theological conservatism, and scientific empiricism, he defended theology as an autonomous scientific discipline. When he began to find his feet, he entered the debates and wrote articles concerning them in *Upsala Nya Tidning*, *Stockholms Dagblad*, and *Helsingen*. He never became an apologist for faith in the same way as J. A. Eklund, an "agitator of the Spirit," but rather presented himself as a modern theologian, a cultural Protestant, or a liberal theologian, depending on one's choice of description. At that time there were not many such people in Sweden; nearly all theologians could be described as traditionalists.

Since the Reformation, nearly all impulses in Swedish theology had come from German universities. At the end of the nineteenth century, however, fresh winds blew from there, but the theologians were late to understand what was going on. Results of the historical-critical method of research were still nearly unknown in Uppsala. There ruled, according to Söderblom, a massively fundamentalist faith. The professors did not guide theological development since they were not independent or creative scholars. The academically more alert Söderblom could not expect much from his teachers. The faculty did not lack gifted personalities, but virtually none of the professors did more than was required of them. The warm-hearted and well-traveled hymnologist Carl Axel Torén was Dean of the Cathedral and also an instructor in practical theology. The exegete Otto Myrberg was a learned, cosmopolitan, and musical scholar in many areas. In his view of the atonement he had collided with both C. J. Boström and Viktor Rydberg. Söderblom ranked Robert Sundelin as a scholar of a higher level. His historical and source-critical method attracted his young student to church history. Martin Johansson was an exegete, but served as a professor of dogmatics and would soon exchange his professor's chair in Uppsala for the bishop's seat in Härnösand. The professor in theological prenotions was the unobtrusive Johan August Ekman. At the turn of the century, after a short time as bishop in Västerås, he succeeded Anton Niklas Sundberg as Archbishop of Uppsala.

The professor most appreciated by the students was Waldemar Rudin. He had an impressive beard and good-natured eyes, was a chaplain to the king, and was a radically pietistic mystic. He had had responsibility for the Swedish Evangelical Mission's work in Africa but had been forced to leave that work when he was accused of heresy. Only after a long wait did he become a professor. Because of his tentatively open view of biblical criticism, he was sharply criticized in the neo-evangelical circles to which he belonged. Rudin was saintly, a visionary and a naïve ascetic who was more taken by the experiential dimensions of faith than by academic problems. He knew his Bible and his Kierkegaard and was sensitive to what really mattered to the students. Söderblom thought a great deal of him. He was impressed by Rudin's openness toward the inexplicable elements of authentic mysticism and he shared his musical interests. Rudin was the only member of the theological faculty who participated in the ongoing debates among the students on faith and morals. On Sundays Nathan often walked all the way to Uppsala-Näs to hear Rudin preach. He felt at home, as Rudin's preaching reminded him of his father, although Rudin was milder in his approach. Rudin had, however, the same passion as his father to draw the souls of men and women to God. He was a model of the kind of authentic piety that Nathan longed for. In spite of their age difference, they became friends for life.

The other professors were not up to the task for the receptive and serious student. They were mired in out-of-date thought and structures and were incapable of leading him into new times. Accordingly, it was outside their lectures and seminars that he tested new thoughts, discussed modern theology, and battled with his own problems of faith. His talents, quick pace of study, ability to express himself, and lack of nervousness over examinations, when taken together, could even give rise to a certain hostility. The driven young man from Hälsingland was not always easy to take.

Usually it took some years before students became involved in many of the activities of university life. When Nathan undertook such activities, it was with a vengeance. He became involved in one student group after another. This began cautiously with the Saturday Union in which students gathered for conversation, Bible study, and prayer. Soon he was also to be found in the Student Missionary Association, the Student Abstinence Union, the Patriotic Student Association, the conservative Heimdal Society, the Academic Union that he helped establish in 1888, the Young Men's Christian Association, an association for the preservation of provincial dialects, and Orphei Drängar, the male chorus. He was also, like all students of theology, a member of the Theological Union. It was not long before he became president and curator of the Gästrike-Hälsinge nation, and then president of the whole student body. In his ten years of study at Uppsala, Söderblom had his hand in almost everything that went on at the university. There were only seventeen hundred students. He was known by everyone and was friends with most.

3

Afflicted and Born Again

A new light fell over Scripture. We began to perceive something of the consistency in God's work through the centuries.

Nathan Söderblom, 1926

On an April day in 1888, a brand new book is lying on Nathan's desk in his student room. It is the first collection of poems by Verner von Heidenstam, who has returned after years of travel in the Orient and been greeted as a poet of promise. Nathan reads and reads. He can do nothing else. One day, two days — his eyes and his mind take in this poetry as though it were a refreshing drink. It is unusual yet much longed for, exotic yet familiar. The 1890s were on their way. This would be Söderblom's decade.

* * *

The Uppsala Student Missionary Association was a small circle, but it meant a great deal to Söderblom's international orientation and spiritual development. Here was a place where he made friends and showed what he could do. The Theological Association, to which all theological students were expected to belong, dealt with more theoretical questions. Teachers and students sharpened their arguments and their defense of Christianity against the onslaught of the natural sciences. When historical-critical biblical studies began to receive attention, the debates heated up. One evening, a theological student asserted that Moses himself, in spite of well-founded objections, wrote the Pentateuch. He was so sharply torn to pieces by Sam Fries and Nathan Söderblom that a few professors had to quiet down the debate. On another occasion, Söderblom was asked how the similarities between the three synoptic Gospels could be explained if the evangelists did not know each other or have access to the same written sources. He responded that there was such a clear gospel tradition in Jerusalem that

Matthew, Mark, and Luke could write independently of, yet also similarly to, each other. Once, when one of the faculty members led the discussion, Fries and Söderblom sarcastically asserted that some candidates for ordination were vassals whom he led around by the nose like a mute herd.

The one who reported on these episodes was Söderblom's best friend Samuel Fries (not to be confused with Karl Fries). He was a rather irascible and opinionated but promising student. He had set his sights on becoming a professor of Old Testament exegesis. Fries was well read and wildly productive, but he was dismissed by his teachers as all too radical and questioning. In frenzied tempo he took one examination after the other. Within nine years he had written his doctoral dissertation. In his free time he wrote long, detailed, and well-reasoned love letters to his fiancée, Anna Fagerlin, the daughter of a landed property owner who lived just hours from Uppsala. The letters dealt with theological questions of all sorts. He described student life in general, but mostly the moral and theological debates that were always going on. She read, learned more and more, and answered patiently and affectionately. With his love he brought her into a theological world dominated by men. The two were compared to Abélard and Héloïse, who at the beginning of the twelfth century donated to world literature their love letters, interwoven with theology. For Anna's sake, Fries wanted to be more learned than all the others. His courtship took the somewhat peculiar form of erudite theological inquiries. Intellectually she was his equal and she encountered him with opposition and critique and became, as he called her, "a fairy of truth." He had significant intellectual gifts and was strong, secure, and self-confident, but it was in tender-hearted dialogue with Anna that he developed into a theologian.

Sam Fries was active in the Theological Association, but it was another forum that meant much more to both him and Nathan. In 1888, they formed, together with Nils Johan Göransson, an informal discussion group, occasionally including others. In Viktor Rydberg's romantic narrative of 1891, *Vapensmeden* ("The Armorer"), it is reported how Gudmund gathered three friends into a group, *Fritt ur hjärtat* ("Free from the Heart"), where all sorts of theological and metaphysical questions were discussed. That is precisely what Sam, Nathan, and "Göran" did. After reading *Vapensmeden*, they called their little group "Free from the Heart." Their conversations created a deep and enduring friendship with modern theology as the focus. They desired not only to renew the theological faculty but — in youthful arrogance — also to reform the whole church. Close masculine friendship was common to the times and to the university, but these three distinguished themselves from others by devoting themselves exclusively to theological and literary discussions rather than to sport or entertainment. They urged each other to take independent positions on controversial questions and to orient themselves in a new and unknown theological landscape. Fries was without compromise. He had given up Lutheran orthodoxy, had no time for the burdens of pietism, and had no inclination toward mysticism. Göransson was more introverted and silent, ironic and self-critical. With time he became moderately conservative. When Fries advocated something, Göransson took the opposite position, while Söderblom sought a middle way. He admired Fries, but trusted Göransson's judgment more and was more personal in his correspondence with him. The group met on Sunday evenings for disciplined and deep personal conversation concerning what they had read, thought, and done during the previous week. This continued for many years, although the intensity faded. Everything was dealt with, certainly the possibility of academic careers, which all three hoped would be realized. Many years later Söderblom wrote to Fries, "God has so wonderfully brought our destinies together that I could not imagine a closer bond of fellowship."

Fiction was important to these three conversation partners. They continued to read the theologically well-traveled Viktor Rydberg, who was so highly regarded by the generation before Söderblom, even though his thinking was increasingly becoming obsolete in the light of philosophical materialism and biological evolutionism. The Christian idealism to which he gave expression at the university jubilee in 1877 could still stimulate a few students, but it was actually passé. Many held Rydberg to be one of the country's leading cultural personalities, but the furor aroused by his book of 1862 *Bibelns lära om Kristus* ("The Bible's Teaching Concerning Christ") had not been forgotten. In that book he had denied the doctrines of both the Trinity and the divinity of Christ. At the end of the 1880s, however, he found new acclaim as a poet. Poems such as *Den nya grottesången* ("The New Grotto Song"), which dealt with the conflicts brought about by industrialism, were naturally discussed by the three friends.

They also read Søren Kierkegaard, Henrik Ibsen, and the Norwegian Bjørnstjerne Bjørnson, who challenged their caution and raised the question as to whether their commitments were really burning. Naturally, they also read the decade's most prominent and controversial figure, August Strindberg, who had lashed out at Uppsala University as being a bulwark for an outdated ordering of society in a short story collection of 1877. Heidenstam came with something else. In his poetry Söderblom felt a warm fantasy, a resilient attraction and yearning that caused him to read and reread the poems. Heidenstam gave "honor, guidance, nourishment" to a patriotic way of thinking. For Söderblom, who was the most artistically inclined of the three, literature had a more than general interest. Throughout his life — in major addresses, insightful literary essays, and extensive correspondence and conversations with notable authors and artists — he allowed poetry, paintings, and music to interpret existence. He could not distinguish between Christianity and culture, for he saw traces of God in all creative art.

The historical-critical study of the Bible also reached Uppsala, requiring a reconsideration of fundamental Christian beliefs. This led to one crisis of faith after another among those who were to be ordained. In Free from the Heart, Söderblom came into contact with modern German theology. He discovered Julius Wellhausen's *Prolegomena zur Geschichte Israels (Prolegomena to the History of Ancient Israel).* The book had been published in 1878 and had been a trailblazer in Germany, but it took ten years to reach Uppsala. Wellhausen integrated Israel's religion into the larger history of Oriental religion. His source-critical analysis of the Pentateuch showed that those five books had been formed over a period of several hundred years. This forced Söderblom to come to terms with his own view of the Bible. He read everything that he could find concerning historical criticism. The ball was rolling. He considered positions that were seen by many to be incompatible with both traditional church teaching and revivalistic piety. He was strengthened in his views by the liberal rabbi Gottlieb Klein, whom he came to know in seminars with the professor of Semitic languages Herman Almkvist. Fries had no problems combining faith with the new way of understanding the Bible, but for Söderblom it was otherwise. For him, the Bible was not just another book of history, but he realized that it could not have been dictated word for word by the Holy Spirit. Certain books possibly did not at every point convey God's revelation, but the Bible as a whole must be regarded as a channel for that revelation. Söderblom endeavored to bridge the gulf between the critical study of the Bible and the literal faith he had inherited from his home. The pious Waldemar Rudin helped him.

He pointed out that one should not forget that behind all revelation stood the single, eternal divine reality.

Söderblom found himself in a quagmire. His "crisis of faith" was looming. It had theological, intellectual, and existential dimensions. It took him more than a year to pass through this fire. He struggled with questions of sin and guilt, and above all he felt a lack of meaning in life. During several anxious weeks, when the faith of his childhood was on the verge of collapse, he doubted that he could continue studying theology or even call himself a Christian. In a sermon of 1905 he described his crisis of faith: "Doubt and moral anxiety became a prison. Enclosing walls shut everything out. My spirit fell to pieces and cried, trembled and sank in exhaustion. Sleep came heavily after long, frenzied prayer. Were those prayers meaningless, solitary cries in empty space?" Yet he did not stop praying for fear that his faith might become a cold rationalism.

The infallibility of Scripture had been the ground of his faith, but if the Bible were only a human book filled with contradictions and incorrect historical narratives, permeated by primitive religious and moral judgments, where could he turn? How could he believe? Nathan felt himself completely empty in his unsatisfied hunger for a living faith. He wrote about this dismal time in his diary, about his "Jacob's struggle," which left him full of uncertainty. He found a bit of consolation in the eighth chapter of Romans where it is asserted that the Spirit helps us in our weakness, and that when we do not know how to pray, the Spirit intercedes for the saints according to the will of God. But could he trust words like that and apply them to himself? In a sermon he preached in San Francisco more than twenty years later, he described how he had felt life's burdens to be ever heavier, guilt more crushing, anxiety more dreadful. For hours into the night, he fell to his knees and prayed and called out from his heart in wordless sounds. Even though this went on for weeks and months, others did not notice it. He did not tell others about his spiritual struggles, nor did he feel that there were any answers to his prayers.

One evening in the fall of 1889 he came across a review by Julius Kaftan of a book on the Christian understanding of providence in a German theological journal. The article was not particularly noteworthy, but it placed modern biblical criticism in a new light. Suddenly, Nathan saw — not as a stroke of lightning but in the clear light of day — that God has not revealed himself only in words and writings but in the acts of sacred history, which reached their climax in Jesus Christ. Much later, and even at the end of his life, Söderblom described this decisive event: "I did not understand everything. But the kingdom of God and its acts became central. There was light in the room where I sat and joy came over me. It was not a book that we had to trust, but that God through Christ has established his kingdom. To that act of God also belonged the birth of the Bible. Christianity was no longer just a religion of the book, it was rather a historic revelation fulfilled in Christ."

With astonishment he saw what the question really was. Revelation was not a word in a book or a doctrine that at every point must be agreed to by Christians, but rather a narrative concerning a living and active God who through Christ seeks to gather all people into his fellowship. The Bible as such is not the Word of God, but the Word of God is found in the Bible. This insight was the beginning of a solution to his intellectual and academic problems. But his personal crisis of faith was not over. He lived with that crisis daily, struggling with the question of whether he had a correct conviction of sin and desire for forgiveness, if he was secure as a child of God. A world-renowned evangelical missionary, Hudson Taylor, founder of the China Inland Mission, on a visit to Uppsala challenged Söderblom. How could he have such an assurance that he could then transmit to others?

Nathan intended to celebrate Christmas at home in Norrala, but he did not look forward to meeting his father. Their relationship had been harmed and a confrontation seemed inevitable. But after Christmas he wrote in his diary: "I was nervous about going home. There had already been disagreements between my father and me. I feared that I might lose respect and devotion for my dear, self-sacrificing father." His mother Sophia was sickly and weak, his brother Svante was far away in California, and the entire family was full of dissension. But Nathan's worries were for nothing. Christmas was one of the "most delightful, happiest."

He was reconciled with his father and the wounds were healed. Nathan felt an outright joy, but he would no longer let himself be dictated to by his father, even though he was attached to him and was totally dependent on him economically. But something else happened that Christmas. A woman who lived on a neighboring farm loaned him a Swedish translation of *Grace and Truth* by the Englishman William Paton Macay. The book was widely circulated in revival circles and had appeared in more than seventy editions. The foreword to the book included a letter from the evangelist Dwight L. Moody. Nathan knew of this evangelist since a "Moody fever" had been loose in Sweden for about fifteen years. Together with Ira D. Sankey, Moody had conducted successful revival tours in England. Their new evangelical message had awakened a strong response and a number of Moody's books and Sankey's hymns had been translated into Swedish. Nathan was interested in the Macay book since he had received an invitation to a student conference at one of Moody's schools in Northfield, Massachusetts.

In his book, Macay described an "order of grace": being convinced of sin, confessing a separation from God, turning toward the cross with trust in Christ's redemption, and personally accepting salvation. Nathan was especially moved by a reference to the serpent in the third chapter of the Gospel of John: "And just as Moses lifted up the serpent in the wilderness, so must the Son of Man be lifted up, that whoever believes in him may have eternal life." As they wandered in the wilderness, the people of Israel complained about both Moses and God. Poisonous snakes had then appeared, biting people fatally. When the Israelites showed signs of regret, Moses formed a bronze snake and set it on a pole. When those who had been bitten looked up to see the bronze snake, they lived. How many times had Nathan read this text both in Greek and Swedish, studied it, and perhaps even preached on it without understanding? Now the words suddenly took on life. In a flash he saw clearly that the cross had completely changed the relationship between humankind and God. Those who encounter the Savior's glance would be saved. The way to freedom from sin and guilt was simple: to look at the crucified one with confidence. Anxious brooding, good works, or intellectual acrobatics could not help; only to look toward Jesus the crucified could. With him the whole world had changed, for the cross had been raised in the midst of history. Nathan had been blind toward this reality. When now he began to see this, his joy was so great that his heart almost broke. "A light spread through the room. Life and the world shone in undreamed light. Tears burst out, but they were tears of joy." Nathan did not need to read further. He gave himself over to God. This happened in the Norrala parsonage on January 18, 1890. He had been born again. This conversion was "the most amazing thing that happened to him in a long life," Söderblom wrote in preparation for a lecture he was to give in Scotland in 1932. But he said nothing about his experience to his father, perhaps because he wanted to be free of him.

What had stirred up Nathan's anxiety was the view of modern theology that the biblical books were not the result of divine dictation but were edited texts determined by particular times. If the Bible was not infallible, how could it be God's revelation? In Söderblom's time, this question was a part of many students' struggle of faith and to doubt seemed to belong to a young man's — in contrast to a young woman's — development. To be an authentic Christian, one's faith had to be tested. For Söderblom's fellow student J. A. Eklund, it was radical naturalism that caused his foundations to tremble. When the hymn writer Natanael Beskow was beset by doubt, he gave up his calling to be a missionary and left Uppsala to become a painter. Einar Billing, five years younger than Söderblom, after having read Wellhausen found himself in the same sort of crisis. "Never will I forget the anguish into which this study brought me. It was like an earthquake: everything seemed to cave in under my feet," he wrote in his episcopal letter to the Diocese of Västerås in 1920. Söderblom reported on these struggles for a later generation of theologians: no one provided clarity or solutions, no one led the way. We were reduced to prayer, to solitary struggle with God. He must help us when the truth of Christianity totters or falls to pieces. For us it was not an inheritance or an easily purchased insight but a revelation from God himself when the question of Christianity's truth shifted from questions about the infallibility of books or words to God's living revelation in history, fulfilled in Jesus Christ and continued in every redeemed soul. A new light fell over Scripture. We began to sense something of the continuity in God's work over the centuries. Academic freedom and rigor became for us a religious duty, an honor that we were debtors to the God of truth and to his witnesses in the holy scriptures.

In retrospect he, like Eklund and Billing, viewed his crisis of faith as a presupposition for a "mature and manly" faith, as they put it. He asserted that it really was only the one who had battled with God who had the right to proclaim the Word and make judgments on theological questions. To have overcome doubt was a necessary requirement for authority as a teacher of theology and as a priest. In this there was an echo of Luther, who referred to his inner *angst* as a guarantor of his painfully won spiritual assurance. How could one who had not experienced the travails of a distressed conscience, the tribulations of melancholy, or the hell of rejection know what is necessary for salvation? Söderblom followed a path that had been well worn by Norrland pietists. He could recognize himself when preachers of all kinds admonished people to set their gaze on Jesus. Jesus did not belong to the past; he continued to encounter those who left old securities behind, turned themselves over to God, and moved on to the future.

After having reached this insight concerning the spiritual content of the cross, the vicarious suffering and death of Jesus became the core of Söderblom's theology. He gave up his introverted concern for his own soul; from now on it was Christ alone who mattered. His personal conversion was fully in line with the experiences that revivalists back home in Hälsingland shared. He was "born again" and soon he would hear the greatest of all revival preachers, Moody himself.

4

With Moody and Mott in America

> Lord, give me humility and wisdom to serve the great cause of the free unity of Thy Church.
>
> *Nathan Söderblom, 1890*

It is a revival meeting on the East Coast of America. The preacher, Dwight Lyman Moody, sits on the platform as though he were enthroned, a sixty-two-year-old steady, angular man with close-cropped gray hair. As he prays and Ira Sankey sings "The Ninety and Nine," there is movement in the hall. It seems as though Sankey never sang that song without some soul being moved or finding peace. The melody is like a trumpet fanfare, but his voice has become the worse for wear, hacking and hard. What should be heard in melodious tones is replaced by the old singer with violent bathos. The music goes from a whisper to a thunderous forte as he mercilessly lets loose on the heaving and puffing tracker organ. Great tears roll down like clear pearls over Moody's bearded cheeks. Half a year later, he is dead. Nathan learns the five verses by heart. He sings the song many times and attempts to have it included in the Swedish hymnal. It is a sensation when he spontaneously breaks into the song during a large banquet in his honor in New York City thirty-three years later. All of America can hear him singing on the radio.

* * *

When Nathan Söderblom informed his father in the fall of 1889 that he had been invited to the United States of America the next summer, his father reacted negatively. He could not approve of such wasteful extravagance. Yet even though Nathan was accustomed to following his father's wishes, this time he was not willing to give in. He wanted to travel to America, and he did. This journey was to determine the direction of his life.

A doctoral student from Yale University, James Reynolds, had come to Uppsala to locate a Swedish delegate to an international student meeting that was to take place on the East Coast of America the following summer. Karl Fries, who was himself a doctoral candidate in Semitic languages and who intended to be a missionary to Ethiopia, was the secretary of the Swedish YMCA. He nominated Nathan Söderblom to be that delegate with all expenses paid. Before he left, as we have seen, Nathan had been struck by a deep crisis of faith. In the warm revivalistic milieu of Northfield, Massachusetts, he would meet many who had had similar struggles and who were sympathetic to his spiritual experiences.

Nathan was twenty-four when he boarded the train on a spring day. He had never been south of Stockholm and obviously he had never been out of the country. Psychologically for Swedes, though, America was not a distant land during that century of emigration. It was, rather, a neighboring country. Nathan had an uncle and a brother in California and, like other Swedes, he was attracted by what he heard about freedom and opportunity in the United States. His travel notes were filled with on-the-spot accounts and thoughts, a lively and informative description of things that some would compare to Linné's diaries from his journeys of discovery through the Swedish countryside 150 years earlier. When his train passed through Lund, the Uppsala student sneered that "it would be impossible to live down here in Skåne. One would become fat and healthy, but also sluggish with no energy." How poets could be born there was inconceivable. He could not imagine that that part of the country could produce people with passion in their hearts and wide mental horizons. No, such people were born farther north.

His journey continued on a little vessel from Copenhagen to Lübeck and then on the steamship *Rugia* from Hamburg to LeHavre and on to New York. Nathan described everything he encountered on his long journey, including poor working children, Ardennes draft horses, and a funeral procession of one hundred French nuns. He was curious about everyone and everything. He was suspected of espionage in France and came close to being arrested, but at the last minute he was released. On board ship, he met extremely poor emigrants who possessed no more than the clothes on their backs as well as wealthy businessmen, dancing gypsies, and beautiful young women whom he looked over carefully, especially a Miss Kaderly. In one of the salons, she would entertain with song while he accompanied her on the piano. Her gentleman friend was hard for him to bear, an egotistical scholar of some kind. Nathan described an enjoyable interlude he shared with her on the afterdeck, which included German folk songs and a deep conversation about Franz Liszt. She was a bit taken with herself but she had personality and lovely sincerity. One can imagine that Söderblom could have won her away from her friend — who had eleven hundred footnotes in his dissertation. But now there were other things to occupy him. After twelve days at sea — sumptuous meals, new friendships, concerts, lectures, and deck games — the ship arrived in New York.

He was met at the pier by leaders of the YMCA, who showed him around. The YMCA had come to the United States from England in 1851 and had subsequently become a worldwide organization with many centers, especially in New York. It centered on social concern and attracted young men who had chosen Jesus Christ as Lord and Savior in accordance with Holy Scripture and who desired to be his disciples in faith and life, spreading the Kingdom of God on earth. In New York, he was able to visit several places of activity where care was being shown to different groups, from French immigrants to Chinese railroad workers. It was "a blessed institution" and Nathan was deeply impressed. Back in Uppsala, he was to become chairperson of the local YMCA group. What he did not yet know was that the ecumenical movement, with which he would be associated as a leader, was to get much of its inspiration and steadiness from the YMCA.

Nathan traveled to New Haven, Connecticut, where he stayed for several weeks as the guest of James Reynolds's family. James's father was pastor of a Congregational church. Elizabeth Campbell, a sister-in-law, also lived with the pastor and his wife. She was married to an important newspaper publisher and had herself made many trips to Europe. She gave Nathan an intensive course in spoken English. The pastor took him to different academic events and arranged for him to meet a few Yale professors who had interests in Swedish theology. Nathan also took part in a conference on church publications at which Newman Smyth was a leader. He had a generous ecumenical outlook and held that the Christian press should foster Christian unity before its own interests. "Good," wrote Söderblom concisely in his diary and added to his word a prayer: "Lord, give me humility and wisdom to serve the great cause of the free unity of Thy Church." Evangelical freedom and an acceptance of different expressions of church life were a presupposition of Christian unity — that was to be Söderblom's ecumenical program. In recognition of his prayer, one can identify June 19,

1890 as the introduction to his life's work, even if it would be a few decades before he was seriously to make his ecumenical contribution.

Söderblom was overwhelmed by the Reynolds family's naturally polite, generous, and cultivated style. Mrs. Campbell, their relative, gave him the impression that women in America were independent and well educated; they seemed to play a totally different role than women in Sweden. He admired her greatly. Never before had he met a woman with such broad knowledge and character. She had viewpoints on everything. Her judgments were based on scrupulously sharp observations and supported by mature convictions. She was the most entertaining woman he had ever met, agreeable like few others but not at all distant, even though she exceeded others with respect to sound reasoning and her many various interests. She understood not only the literary but also the political world. She could handle horses and had made a fortune in California real estate. She also spoke with and placed service people on the same level as herself. Moreover, she was a pedagogical genius and a simple, believing Christian. However, she would not hear of giving women the right to vote. The proper territory for women was "the inner." By supporting their husbands and sons, women had greater power than would be given them by access to the ballot. Furthermore, there was the risk that giving the right to vote to women would increase the power of Roman Catholic priests since Catholic women were inclined to obey their priests in everything. In admiring, nearly amorous terms, Nathan described Elizabeth Campbell: "The waves of her hair are pleasing with no coquettish affectations. The nose is not perfect, but her face is attractive, her eyes have a blue, intelligent gaze, especially when she smiles or laughs in a quietly melodious way that makes her appear youthful in spite of her fifty years. She is a superior individual, a genius." She possessed everything that his deaf and unhappy mother lacked: urbanity, education and wealth, an encompassing social engagement, and not least, personal charm. Nathan often met men to whom he would attach himself as he would to his father. Rudin was one. Soon he was to meet another, D. L. Moody. But he also dreamed of a mother who could give him more than he ever received at home. Elizabeth Campbell fulfilled those dreams and gave him a view of women as equal to men — intellectually, socially, and politically engaged. The well-established New England family who were hosts to the Swedish student conveyed a positive and uncritical picture of the United States, including its church life. This followed him through the years and was strengthened time after time, especially when he came back to America thirty years later.

The student conference took place at the Mount Hermon School, a boys' school in Northfield, Massachusetts, on the Connecticut River, which the world-famous evangelist Dwight L. Moody had founded. Nathan recognized the landscape. If one only changed the broad-leafed trees to birch trees, it could have been the valleys and hills of Hälsingland. He also felt at home in the warm spiritual milieu where the cross of Christ was at the center and where uplifting revival preaching and simple and sincere music gripped the soul. The meeting lasted for two weeks with Bible study, services of worship, and lectures in the mornings, a long recess for sports, swimming, conversation, and prayer in the afternoons, and then an evening gathering, often with inspiring themes on mission. The lectures, according to Söderblom, were mediocre, especially when they took on apologetic tones. But he was "born again" and approached everything openly.

The meeting involved around 370 people. Most were Americans and Canadians, but there were also seventeen students from Japan, two from China, ten from Great Britain, two from France, and one from Germany. Nathan was the only delegate from the Nordic countries. Two Sioux Native Americans made an impression on him, as did students from Yale and Harvard. Like them, he spoke in condescending tones about the "so-called" students from the American southern and west coast states. Christian groups were already organized on many American campuses. Their goal was to spread the student movement to other countries.

The delegates to the Northfield conference were mostly young men from the white, upwardly mobile, Protestant middle class and all of them focused their attention on Moody. He, in sharp contrast to them, came from an extremely limited background, had a poor education, and after his conversion had reluctantly been received into a prominent Congregational church. The first impression this "farmer" — as he called himself — gave was unpleasant and nearly repulsive, but when one got to know him, he proved to be an impressive and gifted Christian personality. Söderblom used strong words to describe Moody. Love toward God and all the unredeemed was the dominant force in his life. He had an unselfishness that not even the bitterest enemy of Christianity who came into contact with him could deny. Moody was truly a child of God, natural and uncomplicated, a man for whom there was no difference between knowing and doing.

To Karl Fries Söderblom wrote: "This man is remarkable, a new chapter in my life." He asked himself how this simple preacher had attained such great influence and was received everywhere with such respect. Moody never propagandized for a particular church group — his listeners were uncertain of which church he belonged to — and there was almost nothing he hated more than proselytism and sectarianism. Wherever he went, he sought to cooperate with local congregations. He urged newly converted people to quickly join a local church, most desirably one they could call their own, and remain there. He was a brilliant speaker and made use of down-to-earth, concrete, powerful, and original language. He allowed no carelessness, even if he preached the same sermon many times. He was always well prepared, thinking everything through to the most minute detail. Söderblom was both impressed and inspired and made a note that he wished to follow Moody's example. From Moody he learned how to capture an audience's attention: by being extremely well prepared so that he could speak from the heart and not from a manuscript.

This evangelist to the world did not make his appearance alone. Ira D. Sankey, who composed twelve hundred spiritual songs, participated in his campaigns. Moody's own publishing company saw to it that these songs were spread throughout the world. Moody and Sankey were like an old pair of horses, the best of friends. One could scarcely name one without naming the other. One evening, Moody requested Sankey to sing the song about the ninety and nine sheep and the shepherd who with bloody feet and hands torn by thorns sought and sought and finally found the lost sheep:

> There were ninety and nine that safely lay
> in the shelter of the fold.
> But one was out on the hills away,
> far off from the gates of gold.
> Away from the mountains wild and bare.
> Away from the tender Shepherd's care.

The text was written by Elizabeth C. Clephane. Söderblom learned the five verses by heart and he loved singing the song. The evening meetings in Northfield were filled with such songs. Young men gave themselves over to the Lord, yet in spite of the concentrated atmosphere there was not an ounce of sentimentality: "It was a muscular, powerful Christianity one came into contact with, a Christianity with no unctuous salve or a trace of Sunday," he wrote. There was "a breath of the unity of Christ's church" and no one could avoid "knowing the *universalism* of Christ's kingdom along with the breadth of a Christian's responsibility."

That summer Söderblom met several people with whom he would later have much contact. One was the American Methodist John R. Mott. He was the same age as Söderblom. Among all the participants at the meeting, he was the one who made the strongest impression. That was true in both directions: Mott paid especial attention to the man in the white student cap. They were to become two of the growing ecumenical movement's strongest leaders. Mott would play a leading role in the YMCA and then in the World Student Christian Federation and the World Council of Churches. In 1946, he was awarded the Nobel Prize for Peace. After Söderblom's death, Mott recalled him: "The openness of his face, his cheerful disposition, lively ways, and winning personality marked him as one who would capture a place in the hearts of the students at Northfield. In the space of ten days he had bound himself in enduring friendship to many in the quite different groups that were represented there." Mott recalled Söderblom's personal charm, freshness of spirit, hopeful view of life, and gift for friendship. Even if Mott's picture was colored by many subsequent encounters, he formed his lasting impressions when both were young.

The other person who would have great meaning for Söderblom was the Frenchman Wilfred Monod. He belonged to a large family of Reformed pastors and would soon be drawn into the Christian social movement centered on Tommy Falot and the highly influential journal, *Le Christianisme Social.* Monod went through, at the same time as Söderblom, an inner crisis brought about by the eternal question of how God's almighty power could be reconciled with all of the evil present in the world. Monod was more radical than Söderblom. He distanced himself — in light of realities in the world — from the view that God could be the good Creator, but thanks to a personally piercing experience of Christ, he could still maintain faith during the violent religious conflicts that broke out in France at the turn of the century. For Monod, as for other Reformed church leaders in France, the dogmatic differences between churches had little meaning; the decisive factor was cooperation in solving social questions. He was one of the founders of Fédération Protestant de France and came to play a central role in the socially concerned wings of the ecumenical movement. When he and Söderblom reestablished contact with each other in the 1920s, their friendship was deepened and scarcely anyone came to stand nearer to Söderblom on the spiritual level than Monod. In 1926, Söderblom wrote after a "holy" visit with Monod and his wife in Paris: "Where are there any people nearer to the Christian ideal than these two — we nearly talked each other's heads off and we also sat together in silence." This lifelong friendship began in the circle around Dwight L. Moody and was strengthened by the fact that Monod had once visited Sweden and learned something of Söderblom's homeland. They met for the last time in 1930 in Chêxbres where they — frail as they both were — presided at the eucharist together.

It is scarcely possible to overestimate the significance of this journey to America for Söderblom. He was there for two months. His horizons were broadened and he was incorporated into an intellectually cultivated upper class of evangelical Christians who de-emphasized doctrinal differences in favor of practical cooperation and mutual respect. For the first time, he moved outside the boundaries of Lutheranism and a state church. He came to value the American churches' variety and independence and also came to the conviction that faith, theology, and social action must go hand in hand. In New York, he witnessed examples of Christian social responsibility. At Yale, he was exposed to modern, open, and results-oriented academic research. In Northfield, he was impressed by the students' eagerness for mission as well as their organizational gifts. He learned to know a nonconfessional "alliance Christianity" permeated by an entrepreneurial spirit.

Concentration was not on mossy church tradition but on winning people for Christ. The churches in the United States had created influential institutions and church leaders were taken seriously even in the White House. The American churches had come to influence the free churches of Sweden. Söderblom wished that the tradition-bound Swedish state church could learn from the modern Christianity he encountered in New England.

During these summer weeks he matured as a Christian, uniting individualism and universalism, inwardness and intellectual integrity. He experienced deep communion across confessional boundaries. Northfield was not so much a theological conference but simply a meeting with Christian content marked by prayer — individually, in groups, or everyone together. It provided a model for Söderblom's own meetings and solidified his conviction that prayer and worship were most crucial when Christians were to do anything together.

Back in Uppsala, he continued with his studies, having two years left before his basic theological examination. His wrestling with modern theology was far from finished. He continued to serve as editor of *The Messenger* and he also spoke widely concerning American Christian students and their keenness for mission. He practiced the piano and took lessons in harmony. After having sung in Allmänna Sången — the oldest student choir in Scandinavia — and having led the choir of his nation, Söderblom joined the internationally well-known male chorus, Orphei Drängar, the Servants of Orpheus. In the summer of 1891, that chorus toured nineteen Swedish cities, giving twenty-one concerts in four weeks. The conversations in Free from the Heart continued, penetrating more deeply, especially into German theology. And at the same time, he was more and more drawn into the leadership of his nation and of the Uppsala student body as a whole.

Karl Fries saw to it that Söderblom continued with his international activities. Söderblom traveled to Amsterdam as the Swedish delegate to an international YMCA conference. This strengthened his conviction that the gospel is intended for all people, but also that the only way this could happen was if individuals encountered Christ. In his report on the Amsterdam event he emphasized that the cultural differences within the group did not lead to division but rather made the meeting both richer and stronger. It was only within the richness of diversity that Christian unity could grow.

The following year, 1892, he attended a student meeting in Horten, Norway. Following the American pattern, this Christian student conference was held even before local unions were formed. This conference was a rare instance of Nordic Christian fellowship and at the beginning mostly Danish and Norwegian students participated. Finland was still a Russian principality and in Sweden the Student Missionary Association was skeptical concerning a Nordic meeting that was "for us foreign in manners and customs." Nor did the Association have much to do with the growing Student Volunteer Movement with its Anglo-American character.

After his journey to America, Söderblom took a different position. Even though at specific points he was critical toward other forms of Christianity, he was eager to see the international student movement develop on Nordic soil. At Northfield, the students had discussed the possibility of gathering all the world's Christian students into a large common fellowship. He hoped that that would happen at Horten, but it turned out not to be the case. The World Student Christian Federation (WSCF) was founded in 1895 at Vadstena in Sweden. Söderblom was not only present at Horten, he was one of the conference lecturers. Referring to his own experience, lively and personal, he spoke in a different way than the Danes and Norwegians had expected. In him they encountered a Christianity that proved that a "Swedish spirit" could hold great riches.

Söderblom was on his way. He had learned much from the expansive American understanding of Christian work in the world. In Amsterdam he encountered Christians from the British colonies who emphasized social responsibility. In Horten he had begun to sense how Nordic Christians, in spite of different traditions of piety, not only had a common spiritual, confessional, and cultural history, but also had received a special call from God to bring together the world's Christians. All of this would provide the basis for his international ecumenical work. First, however, he had to deal with a number of problems concerning God's revelation to the world, take up his doctoral study of ancient Iranian religion, and establish himself as a public student leader. The years 1892 to 1893 would be decisive for his future.

5
With Words at His Command

> It angers me when well-intentioned people call the times evil and anti-Christian because they are backward looking. It is a wonderful time that we live in, filled as it is with power both for good and evil.
>
> *Nathan Söderblom, 1891*

NATHAN HIRES A HORSE AND SLED and drives one Sunday morning a couple of hours to Enköping with his Anna. He is at home in the saddle and the horse trots along the road through a snowstorm past Balingsta, through Lagunda and the northern part of Trögden to Judge Östlund's farm where there are stalls for horses. They are barely on time for High Mass at the Church of Our Lady. Söderblom is the celebrant and Fries preaches. After the meal at the rector's home, Free from the Heart meets. Anna does not remember much of the conversation concerning Jesus of Nazareth and the Christ of the church, but she does recall the atmosphere. Fries is so excited that he almost stammers. Göransson sits quietly and meditatively, slow to express his arguments. Söderblom sees things more deeply than the others and brings their viewpoints together. She adores him.

* * *

In the 1890s, to call someone "Ritschlian" was an easy way for conservative theologians and fundamentalist preachers to dismiss a person as a heretic on the brink of damnation.

Some described Söderblom as a Ritschlian even though at essential points he clearly and definitely distanced himself from Albrecht Ritschl. He never, however, completely rid himself of that label. When he, along with Fries and Göransson, began to read Ritschl's great books, *A Critical History of the Christian Doctrine of Justification* and *Reconciliation* and *History of Pietism*, he became enthusiastic. He found the arguments to be cogent, supplying a new language and means for encountering the demands of modern times. That he was captivated by Ritschl was, however, a surprise considering that the professor from Göttingen was his exact opposite in almost all respects, a wooden and distant intellectual who completely lacked both Söderblom's feeling for the interior aspects of religion and his artistic and creative style of working. Nevertheless, after Schleiermacher Ritschl was nineteenth-century Germany's most influential theologian. That was reason enough to study his work, not to mention understanding the controversies surrounding that work.

Ritschl died in 1889 at the age of 69. Only toward the end of his life were his works studied in Sweden, but his reputation preceded him. Many rejected his theology without even having opened his books. Professors in Uppsala did not dare to defend him and even fewer attempted fully to comprehend his complicated reasoning. But he did have at least two devoted Swedish disciples: the old professor in Lund Pehr Eklund, and the young *Pastor Primarius,* Dean of the Stockholm Cathedral Fredrik Fehr. Söderblom met Fehr on Good Friday 1892 when he and his friends went to Stockholm, participated in High Mass at the Cathedral, and then were invited to dinner with the dean. In these three students from Uppsala Fehr found soulmates. Fries wrote exuberantly about their meeting. Everything about the young priest merited superlatives: his sermon, his simplicity and approachability, his well-appointed home and large library. Fehr had met Ritschl personally and carried on correspondence with several of his students. He wanted to spread Ritschlian theology in Sweden by every means possible, including confirmation instruction for young people. He was persistent and controversial and although he encountered considerable opposition, he was regarded as a popular preacher whose intention was to reach the educated.

According to Ritschl, the Christian faith does not rest on teachings and dogma but on a religious certainty grounded in individual experience. It is by means of an inner experience of salvation that humans can understand the objective validity of the biblical message. God revealed himself in Jesus of Nazareth and in him and in the primitive church, a new epoch of history had its origin. As a consequence of Christianity, a new world ethical community, "the kingdom of God," was to arise. But neither this kingdom of God nor humanity's destiny could be realized unless humanity itself was liberated by divine forgiveness. Ritschl believed that the true essence of the Christian religion is love as revealed in the historic Jesus and made visible in the practical love for neighbors exercised in common social contexts and in every person's daily existence. Love is the heart and pulse of Christianity. The kingdom of God is to be realized on earth in the form of an ethically cultivated and advanced society. Jesus has made it possible for those who follow him to implement God's loving will in spite of their own shortcomings. Historical knowledge supports Christianity's uniqueness and universal significance. Ritschl was a systematic theologian; however, he did not develop his system on the basis of a philosophy of religion but rather on the basis of an evolutionary view of history and a this-worldly ethic of the kingdom of God. By making the person of Christ found in the gospels into an authority over all authorities, he gave inspiration to both ecclesiastical and theological work.

Söderblom worked to make Ritschl more known in Sweden. In an article in *Svensk Tidskrift (The Swedish Review)* concerning Christianity and the spirit of modern times, he presented Ritschl's theology as a way to deal with the problems of society. With a purely religious experience of Christ as a basis and a view of truth determined not by dogma but rather by how a person estimates his or her own experience, it becomes possible to protect human freedom from the shackles of deterministic materialism. Nature's chain of cause and effect encloses people like shackles of iron and this imprisonment is humanity's authentic predicament. Religion, however, is able to set free humanity's ethical resources, showing that people are more than matter. In actuality, religion is neither morality nor a view of life, but is its own category. This is the source of humanity's freedom and value. If religion is suppressed, society suffers, for its deepest humanity is jeopardized.

When Hjalmar Danell defended his dissertation on Albrecht Ritschl's doctrine of sin in 1892, Nathan Söderblom — perhaps because of his *Svensk Tidskrift* article — was chosen to be the opponent. Söderblom asked Fredrik Fehr to attend and on the basis of his knowledge, to oppose Danell from the audience. This became a minor scandal. Fehr's critical comments were met with hoots and catcalls, causing him to leave the university shocked and distressed. Söderblom caught up to him at the Uppsala railroad station and attempted to smooth things over. His contacts with Fehr subsequently became more personal, which meant that he himself was seen as an uncritical fellow traveler of Ritschl. Before Söderblom had taken his first theological degree he had translated the first part of a book on Ritschl who, at that time in 1893, was still largely unknown in Sweden. It was written by a Frenchman and had been well received even in Germany. Söderblom did not simply prepare a translation; he went through Ritschl's writings in order to provide exact references in the book.

It was at this point that his admiration for the controversial German theologian reached its high point. During the years that followed, he became more critical. However, his view of the connection between revelation and history, inspired by Ritschl, remained and was to become a foundation of his theology. God had not made himself known in some supernatural way from beyond the universe's appointed order, but had revealed himself in and through humankind's continuous history. By scientifically studying history, humans could gain insight into its deeper meaning. Similarly, if one studied other religions objectively, Christ would appear in an ever clearer light, for he stood in the midst of all human history, not at its side.

Söderblom wanted to be a modern theologian, but he did not want to be called a "Ritschlian." Even if he willingly adopted positive elements from Ritschl, he remained critical of the fact that Ritschl had no feeling for religion's inwardness and was strongly suspicious of mysticism, which he held to be un-Lutheran. Söderblom could not accept Ritschl's rationalistic dismissal of faith as the soul's personal fellowship with God as "metaphysical," nor could he understand how Ritschl could be so blind regarding elements of mysticism in Luther, elements that permeated the reformer's whole life. In Ritschl he also missed the eschatological dimension in God's promises and he could not agree that the kingdom of God could be reduced to this world. However, he was grateful that Ritschl gave him a new view of revelation and placed Christ at the center of everything without allowing old dogmas to separate him from human contexts. Above all, Ritschl directed his attention to the young Martin Luther and allowed him to read the reformer without the lens of Lutheran dogmatism. Ritschl emphasized freedom as the distinctive feature of Christian faith and he brought to the fore Luther's writing of 1520, *The Freedom of a Christian*. Söderblom virtually memorized that treatise on his way to America in 1890.

In 1893, at a summer course in Uppsala, Söderblom lectured on the basic ideas of the Reformation. In respect to Martin Luther's understanding of Christian freedom, Söderblom confronted the prevalent interpretation of Luther from within. After describing the background of the Reformation, he focused his lectures on the young Luther's own spiritual experiences rather than explicating Lutheran doctrine. For Luther, faith was trust in God, not intellectual certainty. Luther was not at all especially bound to the letters of the Bible or to church doctrine. Concerning the Letter of James, which is full of admonitions to good works, Luther could say that James was mad. In Luther's exposition of the articles of faith there was little trace of the doctrine of the Trinity and he left it to sophists to quarrel over the doctrine of Christ's two natures. If Luther had had the same tools of historical research as later generations, he would, in Söderblom's opinion, scarcely have surrendered points of doctrine that contradicted reason. Certainly there were elements of medieval superstition in Luther, but he approached the old dogmas with a young, fresh faith and exploded them from within.

Revivalists and church authorities alike continually referred to Luther. Since childhood, Söderblom had heard preachers — not least his own father — pile up quotations from Luther, one upon another. In regard to Luther, Ritschl and the pietists seemed to find each other, only to quickly go their separate ways. Ritschl emphasized Luther's carefree freedom in relation to the Bible and his undogmatic view of the person and work of Christ, while the church and the pietists were deeply marked by a conservative and dogmatic interpretation of Luther. This latter view had become untenable in the society now being born. In contrast, Söderblom relied on the historical-critical method of biblical research, a view of history as the revelation of God, and the engagement of theology with the past in order to encounter modernity while at the same time holding fast to Christ as the foundation of faith. Scientific knowledge was not a threat to faith, but it had its limits. Trust in God and union with him lay outside the realm of empirical knowledge.

Luther had reawakened the living religion inherent in Christianity. It had been pushed aside and smothered by moralism and dead doctrine, covered by both impurities and affectations. He had found his firm footing in the gospel and broken the logjam. For Luther, the gospel was not a matter of dogma or law, rites or teachings; it was living religion and thanks to him, it had been born again. When he criticized the state of things within the church, he relied on Christianity's central religious content. To discover the authentic Luther, one must seek him in that content. Doctrine affects only the exterior. Religion actually involves human existence and the faith or doubt that either supports or crushes a person. Luther declared what faith is: *Ein Gott zu haben, dass heißt etwas haben, worauf das Herz gänzlich trauet* — to have a God means having someone who can be relied on with the whole heart. Confidence and reliance are eloquent expressions for the evangelical confession. Confidence makes dogma relative. Confidence does not rest on a teaching or a theoretical view of life but on life as lived and experienced. This can be recognized even outside the Christian context.

Söderblom appeared to be a young, radical Uppsalan who thought he had Luther on his side. By making a sharp distinction between faith as assent to doctrine and faith as trust and by rejecting biblical literalism and dogmatism, he saw himself as being authentically Lutheran. No one doubted Söderblom's loyalty to the Church of Sweden and his eagerness to renew that church, but his interpretation of Luther was problematic for those inclined toward traditional formulations of doctrine. His lectures were published, and he sent them to the nestor of the church's traditionalists, Bishop Gottfrid Billing, who that same year had ordained Nathan. The answer was: "Keep on studying Luther but put aside the German glasses: through them you see some points very well, but they prevent you from seeing a great many others."

For Söderblom, this new discovery of Luther and his encounter with the Roman Catholic doctrinal tradition was of great significance. He spoke incessantly of trust as the gift of the gospel and as a necessary condition for his own service. All narratives about Söderblom describe a confident person who held his own against all difficulties and maintained his balance even in the face of opposition. His life's theme was that of a Christian person's freedom. Submission was the basis of freedom: only the person who completely places himself in God's service is free. His own surrender to God had cost him a great deal. Thus he valued his newfound freedom even more.

As we have seen, standing up for modern theology in Sweden had its risks. It was not easy to convince traditional believers that such theology could be associated with authentic Christian faith. Söderblom's position was made even more difficult because he was so troubled by pious speech and religious sentimentality that he consciously tried to steer clear of the usual "big words" of Christianity. There was a great deal of that vocabulary around as revivals began to lose strength and preachers lost their power; they raised their voices in order to convince people of their arguments.

Söderblom was not only fearful of using pious words but was also reluctant to speak of his own spiritual experiences. When he later described those experiences, he did so in the third rather than the first person. He sought an everyday and natural language in order to win his own generation's attention. Those who were at home with an introverted religious vocabulary saw him as alien to what they considered "classical" Christianity.

There was, however, one person who was attracted to his way of speaking — Anna Forsell. She had grown up in a liberal Stockholm home in which Unitarian literature was often read. She had been confirmed by Fredrik Fehr and had Viktor Rydberg as a teacher before she herself became a substitute teacher in Halmstad in order to finance further studies. One of her students, Klara Johansson, who later on became an influential literary critic, painted a picture of Anna in a few lines:

> There is something between heaven and hell
> In that sweet little Anna Forsell.

Scarcely twenty years old, Anna moved to Uppsala in 1891. She was an independent young student with bright intellectual and musical gifts. She studied aesthetics, literature, art, and above all, history with the greatly admired Harald Hjärne. Throughout her life she had a liberal view of Christianity and occasionally described herself as a "forecourt Christian." Fehr remained her spiritual authority and the modern theology of the 1890s was her lifelong guiding star. She was a doubter who did not give in to the dogma of previous generations and she was, additionally, quite uncertain about the sacrament of Holy Communion. There was a trace of alienation between her and ecclesiastical tradition, old-fashioned forms of expression, and rigid organizational structures. She could not abide the assertive sentimentality of pietism and its hypocrisy sickened her. She met Nathan the first time in October 1891. They were engaged after a short year and they married in April 1894.

They shared a few eventful terms at Uppsala. He was chairman of the local chapter of the YMCA, but he gave more time to his prestigious position as first curator of the Gästrike-Hälsinge nation. He was admired as a humorous and quick-witted speaker and as an advocate for the small nation. He was so popular that in the autumn of 1892 he was elected president of the university student body. It was customary for that position to be occupied by the first curator of a nation and the vote was political. Söderblom had been a member of the conservative student union Heimdal ever since it was established and he was also part of the Patriotic Student Union, which chiefly had national defense on its agenda. Consequently, he ran and won as the conservative candidate. One of his first tasks was to speak at the November 6 observance of the death of Gustavus Adolphus in 1632 at the battle of Lützen during the Thirty Years War. On that day, in a way now inconceivable to us, he began — as he did for many years — to praise his hero king in both word and writing. He saw Gustavus Adolphus as one of the greatest among the geniuses or saints who led humanity toward the goal determined by God. Not even when the First World War drowned Europe in blood, as had the Thirty Years War, did he change his mind. The "Lion from the North" had saved the Reformation and with it the freedom of the individual.

Short in stature, with broad shoulders and blond hair fluttering in the wind, Söderblom stood at the obelisk in front of an enthusiastic crowd outside Uppsala's Trinity Church. Against the leafless trees, torches burned in the dark November night. His light voice was strong enough to be heard even when it sank to a whisper. His speech was elevated and filled with thanksgiving for the king who had liberated the people's power so that it "became a joy to live and be Swedish." What was it that gave the king such greatness? When the European culture was threatened by constraint of conscience and violence, the Swedish king brought a fresh wind from the North that gave rise to a new birth of freedom. Gustavus Adolphus united the Swedish people; he regretted the death of others more than his own; and he was a ruler who cultivated friendship and found his strength in the God of love revealed by Christ. In the spirit of this king, Uppsala students could not dwell as "unworthy parasites in the banquet halls of national memory." No, they should honor their fatherland with the best of their thinking, struggles, purity, and morals. This should be their gift to the world. Söderblom wrote out his speech in a small parchment notebook with a laurel wreath and green ribbon on the cover and gave it to Anna.

Some weeks later he spoke in memory of King Charles XII who, after waging war all over eastern Europe, was killed while invading Norway in 1718. Rhetorically, he asked why one should celebrate the memory of this warrior king whose greatness now seemed so strange. Because, he answered, the students would not allow restricted mediocrity to limit their perspective. They expected great things and they were willing to do great things for everything that made life worth living. This was an unexpected allusion to the Baptist missionary to India, William Carey, whose words, "Expect great things from God; attempt great things for God," had given fire to the Protestant missionary movement just a hundred years earlier. For Söderblom the warrior king Charles XII was no hero, but by interpreting him with the help of the peaceful missionary he could concur with the cheers. More surprising were the cheers that followed for Anna Forsell. In a letter to an aunt, she described how after the meeting Nathan marched with the chorus, as was the custom, to the bridge called Dombron to cast torches into the Fyris river. Then the two of them went off to the side of the crowd of students and pledged themselves to each other. Up to that time he had called her "Miss Forsell," but now he said, "You have my life in your hands." Nathan had just completed his first examination in theology.

He had spoken on many occasions and, to be sure, he had preached, debated, and lectured, but he had not been noted as an especially talented speaker before he began officially to represent the student body. Within a year he was known and acknowledged as one of Uppsala's most splendid orators. Suddenly, he was in the center of things, acknowledged as brilliant and shining.

A twenty-six-year-old Söderblom now belonged to the Uppsala establishment. His approach to life had changed. He was identified as "tomorrow's man." In Norrala, his old father struggled on, fettered by the literalistic biblicism that shaped his pastoral vocation. Nathan had the same background, but he had become free and self-confident. He created a social platform, cultivated friendships with people of growing power, and entered into the world of the press. He was confident in himself and saw his future as being that of an influential professor, with the church as an alternative career path. The church still had a strong position in Swedish society, even though various popular movements lessened its ideological monopoly. His popularity and power affected Söderblom and questions of the future determined his self-image. He expected a great deal from himself and desired to use his influence to change things, not to preserve them.

Lydia Wahlström, who led Uppsala's women's union, received help from Nathan in defending female students when they were accused of using alcohol or tobacco and of casually being with male friends at night. Wahlström, who came out as bisexual in the 1940s, wrote in her autobiography that in her experience, love usually began with an "admiration of intelligence." That was also true of her relationship to Nathan. He was anxious for more "contact and understanding between young women and male students." In the Sweden of that time, which was not behind Victorian England in respect to double sexual morality, neither of them had anything good to say about the ongoing propaganda for free love. But she recalled how on a sparkling moonlit night, which was made for the heat of youth, they strolled in the woods and he leaned against a fir tree and sang a popular Danish song in his deep tenor. That he was engaged did not stop them from being "violently intimate." How much she admired him can be seen in a long poem she sent to him the same year. In six verses she wrote prophetically about Nathan's call to struggle for truth in the footsteps of Saint Staffan of Hälsingland and Martin Luther.

Lydia Wahlström was deeply influenced by Nathan Söderblom and expressly chose to ally herself with the small group of modern theologians in Uppsala. The friendship continued, but the hopes she had for him cooled down when he became archbishop and for a variety of reasons was forced to renounce the radicalness of his youth. She was the second woman in Sweden to earn a Ph.D. As a teacher of girls and a prolific writer, she remained a radical feminist all her life, fighting for women's suffrage and later for the ordination of women. No woman, other than Anna Söderblom, played a more prominent role in Swedish church life at the beginning of the twentieth century.

At Christmas 1892, Nathan took Anna to Norrala to introduce her to his family. Their train arrived in the evening in Söderhamn where a sleigh drawn by a horse called "Balder" awaited them. They wrapped themselves up and Nathan took the reins and the horse — snorting and white from hoarfrost — trotted through the Norrala valley. Farmhouse windows glistened as the starry heavens illuminated their way. Stockholm-bred Anna had never before been in the countryside during winter. Nor had she ever seen so stately a parsonage as the one in Norrala, a red two-story house with two detached wings and outhouses. In the large living room there was a fire, burning kerosene lamps, and blossoming potted plants. On the square piano there was a copy of the spiritual songs, *Sions Toner*, "The Songs of Zion," and on one wall hung portraits of Luther and Melanchthon. The old rector sat in his study by a glowing lamp, writing in an elegant style. With a warm smile he received them. Anna would remember his lively blue eyes, grey streaked hair, and small lips that could smile and joke, scold and console, and above all things, bear witness to a fervent love for Christ and a firm faith in the atonement. He was unlike anyone she had ever met, stern but tender, a man of anxiety and restlessness. He could not take time to eat with them, but in the evening he gathered everyone for prayer. Nathan's mother Sofia, who was becoming more and more deaf, was delicate and lay in bed but remained clear in her thoughts and eager to read and understand the things that Nathan wrote. His two sisters lived at home — Elsa was just nine years old. They mostly kept to themselves in their mother's room.

Anna had grown up in a totally different milieu. Her father, Captain Carl-August Forsell, like his own father, had sailed the seven seas. When young, her mother Axeline Åberg sang and played with him when he came sailing in on his ship the "Knut Åkerhjelm" from foreign lands. When his ship had sunk in the China Sea and he had nearly drowned and when he had suffered shipwreck for a second time off the coast of Norway, he returned to land for good. At the age of forty-three, after an engagement of seven years, he married Anna's mother. After that he held a modest position as a supervisor in the Stockholm harbor. Axeline came from a line of wealthy mine owners in Värmland, but her father suffered bankruptcy and everything in their home was lost. Axeline, who played the piano well, bought her own piano at the family auction. They had an existence of privation but still her parents managed to create a beautiful home life for themselves and their three children. Anna's brother, John Forsell, became well known as a singer and opera director. Her sister was deaf and sickly. Their parents were internationally oriented, eagerly spoke English with each other, cultivated liberal values, and had a warm faith. They saw to it that Anna received the upbringing and education that their circumstances allowed, but her university studies at Uppsala were limited to a total of one year. Nathan also had seafarers in his family, but what he most shared with Anna was a light and open view of Christianity, which was to lead them into the modernity of the twentieth century. The two had many common starting points: Fehr's liberal theology, the warmth of Christian revivalism, intellectual struggles, and an international perspective. Shortly before they traveled to Norrala, Nathan visited Anna's family in Stockholm for the first time. There, John Forsell sang both Mozart and Schubert for them. Two musical families were united, but the distance from Beethoven's "*An die ferne Geliebte*" ("To the Distant Beloved") to Oscar Ahnfelt's "*Ängsliga hjärta, upp ur din dvala*" ("Day by Day, and with Each Passing Moment") was great indeed. In Norrala, Anna met a pious, old-fashioned, and spartan family with conservative traditions and calloused hands. To her it was another world.

Now Anna, together with Sam Fries's fiancée who also was named Anna, was introduced to the group Free from the Heart at a meeting in Enköping. For both Fries and Söderblom it was clear that the two women should not only be present but should also participate in the discussions. Nils Johan Göransson, who had been ordained and was an assistant priest in Enköping, was at work writing an essay on a German pastor, Christofer Schrempff, who had rejected the historic creeds and had been defrocked. Göransson's work was so sympathetic to its subject that he would himself be accused of heresy. Fries was totally taken up with writing a book on the history of Israel. When it came out in 1894, there was a citation on an endpaper from the Archbishop of Canterbury written on the three hundredth anniversary of the Uppsala Synod of 1593: "I wish that the whole power of the word of God revealed in Holy Scripture, transmitted by a faithful and enlightened clergy, and illuminated by the light shed by the advances of scientific criticism, may through the grace of the Holy Spirit bear fruit in the lives and minds of a truly Christian people." These words made an indelible impression on the three friends and became a motto for their attempt to unite faith and academic criticism.

Fries' sharp attacks on Uppsala traditionalism did not fall on fertile ground and he never, in spite of many attempts, became the professor he so deeply wanted to be. Göransson was more willing to fall in line and in due course became professor of systematic theology. We already know how things developed for Söderblom. When the group met in Enköping he was in the process of selecting a field for further studies. He had dropped his plans to devote himself to church history because of the time he had taken for his travels to America. He had laid aside the thought of working in dogmatic theology. Writing a dissertation in the field of the history of religion increasingly appealed to him. But his responsibilities as chairperson of the Uppsala student body continued to demand much of his time.

In 1893, Söderblom had three opportunities to demonstrate his extraordinary gifts as a public speaker: at the honoring of the veteran student singer Gunnar Wennerberg, who had written many of the songs sung at the Last Day of April celebrations; at the three hundredth anniversary of the

The "Free from the Heart" society. Back row: Nathan Söderblom, Samuel Freidenfeldt (who sometimes participated), Samuel Fries. Front row: Anna Forsell, Nils Johan Göransson, Anna Fagerlin. 1893.

Uppsala Synod of 1593 when Sweden officially became a Lutheran nation; and at the Gustavus Adolphus festival on November 6. The anniversary turned out to be a magnificent celebration. In his speech, Söderblom paid tribute to King Oscar II who was present along with some German princes whom he addressed in their own language, which moved them so deeply that one of them considered awarding him the German Order of the White

Falcon. Whenever Söderblom ascended a podium, he conducted himself with remarkable openness. He was charming and poised and he modulated his sonorous voice in a way that touched his listeners without making them feel manipulated. He prepared carefully and practiced his speeches so that he would be able to occupy the entire stage.

This was also the case when he now, for the second time, addressed the students at the Gustavus Adolphus celebration. In the midst of his words praising Sweden as "a bulwark newly born in the Reformation" and Gustavus Adolphus as "the preserver of Protestantism's national freedom," he inserted thoughts that were to mature into a great ecumenical vision. He expressed his hopes that a quarrelsome and ossified Lutheran orthodoxy might give way to a free and dynamic Christianity. Then the Protestant churches could unite with the Nordic people in regaining the initiative. That Gustavus Adolphus planned for a union of all Protestants was a "reminder of the difficult youth of the Reformation and a foretaste of the spirit of coming times." It was as though he were questioning himself: "To the North, the gaze of hope is turned once again. Is the North again to give a watchword; will the world in the next century behold a new and higher Gustavus Adolphus epoch? Whatever happens, it cannot be without the renewal of religion."

The speech was not quickly forgotten. Söderblom had carefully studied the way his greatly admired history professor Harald Hjärne appeared and expressed himself. He admitted without hesitation that he was deeply impressed by Hjärne's rhetoric. He was still something of a follower. It would take a while before he found his own unique style, which would be characterized by expressive clarity and liveliness.

Söderblom spoke as a pastor. On March 5, 1893, the actual three hundredth anniversary of the Uppsala Synod, Bishop Gottfrid Billing had ordained him in the chapel of the Ersta Diaconal Institution in Stockholm. Since Söderblom intended to seek a position as hospital chaplain in the Ulleråker mental hospital, it was necessary for him to be ordained. Archbishop J. A. Ekman was prepared to perform an individual ordination, but when he learned that Billing, who was also a member of the Swedish Parliament, was to ordain a priest from the Linköping Diocese, he asked him to ordain Söderblom at the same time. In a long letter to his parents, Nathan reported on the festival "in the most beautiful chapel on Stockholm's most beautiful point." His fiancée Anna and her family were present, as were his sister Hanna, Adolf Kolmodin, and the Director of Ersta, "the fine old man" Johan Christoffer Bring, the latter two men holding leading positions in the evangelical movement.

Billing, then Bishop of Västerås, made a very positive impression on Söderblom. He described the bishop as "our church's mightiest personality" and continued, "There is something really powerful about him, but at the same time fresh and wholesome." He referred to him as "the coming Archbishop." He carefully reported on his ordination sermon, which concluded with words concerning confident freedom in Christ and steadfastness in the priestly calling. Söderblom was given the position at Ulleråker. In addition to a salary of eight hundred crowns a year, he was provided with both food and an apartment. The work was not really demanding, so he could continue with his studies.

That he was ordained did not mean that he uncritically accepted the church's faith, confession, and teaching or that he submitted to all its ordinances. Söderblom was not inclined to suspend his theological independence. Just a few weeks after his ordination, his friends from Free from the Heart were with him. They spoke again of the German pastor Christoph Schrempf. Had his dismissal from the ministry shown that no one could enter the service of the church without completely accepting its teachings? Fries had previously been of that opinion and so had Söderblom — but no longer. Why should they let the bishop and the cathedral chapter set the norms and have the last word in questions of doctrine? "*I* myself declare what are the norms," Fries wrote in a letter to his fiancée and added, "Even Nathan agrees." If a person like Fehr could remain in his position, they could be confident about the future, even if they followed their own convictions.

Söderblom took care of his pastoral duties at Ulleråker with, as it were, his left hand. It was six months before he presided at Holy Communion for the first time. He gave no more time than necessary to his work there, for in addition to still being head of the student body, he had to give priority to his studies in the history of religion and write his doctoral dissertation.

6

The Pastor in Paris

> At the moment I have the task of begging both for Strindberg, who has been abandoned by his second wife and now is sick and wants to be in the hospital, and also for a Swedish sculptor, one of the most distinguished.
>
> *Nathan Söderblom, 1895*

AN ICY RAIN IS FALLING. The wooden cobblestones on the Champs-Élysées are slippery. The heavy working horses slide. The omnibus is filled at evening time. People wait at the bus stop, shivering but patient. The faint light from the gas lamps is lost in the wet darkness. One more comes. The horse driver sits high up in his seat. "Allons les numéros: cinquante huit, cinquante neuf, soixante, soixante et un. Complet!" Nathan is on his way home. He has been studying early Persian with Alfred Meillet and visiting an ill and lonely stonemason from Sweden.

* * *

The first chair in the history of religion was established in Geneva in 1873. It was not a recognized field of study in Sweden. A few theologians had begun to study the Jewish-Christian tradition from a historical-critical perspective and even that started a debate. If someone wanted to study other religions, it was necessary to learn Semitic and Indo-European languages such as Arabic and Persian. That could only be done in the philosophical faculty where one could also study Sanskrit. Cooperation and trust between the two faculties was shaky. Fries wrote his book on the history of Israel at the urging of the professor of Semitic languages. It was repudiated immediately by the theologians.

Since 1877, there had been a professor of "theological prenotions and theological encyclopedia" at Uppsala. The peculiar word "prenotions" was used to refer to the history of religion, the philosophy of religion, and the psychology of religion. The subject had an apologetic purpose, to explicate Christianity's relation to other forms of faith and theology's relation to other forms of knowledge. At this time, the chair was held by the person who was to become archbishop, J. A. Ekman, whose previous academic work had been in biblical studies and church history. In Germany, England, the Netherlands, and France the situation was different. In those countries, scholars attempted to lay bare — without presuppositions — Christianity's roots in the history of religions. In England the theory of evolution had stimulated the study of Christianity's relation to other religions. Söderblom, who initially considered taking up church history or biblical studies, was determined to attempt something totally new. He wanted to put into practice what he had learned from Ritschl in a study of the connections between Persian and Judeo-Christian eschatology.

It was not Ekman who awoke in Nathan an interest in the history of religions. Ekman devoted himself to Christian apologetics and he had a completely out-of-date view of other religions. He was not knowledgeable, but was prejudiced, and disparaging in his view of "heathendom." Their ignorance of God had led to sinful depravity. Ekman could seriously discuss whether or not the nakedness of heathens was proof of their immorality. He held that their lack of modesty was worse than that of civilized people, but he would also reluctantly admit that the nakedness of people of color was less shocking than that of white people. Söderblom, who was far less prejudiced, had nothing to learn from him.

His interest in the history of religion went further back in time, to his years in the Student Missionary Association. The members of that association frequently discussed both the latest research concerning religion and the question of how the task of Christian missions could best be carried out among the awakening religions of the world. His study of Ritschl had taught Söderblom that the more generously, unreservedly, and honestly one acknowledged that which is good, true, and moral in other religions and the more substantively one endeavored to understand the faith present in those religions, the clearer it became that Christianity was unrivaled and irreplaceable. The study of religion could be the best defense of Christian faith. In contrast to much Christian "apologetics," which was based on an infallible Bible that negatively viewed others' worship and religion, Söderblom wanted to show that an academic, inductive study of religion would positively enforce the conviction that the full truth is found in Christ. He himself had experienced how critical study had supported his own wavering faith and how modern theology had liberated him to take an active stand for Christianity. He was not fearful that academic research would threaten a living Christian faith.

One day on the train between Stockholm and Uppsala he read *Sjæledyrkelse og Naturdyrkelse (Worship of the Soul and Nature Worship),* by the Danish free-thinker Hans Sofus Vodskov, one of Scandinavia's most prominent Darwinians. Reading this book convinced Söderblom that the history of religion should be his field of study. He approached these studies with an apologetic intent. Today, Söderblom would be considered neither objective nor neutral. He had no interest in keeping his distance from religion in order to "objectively" observe it. On the contrary, he held that the scholar should be sensitive to religion and if possible have one's own religious experience in order to understand the faith of others. It might be that he chose the history of religion with the thought that this field would offer him an academic career, but he was genuinely interested in the subject, not for sociological reasons but as something authentically human.

He was determined to write his dissertation on Iranian religion. On a visit to Fredrik Fehr he had found an issue of the journal *The Thinker*, which included an article on Zarathustra and Israel. On the basis of this article, he decided that the Persian prophet would be the subject of his specialized study. The choice of this field and subject was not as far-fetched as it might seem. For several years, Söderblom had been occupied with the question of the historical roots of the Old and New Testaments. Had the Bible appeared simply in one process of divine revelation as theologians had long since taken for granted, or was the Bible actually the product of many concurrent factors? Some of its writings might have been "primitive," while others could have been transmitted to Israel from powerful cultures such as Babylon, Egypt, Persia, Greece, and the Roman Empire. The most interesting question was if there was a Persian or Iranian influence on the Old Testament. The German "History of Religions School" held this to be the case, but in order to get a clear answer it was necessary to go to the sources. And that presupposed a solid knowledge of the ancient Persian language.

Zoroastrianism as such was no threat to Christianity and its prophet Zoroaster, or Zarathustra, had come to be of great interest. His writings were beginning to be translated into Western languages. Some scholars were of the view that he at least indirectly had an influence on Hebrew eschatology. Early in the 1880s, Friedrich Nietzsche had written the philosophical novel *Also sprach Zarathustra* (*Thus Spoke Zarathustra*), which had become something of a cult book among European intellectuals. Since Nietzsche accused the Germans of being vulgar, materialistic, and philistine, the book was well received in France while the Germans were more attracted to Nietzsche's theories concerning "the will to power." The book was translated into Swedish in 1897. However, for Söderblom, Viktor Rydberg's *Undersökningar I germansk mytologi* (*Investigations in German Mythology*) was more decisive. It contained many comparisons between German and Iranian thought. The discussion circle Free from the Heart had not only taken its name from Rydberg — the group idealized him. Söderblom was to cite him more than once in his doctoral dissertation.

As a field of study, Persian religion was virgin territory. The basic texts were written in Avesta or Pazand, a most difficult Middle Persian language that had neither a lexicon or developed grammar. The linguistically gifted Söderblom took on the challenge. After celebrating Christmas in Norrala, at New Year's 1893, he began to seriously study ancient Persian. He received help from the same-aged linguistic scholar Karl Vilhelm Zetterstéen, a student who already was well known for his abilities and who in time would become a celebrated Orientalist. When Söderblom had been ordained and was serving as hospital chaplain in Ulleråker, Zetterstéen would walk there in all kinds of weather. In the hospital's spacious library he would teach Söderblom the basics of the language. The study continued during the summer. In the late fall, Söderblom began to write his thesis on Zoroastrianism or Mazdaism. In light of his continued service in the hospital, his presidency of the Uppsala student body with all that that involved, and his studying Persian, it is not surprising that his time was at a premium. Nevertheless, he continued to sing in Orphei Drängar and together with Anna he also went to concerts, the theater, and parties at the Uppsala nations. He now was among the most well-known people in Uppsala, had a close friendship with Harald Hjärne, was a frequent dinner guest at the archbishop's residence, and seemed involved in all sorts of things. According to Lydia Wahlström, he was "lively and talkative to the point of nervosity," always happy and in "high spirits."

One day in June 1893, Nathan sat in His Majesty Oscar II's reception room at the castle in Stockholm. He was there, as head of the student body, to inform the king about the coming anniversary of the 1593 synod in Uppsala. The newly named Professor of Pastoral Theology at Uppsala, Henry William Tottie, was also there in order to thank the king for his promotion. He mentioned to Nathan that the Swedish priest in Paris had been chosen rector in Skövde and the Paris position was now vacant. Söderblom could not stop thinking about that. He had been ordained for only a few months and really had no pastoral experience to speak of, but he longed for a regular position and the possibility of raising a family. What could be better than France? Since the imprisonment of Napoleon III in 1870, France had been the only republic in Europe. It was a suspect nation in the eyes of people who were still ruled by emperors and kings, princes and dukes, who were often related to each other. Christian IX in Copenhagen was called "the father-in-law of all Europe." Queen Victoria had led the British Empire for nearly sixty years. Her grandson Wilhelm was kaiser in Germany and his cousin Nicolaus was czar in St. Petersburg. Kaiser Franz Josef was at the head of the feeble Hapsburg Dynasty. Protocols and regulations were as rigid as those of the Roman Catholic Church. France alone had broken with its monarchy in order to pursue a different political future.

If there was a city that captured the young chaplain's imagination it was Paris, not only because it was the center of modern culture but also because some of the world's leading historians of religion taught at the École Pratique des Hautes Études. One of them was James Darmesteter who was regarded as the world's leading scholar of early Persian literature. The world's only significant journal of the history of religion was published in Paris. The Guimet Museum, with its extensive Central Asian collection, was also there. Moreover the Protestant faculty of theology, which had recently moved from Strasbourg to the Sorbonne, was by no means as conservative as the faculty in Uppsala.

It was impossible to resist all of that. Anna was of the same mind. After the Reformation celebration, which was such a personal success for him, Nathan completed his term as president of the student body and courageously went to the archbishop and asked that he be given the post in Paris. Söderblom did not hide the fact that at the same time he intended to continue his studies in the history of religion. The stern archbishop, Anton Niklas Sundberg, rejected the proposal. It would not be possible to unite so demanding a position with advanced studies. Yet, in spite of the great differences between the two men, he marveled at the goal-conscious and well-spoken twenty-eight-year-old and finally gave in. Söderblom was called to be priest to the Norwegian-Swedish colony in Paris and, during the summers, priest also to seamen in the port cities of Calais and Dunkirk.

In March 1894, he planned for the printing of his dissertation, but it was only half completed and the faculty would not receive it for judgment. It is difficult to know both how much ancient Persian he had actually learned and whether the faculty would have approved the thesis if it were complete, but it was apparent that for the first time, he had taken on more than he could manage. He had had too short a time and his life was so split up that he could not achieve any genuine results in his research. Yet he remained convinced about going to Paris. He had also traveled to America before he was finished with his essay on church history. That journey had changed his life's direction and he had never regretted it. Now he was in a similar situation. He simply could not miss the opportunities Paris would give him. Somehow things would work out for his academic career. And that turned out to be the case. He was able to complete his studies in Paris, even though he gave more of his free time to more immediate matters than to Zoroastrianism's teaching about the last things.

In the midst of all this, Söderblom had yet another spiritual experience. One Sunday when he had presided at worship — it was March 11, 1894 — he was in the library at Ulleråker. He was suddenly struck by a tremendous feeling of the holiness of God. He saw that God was mightier and more demanding than anything a person could imagine, that God was like a consuming fire. The experience was so traumatic that he could not remain on his feet. He grasped the edge of a table, fell to his knees, and tears streamed down his cheeks. He sighed and groaned, and only gradually did he calm down. Anna Forsell witnessed all of this while feeling totally outside of it. For the rest of his life he remembered this event. "It is crushing to meet the living God," he wrote. Together with the events of an earlier year, this became his most basic religious experience. Its memory became to him an incomprehensible means of grace. He had not only seen the suffering, crucified Savior but also the judging Son of Man. This personal experience of God's irresistible grace and annihilating holiness — *mysterium tremendum et fascinans* — became a base point for his entire spiritual life. It could not be compared to anything else. It gave him an enduring certainty of the presence of the living God.

In *Jesus' Sermon on the Mount*, a small book he wrote in 1896 in Calais, he made reference to this experience: "A person who once has felt the hand of God, its mighty and irresistible grasp, and realized how infinitely greater and stronger he is than we thought or believed, he may perhaps glide along far from that grip, be weak or even unfaithful, but his conscience is eternally marked for salvation or condemnation. No reality of life, no new knowledge or event can obliterate the mark of having encountered God." In his university sermon of 1905, *De stackars dödlige* ("The Poor Mortals"), Söderblom dwelt again on that same event: "If one has felt the grasp of God, he can in both small and great ways veer off from the path on which he set out, but he can never forget that grasp and he will always feel the certainty, near or distant, of a guardian and judge — and helper." His conviction that he had personally encountered God helped him to unite his roles as a scholar and a believer. The encounter meant that he could no more doubt God.

He presided at his last service of worship at Ulleråker on April 29, 1894. The same evening he and Anna Forsell were married in the chapel at Ersta. That eight-sided church had been dedicated in 1872. From her home in Stadsgården near the harbor, Anna had sometimes gone up the steep steps of the church in order to sit beneath the balcony to hear the captivating messages of J. C. Bring who gathered many of Stockholm's committed pietists around his pulpit. She remembered how Ersta's devoted deaconesses, who maintained stricter practices than others, exercised a "world-denying piety in sacrificial works of love." Stockholm's most prestigious assembly hall for the evangelical establishment was the mighty Blasieholmen Church. Ersta was the center for practical good works. At Ersta Nathan had been ordained by Gottfrid Billing who was anything but a pietist. There they were married with Fredrik Fehr, who was surely not highly esteemed in revival circles, as officiant.

Even as Anna and Nathan sought the inner piety that warmed them when they were younger, they also wanted to demonstrate for themselves and their wedding guests that they now intellectually and spiritually belonged to another world. Jonas Söderblom had been invited to officiate but refused to "risk health and life" by traveling to Stockholm. Anna, of whom he was deeply fond, attempted to convince him to come, but she did not succeed. A small wedding reception was held in Anna's home. Friends from Free from the Heart were there, as were Nathan's mother and his sister Hanna.

The next evening the newlyweds took the night train to Copenhagen. They stayed one day in Berlin where they visited Adolf von Harnack and listened to lectures by Julius Kaftan and Otto Pfleiderer. Not even on a honeymoon could time be wasted. On a Thursday evening they arrived at the Gare du Nord. Neither of them had ever been to Paris. They observed men and women who streamed in every direction, corseted women in elegant dresses, stylish mustached men in promenade capes and high hats. There were swarms of carts and horse-drawn cabs, omnibuses and trolleys pulled by muscled horses. It would be several years before a few dusty and chugging automobiles driven by chauffeurs with peaked caps and gloves that reached to their elbows would appear.

For fifty years the whole city had been a gigantic building ground. It was becoming the Paris we now know. Up to the middle of the nineteenth century it had been a dilapidated, smelly, medieval city with narrow lanes, malaria, and unclean drinking water. Napoleon III assigned Eugène Georges Haussman to create *la ville lumière*. Tens of thousands of people were forcibly relocated as their homes were torn down. Railroad tracks were laid. Stations, warehouses, churches, and hotels were erected, as well as the opera house and market halls. The city was given broad avenues, green parks, and apartment houses of quarried granite. For the exhibition of 1889 — a hundred years after the French Revolution — the 320-meter-high steel Eiffel Tower was constructed, the tallest structure in the world at the time. When the subway between Bois de Bologne in the west and Bois de Vincenne in the east opened, Paris was already a modern city of three million, self-confident and attractive. It was Europe's center for art, entertainment, and fashion in the same way as London was the center for society and Rome for antiquities. Germany, where both Richard Wagner and Richard Strauss were born, led the way in music. Germany had conquered Alsace and Lorraine in 1870 and France was eager for revenge. People placed flowers at the statue representing Strasbourg in the Place de la Concorde and dreamed of the day when France would be Europe's cultural power. Anna and Nathan Söderblom got to experience the finale of the transformation of Paris, which culminated in the World's Fair of 1900.

They could not resist being smitten by the optimism that reigned. However, during their seven years in France it was not progress that created the big headlines but something totally different: the Dreyfus Affair. In 1894, Alfred Dreyfus, a Jewish artillery officer, was accused of having given defense secrets to Germany. A scandalous trial led to violent opposition throughout all of France and exposed a deep and broad anti-Semitism, not least within the Roman Catholic Church. Söderblom, who for ten years had counted the Stockholm rabbi Gottlieb Klein among his closest personal friends, was deeply troubled. He followed the Dreyfus Affair daily and condemned the Catholic clericalism and ultramontanism with its emphasis on the pope's supremacy in all questions in the same breath as anti-Semitic chauvinism. But the Dreyfus Affair also united conservatives, republicans and monarchists, idealists and naturalists — in a common struggle for justice. Not until 1906 did Dreyfus receive redress, and then only halfheartedly.

There had been a Swedish congregation in Paris since 1626. During the time of Napoleon its work had been suspended for half a century, but it was taken up again in 1859 and as Sweden and Norway constituted a Union at the time, it included both Swedes and Norwegians. The Sofia Chapel was dedicated in 1878, poorly located on Boulevard Ornano behind Montmartre. The threadbare furnishings, with a white statue of a welcoming Christ in the choir, pleased no one. Fifteen years later, Calais was also given an undistinguished chapel.

Now Anna and Nathan were not only to create a home together, they also had to learn their roles as a clerical family, expatriate Swedes, and soon as parents. Anna could have developed her own career but without hesitation devoted herself to Nathan. She suppressed her own interests and supported and encouraged him in whatever he did, became an unpaid worker for the congregation, took care of the home, and raised the children. She insisted that a woman, by deepening her femininity and concentrating on the working areas that "were most suited to her nature," would best contribute to society and humanity. She lived through her husband, convinced that home and children were a woman's given calling. With joy she undertook all of the tasks that she was expected to carry out. His expansive personality, thousands of commitments, and increasing reputation would totally permeate their life together. She spoke and wrote of him in the third person as "the pastor," "the young professor," or "the archbishop." He was demanding and self-assured, driven by uncompromising expectations of himself, and he had a great need for approval. Anna was his intellectual conversation partner who kept him down to earth, read his manuscripts, discussed his lectures, criticized his sermons, and quieted down something of his impetuous lifestyle. It was for her eyes that he spoke, even if she was not sitting in front of him. For him it was true love if one reached self-realization in the destiny of the other. When Anna came to Paris she was only twenty-three years old, charming and newly married. Before the children came, she could spend all her time with Nathan, learning to know the congregation as well as he.

For the first year they lived in temporary quarters before they found a small apartment four stories up on Rue Malleville near Parc Monceau. The house was built in 1864 and had six floors. The apartment had five small rooms of which their domestic servant Adèle had one while Nathan's desk and his many books filled another. The kitchen was small and crowded. There was water and a drain but nothing more. "The bird's nest," as they called it, was suitable for a young family with few requirements. Soon the home became a meeting place for Parisian Swedes where they ate, talked, and practiced choir music. To gather people in the faraway Sofia Chapel was nearly impossible other than for funerals and major events. During one of his first weeks in Paris Nathan had to bury a young artist who had taken his own life. It was very difficult, but in his funeral sermon the words "I know that my Redeemer lives" from Handel's *Messiah* resounded in a way that touched all of the Nordic painters, sculptors, and musicians who were at the service. During the long procession to the cemetery of St. Quen several of them began a friendship with Söderblom that would widen, deepen, and continue back in Sweden until his own death.

Before their thirteen crates of household goods landed at Calais and they had moved in, summer had begun and Söderblom had to take up his duties as seamen's priest. In the attic of the small chapel in Calais there was a modest apartment, not much more than a cubbyhole with a skylight. The ocean breeze brought with it the scent of tar and seaweed, sour fish, rotten wood, and horse droppings. While Anna spent her days in the seamen's reading room, Nathan visited the boats. He went around the harbor area and invited those he came across to come to church. As a high school student he had sometimes been on board freighters in the Hudiksvall harbor and both he and Anna had sea captains in their families, so seafaring was nothing strange to them. Nathan lay his academic work aside, adjusted his speech and habits to that of seamen, and made conversation with all the Scandinavians who came his way. Many Swedish and Norwegian freighters came to the French seaports, often loaded with timber.

When autumn came, it was time to seriously begin parish work in Paris. If Söderblom's predecessor had built the chapel, he wanted to build the congregation. At the beginning, however, it was not easy to come in contact with the three to four hundred Swedes and Norwegians who lived in the spread-out capital of France. He wanted to be a priest to all and took himself by foot, wagon, and horse-drawn cab to the homes of artists and au pairs, maids, manual laborers, and diplomats and won their trust. Anna shared the work with him and was able to provide both a space and food for those who came to their home every Monday evening. In point of fact, she was rather shy and more suited to intellectual work than to practical activities and she also had a bit of melancholy, stronger than that which at times marked him. The difficulties in gathering people for worship caused them both to despair. They had expected that many would come, but social needs were evidently greater than spiritual ones. The priest had no other choice but to try to help as many as possible. Those who were unemployed, who had drowned their money in drink, or who needed help with clothes and medical care sought him out. A ballet dancer needed a new spangled skirt and it was only he who was there to help out. He had no allowance for such things. The parish's relief funds ran out when he was inundated by people in need, so Söderblom soon became the best-known beggar in the Swedish colony. As gullible as he was, it happened sometimes that he was deceived, but he took that risk. Faith and works must go hand in hand, otherwise how could he be reliable as a priest? In America, he had learned how social work could be organized. Slowly the number of people at worship increased, but there were many who found their way to the priest's home rather than to church.

One day the Norwegian author Jonas Lie and his wife Thomasine came to see Söderblom. Anna and Nathan had read his books and admired him greatly. Lie attended church regularly even though he missed a more mystical attitude toward the eucharist. This time, however, he came to appeal on behalf of August Strindberg whose hands had broken out with eczema as a result of his experiments in alchemy. He needed to be hospitalized but was so destitute that he could not pay. Söderblom raised money and saw to it that the bill was paid, but he never met Strindberg in person. Seventeen years later, shortly before the then world-famous author's death, he received a letter with a word of thanks and a thousand crowns for the relief fund of the Paris congregation. This moved Söderblom to tears. In his reply to Strindberg he wrote, "I will not and cannot tell or even indicate the gratitude I have felt toward you for many years." One year earlier he had suggested to the Swedish Academy that Strindberg should receive the Nobel Prize in Literature, but before that could happen Strindberg died. Söderblom conducted his funeral.

Anders and Emma Zorn had moved to Paris in 1888. He was an illegitimate son from the edges of Swedish society who had married well and had adopted gallant and worldly wise ways. He did not have much formal education and was a bit awkward in conversation but tried both English and French even if he was uncomfortable doing so. The couple traveled for long periods of time and he made a fortune as a portrait painter in America. Their permanent address was Boulevard Clichy 71 in a part of Paris where many Swedes lived. When Söderblom arrived in Paris, Zorn was established, well known, and wealthy. His large apartment was fitted in a refined and affluent way with woven tapestries, baroque furniture, and fine art. He had taken on continental and extravagant ways. He would ride a white horse through the Boulogne Forest dressed in a British suit with a gaudy scarf. He was eager to appear as a gentleman. With time he had also become politically conservative, but that did not stop him from simultaneously keeping his distance from both the Academy of Art and from everything that might be regarded as philistine. He was very much aware of himself and was internationally far more well known than any other Swedish artist. In Paris he moved among art collectors and men of finance and he knew more French artists than he let on. He preferred to associate with the large number of Scandinavians who came to Paris toward the end of the nineteenth century. Among them he had the reputation of being a mannered snob who was all too "full of himself." Zorn was one of the artists whom Anna and Nathan soon came to know.

There were certain similarities between the Zorns and the Söderbloms. The men had grown up in the colorful rural culture of Dalecarlia and Hälsingland; they were deeply rooted, extroverted, virile, musical, and very much self-aware. Their wives came from Stockholm's middle class, were obliging, well educated, and knew how to comport themselves in fine salons. Zorn returned to Sweden in 1896 while Söderblom remained in Paris, but they stayed friends for life.

Soon the pastor and his wife began to feel very much at home in the studios of Montmartre. There were more Nordic artists in Paris in the

Many years after Paris (left to right): Nathan Söderblom, Helge Söderblom, Erik Lamm, Magda Nachmanson, and Emma Zorn on the porch of the Zorn home.

1890s than at any time previously. The city, of course, was Europe's artistic center. Anna and Nathan came to know many of them — for example, August Hagborg who painted remarkable scenes from Normandy, and Carl Wilhelmsson who would soon return to Sweden to paint the barren landscapes of Bohuslän. They also came to know Alfred Wahlberg who was much older, a musician and painter who had been inspired by Emanuel Swedenborg and who participated in Nathan's Swedish services; he was an unpretentious person of taste who happily associated with the priest's family. Nils Forsberg was a poor artist who had been in Paris since 1867. He had become well known for his painting, "A Hero's Death," which was inspired by a single soldier who alone held off the Germans in the French-German War of 1870–1871. When Söderblom met Forsberg he was at work on the imposing painting "Gustav Adolf before the Battle of Lützen," which now hangs in the Gothenburg Museum. Söderblom, who had enthusiastically hailed Gustaf Adolf as king, was deeply moved when he saw the picture of the king at prayer with his head bare and his face gazing upward. The painting made incarnate the "powerful feeling of vigor, manly evangelical faith, and willingness to sacrifice by which the heroic king revealed the secret of the Swedish army's strength," wrote Söderblom. Later, Forsberg presented him with a portrait of himself as a young priest in the pulpit with uplifted head, strikingly like Gustav Adolf.

That was not the only time that one of his artistic friends from Paris used him as a model. In Calais he was also depicted by Otto Holmström, a bohemian who shared living quarters with Nathan while his family was in Sweden. He painted an altarpiece for the chapel: Jesus preaching from a boat on the Lake of Geneseret. In that painting, the shore was a landscape of Sweden's west coast where a fisherman's shack could be glimpsed. As models Holmström used an old Norwegian sea captain, the two sisters who were caretakers of the church, a Danish telephone engineer, and some children. Söderblom also appeared in the painting, wearing a cassock, for even a priest needs to listen to the Savior's words. The sculptor Christian Eriksson from Värmland depicted Nathan both as Archbishop Jakob Ulvsson for a statue outside the Uppsala Cathedral and at the main office of the Sundsvalls Bank on Fredsgatan in Stockholm where a manly and genuinely Nordic figure was to appear. That sculpture, according to Anna, was one of the most characteristic representations of Söderblom, who made a deep impression upon artists. Actually, artists were at the center of his congregation even if they seldom came to worship. Many of them would remain his friends through the years: sculptors such as Harald Sörensen-Ringi, Carl Eldh, and Carl Milles; authors such as Jonas Lie; composers such as Hugh Alfvén and Emil Sjögren; a violinist such as Sven Kjellström. For a time, Anna's brother, the singer John Forsell, was also a part of that circle in Paris. She had an especially close relation to women artists such as Ida Matton, Julia Beck, and Ingrid Lamm.

If they did not come to church, the priest would go to them. He baptized the first child of sculptor Christian Ericksson and his young French wife; the event culminated in a great feast. Some months later, in pain, he buried the baby. After a few years, however, they were again to gather in the artist's home when three more children were baptized at the same time. The Söderbloms had themselves lost their first child during a late miscarriage, and then their third child, Ingrid, died. They knew what sorrow was and they felt strongly bound to the earth, which had received their beloved.

Anna and Nathan saw Paris with the eyes of artists: there were festivals, expectations, and successes, but just as often miseries and misfortunes. They felt a unity with these creative and sometimes harried people, for they were themselves artists and each one of them could have been an author or musician. When their modest salary allowed, they went to the theater, concerts, and exhibitions. Nathan Söderblom often had errands at the Swedish Embassy and he frequently guided prominent Swedes around Paris. He met Alfred Nobel, won his confidence, and discussed the formation of the contemplated Nobel Foundation with him and also his drama "Nemesis." The play was published soon after Nobel's death, but Anna Söderblom was nervous that its content would jeopardize Nobel's reputation; therefore, nearly the entire printing was destroyed. Söderblom conducted a memorial service in San Remo before Nobel's body was taken to Sweden.

Söderblom also learned about the long working weeks of domestic workers, the struggles of laborers to make a living, and the fate of seamen who were at the mercy of ship owners. In Uppsala he had associated with students, docents, and professors. In Paris he came to know people in the working class. He had pastoral responsibility for them and could not avoid thinking about how their experiences related to Christian faith.

7

Social Christianity and Christian Socialism

> Why should the Social Democrats always be the first to recognize the misfortunate in society and oppose injustices?
>
> *Nathan Söderblom, 1896*

One summer he lives in a shed with a dirt floor in Coulogne where a Swedish businessman runs a sawmill. Söderblom goes around among the Swedish workers in his wooden shoes, cotton tunic, and a floppy hat. He looks like Leo Tolstoy, although without a beard. He has read how the Russian author in an earlier day interpreted the teachings of Jesus and he definitely distanced himself from Tolstoy's revolutionary vision, anarchic idealism, and moralistic asceticism. The pastor sits at a packing case, which he uses as a desk to write his own book concerning Jesus's Sermon on the Mount.

* * *

Archbishop Sundberg had had it right: the work of an expatriate pastor was so demanding that it was unrealistic to think of doing something else at the same time. Helge, Brita, Sven, Ingrid, and Staffan were all born in Paris in the space of four and a half years. Ingrid died before she was two years old. Their home was small, his salary low, and both family and work required more and more of him. In spite of that, Nathan held to his intention to finish his studies in the history of religion. Already, in the fall of 1894, before he had really gotten into his parish work, he registered as a doctoral student in the Protestant theological faculty at the Sorbonne. To his disappointment, the veteran linguist Darmesteter died just a few weeks later, but he took up his studies in ancient Persian with other teachers. He was not given a historian of religion as his adviser, but rather the reformed dogmatician Auguste Sabatier, who had been a professor at the University of Strasbourg before he served in the German-French War.

When the Germans occupied Strasbourg, he refused to return to his position, but in 1877 the whole faculty moved to the Sorbonne and he resumed his professorship. Sabatier was a pious man who had left his conservative inclinations behind in preference to a nondogmatic interpretation of faith based on the individual's experience. The relationship between Christian faith and modern culture was a crucial issue for him. His individualistic, experiential Christianity fascinated Söderblom. He was captivated by Sabatier's elegant, broad-minded, and cultivated lifestyle and looked up to him both spiritually and intellectually. Sabatier introduced Söderblom to French Calvinism, but also mediated its antipathy toward the Roman Catholic Church. He became yet another father figure in Söderblom's life, even though he was so different from Papa Jonas in Norrala, Dwight L. Moody in Northfield, and Waldemar Rudin in Uppsala. He became even more so when Fredrik Fehr, who meant so much to both Anna and Nathan, to their great sorrow died in May 1895 at the early age of forty-six. He had married them one year before a heart attack ended his life.

Sabatier became a personal model. Söderblom described him as the French-speaking world's foremost theologian and the best academic lecturer he had ever heard. When Sabatier published *Esquisse d'une philosophie de la religion* (*Outlines of a Philosophy of Religion*) in 1897, Söderblom's enthusiasm knew no bounds. "I read and rejoice," he wrote to Tor Andrae. "I do miss a few things, but it is barbarous to speak of them when we have such a masterwork, consummated by a great and living and warm personality in this beautiful and accomplished form. This work seems to me — to me personally — the most remarkable volume that has come since Ritschl and Harnack's *Dogmengeschichte* (*History of Dogma*)." As a personality, Sabatier was richer than Ritschl and he was less dogmatic than Harnack. Söderblom had encountered a magnificent person who for him was nearly the ideal theologian. "I can compare no one to him," wrote Söderblom. Sabatier was a living person, not a fossil of any sort. His secret was that he was simultaneously a historical and a dogmatic theologian, a literary scholar and a journalist, without being a dilettante in any of those areas.

In exquisitely beautiful language, Sabatier spoke of the Protestant religion as the prayer of the heart directed toward God, *le Dieu intérieur*, and of a faith that liberated humans and made them mature. In contrast to the authoritarianism of Catholicism and the biblicism of Protestantism, Sabatier put forth a vision of "the religion of the Spirit." Religion did not belong to reason, but to the heart. It was its own domain separate from science, although historical-critical and psychological methods were to be used in the study of religion. With religious experience as the norm, even scholars in dogmatics should objectively expose what is genuine and enduring. Dogma was thus secondary to experience and every representation of God had a symbolic character. Every expression of faith and dogma was determined by its historical and cultural context. The divine life itself, therefore, could be clothed in varying symbols. Visible signs and spoken words pointed toward an enduring but invisible spiritual reality. Since they were not absolute, a person could hold to the ancient Christian symbols without compromising the individual soul's freedom. For those who distinguished between form and content, tradition was a support and not a burden. That inherited external forms could be united with inner renewal strengthened Söderblom's attraction to ritual and contributed to his ecumenical generosity. He translated Sabatier's entire book into Swedish. This did not mean that he subscribed either to Sabatier's so-called symbolic fideism or to his evolutionary view of religion. He also saw the problem of subjectivity, which arose when authority was transferred from the church to the individual. Sabatier spiritualized religion in a way that was alien to Söderblom, but his way of thinking was nevertheless liberating. Sabatier gave him a language for his own thoughts concerning prayer, religion, and ecumenism as well as a more radical understanding of the role of the church in society.

Söderblom was at root a conservative person, but he desired to see everything from different perspectives and he was as eager to speak with workers as he was to participate in academic hairsplitting. When he was growing up, class distinctions were integral both to thought and society. He had been both frightened and fascinated by socialist agitators in Uppsala, since he actually had the feeling that they were to possess the future. When he came to Paris he still had not thoroughly considered the connection between Christian doctrine and social justice, but there that question was raised so powerfully that he had to take it seriously. He became political, but he never gave in to party politics and never became a party member. He probably voted only one time in a political election. That was in 1914.

Socialism was international. Its banner was a clear red symbol for the blood that courses through every person. The Second International had been founded in 1889 in Paris on the centennial of the French Revolution and it gave rise to growing fears within the ruling class. For socialists it was a fundamental dogma that if resources and power were amassed by capitalists, workers would be impoverished to a corresponding degree. Their increasing misery would sooner or later lead to the collapse of capitalism. Socialism was both a means and a goal. The question was whether the revolution should be carried out violently or through reform and cooperation with middle-class parties. For those who chose the latter way, the right to vote was decisive for coming to power. On this point, the French socialist movement was divided, but during the year before Söderblom arrived in Paris, the democratic socialists had had great success and had won thirty-seven seats in the House of Deputies. Their great leader was Jean Jaurès who was young, dynamic, interested in everything, and so skilled a speaker that even his opposition admired him.

The city was awash in social unrest. Demonstrators moved along the avenues with music, streamers, and red banners. The result was hatred toward Christianity and especially toward priests. "The city of light" with all its manufacturing and industry had an underside of misery, prostitution, and child labor. "The connections I occasionally have with workers are remarkable. I am encountering an unknown and far-flung world that awakens horror in me," Söderblom wrote to Göransson. It had been fifty years since the Communist Manifesto of Marx and Engels had begun to circulate and conflict between social classes had become the great issue for society. Political socialism was in principle this-worldly. It had an atheistic signature and allowed no place for religion. The church, capitalism, and the military were identified as the proletariat's great enemies and as the means used by the upper class to keep the workers in their place. Communists and socialists were convinced that the church's self-interest would be a future hindrance to progress for the working class.

The churches did not refute the criticism. All too late did they begin to sense their responsibility and contribute to the betterment of the situation for workers, the *lumpenproletariat* of the mobs and the slums, the "dirty proletariat." In England, however, at the end of the 1870s the blue-edged red banner of the Salvation Army had become a feature of the streets and ten years later, a wave of socially directed Christianity broke over the continent from Great Britain and the United States. It would become an alternative to revolutionary socialism, supporting the demands of workers for free time on Sundays and shorter working hours, and encouraging the gradual improvement of working conditions. Söderblom was swept along. Everything that went by the name "socialism" did not need to be seen as a denial of God.

To be a modern theologian was for many tantamount to engaging in social and political questions. The passionate debate between theologically conservative and liberal Christians had a political undertone. David Friedrich Strauss's book of 1835–1836, *Das Leben Jesu, kritisch bearbeitet* (*The Life of Jesus Critically Examined*), had appeared as a kind of manifesto against the church establishment. Liberals used Jesus's teaching about the Kingdom of God as a way of getting at social questions. This was interpreted by conservative Christians as a repudiation of both hierarchical "rules for the household" (*Haustafeln*) and the doctrine of the two kingdoms. A sharp polarization occurred in the Germany of Bismarck and Kaiser Wilhelm; in Sweden, the Lundensian high church movement defended the prevailing orders. Christian socialists were criticized for playing into the hands of the enemy. Lutherans had read about Jesus through the eyes of Paul and commonly interpreted Paul in Luther's way. Liberal theology was determined not to allow Luther — and behind him Paul — to hide what they saw as the true life and teaching of Jesus. It was the Jesus of the Gospels who inspired them, by his words and deeds, to take the side of the working class.

Söderblom met homeless people underneath the bridges of Paris and sailors in Calais who were without legal rights. He was friends with rebellious artists in Montmartre and he came to know descendants of the Huguenots who were always being forced to defend their rights in relation to the Catholic majority. In 1892 in Uppsala, he had published an article on Christianity and the modern workers' movement, which he surely had taken mostly from the work of the German ethics professor Wilhelm Herrman, in which he held the church responsible for, with the aid of the upper class, contributing to widening the gap between it and the workers. At the student meeting in America he had come into contact with the socially engaged French theologian Wilfred Monod. In Paris he met other Protestants who, in accord with the reformed tradition, were more activist than Lutherans and who had formed solidarity groups with leftist tendencies. Such groups had contact with the young socialist leader Jean Jaurès who, since his Marxism was not doctrinaire, was open to cooperation with Christian social movements.

In a September 1900 letter to Sam Fries, Söderblom clarified his own position. The socialists were, he wrote, a striking power, youthful and fresh, remarkably organized, and with a deep reserve of idealism. Numbers of them possessed something of early church enthusiasm and its feeling for solidarity. In contrast to others, they had never yielded in the Dreyfus Affair. No one stood nearer to evangelical Christianity than socialists with the idealism of Jaurès. Apart from evangelical Christianity, Söderblom was not aware of a more satisfying phenomenon than the organized socialistic workers' movement. He hoped that church leaders would have the vision to apply Jesus's words, "He who is not against us is for us."

After the fall of Napoleon III in 1871, France had again become a republic. It was, however, dominated by conservative monarchistic Catholics, except in Paris where free thinkers and revolutionaries who were vigorously opposed to the church had the power. In the bitter conflict that arose, many socialists were imprisoned by the government. "Les communards" responded to the arrests by shooting twenty-four priests and the Archbishop Georges Darboy together with forty-nine others who had been taken hostage. When the basilica Sacré Cœur was erected, it was a kind of penance from both sides for the violence. The struggle between church and state swung back and forth until the government determined to effect a radical divorce in 1905. Söderblom experienced this struggle from a Protestant perspective and in light of the Dreyfus Affair. He could not find anything good to say about the reactionary Catholic hierarchy. Pope Leo XIII had, however, shown himself to be more progressive in social matters than most Roman Catholics of his time. In the encyclical *Rerum novarum* of 1891, he had attacked unrestrained capitalism, demanded that the state should intervene on workers' behalf, and argued for equitable salaries and for the right to organize. Consequently, he was viewed by many as being more democratic and liberal than he actually was. The encyclical put wind in the sails of Catholic social movements all over Europe. They dedicated themselves to comprehensive charity and created strong social institutions, but nevertheless, they remained relatively marginal. The political agenda was determined by atheistic socialists. The working class turned its back on the church. Socialism became its gospel with promises of bread and justice. In France, the powerful and reactionary Catholic ultramontanists continued to dominate the scene.

Söderblom sought out "modernists" who shared his criticism of the Catholic Church. One of them was Abbé J. A. Lemire. He was the leading person in the Catholic social movement. Another was Marc Sagnier who founded the liberal democratic organization Sillon. That movement saw rapid growth among seminarians and young priests and was supported by many bishops before it was forbidden by Pope Pius X in 1910. In Belgium, where the well-established worker's party made considerable progress in a population with greater illiteracy than any other European nation, he also had contact with the Catholic social movement. During a weekend visit to London in August 1896, he devoted Friday to studying social work, Saturday to observing the Socialist Congress at Crystal Palace, and Sunday to worshipping in Westminster Abbey, officiating at a Swedish funeral, participating in a Baptist service at the London Tabernacle, and preaching at the Swedish seamen's church. On Monday he rounded out the whole visit by having a look at the Assyrian collection in the British Museum and visiting Parliament. Every minute was filled, but his actual task was to learn something about "Christian Socialism" in England. Inspiring socialist pamphlets depicted muscular men in blue shirts followed by indomitable women with curly hair, but the real conditions of the working class were different: coal dust, child labor, and extreme poverty. The worker's movement in England, as nearly everywhere else, was led by well-trained people who were equipped with ideas and energy. This was even more true for the Christian Socialist movement, which was entirely led by highly educated people.

In spite of all that he was exposed to in France and England, it was certain socially aware Lutherans in Germany who meant the most to Söderblom and his development in this area. In the late fall of 1896, when his first child Helge was only a few months old and daughter Brita was soon to be born, he was invited by a pious but somewhat perplexing businessman, who on his own had taken up the study of theology, on a study trip to Germany. This was the first time Söderblom had been there apart from a single day's visit to Hamburg and Berlin. He was captivated by the nature, culture, and history and was especially happy to walk in Luther's footsteps. In spite of his love for France, he felt more at home here. The culture was closer to that found in Sweden and it had been German theologians who had shaped his way of thinking. In a letter to Göransson in January 1895 he wrote, "We who are 'Germanic' are the most prominent generation for peace. Will we possess enough vigor and originality to produce the new religion which the times need?" It was clear to him that religion must include a trustworthy dose of socialist values if it were to speak to its time. He took the occasion to listen to some German theologians who were of the same mind, among them Wilhelm Hermann in Marburg. Visiting the Lutheran city of Eisenach and the Wartburg Castle was a great experience, but the goal of the journey was an evangelical social ethics congress in Erfurt. By means of a press card from the conservative and Germany-friendly Swedish paper *Nya Dagligt Allehanda*, he was admitted to the congress.

The German socialist party was the oldest and largest in Europe. It was — in spite of its Marxist rhetoric — pragmatic and reformist, yet reluctant to make common cause with any other party. Consequently, it had less political influence than might have been expected considering its significant number of voters. With 1.4 million votes in 1890 the party became a serious threat to the churches. In line with the British model, Adolf von Harnack then formed an evangelical social conservative movement. One of its most prominent leaders was Adolf Stoecker who was chaplain to Kaiser Wilhelm, conservative in all respects, and clearly given to anti-Semitism. He had unsuccessfully attempted to establish a Christian social party in order to counter the Social Democrats.

Another leader was the more liberal Friedrich Naumann who published the journal *Die Hilfe*. Söderblom had read that journal and thus traveled to the congress in Erfurt with high expectations. He was not disappointed. Here he encountered a Christianity as he would have it: energetic but not "methodistic," virile but still rather quiet, inward but not introverted or pietistic. Naumann, who later would distance himself from the church, awakened Söderblom's great admiration. He was able to speak both to world-famous academics and to unschooled workers. With gifts for simple and expressive speech, consistent argumentation, and a warm heart, he captured the attention of everyone. He emphasized that a Christianity that forgets its friendship with Jesus, who was himself a friend to the suffering and the poor, does not amount to much. Yet Christians seem content with giving charity instead of being representatives of justice and mercy. They should pay attention to the social movements, for if Christianity does not stand up for its highest ideals, it has no future.

During his years in Paris, Söderblom wrote approximately forty articles for Swedish newspapers, perhaps mostly to augment his low salary. Most were published in *Nya Dagligt Allehanda*. His reports from the congress in Erfurt were given a great deal of space in that paper. He admonished thoughtful and upright people, without respect to parties, to act to change the miserable situation of workers. It must not be only the workers movement or the Catholic Church that struggled for justice. Yet Söderblom was not prepared to give political power to the working class. He wanted a socially conservative solution to the problems of society. He did not deny the necessity of class struggle and he defended the freedom both to form unions and to strike, but as a Christian he kept out of party politics seeking, rather, to convince those who had control over great wealth to take responsibility for the poor. He set the command to love against greed and exploitation and hoped that conscience would drive those in power to acts of sharing. And there was, indeed, much philanthropy going on at the time.

In retrospect, his way of looking at things might seem politically naïve, but in the aggressive class struggle that was underway, it was clearly radical for a young priest to publicly show solidarity with the workers' demands even if he did not go along with their methods or utopian goals. In his reports from the Erfurt congress, Söderblom for the first time pointed out the connection between the church's social responsibility and its unity. They were little more than initial intimations, but a few decades later they were to develop into a picture of evangelical Christianity united by a common social program. The congress was an event in the area where the monk Martin Luther came to his evangelical faith, and it was where Söderblom first experienced how Christians of different traditions could be united in a faith that the power of the gospel could bring about social renewal.

During this time he was writing his first book, which was published in 1898, *Jesu bergspredikan och vår tid* (*Jesus's Sermon on the Mount and Our Time*). He should have given priority to writing his dissertation, but he could not avoid first writing this book, which had initially taken shape as a lecture to Protestant theologians in Paris in 1895. Reading Tolstoy had awakened his interest in the Sermon on the Mount and like many others, he wanted to make a contribution to the perennial discussion about the Kingdom of God. He approached the Sermon with questions: Was it not too idealistic to believe that whoever wanted to could follow its admonitions? Is there anything in the Sermon that can be taken literally or must one go through a long process of interpretation? If the Sermon on the Mount is beyond actual practice, would it not be better to reduce it to understandable points that can be realized? Should it not be read as an eschatological text that reflects the primitive church's expectation that Christ would soon return rather than as instruction in social ethics?

The book also dealt with a number of other matters: the relationship between theology and the church, Catholicism, Luther, marriage, prayer and miracle, revolution, war, and the struggle against evil. He used material from many sources, but emphasized ideas that were specifically Christian, Protestant, and Lutheran. The chapter on the Sermon on the Mount actually took up only one-tenth of the book. Critical as he was toward all fundamentalism, he attempted to show that correct biblical interpretation presupposed a careful scholarly study of the text. Whoever was really devoted to such study could not, as liberal theologians did, describe the Kingdom of God as embryonic for a perfect earthly society, nor could they, as the social gospel movement in the United States did, conclude that the Kingdom is the sum of all the good things that humans strive for here in this world. There were theologians who were against looking at things in such this-worldly manners. One of them was the German Johannes Weiss, whom Söderblom had read. For him the Kingdom of God had nothing to do with social progress but was, rather, an eschatological promise that would be fulfilled at the end of time. Whoever believed that the Kingdom could be realized within the present world order built that view on poor exegesis that reflected the optimism of the Enlightenment. It had little support in the Bible.

Weiss was out of step with his time, but Söderblom took him seriously. Since his own doctoral work dealt with Persian views of the last things, everything that concerned eschatology awakened his interest. He welcomed Weiss's interpretation as reasonable and as a source of inspiration for a more just society. Yet the Kingdom of God did not belong only to the future. It was also present in the midst of human life and had been revealed through the "signs of the Kingdom of Heaven," which Jesus had pointed to. Söderblom rejected both Tolstoy's revolutionary interpretation of the gospel and the attempts of others to translate the Sermon on the Mount into this-worldly laws. He also denied the view — as held by the Catholic Church — that higher demands could be placed on some people than on others. Instead, in keeping with Luther, he realistically distinguished between two kingdoms — one directed by worldly law, power, and force, and the other guided by the absolute demands of Jesus in the midst of a world of sin and relativism. Both kingdoms, however, were placed under the rule of God.

In 1897, in connection with the twenty-fifth anniversary of the coronation of Oscar II, a large artistic and industrial exposition took place in Stockholm. A dream city was built up in a park and one event succeeded another; a number of conferences on different themes were held. Samuel Fries, together with the Swedenborgian Albert Björck and the rabbi Gottlieb Klein and with the help of Nathan Söderblom, arranged a rather pretentious conference on the academic study of religion held in the Riddarhuset, the House of the Nobility. The initiative for this had originally come from Björck. He had been inspired by the Parliament of World Religions held in Chicago in 1893 where the Church of the New Jerusalem, the Swedenborgians, had played a central role. But Fries was not out to launch a universal religion; such already existed in Christianity. Rather, the conference was to show the meaning of the modern study of religion for the church, and it was marked by a number of Christian events. Klein was the only representative of another religion. With the exception of Waldemar Rudin, the Uppsala theological faculty stayed away, as did the bishops, also with one exception: Knut Henning Gezelius von Schéele was chairman of the event, and he also supported the event financially. The international feature of the conference was limited to Professor Auguste Sabatier and a handful of historians of religion whom Söderblom was able to get to Stockholm. There were 318 participants in the conference of whom, surprisingly, more than 100 were women.

Nathan Söderblom traveled to Stockholm to present one of the main lectures at the conference. He did not speak about his own research, as might have been expected, but rather took the occasion to present a long lecture concerning religion and current social developments. He lifted up themes in social ethics, which he would subsequently follow in his ecumenical work. His starting point was that religion and social development in principle are independent of each other, but that they nevertheless influence each other, especially in the area of morality. Christianity is transcendent and its primary task is the proclamation of the gospel. If the church downplays that mission in favor of social or cultural work, it has lost its way. Christians have an inescapable social responsibility, but it is secondary.

Söderblom was intimately familiar with social currents in Europe and well read in Marxism. He believed, however, that political socialism should not be mixed with Christianity and he was surely not an advocate of revolution. Christianity must hold itself to its own principles; it would lose itself if it became subordinate to other entities. Protestantism had often organized itself in accordance with middle-class needs and reflected society's general values, but it was better advised to bring about change through socially engaged theologians. The gospel had its best friends among the poor, and the more economically privileged must take responsibility to include them in a Christian fellowship.

The Swedish Social Democratic Workers Party had been formed in 1889. Hjalmar Branting was a member of the lower house in the Riksdag, the Parliament. Söderblom regretted the Social Democrats' lack of realism in their concept of humanity. They believed that it was within human power to improve the conditions of existence, but Söderblom had no illusion that humans could achieve justice by their own strength. If, however, the gospel liberated people to place love and solidarity first, society could be changed from within. It was an urgent task for the church to create congregations without the conflicts that marked society. Through a Christian concern for people, the church could influence the formation of law in society and contribute to a life fit for all human beings.

Söderblom had a genuine and instinctive concern for the marginalized, whether they lived in Paris or Stockholm. They should not have to experience the church as an inaccessible institution or socialism as empty agitation, but rather as sources for personal fulfillment. He wanted to enter into the situations of the workers in order to share the gospel with them. The church had both spiritual and material resources and the potential for change, but it did not use them. Consequently, workers voted with their feet and left the church, and thus lost the best means of solution for the evils of society. The church did not even see the problem, although the situation clamored for thorough analysis and action.

By the standards of the church, the lecture was radical. Six years earlier, Archbishop Sundberg had lectured on socialism at a gathering of clergy. He had, without at all distinguishing between communism and socialism, spoken of them as the most dangerous of all ideologies and urged the priests to take positions on the front lines of the battle against everything "socialistic." Söderblom struck a different tone. He spoke with sympathy and solidarity. His emotional engagement with the workers was even more apparent when, a few days later, evidently in a completely improvised way, he addressed a large group of students.

During a celebration for Oscar II in the Botanical Garden in Uppsala he saw how one person in the glare of the fires cast a large, dark shadow on the wall of a greenhouse. This triggered his imagination. When, the following day, nine hundred students went on an excursion to Skokloster Castle, Söderblom was among them. Suddenly, he took a place on the castle steps and called the crowd to order as though he were still chairperson of the student body. Some of the students did not recognize the passionate priest who addressed them with an extraordinary question: "Did you see him? He appeared to me yesterday, just as we ordinarily see him, at a distance, shapeless, without contours, frighteningly enlarged." He had himself just recognized him. Perhaps it was a stonemason from a street nearby or, for that matter, any physical laborer at all, whom the privileged students seldom even noticed but whom they should learn to know and love. For it was loyal workers who made the students' celebration possible. "Therefore I request from all of you a commitment to solidarity with all of those in our Swedish land who work with their arms or their heads." So he concluded and — on the doorstep of a baron — called for a cheer for "our country's true nobility who bear the burden and heat of the day."

When Söderblom returned to Paris it was high time for him to complete his doctoral dissertation. There was a need for speed since J. A. Ekman had unexpectedly been elected bishop in Västerås and his much coveted professor's chair in Uppsala suddenly stood vacant. Söderblom had considered changing his field from the history of religion to New Testament, leading him to devote so much time to the book on the Sermon on the Mount. But now he aimed exclusively at the history of religion in order to possibly succeed Ekman. The time was short and a great many things intervened: preparation of another congress on the history of religions in connection with the Paris World's Fair of 1900, celebration of the turn of the century with his congregation, receiving all sorts of dignitaries who were continually coming to Paris. Nevertheless, he succeeded in completing and defending his dissertation. His time appeared to be more flexible than that of others and he was accustomed to having many irons in the fire.

The years around the turn of the century were golden years for the history of religions. Knowledge of world religions increased dramatically because of careful scholarship. Every religion was being dealt with on its own terms. There was no "religion in general" even as there was no "humanity in general." All religions had their own cultural expressions. Religion did not consist of a number of truths to be evaluated. Religion affected actual lives in all of their expressions. Söderblom was suspicious of attempts to create order out of miscellaneous variety by trying to organize the manifestations of religion in some sort of evolutionary hierarchy. He was an outspoken individualist who acknowledged the uniqueness and integrity not only of churches but also of world religions.

He intensified his linguistic studies, consulted leading historians of religion in Belgium and the Netherlands, and in 1899 wrote a major essay on "guardian angels" in Mazdaism, which he dedicated to his old Uppsala friends. Then he concentrated on completing *La vie future d'après le Mazdéisme à la lumière des croyances parallèles dans les autres religions: étude d'eschatologie compare* (*The Future Life according to Mazdaism in the Light of Parallel Faiths in Other Religions: A Comparative Study of Eschatology*). Behind that long title there was an impressive doctoral dissertation of 450 pages, written in Swedish and translated into French by the Catholic journalist Barbie de Quirelle, who also kept Söderblom informed of developments in the Roman Catholic Church. The dissertation was a comprehensive essay in comparative eschatology, that is, the study of the last things. It dealt with Persian conceptions of heaven, hell, and eternal life; it discussed the destruction and reconstruction of the world as an eschatological event; and it offered comparisons with other religious notions in the Eastern Mediterranean area. Most of the material was actually taken not from Iranian religion but rather from a large variety of other religious sources. The final section of *La vie future* was devoted to eternal life from a Christian perspective, concentrating on Martin Luther. In conscious opposition to the general trend in biblical studies of the time, Söderblom held that the Christian view of eternal life had its background in Judaism and not in Hellenistic or Iranian notions. Finally, Söderblom gave an account of what he had learned and then drew his own conclusions. He had come to just the point he wanted to prove: the Jewish-Christian faith in God stood on its own legs.

The defense of the dissertation took place on January 24, 1901, long after he had made his application for the open professor's chair in Uppsala. He received the highest grades and congratulations came to him from all directions. Not only was he the only foreign student but actually the first and only student to receive the degree of Doctor of Theology at the short-lived Protestant Faculty at the Sorbonne. A celebration was surely called for. A ceremonial, although by French standards quite frugal, feast took place with twenty-five guests, including Consul General Gustav Nordling, in the Swedish-Norwegian Society's locale, which was decorated to the fullest with flowers. The artist Julia Beck, one of Anna's friends, painted personal place cards for the guests. Scandinavian music was played and sung. The revered and beloved Auguste Sabatier was for the last time present in a large group before illness took its course. In a letter to his father, Nathan described Sabatier: "His disposition is so holy, so free from arrogance and worldliness and so full of love, that he appears to be sent from the higher life. I can not go along with everything in his theology, but I am deeply attached to him." Sabatier died in the middle of April.

The academic way now lay open. Söderblom could have become professor in Leiden in the Netherlands, but his eyes were set on Uppsala. And there he went. He had much more in his portfolio than his doctor's degree: thorough knowledge of the state of things in France, a Christian understanding of society, and personal friendship with many French intellectuals and Nordic artists and authors. But above all, he had become European through and through, spoke French like a Frenchman, and communicated fluently in English and even more in German.

8

The Young Professor

> The meaning of life shines forth only for the vigorous will, the vision of the longing heart.
>
> *Nathan Söderblom, 1899*

HE LECTURES AT EIGHT O'CLOCK IN THE MORNING. With melancholy complaint he recites Babylonian penitential psalms: "Great are my sins, many are my misdeeds. Let your liver be silent. I shake like a dove, I feed myself with sighs." He emphasizes the sympathetic and authentically religious aspects of Mohammed's personality. He speaks of the winding way of revelation from Mount Sinai to Uppsala. He draws a picture on the blackboard: faith and criticism stand as quarreling parties before the judgment seat of science. Christianity has nothing to fear.

* * *

Academic study and research were his greatest joys throughout life and a way to hold his demons at a distance, but it was not at all clear that he would be a professor. Openings were few and the appointment process was complicated and arbitrary. As the decision neared, he felt inadequate for the task. Perhaps he was more suited to be a parish priest? The conservative faculty at Uppsala would scarcely propose someone who stood so near to Fehr. But nevertheless, he applied. Then he could only wait while the experts studied the academic work of all the applicants and proposed two candidates who would then each present two public lectures before names would be sent to the University Consistory. The Consistory would then choose one name to be sent to the king for a final decision. Of the five who sought the position, J. A. Eklund and Nathan Söderblom were considered best qualified. Eklund had been Ekman's docent and then interim professor while the appointment process was carried on. He had written a critical review of Sabatier's *Esquisse d'une philosophie de la religion* (*Outlines of a Philosophy of Religion*), which Söderblom had translated, and he indicated that the choice between himself and Söderblom was a choice between two schools of thought and not simply between two individuals.

In November 1899, Söderblom came home from Paris to give his two lectures. With rapid, slightly stumbling steps he went to the podium, drank a glass of water, and began to speak. The students listened intensively. "The voice rang out like a spring brook, and the r-sound hummed at supradental combinations," wrote the hymn writer Emil Liedgren. One could ask whether or not his Swedish was infected by French and object to the language on phonetic grounds as he lectured with great precision from notes written on small loose papers. There was also talk of "playing to the gallery." The first lecture dealt with the significance of Schleiermacher's *Reden über die Religion* (*On Religion: Speeches to Its Cultured Despisers*), the second on the temptations of Jesus, Buddha, and Zarathustra. In these lectures, which actually built on the work of Rudolf Otto and Rudolf Seydel, Söderblom emphasized four of the basic theses which were always to guide him: that religion is independent in relation to metaphysics and morals; that theology must confine itself to the prophetic tradition and Christ; that all religions are revelations of God; and that each religion has its own individuality, comparable to that of humans.

During his visit to his homeland, he also attended to other matters. He visited Norrala where his old father was still rector, and he delivered a university sermon in the largest of the lecture halls to an overflow crowd. Söderblom stood there like a prophet and admonished the students not to attach themselves to the past but rather to look forward in Jesus's name. Far more attention was paid to another appearance, three weeks later. The Uppsala student body had arranged for a November 25 Nordic festival "in memory of the fathers." It was to mark the approaching turn of the century. The poet Erik Axel Karlfeldt, and the theologians Hjalmar Holmquist and J. A. Eklund — Söderblom's competitor for the professorship — had promised to participate. The history professor Harald Hjärne was asked to summarize the nineteenth century but was unable to attend.

Söderblom was drawn in as a substitute. Protests were quick to come: three theologians on the stage were too much of a good thing when what was being celebrated was a century of rationalism, natural science, and industrialism. Söderblom had three weeks to prepare his speech. To the clatter of a trumpet fanfare he took the podium and captured the attention of everyone. In an exuberant and sparkling speech, he summarized the past century's hopes and disappointments and opened the doors to the twentieth century. It was the same Nathan Söderblom they remembered from the past: youthful, fresh, and energetic, now with his Swedish patriotism clothed in French ésprit and his candid piety supported by continental theology.

His opening words were to become a classic in the annals of Swedish rhetoric: "Over the century three messengers of peace came soaring in, doves of peace who after many false directions and long imprisonments had forgotten their far-off home in Israel. They had blood on their wings . . . the three were called freedom, equality, and fraternity." Even though they are misused and have fared ill, the enthusiasm these slogans have awoken will endure. Freedom, equality, and fraternity, prophesied Söderblom, will need eagle's wings to fly during the twentieth century.

The Revolution had failed because of Napoleon's arbitrariness. In opposition to this power-mad genius, Söderblom placed the gentle philosopher Immanuel Kant and German culture, which, with its loyalty to the king and an organic view of the nation, had a solid future if only it could do away with the "sickness of nationalism." He hailed the progress of science and its discovery that everything in nature is interconnected, but he warned against a mechanical view of the world that has no room for religion but lives in estheticism's original sin of denying both good and evil. The nineteenth century had been the century of liberation. Söderblom urged his listeners to go further in the same direction: "Let us strictly and with precision use scholarship's own method, chaste as a virgin without lust, bold as a man facing tremendous opportunities." It is now important to set sail in God's providence and not abandon Jesus of Nazareth. With Kant and Goethe as guides, the students should go forward listening to the cantata composed for the Uppsala Jubilee twenty-two years earlier by Viktor Rydberg, a wise visionary in the land of pine forests who had inherited Faust's world-encompassing curious mind but never renounced his spiritual heritage:

> Let thy selfishness be chidden,
> Let God's image in thee hidden
> Toward His perfect likeness tend

With each age and generation.
So shalt thou through desolation
Wind to Jordan at the end.

Referring to Ibsen's *Brand*, Söderblom asked: Do you dare to hear without prejudice the call for more religion and more Christianity — a call that arises from the sickness of the time? Students must listen to Søren Kierkegaard and Leo Tolstoy and follow the solitary wanderer who climbs steep steps to reach the heights where the view is clear. "Development" was a word of the times. Söderblom gave the word content: "Being is not seized in repose. Its image is not a temple of marble, in whose cool cloisters the spirit finds delight and rest. Being is seized in daily life, in becoming, in what ought to be. Its image is of an ascent to the heights." Development is, and must be, a contest in which strength wins. And this strength is the suffering of righteousness, and the greatest strength is sacrificial love. In this strength, centuries are joined one to another with no break in the chain of faith, hope, and love.

As speakers, there were similarities between Johan Olof Wallin, the early nineteenth-century Archbishop of Uppsala and a well-known orator and hymn writer, and Nathan Söderblom. They both had a brilliant feeling for the rhythm and musicality of speech and a charismatic charm at the podium. They were fully assured that religion had the answer to the social and political questions of the day. They were admired, but also criticized. Söderblom's rhetoric was studded with risky metaphors and references to people and events, clear-eyed analyses and daring conclusions. It was permeated by confessions of God as the God of history and Christ as the fulfillment of history. Difficult, old-fashioned, and pompous words were piled on each other. It was so warm in the auditorium that some fainted, and it was not easy to follow his overloaded speech. Yet his candid impact and his faith in the future gripped his listeners. Here spoke a European out of his French and German experiences, and he lifted the festival to unexpected heights.

The students wanted him back in Uppsala. He did come, but it was March 21, 1901 before the theological faculty made its decision. By that time he had submitted his dissertation to the Sorbonne and been hailed by historians of religion in many countries. The four members of the faculty who voted for him could feel satisfied that they had saved this splendid scholar for Uppsala. To the very end, the outcome was unclear. Fries and Klein were anxious and all sorts of rumors circulated. Two professors favored Eklund. Söderblom prevailed because of his knowledge of Persian.

He rejoiced, but his joy was mixed with sorrow. In mid-April, Auguste Sabatier, who was so close to him as teacher and friend, died. In June of the same year, his father also died. The train journey from Paris to Norrala took three days and Nathan reached home just before it would have been too late. When he came into the room, the old priest awakened from his silence. At his deathbed they had a conversation about holding fast to the Lutheran faith and to the Apostle Paul's words, "I do not mean to imply that we lord it over your faith; rather, we are workers with you for your joy" (2 Cor. 1:24). It was a conversation to which Nathan would often return. The father and the son had been reconciled; the task of proclaiming the gospel had been handed over from one generation to the next.

Nathan was thirty-five years old. His life was taking a new turn. His dissertation had been approved and the chestnut trees had shed their blossoms in the Tuileries and he had followed his father Jonas on his last journey. Then on July 5, 1901 came the expected appointment to the professorship and it was time to return to Uppsala. After seven years, the Paris congregation took leave of its pastor and his family. With a gleam in his eye the wholesale dealer Sigurd Løchen said, "Those up there in Uppsala sent us a young student to be our pastor. We are sending him back as a professor." It was an emotional farewell, for even if the Söderbloms at times longed for home, Nathan and Anna loved Paris and its people. The congregation also had learned to treasure the young priest whose like they would not see again. With thanks they were presented with a silver tea service and they discovered that the sugar bowl was filled with gold coins. This allowed them both to leave Paris without debt and to pay for their move home. The family returned to Uppsala's chillier climate and dry academic milieu, but also to relatives and friends and imposing tasks.

The oldest of their four children was now six, and Anna was once again pregnant. They moved into the rectory at Stabby, two miles from the university. It belonged to the Holy Trinity parish, which was his prebendary. He could have chosen to serve in Old Uppsala but he preferred to be a priest in the midst of the academic milieu. Even if the parsonage was built later, it had a lineage back to the sixteenth century. In many ways it was similar to the rectories of Hälsingland: a red-painted six-room house on one-and-a-half levels, a detached wing fit to live in, and a wagon shed nearby. In the rectory's yard there were large elm trees with birds' nests. The road into the city had deep ruts that were filled with mud when it rained or snowed, which it seemed to do much of the time. Farther along there were groves of oak trees, meadows, and pastures; the city was much smaller in those days. There were no streetlights and the rectory had no electricity or running water. Söderblom quickly ordered from the Royal Telegraph Service a telephone with a direct line to the phone station in Uppsala. He was not ready to be totally cut off from the world around him. When in September darkness began to envelope the house, Anna and Nathan must sometimes have longed for their "bird's nest" on Rue de Malleville.

On Anna's thirty-first birthday, September 24, 1901, Söderblom gave his inaugural lecture in the university aula. The procession glided in and Söderblom took his place at the podium. Over it shone the golden script of the university's venerable seal: *Gratiae veritas naturae*, which can be translated as "The Truth of Grace Is Nature's" or as "The Truths of Grace and Nature Are One and the Same." But the times had changed since the seal and its motto were adopted in 1601. The self-evident unity between faith and knowledge had been broken. In his lecture, Söderblom attempted to show how the two belong together, making peace between doctrinally bound Christian theology and secular science. There was a continual discussion concerning the place of heteronomous confessional theological instruction in a university characterized by autonomous, empirical research. Söderblom was unequivocally committed to a view of theology as a field of autonomous research.

His predecessor as professor, J. A. Ekman had, a few months earlier, succeeded Anton Niklas Sundberg as archbishop. When Söderblom lectured on "the general history of religion and the theology of the church," in most respects he followed the same line as Ekman. He argued that the study of the history of religion belonged within the theological faculty. There were different opinions about this. Some feared that the history of religion would lose its academic objectivity if it were placed within theology; others feared that the confession of the church and the faith of candidates for the priesthood would be threatened by encounters with other religions. One reason that Söderblom defended the place of the history of religion within the theological faculty was his conviction that a person must have his or her own religious experience in order adequately to understand another religion. To deny this was like saying that someone who was tone-deaf was able to study music. To keep the history of religion within the bounds of theology was a matter of academic integrity. It presupposes that there are common experiences within different religions. The history of religion also serves the church. Christian missionaries needed knowledge of the religions in the countries where they worked in order to adapt their message to the immediate religious milieu. And in a shrinking world, all must learn to associate peacefully with each other, with understanding for other communities of faith. Söderblom had a positive attitude toward religious pluralism and was convinced that Christians, through encounters with others, would also learn better to understand their own religion. Harnack had formulated the thesis that whoever knows so comprehensive a religion as Christianity knows all religions. Against that view, Söderblom set the words of the Orientalist Max Müller that whoever knows only one religion does not know any religion. According to Söderblom a strict scientific approach to research in the history of religion leads to a deeper knowledge of Christianity's distinctive prophetic character. A comparison between the life of Christ and the teachings of founders of religions such as Buddha and Zarathustra would lead to the conclusion that Christianity is the definitive and absolute religion. Thus it was, he held, that the study of the history of religion was needed in religiously ignorant Sweden.

Söderblom maintained energetically that unrestricted academic rigor must mark every area of the study of theology. Research in recent years had given a more accurate picture both of the Bible and church history, not least of Luther. He saw it as the responsibility of the theological faculty to make sure that a new authoritative dogmatism did not arise in reaction to this. Those who believe must humbly and self-critically surrender to reality. The church and the university must agree that truth and reality should be united at the root. Contradictions between different methods of research are basically illusory.

In his lecture he disclosed what could be expected of him as a professor. He identified himself with the approach of neo-Protestantism's liberal theology. He defended autonomous research with its free and unlimited search for truth that — even if it brought difficulties for faith — aimed at reforming church teachings and liberating them from obsolete notions. He was open to hearing God speak through different religions, but he emphasized that in the end, Christ was the fulfillment and crown of them all.

Söderblom did not succeed in convincing all the professors, but the students received him with open arms, especially when, at the end of his lecture in long and passionate remarks, he turned directly to "those whose servant I have been called to be." He congratulated those who had chosen to study theology in order to enter into the service of parish ministry. To make that choice was by no means self-evident. Christianity was under attack from many directions. Many clergy were convinced that they belonged to the last generation before the death of the church. In Uppsala, the number of theology students had shrunk in ten years from 275 to 193. One had to count on a severe shortage of clergy all over. Söderblom encouraged them like no one else, and his words to the students that September day would be quoted for decades to come.

There are today many who pity you, he began, "because you serve what is supposed to be an outdated cause, that of Christianity, or at least — and the distinction must be carefully drawn — because you serve an outdated church. People pity you because you have to wear the yoke of the church's confession around your necks." But I, he continued, "wish to congratulate you with all my heart on your present studies, on studying theology at this time, and on your coming vocation . . . I congratulate you on those who will be your companions: an Amos, a Hosea, an Isaiah, a Jeremiah, a Paul, an Augustine, a Francis, a Luther, a Pascal, a Kierkegaard. And high above all of these, the Master, the Lord Jesus, who grows before our eyes the closer we come to him. He is the one whom you, yourselves set free by submitting to his yoke, are to present to your brethren. In the history of religion the human heart will reveal its deepest secret: its longing for God."

He congratulated the students on their calling to be courageous interpreters of truth and available to all, for "if you are too great to concern yourselves with the smallest person, you are too small to be a minister." You should love people, not humanity, he said, and you should know that as servants of Jesus you have an ally in every person. And he concluded, "May the Lord light the sacred fire in your hearts and preserve it!"

No one who was present that day ever forgot what they had heard. One of them was Gustaf Aulén who immediately decided that he would take part in Söderblom's lectures and seminars. In his memoirs, which he published in 1975 when he was ninety-six years old, Aulén wrote that Söderblom's words struck a new and previously unknown tone for all who listened. No one had ever said anything like this from a university platform, or for that matter, from any other platform. Everyone was grateful, not least himself. Soon Aulén became Söderblom's docent. What those who listened to the new professor that day, however, did not know was that his words were taken from the address that Auguste Sabatier had directed to students in Paris in the fall of 1896. He also had spoken of the holy fire that could not be extinguished.

Söderblom was met with an ovation. With the flags of fraternities, banners, songs, speeches, and white student caps, the spirited young professor was greeted on the steps of the university by many hundreds of students from all the faculties. Eight years earlier he had himself pleaded the students' cause. Now the roles were changed and it was he who thanked them. During the past years, he said, he had learned more of life than was to be found in his theoretical studies. Now he was again in the midst of the students in order to serve them for the rest of his life with all the power God might give him, "a task so beautiful, so high, that I cannot dream of anything higher." He concluded by saying, "If I am given no greater spiritual service, let me at least call to you: Do not forget that the highest and most noble of all knowledge is to know how to live. Do not forget that whatever you become, you can never become more than truly living persons."

The coolness that came after that uncommonly hot summer made the return to academic life pleasant, but Söderblom had long known that his tasks would be difficult. He was not only the youngest member of the theological faculty, but he had been suspect since his student years for his radical theological positions. Some faculty members had not recommended him. He had skillfully argued his case in his inaugural lecture, but not everyone had been convinced. There were some who joked with a bitter touch that he was a professor of heathendom, not Christianity. Jealousy arose when they saw how the newcomer was received. He was not entirely welcome and for a long while, some of his colleagues spoke of him with an unpleasant tone of superiority. Their suspicions did not cease.

He got going with his lectures. He held them in the early morning and that was about the only thing the students had against him. His successor as professor, Tor Andrae, described how it went: "At the stroke of quarter past eight he bounced up to the lecturer's stand with a morning freshness like that of spring, and cast himself quickly into the midst of his topic. His presentation was lucid and lively. . . . He was like no professor in that august faculty, like no theologian of that estimable sort that counts thirteen to the dozen. He was like a character in Strindberg's drama *Mäster Olof* who in a wide-brimmed hat wandered through the streets of the small university town." The first years he lectured on different religions, later on the phenomenology of religion. He often surprised his students by lecturing on Luther's *Small Catechism* in the light of the history of religion, or on St. Francis, or Socrates, or Swedes such as Erik Gustaf Geijer and Pehr Eklund. Many of his lectures later appeared in books. Students streamed to hear him. "His thoughts and expressions occupied us constantly and came to be, without us noticing it, our second nature," wrote Tor Andrae. Students collected everything he had printed and missed no chance to hear him. He quickly became the faculty's most influential teacher, but he stood nearly alone.

This was brutally revealed when Söderblom's best friend, Sam Fries, sought a chair in exegetics in 1902. This was the third time Fries had sought a professorship, something that had always been his dream. In the past, he had received the judgment of "incompetent" from the appointed experts. In order to instruct those who were to become priests, one should have a "firmly grounded faith in the truth of biblical revelation as a whole and in Christianity's fundamental teachings." He was clearly superior to the others who sought the chair in respect to languages, learning, and enthusiasm for research, but he was handicapped in that he was identified with Ritschlianism and was convinced of the autonomy of theological scholarship. That the University Consistory this third time declared him competent by a slight majority did not help. Söderblom emphasized his originality and intellectual sharpness, but he was the only professor of theology who supported Fries. Leading professors of the philosophical faculty, Herman Almqvist, Harald Hjärne, Henrik Schück, and Adolf Noreen spoke on his behalf. This was a moral victory, but the theological faculty chose instead Adolf Kolmodin who belonged to *Evangeliska Fosterlandsstiftelsen*, the Evangelical Mission, and lacked expertise in historical-critical research. For Söderblom, this decision was a great disappointment.

Things got even worse the next year. Torgny Segerstedt, who would become well known as a journalist and anti-Nazi, sought to become docent in the history of religion on the basis of a dissertation on the origins of polytheism. Söderblom had been his supervisor and the disputation took place May 28. It was also intended that Segerstedt would preach in Holy Trinity Church the following Sunday prior to being ordained and becoming Söderblom's docent. But his dissertation was not approved. It had considerable academic merit, but according to the professor of exegetics, Eric Stave, who was supported by Danell and Kolmodin, it was all too vague to qualify someone to teach those who were to become priests. The traditionalists, with their heteronomous view of theology, succeeded yet again in holding back a modern theologian who had an expressly autonomous view of theology. It did not help that the dissertation was praised by professors in the philosophical faculty.

This event developed into a public scandal of considerable proportions that was discussed for a decade. Söderblom was set in his place, receiving virtually no support from the theologians, although considerable support from the leading humanists. The questions continued to be whether the history of religions really had a place within the study of theology and whether one who did not unambiguously stand on Lutheran confessional grounds could be allowed to teach candidates for the ministry. The theological faculty was not open to innovation. Confessional allegiances were too strong and newer views of academic research had not been accepted as they had in other faculties. It was actually no longer possible in any juridical sense to require of teachers of theology any sort of codified allegiance to "pure doctrine," but the idea that unique academic conditions must be allowed to apply to theological research was deeply rooted. Theology was caught between the confessions of the church and the requirements of the academy. Söderblom was deeply depressed but he did not give in to bitterness. He stood squarely on Segerstedt's side and sought, despite this setback, to find a way to keep him at Uppsala. He did not succeed and Segerstedt was called to Lund where a docent's position had been created for him. He later became a professor of the history of religion at Stockholm University where there was no faculty of theology. This event would haunt Söderblom through the years. The friendship was injured and when Segerstedt became editor of the paper *Göteborgs Handels & Sjöfartstidning* (*Gothenburg Commercial & Maritime Times*), Söderblom became a regular target for his sarcastic criticism.

Söderblom had lost two rounds in his battle to shape theology as an academic discipline without confessional boundaries. The program he had laid out in his inaugural lecture had been shot down. He felt opposed and isolated, irritated and rejected, and for a time he considered leaving his position. That summer he developed stomach ulcers for the first time. There were no antibiotics at that time, but Söderblom was not one to give up work, even if he was seriously ill.

9

God Speaks Many Languages

> No religion is a product of culture, rather all religions depend on revelation.
>
> *Nathan Söderblom, 1903*

SÖDERBLOM IS AN INSPIRING DOCTOR FATHER who always comes up with new proposals. He gives his doctoral students complete freedom. All too often, detailed and precise directives can take away individual initiative. He selects a theme of academic significance and shares his own enthusiasm. He suggests that Gustaf Aulén studies Reuterdahl's relation to Schleiermacher and sends him to Pehr Eklund in Lund. He gives Tor Andrae a totally new topic: the Prophet Mohammed. He puts him in contact with the Islamist scholar Ingnác Goldziher in Budapest to get started. The rest of their work they can take care of themselves. He always encourages them but seldom examines their work before the actual disputation.

* * *

In spite of the opposition, Nathan Söderblom did not give up his struggle to identify theology as an independent academic discipline. Many of his colleagues had difficulty putting up with the young, opinionated, intellectually and socially superior professor who had already become one of Uppsala's best-known personalities, but he did not lose courage. If the theologians had difficulty knowing exactly what he stood for, he knew all too well where they felt at home. He did not think like they did, and he often felt himself outside their circle. His large family, lectures and seminars, and his work as a parish rector demanded a great deal of him. A complete revision of the nearly five-hundred-page-long history of religion compendium of C. P. Tiele, professor at Leiden in the Netherlands, took more of his time than he had counted on, but he was still able to write both in the daily press and in scholarly journals. An incidental contribution to a *Festschrift* made him — much to his own surprise — suddenly notable far outside the limited circle of history of religion scholars. It was a volume dedicated to his old teacher in pastoral theology who later became Dean of the Uppsala Cathedral, Carl Axel Torén who turned 90 in the fall of 1903. Söderblom contributed to the volume an important, analytical, and forward-looking article attempting to systematize religions.

The German assyrologist Friedrich Delitzsch had in 1902, in the presence of the kaiser, presented two lectures in which he demonstrated considerable agreement between the Babylonian and biblical religions. He described Babylonian religion and culture as totally superior to those of Israel and asserted that there had been monotheism in Babylon long before it developed in Israel. The Old Testament had such a unique picture of God that it could not be united with any modern consciousness of God. The kaiser did not approve of what Delitzsch said; the theologians even less so. There arose a vigorous debate that even reached Sweden. Nathan Söderblom's article in the Torén *Festschrift* became a major contribution to that debate and it was read throughout Europe. In approximately fifty-five printed pages Söderblom, nearly by chance, made a significant contribution to research regarding religion. In *Uppenbarelsereligion: Några synpunkter i anledning av Babel-Bibel-diskussionen* (expanded edition, 1903; English edition, *The Nature of Religion,* 1933, 1966), he outlined the main contours of his entire study of religion.

The archaeological discoveries of the nineteenth century in Mesopotamia had been welcomed by Christians who were certain that all such finds would support biblical accounts. But now, many Babylonian texts that were parallel to the biblical accounts had been discovered, especially that of the great Flood. All of the eastern Mediterranean area was shown to have been influenced by Babylonian culture and thus there seemed to be good reason to admit that Israel too had been deeply influenced with respect to its religion. Delitzsch, who measured revelation by standards of morality, asserted that most elements of value in Israel's religion were derived from the superior Babylonians. For him, the Old Testament had no unique revelation; on the contrary, it included a great deal of immoral material. What was thus at risk was the Old Testament's trustworthiness as a unique witness to God. Söderblom took this issue as the starting point for his own explication as to how God made himself known in the world of human beings.

In Germany, many, in apologetic fervor, attempted to show that the Jewish world was ethically superior to the Babylonian religion. Söderblom chose another angle of approach. For him, religion did not primarily deal with morality; rather, it gave meaning to life and shielded against despair. Certainly religion involved ethics, but it was much more than that. That which is purely or essentially religious must be given its proper place. Religion was the faith of the heart, touching humans inwardly and determining all of their existence. "Heart" and "inward" were words Söderblom often used when he spoke about participation in the divine life. All religion had its origin in the one God who made himself known in many ways, not only in Christianity. God was *one*, and all genuine religion had the same source. That explained the striking similarities between the religions of the world.

Söderblom distinguished between two sorts of religion, "the religion of revelation" and "the religion of culture." God makes himself known in both, but more distinctly in the former than in the latter. To experience an intuitive feeling of unfathomable presence is sufficient to allow one to speak of revelation. No religion is purely a product of culture, but all religions have their foundations in the experience of being addressed by a power that is beyond all empirical knowledge. Culture and religion walk side by side, although, to be sure, often out of step. If religion is made subordinate to the interests of state, society, or culture, it risks losing its specific character as religion. In such situations, the prophets entered into history. In order to reestablish Israel and restore religion to its proper place, they proclaimed God's absolute holiness and sovereign will. Christians in all times have thus ascribed *special* revelation to the prophets, from Moses to John the Baptist. This revelation had been fulfilled in Jesus Christ who was the greatest of the prophets and who showed the world who and how God is.

For Söderblom, however, the doctrine of *general* revelation was equally fundamental even if it had been obscured over the course of time. He was convinced that God had revealed himself in different ways to all people. This conviction shaped his picture of God and his interpretation of the history of humanity. The Bible and the Christian tradition included not only special revelation, but they also pointed to general revelation. Many Christians, however, had lost the awareness that the same God who spoke to them had also spoken through philosophers such as Socrates and Seneca as well as through other religions. Fundamentalism had stunted their understanding of revelation. Söderblom reminded such Christians that God had made himself known not only through Scripture and Jesus Christ. It was unthinkable that all people shared the possibility of religious experience but that only Christians could come into relation with the object of their faith. That he himself practiced the religion that had the cross as its foremost symbol did not exclude others from experiencing the reality of God in their own way. It was a central and integrating aspect of his faith — but not of his knowledge — that general revelation, however it occurred, was God's self-communication. Such an acknowledgment merited a definite place in the Christian view of faith.

General revelation became, with time, more and more important for Söderblom. Forward-looking as he was, he wrote that in the period of world mission and world communication, when cultures were at last flowing into each other as *one* mighty stream of world history, it was high time that the church made itself familiar with the thought of God's general revelation.

He was, as were all others at the time, influenced by the theory of evolution and the thinking of Herbert Spencer. The same course of development, it was commonly held, which marked nature was also prevalent in society and the religions. People stood at different stages of development. Söderblom gave no credence to that view, but he wanted to show that the religions of culture were by nature other than the prophetic religions. In the prophetic religions — Judaism, Christianity, and Islam, but also Zoroastrianism — revelation was united with their histories. Their founders had conveyed something that was totally lacking in religions of nature and culture. In prophetic religion, faith was directed toward the one, living, spiritual God who was active in history and who revealed himself in history. Prophetic religion did not have its power in rites, organization, or holy books, but in its religious content. It addressed itself directly to the hearts of humans in order to infuse courage and power for life. It presupposed a leap of faith into the embrace of the living God.

One could not know if a religion was "true" by comparing it to others, but rather only by unreservedly giving oneself to it. Prophets such as Zarathustra, Moses, or Isaiah had conveyed the living God's primordial power. That power manifested itself in their consciousness and broke through the opposition between nature and spirit. Their experience of God was other than what was found in religions of nature and culture, which were always at risk of being blurred in pantheism, asceticism, and idealism.

What then was revelation? In general it could be described as an opening toward the transcendent. But for Söderblom it was more: it involved continuity and drama. For the Christian, Christ played the central role. Historical knowledge alone was not sufficient to interpret existence as God's revelation. Natural science could place empirical facts in a context of cause and effect and time and space, but it could go no further. Research could not discover God because God does not appear in a causal chain of secondary, reasonable effects. When God comes to be known by humans it does not happen through observable miracles but rather when the totally natural events and experiences of the faithful *are interpreted* as divinely led. This gives life meaning and purpose. Natural explanations of causality do not dispute the religious view that a certain happening was the result of an active will or a divine intervention. In many religious milieus an inexplicable event was frequently held to be a miracle, as was frequently the case in both antiquity and early Christianity. For Christian faith — according to Söderblom — a miracle was something else, namely that with the eyes of faith one could see what actually happened in that which seemed to happen. In this view he expressly endorsed the position of Erik Gustaf Geijer, the early nineteenth-century Swedish thinker who inspired him to conceive of continuing revelation in history and in the work of creative humans.

The true miracle was thus the capacity to give reality a religious interpretation. This miracle appeared in all religions. But far from all that one encounters in the world of religion was God's revelation. It must be clearly demarcated and defined. An important criterion was religious genuineness, authenticity, or its "inwardness" as Söderblom so often described it. Mysticism in a broad sense was an expression for an inwardness that appears in all living religions. For Söderblom mysticism expressed a positive and personal experience of God. He distanced himself in that respect from Ritschl who certainly paid much attention to emotions and feelings but did not understand that the inner essence of religion was fellowship with God. To the contrary, Ritschl ridiculed what he called an imagined private relation with God and Christ and dismissed all mysticism as neoplatonism.

"Mysticism" was a term of various meanings and it was a confusing concept for describing the experience of that which is mysterious, indivisible, and unfathomable and which we name God. The word came into wide use around the turn of the twentieth century and was much written about, especially by Protestants. From having been viewed very negatively, the concept "mysticism" came to express that which belonged both to the innermost core of religion and to the individual's most authentic experience of faith. Higher estimations of mystical experience had come about in reaction to the Enlightenment's overemphasis on the rational and moral dimensions of religion. Mysticism represented a liberation from dogmatic and institutional religion and a rediscovery of hidden and forgotten treasures. Spirituality was set against materialism. Different forms of spiritualism were given increased emphasis and Hindu-inspired theosophy became fashionable in educated circles. But vogue words such as "mystic," "mysticism," and "mystical" were not easy to define. They could stand for one thing or another: visions, out-of-body experiences, or unity with the divine. The word awakened interest, especially within the emerging field of the psychology of religion, in immediate, personal, and spontaneous religious experiences. In contrast stood the rational, ethical, and collective aspects of religion. The ecstatic stood against control.

For Söderblom, the concept of mysticism offered the possibility of dealing with both the inscrutability of religion and the internal agreements of religion. It was necessary, however, to clarify the word's precise content. This he did by distinguishing between two forms of mysticism: "mysticism of infinity" and "mysticism of personality."

The distinction was decisively important. The type of fellowship with God that was most apparent in the Asian cultures' religions, he described as a mysticism of infinity. It was based on an opposition between body and soul. The goal for infinity mysticism was that the soul be set free and rise into nameless infinity. Personal identity should dissolve into the pure indifference of Nirvana, and consciousness and will should lose themselves like streams in the sea. The mysticism of infinity led to a devaluation of the body and to negative expressions for God — in Buddhism even to a denial of divinity itself. Söderblom would later describe this kind of mysticism as "practical mysticism" since through ascetic and meditative practices it was believed that one could reach the desired goal. In spite of the fact that his evaluation of the mysticism of infinity was generally negative, he yet held it to be a way for God's self-revelation.

The mysticism of personality, in contrast, endeavored consciously to place itself in the service of the living and active God. It aimed, through self-sacrifice and the death of the ego, to grow into the likeness of Christ in order to be totally possessed by God. It did not look for infinite delight, quietness, and rest but rather faced a consuming fire before which the faithful could know only fear and trembling. There was a line of personality mystics from Jeremiah to Paul, Augustine, Luther, and Kierkegaard. They were all drawn into the struggle between evil and good. They did not seek to escape but rather strove for the purification of personality.

Both the mysticism of infinity and the mysticism of personality were concerned with the relation to God, but they had differing pictures of God. One could portray God as a great, still, infinite ocean into which life's disruptions and contradictions flowed together toward a beautiful slumber in his embrace. But for those who experienced God as an overwhelming, burning and holy love who desires and produces personal life, a totally different picture appeared. The picture of God one had determined the meaning one gave to personality. Should personality be deadened and leveled out or should it be recreated and purified so that the ego could be placed in the service of love?

Söderblom did not raise the question of whether God was impersonal or personal in order either to draw a boundary between false and true religion or to attribute advantage to Christianity. The mysticism of infinity and that of personality could be found both within and outside of Christianity. For example, Socrates was not a Christian but he represented the mysticism of personality while within Christianity many examples of the mysticism of infinity could be found. But for Söderblom, general and special revelation corresponded largely to the mysticism of infinity and the mysticism of personality. The line of demarcation coincided somewhat with the indistinct borders between Asiatic religions and those of the monotheistic Middle East. He attempted to determine Christianity's uniqueness in relation to other religions in a way that did not involve deprecation. That was not easy. How could one reconcile Christianity's claim to be the absolute religion with the view that all religions are recipients of general revelation? If there was truth about God revealed in all religions, in what way was Christianity unique?

For his time, Söderblom was uncommonly open to the manifestations of different religions in various cultures, but he never doubted that Christianity, seen historically, was the most outstanding among the religions of the world. It was more complex than the others and presented richer material for study than all of them. "Christianity has everything," he would say. It included all nations with their varying customs and traditions, encompassed both eremites and builders of empires, represented continuity along with renewal, and had the capacity to mediate a quality of life and energy to individuals and also to chart out a final goal for all humanity. Thus he set Christianity as highest among religions with what he felt were incontrovertible reasons.

In *Uppenbarelsens portar* (*The Portals of Revelation*) of 1910 (included in the English work *The Nature of Revelation*, 1933, 1966), Söderblom spoke of this in the form of an analogy: "I am almost as certain that we reach in Bach, in principle, the highest point in music, and that Plotinus constitutes the perfection of the mysticism of infinity, as I am that Christ will never be surpassed nor even equaled in the history of divine revelation. Of course this can have no demonstration logically." He also evaluated different types of religion and made choices between them. For him religion was deeply personal and the perception as to which religion was "best" was in the end equally as subjective as choices between music. To be able to choose the true and the correct is, when all is said and done, a "miracle" given to humanity.

Even if he felt that his structuring of religion and mysticism rested on historical and psychological fact, he knew that the convictions of faith had no actual empirical basis. But whoever set Bach first among composers did not for that reason despise Beethoven, and whoever regarded Christianity as first among religions did not need for that reason to deny the truths that other religions possessed. Religion was *experienced* reality. There was no shortcut to God that bypassed personal experience. Thus, all religious insight necessarily had a subjective element. A religious truth could not be fixed or locked in a book, a dogmatic system, or even a church. "To have a vision of God requires a pure heart and a clear and true personality, not knowledge, not an art or a method. To know him there is needed the heart of a child, not philosophy," he wrote in *Uppenbarelsereligion*. He wrote from his own experience.

The mysticisms of infinity and personality complemented and corrected each other and protected Christianity against anthropomorphic pictures of God and against every notion that a human being could create an adequate conception of God. The God encountered by genuinely searching individuals — within or outside of Christianity — was the Father of Jesus Christ, hidden to all except the faithful. The mysticism of personality did not eliminate the mysticism of infinity but rather fulfilled it. Christianity at its innermost was not a doctrine but an encounter with the Living.

That Söderblom attributed such great meaning to inner experience did not lead him to conclude that outer structure and rites or ceremonies were meaningless. They were essential to communicating the content of religion to new generations and cultures. The essence of religion was not to be found in its outer forms, but without those forms, all religions ran the risk of being diluted and losing their power. Accordingly, long before he became archbishop, he was greatly concerned about the church's worship and above all, about how he should preach in order to reach his contemporaries, both urban people who were well educated but religiously ignorant and also the religiously committed but uneducated people in rural areas. In order to understand the temper of his time, he read a great deal and had a phenomenal ability to quickly capture what was essential for incorporation into his sermons. He often translated his academic work into his sermons. In the context of worship, that work was transformed into an urgently pastoral message.

The questions he dealt with in *Uppenbarelsereligion* often appeared in his preaching. A university sermon, where the preacher was not bound to the lectionaries of the church year, bore the title, *De stackars dödlige* ("The Poor Mortals"). The sermon had a characteristic opening: "We are down here. Is there anyone up there? We are out here. Is there anyone in there, in the heart of existence?" He attempted to answer the eternal question: Is there a spiritual reality, a ground for confidence? He answered with a summary of what he had written in the widely acclaimed Torén *Festschrift*.

In all times and in all cultures humans, no matter how firmly they were rooted in the earth, had devoted their finest, best, and most beautiful thoughts to the search for something more: invisible powers and an invisible world. At times they had been prepared to sacrifice everything on earth for the pure life of the spirit. This was true not only for one-eyed fanatics but even for outstanding personalities such as Buddha and Plato, Plotinus and the great Christian mystics. However, in one single place — the Israel of the prophets — certainty about the supernatural had taken another form than flight from and rejection of the world. There it was understood that all of existence rested in the hands of the One and that life was responsibility and "a fearful but liberating and sanctifying compulsion." Jesus did not speak about the pure life of the spirit or about the ascension of the soul.

That did not mean that the divine reality had been pushed aside. On the contrary. That reality had come so near that evil had become a concrete and practical challenge. All that was alien to God's kingdom must be conquered. In an evil world, humans must with confidence stand up in the service of love since the innermost meaning of existence is life and "the saving victory of God's will."

But what about certainty concerning the reality of God? How many actually live in such certainty and how many only talk about it? Piety and confessional faithfulness did not always follow one another. A religious disposition is characterized by respect, care, devotion, silence, and sanctity before the holy, before humanity's innermost, before God. One does not always find these characteristics among the pious, but sometimes they are found among those who are called the children of the world. There was, said Söderblom, sometimes more of a feeling of spiritual solidarity and better possibilities for common prayer with a person of another faith and history — provided that he or she possessed a religious disposition — than with someone who stood doctrinally close but lacked that disposition.

In his sermon, he reminded his listeners of what ought to be typically Christian, namely tenderness of conscience, incorruptibility, tactfulness, uprightness, truth, mercy, and peace. He then again raised his initial question: Is there a spiritual reality? Is there someone in our inner life, someone who hears and is not merely an echo of our dark senses? Is there someone to pray to and entrust ourselves to? To such questions there is no scientific answer or convincing proof. The only thing he could refer to was humanity's enormous experience, which in spite of all objections held to the certainty of a living world of the spirit. If that certainty becomes a hypothesis for life, it proves itself to be true. He told his listeners that when the veil covering the most holy in his soul was torn apart and he was allowed to see, he saw the heart of God. Not everyone has had such spiritual experiences. But — he consoled his congregation — one could believe even without them, perhaps by carrying faith on from childhood and allowing ethical duties to mature to a blessed necessity, which over time leads to freedom.

When Söderblom described religion in its widest meaning, he concluded that it was finally sanctity and holiness. The decisive line of demarcation went between a religious and a profane view of life. How a person understands and interprets outer realities and inner personal experiences is decisive. The conviction that there exists a spiritual reality is independent of scientific proof, for it stands by itself and is not to be understood as knowledge in any empirical sense. Thus faith cannot be disproved. No matter how evident the effects of religious actions are in the world, religion itself is finally true only for those who can view the world with the eyes of faith.

With such a view of faith and knowledge, it was possible to unite service as priest and professor. Söderblom did just that and neglected neither.

10

The Professor as Priest

> The spirit that we perceive in the church is greater than the total spirituality of all those present and greater than all institutions. Our heart feels this spirit and knows that it possesses transcendental power.
>
> *Nathan Söderblom, 1908*

THE PARSI RASTAMJI EDULJI, who is high priest at the Temple of Fire in Wadia just outside Mumbai, comes to Uppsala. He wants to meet the remarkable person who knows so much and thinks so highly of his religion. He stays in the rectory for a few days. Then Rastamji returns to his temple and cleanses himself of the contamination of the unbelievers' land with the urine of an ox. Söderblom is given a holy baresman, a sacred bundle of sticks, which Zoroastrian priests use in their liturgical service. Is he a man of power and worthy to serve in Ahura Mazda's sanctuary?

* * *

A stone's throw from the Cathedral stood the fourteenth-century Holy Trinity Church, worn down and humble. The parish stretched into the countryside west of the city. Söderblom succeeded Waldemar Rudin as rector and received a large portion of his salary from his prebendary. His vice pastor, Fredrik Nathanael Sandberg, was married to a wealthy woman from Gothenburg who paid for their new, red-tiled parsonage next to the church. Söderblom would also have liked a more modern home, but since he had chosen Holy Trinity for his prebendary, he was expected to move into the old rectory in Stabby. Sandberg took care of the daily business while Söderblom took every opportunity to preach. When he did, the church, which then had a large balcony, was filled to the last pew, mostly with students and other academics. His sonorous tenor voice echoed under the vaulted ceiling. He articulated every word with exaggerated clarity since he was anxious to be understood by every worshiper. There being no microphones, that demanded a great deal.

As a professor of theology he also belonged to the Diocesan Chapter. That gave him good opportunity to learn to know the diocese. All matters concerning the clergy, from parish appointments to discipline problems, and many school questions landed on the chapter's table. Soon he knew what was going on in every parish of the diocese. Archbishop Ekman was not an exceptionally noteworthy person, but he often visited the congregations and had a special interest in Hälsingland. The diocese encompassed a large part of the growing capital city of Stockholm, the fertile farmlands on the level plains of Uppland, the fishing villages and harbors of the Baltic coast, the grandiose parish churches of Hälsingland, and the distant chapel congregations of Härjedalen.

In Stabby, the growing family found itself in an outmoded, cold, and uncomfortably small house. In the children's room on the second floor the beds were lined up, one alongside another. A little pedal organ, which they had had in Paris, was soon joined by a grand piano in the living room where paintings and sculpture, given by artist friends in Paris, also had their place. With walls in a warm deep green color, benches fixed to the walls, simple furniture in red and green, and plants in the windows, which had no curtains, the home stood in contrast to the typical nineteenth-century drab brown and over-decorated bourgeois homes. The professor had a small study where the shelves sagged from the weight of many books. Portraits of Luther, Pascal, and Fehr were crowded together on a wall over a mahogany desk.

One evening each week students were invited to Stabby, fifteen at a time. These gatherings, reminiscent of the open evenings at Professor Sabatier's home or at the rectory in Paris, have often been written about. There was a simple meal, Nathan and Anna read aloud from current books, art was shown, and Nathan sang: Wennerberg, Ahnfeldt, Schubert, and Schumann. The guests joined in singing hymns and revival songs. Music was Söderblom's inspiring companion. He played both the piano and the organ and he listened to music whenever he had the chance. In Uppsala, there were frequent choral, organ, and orchestra concerts. For himself he preferred to play Bach and Handel who were not very well known in Sweden, Beethoven and, less frequently, Mozart. Music was more than healing for him. It provided integration; it was a gospel.

The parsonage was at times filled with guests from abroad, professors from other faculties, or clergy from the city. It became, as parsonages often do, a real center of culture. At home Söderblom allowed his roguish and lively humor to run loose. He was unconventional and generous and willingly reported on his own activities. Like Martin Luther, he gathered his young friends together for table talk. There were many children — five additional ones were born in Stabby — and a singular atmosphere in the old-fashioned parsonage where uncommonly modern people lived. Things, however, were not idyllic. Neighboring tenants were not the best — it was trying for Anna to have her mother-in-law and her talkative sister-in-law living on the property. But the most difficult thing was that Nathan was away so often. Anna felt inadequate and the children became quarrelsome and insecure. The boys especially came to feel closer to their mother than to their father.

Lucie, the daughter who was born in 1902, has written that her strongest and earliest memory was of insecurity. She felt abandoned when her parents were away, and when they were at home the atmosphere swung from happy activities to tones of disharmony. Anna's health was often delicate and Nathan could be low in spirits, especially in the mornings. At times he was struck with a melancholy that bordered on resignation. He wrote in his diary: "Crazy theology which invents purgatory. People do not know what grief is. As if purgatory were enough. Suffering comes in all sorts of ways and it is ingenious, trying everything. I could write a book about this that would sell well and would produce a good income for my heirs." Melancholy was not a part of his public image, but Lucie had reason to complain over his mournful piano playing. By sheer strength of will he controlled his periods of depression. In one of his lectures he quoted Montesquieu: "Studying has for me been the infallible medicine against life's vexations. I have never had a sorrow that cannot be cleared up by an hour's reading." His depressions became worse over the years and plagued him greatly at the end of his life.

In spite of days of depression, he appeared outwardly as a charming, energetic, expansive person who could embrace the whole world. He was overactive in a way that made him seem almost constantly hyper — exhilarated, optimistic, able to concentrate, creative, not needing much sleep. The relationships between melancholy, madness, and inspiration have been discussed since antiquity. He understood Aristotle's question: "How does it come to be that all who are outstanding in philosophy, poetry, or art are melancholic?" German psychiatrists such as Emil Kræpelin had at the turn of the century initiated the study of manic depression. Söderblom showed in his studies of Luther how much he was at home in this area.

He took a great many things with humor, but he was a stern disciplinarian. The children remembered how he could take a cane in his study and give them a spanking. He had inherited his father's strict approach to life. Card playing and dancing were for him like a red cape in a bullring. The children were not to be spoiled. He did not like it when they chattered about daily happenings and he had a hard time understanding that the girls did not help out in the kitchen but were waited on by servants: a cook, a kitchen helper, and a household maid. He expected that Anna should read instead of sit and embroider. She should devote herself to cultural matters. The maids were to take care of the household.

As a parish vicar, Söderblom left his mark. Many remembered both the emotional and intellectual experience of hearing him preach. The sermon was the most important element in every service of worship and he preached often and long. His way and style of preaching changed over the years, but the encounter with the biblical text and the search for an authentic and distinctive language, as well as carefully thought-out formulations and surprising angles of approach were characteristic of him. No one could miss his eagerness and joy in the task of preaching. If a sermon measured up in Anna's critical ears, he would not hesitate to preach it again. For him the difference between a sermon and a lecture was indistinct. He often dealt with a particular theme under an effective title. He had an essay-like style, weaving in many biblical citations, parallels from the history of religion, illustrations from everyday life, and hymns and songs. He could adapt the same sermon for different occasions and days of the church year.

When Söderblom preached, people flocked to hear him. Around the turn of the century, J. A. Eklund, who was then a priest at the Cathedral, gathered the people of Uppsala around his pulpit, but after 1902, when Eklund moved to Kalmar, Söderblom became the favorite preacher for students and the whole city. In 1908 in *Sveriges kyrka* ("Sweden's Church"), he described a situation that, to a degree, could explain his own popularity. He asserted that "wretched preaching" was the weakest point in a generally weak church. Many sermons were so hopelessly dead, sloppy, and inferior that it would be better if one did not have to hear them. They went right over the heads of congregants. Both churchgoers and priests were preached out. He came along with modern speech and thoughtful content and the people in Uppsala very much wanted to hear him.

Jonas Söderblom, his father, had provided his first impressions about preaching. Söderblom would never forget his father's sincerity and seriousness. During his years as hospital chaplain at Ulleråker, Nathan had consciously tried to find a simple and clear language for preaching, a language not overloaded with pious words. Among the seamen in Calais and Dunkerque he had developed a concrete speech of daily life. Professor Auguste Sabatier had also been an important model in homiletics. He had spoken in quiet tones and with crystal clarity concerning the God who people vainly sought in exterior things, but who finally could be found in their own interior lives. As few other preachers, Sabatier had integrated the heart's faith with insightful and urgent social analysis.

Already in his initial sermon at Holy Trinity Church, a few weeks before he gave his installation address with its words for the students, Söderblom astonished his listeners. He spoke about loyally devoting one's self to daily cares and obligations and he reported in rich detail the story of a woman who lived in deep poverty in a ramshackle cabin, but who still could say, "I take the day you send me, and it goes so well." His appeal led to a verse in a song that was popular in rural prayer houses:

> Do the little that you can
> put your heart in it,
> do it all for your Saviour's sake.

The brilliant professor, who had just come from fashionable Paris, preached in a movingly simple way for his academic congregation. He was to continue blending the high and the low, always with warmth and insight and not infrequently with a sharp critique of society. His analysis of the time and his experience-based spirituality were clothed in a flood of metaphors. He could preach playfully and humorously, but if the situation called for it, he would be formal and monumental but seldom sentimental. He often spoke with choppy and incomplete sentences, piling words on top of each other and moving quickly from one image to another. It was not always easy to follow his line of thought. It could go like this:

> Jesus does not stand at an observer's height. He stands in the middle of the crowd. And he knows that it's now. The danger presses. Men and women, do they not see it? At any minute catastrophe might strike like lightning. Save whatever can be saved! The people? He struggled to the end, until it was too late. But of the individual, as many as possible. Immediate instants are precious. The weak one shouts and bustles. The strong become as calm as ever. The express train's engineer in his locomotive, the commander at the battle's turning point, Luther at Worms. High pressure brings a strong calm into Jesus's life. One must make good use of the last minutes. For all the important but unnecessary things he has no time. "Your heavenly father knows that you need all that." There will be time enough to do what must be done. For God's dominion in a person's soul is not a rush job. And the daily work of the Son of Man was God's final recourse. "In the fullness of time he sent his son."

Often it was the sermon's first words that made an impact and captured attention. On All Saints' Day, which along with Good Friday was for Söderblom the most important day in the church year, he once began like this: "Someone is sitting at home sewing. She sews according to a pattern and when the work is finished it is proper and beautiful. But it is created according to a pattern. That's not the way saints are created." The worshipers were gripped by his concrete and liberating humanity. Like no one else, he united Christianity and culture, faith and science. He quoted not only Luther but also revivalist preachers, philosophers, and writers.

He was constantly on the move so that he could at all costs deal with as much as possible. With an iron will he pressed himself to the limit. That could have affected his preaching even if he was able to deal with his stress through his well-practiced discipline, routine, and careful preparations, often long in advance. Yet in spite of all the ideas that were constantly spinning through his head and his capacity for what seemed like simultaneous reading, listening, and writing, he conveyed in every meeting and conference the impression of concentrated presence. He loved to speak, preach, perform, and stand in the limelight. This aroused expectations among his listeners, who were always prepared to hear him speak. For Söderblom, worship was, in the best sense of the word, theater, with the priest in the starring role — a recurring yet always new drama at the intersection of heaven and earth.

He also left his personal touch on the interior of Holy Trinity. When the church was restored in 1905 he saw to it that his theology was expressed in the new appointments. He engaged artists whom he had met in Paris. The sculptor Harald Sörensen-Ringi created a sculpture in relief, which was placed above the old altar. It depicted Jesus and his disciples at their last meal and thus emphasized the eucharist's central place in worship. The relief was framed by two statues: on one side a duplicate of Carl Eldh's "Mother," representing the parish's rural worshipers; on the other side a statue by Sörensen-Ringi of Erik Gustaf Geijer, representing academic Uppsala. "I placed," wrote Söderblom, "on one side Sweden's greatest thinker, on the other side a simple woman of the people with her back bent by the pains of labor. For in the presence of the Lord, who was depicted at the mid-point of the altar, the two, learned philosopher and simple old woman, were alike, humans in need of salvation by God's mercy." When the balcony was taken away, the organ moved, and the vaults and walls washed, the artist Nils Asplund did a large painting of the Good Samaritan on the west wall. Söderblom wanted the congregation, as it left the church, to be reminded of Jesus's words, "Go and do likewise." The art became a sermon and Söderblom's words could be heard. This was not to be the last time that he translated his theology into pictures.

That same year the union between Sweden and Norway was dissolved. This did not come as a surprise, but it affected Söderblom deeply. As a seaman's priest in the northern French seaports and then in the Swedish-Norwegian congregation in Paris, he had learned how the Norwegians, not least the naval officers, despised the union. He must have realized that the breakup of the union was sooner or later inevitable. Sweden and Norway were basically different from each other in respect to social structure. In Sweden there was an immense social hierarchy under the king. Nobility still held a number of key political, military, and economic posts. There was virtually no such upper class in Norway. There a growing radicalism had taken over and for all practical purposes a parliamentary system had been formed even as, simultaneously, party politics also broke through. The left demanded Norwegian independence. To all appearances, small issues triggered one conflict after another. In the spring of 1905, the decisive crisis came that brought with it the dissolution of the union and the naming of a king for Norway.

Like many other Swedes, Söderblom experienced the Norwegians' one-sided cancellation of the union as humiliating. But the Swedes who wanted to put the Norwegians in their place militarily received no support from him. One of them was his competitor for the professor's chair, J. A. Eklund, who was now Dean of the Cathedral at Kalmar. In the widespread unrest that followed in the wake of the continuing Russianization of Finland, Japan's victory in the Russian-Japanese war, and the flaring up of social conflicts in Europe, the question of defense again came to be high on Sweden's agenda. Eklund had a hard time putting up with the even-handed dealing with the situation by the Swedish government and was surely not the only one in church circles who opted for a harder line toward Norway. He did not distinguish himself for compromise or *Realpolitik*. Some compared 1905 to 1809 when Sweden lost Finland. Not infrequently, the pulpit became a place where clergy took positions in this conflict. Two weeks after Norway broke the agreement of union and feelings were most agitated, Eklund preached in Kalmar on "our fathers' land." His sermon was directed to the Norwegian people, emphasizing that it was wrong to protest and that the authorities did not bear the sword in vain. He did not come out in favor of war but he did not speak against it either.

On September 17, when the negotiations with the Norwegians in Karlstad were hanging in the balance, Söderblom preached in his church. In contrast to Eklund, he took a striking distance from every form of military action. We must believe, he said, that the liquidation of the union can take place without bloodshed. He thanked God for what the now generally scorned union had meant for the two peoples and spoke of two brother kingdoms for whom an armed conflict must be excluded. When it appeared that there were Swedes who could think of war as a solution "one must cry tears of blood."

He deeply regretted the breakup of the union but was equally gratified that the issue was solved without violence. Two people above all contributed to this, he pointed out — Oscar II and Hjalmar Branting, the future prime minister. In Uppsala, November 6 was celebrated as a memorial day. As often before, Nathan Söderblom spoke from the obelisk in Odinslund, but this time he did not speak to the student body but rather to hundreds of school children and their parents. He praised the peaceful outcome of the conflict and spoke of Sweden's future: "Let us make our nation a spacious home, brighter, warmer for all who belong there. All, all must be brought in with a wise and venturesome welcome. At last let us share our common responsibilities and common riches." That last point alluded to the vexatious issue concerning the right to vote, which was solved in 1908. But it would be more than ten years before women were also given the right to vote.

The dissolution of the union gave rise to the question of defense, letting loose a wave of Swedish ethnic nationalism. Nationalism was not alien to Söderblom, but his American and French experience had taught him that nationhood should be defined by common citizenship rather than by ethnicity, language, and religion. In an ideological sense, he was a patriot rather than a nationalist, although since his student days he had often praised the heroes of Swedish history. When Orphei Drängar, the Uppsala male chorus, came to Paris in 1900 and the Swedish students at the Élysée Palace sang Nordic songs of spring, his speech overflowed with pride and a longing for home. At the spring festival of the Uppsala student body on May 16, 1902 at Skansen, the famous outdoor museum in Stockholm, he really beat the drums. The right to vote was up in both chambers of Parliament. A strike had occurred and in Stockholm alone 28,500 workers were off their jobs. Against that background, he spoke to Sweden. His words flowed: "Come home to yourselves, people of Sweden," he exhorted. "Come home from false attachments to all things foreign, from furtive or outspoken suspicion toward what is yours and who is yours. Every muscle that can stretch, every heart that can beat, every brain that can work: arise to defend Sweden's welfare and Sweden's future! Do not be ashamed of the soldiers of Charles XII or of Gustav Adolf or of Linné and John Eriksson," he shouted. And he gave praise to fields and forests, industrial cities and rolling trains, school children and heroes alike, as well as to the voice of Sweden heard in poetry and philosophy, in hymns and legislation. He had himself just returned from a foreign country and was not simply swollen by national pride. He felt a need to reestablish himself among the molders of Swedish public opinion and the auditorium was filled with impressionable students in white caps. He felt which way the wind was blowing and ventured with his rhetoric to take the lead.

The turn of the century was the time of the masses with their demands for social justice and democracy, but the media set its focus on particular individuals. The media created heroes. Industrialists, scholars, authors, and artists were lifted up as models. Throughout all of Europe the concept "personality" held sway, a personality distinguished from the crowd with special responsibility for the developments of history. Friedrich Nietzsche with his ideal of the *Übermensch* had given legitimacy to the claim of political leaders and the cultural elite to be chosen. The new middle class hailed these models and identified themselves with their successes. They marveled at the confident explorer Adolf Nordenskjöld who stood on an iceberg in the Northwest Passage with a telescope in his hand and at the aristocratic Verner von Heidenstam standing in the summer on a veranda with his gaze fixed in the distance. Similarly, Ellen Key and Selma Lagerlöf were national icons who demonstrated their nobility with homes that were reminiscent of a past golden age. When Sven Hedin returned from his journey of discovery in Central Asia he was hailed by enormous crowds of people, and thousands of mourners accompanied August Strindberg on his last journey.

Feelings of romantic nationalism grew. Swedish history, the life of peasants, and the Swedish language took on value in and of themselves. Artists, authors, and composers captured the atmosphere. The authentic Swede was defined by the poet Erik Axel Karlfeldt and the composer Wilhelm Peterson-Berger. The province of Dalecarlia became a cultural ideal and "free air tourism," complete with long skirts and hiking canes, offered new prospects. It lay in the nature of things that this kind of nationalism had conservative features and was attached to both the defense movement and the national church. In the developing "Young Churchman's Movement," nationalistic and defense-friendly elements dominated under the influence of J. A. Eklund and the leadership of Manfred Björkquist.

Nathan Söderblom had his roots in the rural culture of Hälsingland. Virtuoso sixteen-part polkas and fiddlers' strings were in his blood. For him they could sound like they were taken from Bach's partitas for the violin. His had an artist's soul with a temperament that responded to folk music even when it modulated to minor keys and became dark and wild. But he did not attempt to hold on to the past. On the contrary, he saw with confidence how creative people made God's intentions visible. He regarded great changes, such as logging in the forests and the building of roads, as good for Hälsingland. But he was unshakably convinced that the nation's cultural and spiritual roots must be preserved if Sweden was to become a good society in which people were prepared to move beyond their own cultural borders. He saw no opposition between loving Sweden and at the same time being cosmopolitan.

He shared these views with Emma and Anders Zorn, perhaps the greatest of Swedish artists at the time. Söderblom spent several New Year's holidays with them in Mora and participated in some of Zorn's summer courses. One time Zorn blurted out, "O this Midsummer's Night, how it inspires us to old heathen nature worship, and how little it has to do with pale Christianity. Even our professor of theology Nathan Söderblom is a veritable sun worshipper on this night. He has watched faithfully with me and spoken only of our old cult." Söderblom was embarrassed; he had not traveled to Mora to engage in customs of folklore, but rather to discuss the folk church's openness to contemporary popular movements. However, he found himself among people who cultivated the national romantic spirit. Among them were not only Zorn but also a number of artists who had moved to the area of Lake Siljan. Anna and Nathan Söderblom felt very much at home in this circle. Zorn, who with his German heritage was half a "foreigner," arranged Dalecarlia's first fiddlers' festival, and Söderblom was there. Söderblom himself later took the initiative for organizing the first such festival in Hälsingland in 1908, and he prepared for it in the most minute detail. Fifteen thousand people came, among them the most prominent residents of the area. Both the prime minister and the provincial governor were there. Söderblom himself was prevented from attending because of sickness. In 1909, however, he was there. The folk musicians expected him to hold a service of worship. In his sermon — it was on Midsummer Day — he coupled John the Baptist together with three Midsummer events: the arrival of King Gustav Vasa in Stockholm in 1523, which is now grandly depicted by a Carl Larsson painting in the National Museum; the presentation of the Augsburg Confession in 1530; and "the world history-making midsummer memory" of Gustavus Adolphus landing in Germany on his way to the Thirty Years War. For Söderblom, it was more natural to preach on God's revelation in history than on nature. Nature's beauty and the greatness of creation were seldom mentioned in his sermons. In this respect, he separated himself from common Midsummer preaching.

In organizing these festivals he had the assistance of his comrade from high school in Hudiksvall and friend from Paris, the violinist Sven Kjellström. They had often made music together. Kjellström had a deep feeling for folk music and took part in the festival year after year even after Söderblom's death. At times, a program of classical music with Kjellström as violin soloist was included.

Should a son of the evangelical revival really encourage sinful music? In the nineteenth century, Nathan's grandfather and other pietists had imagined — not fully without reason — that the violin was the devil's instrument for enticing young people into dance, sex, and sin. Revivalists left their violins hanging on the wall and crushed their liquor glasses. Nathan's own brother Svante fell out of favor with his father and was more or less forced to emigrate to America because he played for dances. But Nathan saw to it that the violins were publicly taken down and used again. The music of the people should sound freely. Some clergy had objections. They were not satisfied with merely criticizing Söderblom; they reported him to the Diocesan Chapter. The fiddlers' festival caused him some difficulties when it came to being chosen archbishop. As if it were not enough that he was a liberal theologian with a positive view of other religions, had he not also opened the door for the sinfulness of the dance halls?

Söderblom rejected the life-denying side of pietism with its suspicion and contempt for what was natural. At the Midsummer meeting in Mora in 1906, he spoke of the tragedy that pietism had not produced one single personality of such freshness and clarity, strength and originality in respect to spiritual gifts that he could be described as a religious genius. An exception might have been the German Herrnhutter Nicolaus Zinzendorf, but he was not virile enough. Pietism had gotten into a "less and less" mentality in its view of life and history. At its beginning, pietism had been warm and comforting, but lacking clear direction it had finally become sickeningly narrow and moralistic. The pietists had no understanding of the church and its spiritual riches; instead they rejected the church and moved into cheaply built prayer houses. Söderblom treasured small pietistic circles that, in their simple ways, made space both for other-worldly spirituality and strict ethical behavior. He, if anyone, was eager that such hearths of warm, personal faith should continue to live within Swedish Christianity. But he regretted that this kind of piety had come to limit people's horizons and did not reach beyond the formation of small cliques. When young ordinands who grew up in these circles spoke ill of the church, it was time to discover the church anew. This was precisely the intention of the Young Church Movement.

11

First Steps in Ecumenism

> Church history has had enough of well meant but doomed to fail attempts to form alliances based on some sort of common adjustments of dogma.
>
> *Nathan Söderblom, 1909*

THE MORNING OF TUESDAY, SEPTEMBER 21, 1909, a visiting delegation of Anglicans celebrates Mass at Holy Trinity Church in Uppsala. The Bishop of Winchester, Herbert Ryle, presides at the eucharist. Nathan Söderblom assists, wearing an old-fashioned black and silver chasuble. He receives communion in spite of the fact that he is not an Anglican. It is the Feast of St. Matthew. Every year as long as he lives, he will remember that event. Thirteen years later, the Church of England and the Church of Sweden establish full communion.

* * *

Söderblom had had an attack of stomach ulcers for the first time in 1903. In February 1906, when he had just turned forty, he again became so ill that Anna nearly gave up hope. He was given morphine and put on a strict diet and when he finally got to his feet, he continued to work at the same intense tempo, even though he really had not returned to health. During the coming years he was sick many times. In February 1908, he was in such a bad way that he had to give up his teaching and enter the Academic Hospital, where he stayed for over a month. It was not certain that he would survive. In May he became ill again and was bedridden in the rectory at Stabby, weak and in pain. Anna and his friends wanted to do whatever they could to save Söderblom, whom they regarded as the country's leading proponent of a Christianity for modern times. He had a large family and very few financial resources. His professor's salary was not sufficient without supplements from lecture honoraria and book royalties. He could not afford to take a leave of absence and there was no health insurance. In order to regain his health, he had to get away from Uppsala for a longer time of rest and care.

He was surrounded by a growing circle of educated, religiously oriented, and wealthy people who wanted to support him and strengthen his influence in the church, even while he was a professor who had not yet begun his life's project. In Paris he had become known for his success at soliciting funds for needy Swedes. Now it happened that generous people could in turn help him. The diplomat Harald Bildt was one of them. He was financially independent, unmarried, musical, and religiously interested. At that time he regarded himself as a theosophist. He had been Söderblom's friend since Paris and he took initiative among his friends to gather funds so that Söderblom could take a leave of absence for necessary rest and care. In Bildt's eyes, Söderblom was "the Church of Sweden's most significant force, certainly the most significant proponent of a progressive Christianity that is suited to the times." That was enough of a motive to help him. Among those who contributed were the landowner Oscar Ekman and his wife Maria. Ekman, who lived at Bjärka-Säby in Östergötland, was a great patron especially of church-related causes. He had already funded a faculty position in Christian apologetics that was related to Söderblom's field. The funding campaign brought in $25,000 (U.S. value at that time) that was given to Söderblom. With the help of this financial aid, he and Anna were able to spend much of the summer of 1908 at a well-known treatment center in Germany. Friends cared for the children. There were funds left over and Söderblom wanted to give it to some cultural cause, but Bildt insisted that he keep the money. The funds had been gathered to "save an essential force for the Church of Sweden." The intention was to further spiritual life and Söderblom was not, according to Bildt, to feel indebted to the givers. You have no right, wrote Bildt, to decline "the possibility of releasing from its yoke your Pegasus, so that your pastoral tasks can be carried out without the pressure that financial worries bring."

While he breathed fresh air, enjoyed the landscape of Germany with its untouched small farm villages, and took pleasure at being in the middle of Europe, he carefully considered how he could best use a large donation that had so unexpectedly been put at his disposal. One day a woman dressed in black had awaited him in the theological faculty's room in the university hall in Uppsala. He would always remember that it was at midday on Wednesday, October 23, 1907. He had never seen her before and did not know who she was. Toward the end of their conversation she revealed, against her will and on a promise of anonymity, her name. She wanted to dispose of some of her wealth and she intuitively felt that she had now met a person who shared the same spiritual values. She read Söderblom's thoughts and felt from the beginning that he was quite skeptical, which did not surprise her. She wanted to give away a great deal of money while keeping her name secret and he, reasonably enough, wanted to know where the money came from. Her wish was to underwrite a number of annual travel grants that could broaden the perspective of Swedish priests and deepen their message, but she would also consider covering the costs of guest lecturers as Söderblom suggested. It was not a small amount she proposed giving, in the day's valuation about five million crowns (or 625,000 U.S. dollars) and there would be more. Söderblom, who was living with illness and constantly had to put up with his colleagues' narrow-mindedness, could not have wished for more in order to realize his dreams. The conversation was a turning point. Completely unexpectedly, he was to receive the resources to do what he had wished to do for a long time: to give his students an international experience and put Uppsala on the world map of theology and church.

It turned out that she was Anna Lindblad and together with her husband she had owned both an old iron works and large forests. They sold all of it and wanted part of their money to be put to good use in the church. She had heard of Söderblom and his good contacts with students. He would be the right person to use the money in the best way possible. On May 8, the Olaus Petri Foundation was established. It would be managed by the university, but all decisions would be made by Nathan Söderblom for as long as he lived. In the foundation's statutes there were directions concerning grants for travel and lectures, but also a provision that gave Söderblom free rein: income from interest could be used for other purposes if they served the foundation's main task, namely, to benefit Sweden in spiritual matters, above all through the church's clergy.

At that time in Sweden the old noble aristocracy, certain wealthy families, and newly rich industrialists controlled a great deal of the country's resources and could use their fortunes as they thought best without taxation. Söderblom became dependent on these sources for carrying out his international projects. The state did not cover his travels, conferences, or other costs and the church put nothing at his disposal. He needed sponsors and thus he developed — in spite of his outspoken sympathy for the labor movement — close personal relationships with many wealthy families, industrialists, and landowners on whose support he could count. Strikingly, there were many women who helped him and he took their wishes to do good seriously. Söderblom assured them that they were both needed and appreciated at a time when their world and their values were being called into question. His undogmatic religion confirmed their sense of spirituality.

Even before the Olaus Petri Foundation was established he began to award scholarships. The first went to Samuel Gabrielsson, a young priest from Dalecarlia. His bishop had disciplined him for his outspokenness by sending him to serve a small community in the forest country between Malung and Mora. Söderblom saw to it that instead he was able to study Anglican church life. Gabrielsson became an energetic proponent for the new Swedish high church movement and also a significant writer of hymns. He concluded his career as rector in Rättvik. Among other early scholarship holders were Emilia Fogelklou who traveled in England, France, and Italy in order to devote herself to mysticism, modernism, and Francis of Assisi. She was the first woman in Sweden to take a degree in theology, a mystic who later joined the Society of Friends. Herman Neander studied Greek and Russian in those countries and became a bridge builder to Orthodox churches. A letter of recommendation from Söderblom opened all doors. Without realizing what he was doing, he was preparing students to make ecumenical contributions. When in late summer he traveled to the treatment center in Karlsbad, Germany, he was weak but filled with confidence. His wife was convinced that the donation from Anna Lindblad contributed to the regaining of his health.

In spite of his doctors' warnings, Söderblom broke off his time in Germany after a few weeks in order to go to England to participate, along with scholars from around the world, in a congress on the history of religion that was to be held at Oxford. He also had another reason for going, a reason that was urgent for him. He wanted to take initiatives in the development of Anglican–Swedish church relations and aimed to make contact with Anglican church leaders who shared his concern.

On the way to England he looked up the Catholic exegete Albert Loisy, whom he had come to know in Paris. Loisy had been excommunicated and lived surrounded by books and chickens in a small village in western France. Encouraged by the more liberal atmosphere during the pontificate of Leo XIII, he had published *L'Evangile et l'Eglise* (*The Gospel and the Church*) in 1902. In that book he defended the Roman Catholic Church by describing how biblical criticism had destroyed the Protestant fixation on "Scripture alone" and made a naïve fundamentalistic faith impossible. It was only through the Catholic Church that a Christian could have an authentic relation to Christ. It was the Church's Christ and not the "historical Jesus" of liberal Protestant theology who was the object of faith. A Jesus "as he really was" and who could be mediated independently of the Church did not exist. In spite of Loisy's good intention his book was listed on the Vatican's *Index Librorum Prohibitorum* (*List of Prohibited Books*). He was banned, together with many other "modernists," not only as heretical but also as punishable, deceitful, and disloyal toward the Church. Söderblom remembered how he and his friends had been opposed by the hardline conservative forces at Uppsala and, just like the Catholic modernists, had been called into question by the church leadership. But that conflict in no way could be compared with what the liberal Catholics had to endure.

Accordingly, on the way from Germany to England, he took back roads to the village Ceffonds in the Haute Marne in order to meet the isolated Loisy. He was very much alone since whoever made contact with him would also be banned. Loisy and Söderblom both had rural backgrounds and broad theological educations. They were constantly engaged in intellectual struggles with the question of the truth of faith. They were both modern theologians, but in their views of the church they diverged. They had much to discuss and their meeting inspired Söderblom to read all that he could find concerning the conflict between faith and academic research within Catholicism. During the following spring, he dealt with Roman Catholic modernism in his lectures at Uppsala.

He did not travel to England alone but was accompanied by the twenty-seven-year-old Sam Gabrielsson who was going to spend the next year there. Before Gabrielsson traveled, he preached in Holy Trinity Church and was present when Söderblom's seventh child, Bror Carl, was baptized. Together with the docents Edvard Lehman and Gustaf Aulén, he was godfather to the child. Some weeks later he met Söderblom at the home of the Swedish seamen's priest in Calais and was sent ahead across the English Channel in order to book rooms at Miss Slatter's hotel for teetotalers in

Canterbury. There they stayed for a few days in order to see the old pilgrim city. Söderblom was deeply moved when he came upon the grave of Archbishop Benson. It was he who had sent greetings to the Swedish Archbishop at the Reformation Jubilee in 1893, which became the motto of the Free from the Heart group and which Sam Fries cited in his controversial book on Israel.

Otherwise, Söderblom spent most of his time in bed on account of his severe stomach ulcers, but he also dictated letters to Gabrielsson and attempted to devise correct formulations and expressions for the first lecture he was ever to give in English when in Oxford. His knowledge of English was limited and he listened to the slang of store clerks, coachmen, and whomever he met in order to learn something of the language and also to get an impression of what was going on in England during that September. A Eucharistic Congress in London's Westminster Cathedral with Cardinal Vincent Vannutelli as the pope's personal legate and six other cardinals present naturally received much attention. The Congress confirmed the pope's hard-as-nails antimodernism line. Simultaneously, Labor's annual congress was going on with delegates representing 1.7 million labor union members. It was less predictable. Söderblom, however, was not able to give these events much attention since he had to go on to Oxford. There he resided comfortably with his own attendant in St. Johns College. He gave his lecture on the Christian Doctrine of the Trinity in comparison with the Triratna and the Holy Triads of Buddhism. He socialized for some days with the historians of religion and also visited the world-famous social anthropologist James Frazer: "small, red-nosed, with eyeglasses and bearded, with short sentences and a magician's wand for a pen." For generations his great work *The Golden Bough* has been read by historians of religion. Nevertheless, for Söderblom, contacts with Anglican bishops were far more important.

He had visited England one time before, but had come to feel more at home in France and Germany and spoke comparatively broken English. He had, however, long desired to deepen connections with the English church and had begun to orient himself in the Anglo-Saxon direction. Among Anglicans he had found a deep sensitivity to historical tradition and great respect for academic research. He encountered there a nondogmatic Christianity and an open view of culture. He had, briefly put, seen much of what he wished for in all churches. But the Victorian spirit was still strong and class distinctions were apparent. Colonialism, which the Church of England uncritically supported, stood at its high point and Great Britain ruled half the world. The church, moreover, was at home in the milieu that we know from the television series *Downton Abbey*. Many bishops belonged to the upper middle class. Half of them had gone to the foremost schools and then studied at Oxford or Cambridge. They did not have much pastoral experience and felt quite at home in conservative circles. But the farther one went from London and "Oxbridge," the more sparsely filled were the church pews. The Anglican Church was losing its grip on the people while the Methodist Church was growing. A few high church priests found their way to the grimy industrial cities, took sides with the workers, and openly fought the class system.

The Church of England was more diverse and marked by contradictions than the Church of Sweden. It accommodated a variety of pieties and included all possible theological positions. Since the start of the century the Anglo-Catholics had gained ground. With pastoral awareness, social engagement, and interesting leaders, they had the wind in their sails, even as it was apparent that the theologically contourless and generally Protestant "broad church" had had its best time. The variety appealed to Söderblom. He wished that the whole breadth of the Church of England would be represented in a meeting with the Church of Sweden.

The Lambeth Conference of 1908 had just come to a conclusion. Every ten years since 1867, the Archbishop of Canterbury had called all the world's Anglican bishops to a conference named after his residence, Lambeth Palace in London. The Conference of 1888 had been an ecumenical milestone. The bishops then adopted what has come to be called the "Lambeth Quadrilateral" with four conditions for eucharistic fellowship with other churches: that Holy Scripture is confessed as containing all that is necessary for salvation; that the Apostles and Nicene Creeds were sufficient expressions of the Christian faith; that baptism and the eucharist were celebrated with the Words of Institution, water, and bread and wine; and that bishops be consecrated in apostolic succession. This declaration stipulated the conditions that might bring about communion with the Church of Sweden. Earlier and more occasional contacts between Canterbury and Uppsala had not led to concrete results. But since the Church of Sweden was also marked by commitment to these four conditions for ecclesial communion, it was high time to bring about an official dialogue between the churches.

The Swedish ambassador in London, Herman Wrangel, had negotiated a request to Archbishop Ekman to send a Swedish bishop to the Lambeth Conference as an observer. Söderblom had Ekman's confidence and he immediately assisted in making this possible. Quickly he saw to it that the Bishop of Kalmar, Henry William Tottie, was given this assignment by the archbishop and the government. Tottie was of Scottish descent and spoke perfect English. He was well informed concerning the Church of England and he was also a moderately high churchman. Moreover, that he had been Director of the Church of Sweden Mission and knew the situation in South India and other countries where Swedish missionaries came in contact with Anglicans made his appointment even more appropriate. He brought greetings from the Church of Sweden in Latin and made such a positive impression on the 242 bishops present that they asked the Archbishop of Canterbury to initiate direct negotiations with the Church of Sweden. Before Tottie traveled to England, Söderblom, in an English edition of *Stockholms Dagblad* that had been published to mark King Edward VII's state visit to Stockholm, had pointed out how the two churches' historic continuity and succession of bishops meant a great deal for the churches mutually approaching each other. The royal state visit thus stimulated interest in closer relations between the churches. The matter was initially seen as an intergovernmental affair, but Söderblom changed it into an interchurch matter.

The Lambeth Conference had come to a close at the beginning of August, a few weeks before Söderblom arrived in England. For him it was crucial to strike while the iron was hot so that the discussions would continue. Completely on his own initiative he approached one bishop after another in order to assure their support. He himself was not a bishop and he was internationally comparatively unknown outside the circle of historians of religion, but with his unfailing self-confidence he managed to get invited to lunch with Archbishop Randall Davidson so that he could lay out his thoughts on "contacts between the churches." The ecumenical seed that had been sown in the Student Missionary Association, at Northfield, and at Paris had matured and the Olaus Petri Foundation had given him the financial ability to begin to realize his plans. From that summer on, ecumenism was to take up more and more of his attention. Where should he begin if not with the Archbishop of Canterbury, who with such great warmth had received a Swedish representative at his important Lambeth Conference?

Davidson had visited Sweden thirty years earlier. He had never forgotten that at that time Archbishop Sundberg had refused to meet with him. Lord Davidson was Scottish and a careful man who was strict about rules and regulations. Everything would take its time. Söderblom was temperamentally always in a hurry and he possessed the courage to attempt things that at first seemed impossible. They were extremely unlike — the one statesmanlike, the other prophetic; the one conscious of the past, the other always looking forward. But Davidson gave Söderblom his full support and that opened the doors to many bishops' palaces.

First, Söderblom met with the moderately high church Bishop of Salisbury, John Wordsworth, who had been chairperson of the Lambeth Conference's commission on interchurch questions. He was learned and well known for his editions of the Vulgate and also of Origen; he also had strong bonds with the Old Catholics and the Orthodox. Now he was turning his attention to Sweden. He set about learning the language and in a short space of time wrote a history of the Swedish church that would come to be used even in Swedish universities. Söderblom was then received by the elegant low churchman and biblical scholar who was Bishop of Winchester, Herbert Ryle. The person who made the strongest impression on him, however, was the Bishop of London, Arthur Winnington-Ingram. He was not primarily a theologian, but he was a popular and much discussed high churchman who gathered drunkards from London's streets, made certain that St. Paul's Cathedral was filled during Holy Week with both businessmen and workers, played tennis with President Theodore Roosevelt, and once preached a sharply critical sermon on the steps of the New York Stock Exchange.

Söderblom had an exhausting schedule during those weeks. He had not yet regained his health and during his last days in England he became ill again. He barely made it to Lund where Anna awaited him. After dinner with Pehr Eklund, with Torgny Segerstedt also a guest, he was overcome with severe pain. Anna and Segerstedt cared for him through the whole night. He improved and back in Uppsala characteristically continued to devote himself to the work of the Olaus Petri Foundation, which was to be the base for much of his ecumenical work. The Olaus Petri lectures became, in the words of Yngve Brilioth, "one of the most important points in the history of the ecumenical movement." In March 1909, the foundation's first lectures were given by the philosopher and subsequent Nobel Prize winner Rudolf Eucken. The birth of the foundation was celebrated in Stabby. Friends Axel Olivekrona, Ulrik Quensel, and Gustaf Ribbing provided silver tableware and candelabras, John Forsell sang Schubert and Mozart, and Sven Kjellström played Beethoven's *Kreutzer Sonata*. The foundation's benefactress was not there — she wanted to remain anonymous — but a large floral bouquet symbolized her spiritual presence.

In September 1909, Archbishop Davidson dispatched an official delegation to Uppsala for a few days' deliberations concerning a limited church fellowship. Ingram was not able to be present, but Ryle and Wordsworth participated and together with Söderblom played leading roles in the discussions. Söderblom had written a general outline for the conversation. They had to pacify those Swedes who were nervous concerning the implications of the venture. The intention was to make contact with the Church of England as such, not with any special wing of churchmanship or piety. Even though the high church Anglo-Catholic movement of the time often set the tone and was eager to extend its influence, it was the Church of England in its whole breadth that approached the Church of Sweden. Bishop Ryle, who led the English delegation, had a warmly evangelical image and was anything but a ritualist. There was no hint that either church should renounce any of its teachings or traditions. They were mature and independent churches that desired to know each other better. Their similar historical experiences and common view of the episcopal office had brought them together. Söderblom was of the view that historical continuity was more organic and harmonious in Sweden than in England and the Church of Sweden had never been subordinate to the powers of the state in the same way as had been the case at times for the English church. If the Church of England were on occasion to demand changes in the Church of Sweden as a condition for ecclesial communion, they must be decidedly rejected. The Swedes clearly acknowledged that apostolic succession was a fact which they certainly valued highly, but it was not a condition for regarding a church or a service of worship as truly Christian.

The English delegation was received in high style at an audience with King Gustaf V, at the laying of wreaths at the graves of Gustav II Adolf and Oscar II at the Riddarholm Church in Stockholm, and at lunch with the Crown Prince and Princess. No one could miss the fact that the meeting between the two state churches also had an international political dimension. That Russia and Germany overinterpreted that dimension was a fact to be avoided. In the delegation from England, apart from Wordsworth and Ryle, there were two theologians and also the American bishop Gershom Mott Williams and his chaplain, the Swedish descendent Gustaf Hammarskjöld. The Swedish delegation consisted of Bishops Ekman and Tottie together with Professors Lundström, Billing, and Söderblom. Gustaf Aulén was also present, mostly to help Wordsworth locate material for the Swedish church history that he was writing.

These twelve men assembled in the session hall of the Diocesan Chapter, gathering beneath the portraits of bearded archbishops going back to the Uppsala Council of 1593. This was an event of historical importance, one of the world's first official interchurch dialogues. It took place with the full consent of the governments of the two states and the delegates were aware of the seriousness of their task. Everything went according to a strict protocol. Things that are now taken for granted as routine in ecumenical contexts were then regarded as matters of great significance. On the agenda were issues such as the nature of ordained ministry, the diaconate, and confirmation, but above all were the questions of mutual recognition of the episcopacy and apostolic succession, which for the Anglicans were conditions for every form of sacramental fellowship. Could they accept the Swedish view that neither church structure nor the ministry were instituted *jure divino* and did not require the same form everywhere? Could they agree that the form of the church was a matter of human institution adapted to historical and cultural circumstances? It would have been both short-sighted and ill-informed not to value the continuity of the unbroken line of bishops possessed by the Church of Sweden, yet scarcely any church leader or theologian in Sweden would assert that the office of the bishop or any other external matter was essential to the church being the church and a mediator of the grace of God. The church historian Herman Lundström convincingly showed that the bishops of the Church of Sweden surely stood in apostolic succession. The results of his research would satisfy the Anglicans. They acknowledged, further, that the Swedes had a different estimate of the necessity of succession than they did.

There arose, however, a totally different issue that disrupted the discussions and required considerable diplomatic skill if the whole endeavor were not to become problematic. Swedish immigrants to America had come together to form the Augustana Synod in 1860. This group had developed into a consciously Lutheran communion influenced by low church revivalistic tendencies and it had no desire whatsoever to be led by bishops. Because of family ties, language, and the Lutheran confession, the Augustana Synod was better known in Sweden than the Anglican Church. In the United States, however, Swedish immigrants had for a long time had connections with the American Episcopal Church. Clergy in the Swedish colony in Delaware had been recognized by the Episcopal Church and they had absorbed their Lutheran congregations when the colony was dissolved. When the Augustana Synod was formed in 1860, the Episcopal Church continued to attract Swedish immigrants to their parishes. Relations became strained and Swedish Americans were deeply suspicious of contacts with the Anglicans. For his part, Söderblom regarded the Augustana Synod as a branch of the Church of Sweden, hoping that in time the Synod would adopt the episcopal office in accordance with the Swedish tradition.

Bishops Tottie and Ryle chaired the meeting and Söderblom was quite silent except when the American situation came up. The competition between the Episcopal Church and the Augustana Synod was a fragile issue that engaged him deeply. He regretted that words like "diocese" and "bishop" gave rise to a kind of fear among Lutheran Christians in the United States. If they had only adopted the office of the bishop, the proposals of the Episcopal Church would have subsided. Given the situation, he could not disregard the unease that the Augustana Synod felt at the thought of closer English-Swedish church relations. Accordingly, he saw to it that Father Hammarskjöld did not take part in the discussion and he himself pleaded the cause of the Swedish Americans. He had prepared well and presented his arguments forcefully. In a laconic entry in his diary he wrote, "Now I got going." He maintained that the Augustana Synod was founded by pastors ordained by bishops in Swedish orders and that the Synod actually was the Church of Sweden in America. The hope of the Episcopal Church to absorb Augustana into its structure was completely futile. Söderblom also pointed out to Bishop Mott Williams that the Augustana Synod was extremely low church and followed a strict Lutheran orthodoxy. The Swedes rejected the proposals concerning the Americans, but in all other matters, the two delegations were in full agreement.

Church fellowship between the Swedish and English churches had its own value, but it could also untie knots in other parts of the world. One such place was South India where the Lutheran church needed to ordain Indian clergy. Since it had no bishop, mission officials thought they could be ordained by Swedish missionaries, but the colonial authorities did not recognize such ordinations. There had to be a bishop. In South Africa, where Swedish missionaries supported the English in the Boer War, the churches had also come in close contact with each other as, naturally, was already the case in London. Now the possibility of practical cooperation opened up. The negotiations of 1909 were so fruitful that they laid the basis for the eucharistic fellowship between the two churches that was established in 1922. Seventy years after that, in 1992, the signing of the Porvoo (Borgå) Common Statement established full church fellowship between the Anglican churches of Great Britain and Ireland and the Lutheran churches in the Nordic and Baltic countries.

One evening during these talks, Canon Arthur Mason gave a public lecture regarding the Church of England. He spoke of three principle streams or lines among Anglicans. The first was the considerable appreciation of Anglicans for the Orthodox and Roman Catholic Churches, mostly concerned with the question of the ordained ministry and matters of institutional and sacramental practice. The second was the Anglicans' relation with evangelical movements that had conversion and personal faith as their chief goals. This line was suspicious of all who valued the church and tradition over the Holy Scriptures. The third line defended freedom of thought and action, did not feel itself bound by old rules, and was not much concerned with dogmatic distinctions. For this line, it was equally as important to support art, culture, natural science, and social welfare as it was to conduct worship. None of these three lines could be isolated; they influenced each other and each had a legitimate place in the church. Mason, who was Vice Chancellor of Cambridge University, himself emphasized especially the importance of freedom of the intellect.

Söderblom had great appreciation for the Church of England, a church that united respect for history and institutional structures with confessional independence. It had simultaneously a strong interest in religious scholarship and a social responsibility that sought to eradicate much of the prevalent class distinctions. He valued Anglo-Catholicism's spirituality, social energy, and intelligent spokespersons, but he distanced himself from the emphasis on the sacrificial character of the mass, the liturgical snobbery, and the disdain for academic research that also were found in these circles. He warned Swedish priests against identifying with unevangelical English high church practices, which he called "county constabulary rules," even as he was pleased that a modernist ecclesiology, which would not let itself be identified with the hierarchical structure of Roman Catholicism, found support and a home in the Anglican church. The Church of Sweden did not lag behind the Church of England when it came to continuity, the office of the bishop, or liturgical tradition. Together these churches were primed to sail with the winds of the general consciousness of the church that were blowing through the Protestant world, leading Reformation Christianity to a deeper understanding of its heritage and its task. In the Church of England he encountered an "evangelical catholicity," which he wanted to see more of in the Church of Sweden. It brought general tradition into contact with evangelical freedom and identified the office of the bishop as the sign of unity.

12
The Student Awakening

> Christ never founded a church or a religious institution. He lived in the dominion of God and expected its realization in human hearts and in the world. Only as long as the church preserves and cares for that legacy does it possess legitimacy.
>
> *Nathan Söderblom, 1909*

A NATIONWIDE STRIKE BREAKS OUT ON AUGUST 4, 1909. *In the well-educated city of Uppsala, the striking workers ask for lectures of various kinds. Nathan Söderblom is asked to speak in a public park about the church from the perspective of the history of religion. Many come to hear him, but it begins to rain. Söderblom then marches the hundreds of workers to Holy Trinity Church, which is filled to the last pew. The workers' brass band plays. Söderblom describes how since the thirteenth century, men and women, workers and intellectuals, have knelt together in that church in common respect for the holy. He points to what is inscribed on the pulpit: "The truth shall make you free." Then he speaks uninterruptedly for two hours about the history of Christianity in Sweden, the world's religions, sacrifice, struggle, and the cross as the way forward. It is completely silent in the church. Outside it continues to rain.*

* * *

There was not much intellectual ferment among the teachers in the theological faculty. Modern theologians had difficulty in being heard and Söderblom did not get the intellectual stimulation he needed. He turned toward the historians, literary scholars, and philologists. Harald Hjärne, the tremendously learned scholar who had been his teacher, had become his personal friend. Linguistic scholars helped him with the translations of original texts for his book *Främmande religionsurkunder (Sources of Foreign Religions)*. He himself had plowed through opaque early Persian texts and come to an almost devout respect for philologists. The productive professor of literature Henrik Schück, who was named university rector in 1905, willingly walked all the way to Stabby for conversations with Söderblom who was also an essayist and literary critic of note and who had published several literary biographies. In 1908, Söderblom wrote a long essay entitled "Oscar Wilde och hans Kristusbild" ("Oscar Wilde and His Picture of Christ") for the journal *Ord och Bild* (*Word and Picture*). In light of the scandal over his homosexuality, his time in prison, and his death in a shabby hotel in Paris, there were few who dared approach Wilde's literary production, but Söderblom analyzed in depth the individualistic and romantic picture of Christ that emerged sharply for the humiliated poet when he was in the Reading Gaol. The year after that, Söderblom wrote "Strindberg och makterna" ("Strindberg and the Powers"). Three years later, that essay was followed by "Skuld och försoning" ("Guilt and Reconciliation"). He took the religiosity of Strindberg's final year with utmost seriousness. Few had Söderblom's candor in painting a portrait of "one of the world's lost human souls most under the grip of the powers."

He also wrote biographical portraits of the historian Erik Gustaf Geijer, the great preacher Henric Schartau, the philosopher Friedrich Nietzsche, and the bishop and famous romantic poet Esaias Tegnér. His perceptive speech at the funeral of the controversial poet Gustaf Fröding in 1911 aroused a great deal of attention. It was common in those times to analyze the thinking of great personalities. Söderblom placed all sorts of cultural matters in a religious perspective in order to illuminate the most intimate and provocative points in the world of the imagination. He was convinced that Jesus had a friend in all thoughtful and knowledgeable men and women. No sharp distinction was to be made between church and culture. With humanists, lawyers, and medical doctors he developed close friendships marked by intellectual exchange. It was they who, one day when the theologians turned their backs, would see that he was chosen archbishop.

While there were theological ties between Uppsala and Germany and students used German textbooks, the Church of Sweden itself was still cut off from the surrounding world. Contacts with Christians in other lands largely passed the church by. The growing free church movement, to be sure, had extensive contacts with American groups. The student Christian movement, which was established in Uppsala in 1901, was heavily influenced by Anglo-Saxon nondenominationalism and not much by Lutheran tradition. Some knowledge about Christians in Africa and Asia was conveyed by missionaries, but the ecumenical movement was in its infancy and knowledge about other churches was, to say the least, minimal. Even cooperation between the Nordic churches was extremely limited. With his orientation toward France and his European perspectives, Söderblom felt isolated in Uppsala. His was a restless spirit with an insatiable need to be at the center of things. The theological faculty was too narrow, the church too old-fashioned, and Sweden too provincial. He had to break his isolation. It was largely to his credit that the Church of Sweden began to orient itself outward and to learn to know others besides German Lutherans and Swedish Christians in America. By invoking the seventeenth century, he began to convince even conservative Swedes that the Church of Sweden had a call from God to build bridges between the churches of the Reformation.

After Söderblom became professor, Adolf Kolmodin, who was opposed to historical-critical research, was named chair in the New Testament department. Otherwise, the composition of the theological faculty remained unchanged until the appointment of Einar Billing as tenured professor. Billing was five years younger than Söderblom and had been an instructor in dogmatic and moral theology for a number of years. For him, as for Söderblom, the relationship between Christianity and history was a central theological problem that could be solved only by a broadened and deepened view of God's revelation. God had made himself known through the biblical witness, but he is also the God of history who reveals himself through human experience, historic events, and progress in development. The task of theology is to interpret divine revelation in all of its breadth and to show how Christ is the consummation of everything. Söderblom preached a God who was dynamic and present in the manifoldness of the world, and Billing continually emphasized that the forgiveness of sin was God's work in the present and not a mere paragraph in a system of dogmatic theology.

Billing was the youngest among the professors, Söderblom the next youngest. Each had taken his doctorate at the turn of the century, Billing with a dissertation on Luther, Söderblom on early Persian religion. Together they became prominent figures in Swedish theology. It has been said that Söderblom was the broadest and Billing the deepest theologian ever present at Uppsala at the same time. They influenced church and theology perhaps more than all the other theologians combined. Billing was the systematic thinker who intentionally and laboriously built a unified and comprehensive theology, which he set forth only after extremely careful testing. He was single-minded and burrowed deeply into things, while the encyclopedic Söderblom ranged over wide areas, intuitively immersing himself in different issues and acutely narrowing things down to essential matters. His field of vision stretched to Babylon and Benares, while Billing confined himself within the bounds of the parish.

As researchers, teachers, and personalities they were like night and day: Billing, somber and uncertain of himself and not given to trivial conversation; Söderblom, impulsive and nearly manic with energy. They had a deep mutual respect and could both correct and complement each other. Gustaf Aulén, who first was docent to Söderblom and then to Billing before he became professor at Lund in 1914, had no doubt that their scholarship changed the theological situation in Sweden. He himself united Söderblom's universal and Billing's local perspectives and more than any other scholar preserved and renewed their theological legacy after them.

In 1908, Söderblom published several lectures and articles on the church. He called the little book that resulted *Sveriges kyrka (Sweden's Church)*. It concluded a bit prophetically: "Does my faith cause hearing problems? No, I think I hear correctly. From different directions I can hear sounds indicating that bells will ring out and call us once again to High Mass in Sweden's church." He was completely correct. J. A. Eklund, who was then Dean in Kalmar, had set the ball rolling at a student meeting in Huskvarna in 1907. There he lectured on the theme, "Youth and Our Evangelical Church of Sweden." His view of the church was more historically and ethnically determined than that of Billing and it seemed to most people, especially those in southern Sweden, to be something new. With the shortage of clergy as the background and the emotional reaction to the dissolution of the union between Sweden and Norway fresh in people's minds, Eklund stoked the fires and sought to awaken slumbering church people to spiritual life. Lack of love for "the Swedish" had rendered the priesthood unthinkable to many, but Eklund saw before him a reborn church and listed a number of past heroes, reformers, kings, and scholars who were part of that rebirth. He directed a passionate appeal to the students to open their hearts to Sweden's people and their church. He was not simply looking back: his vision was toward the future and his call was directed toward young people. Eklund's lecture was a call to battle. The gauntlet was thrown down and the leader of the student movement Manfred Björkquist provided the watchword: "Sweden's people — a people of God."

Einar Billing was also at Huskvarna. He gave two lectures on the atonement and began to lay the theological foundation for a new understanding of the church. His emphasis differed from that of Eklund. Billing was not nostalgic, nor was he militant; he was deeply reflective and goal driven. The mission of the church in the present time, as he saw it, was to reach out to all with the message of the forgiveness of sin. To fulfill this task, the "folk church" ("peoples' church") with its traditional self-governed parishes was the ideal ecclesial structure. The folk church included everyone and should proclaim the gospel to all. More: it *was* the forgiveness of sin for Sweden's people.

In low-church Uppsala, ecclesiology had not been discussed since Boström's time. His idealistic view of the state church had had its day, even if one could hear echoes of it here and there. In Lund, the situation was different. What was labeled "Lundensian high-church views" had for half a century implied a defense of the state church institution with its ministry, theology of orders, and Lutheran confessionalism. But in Uppsala, the state church was heckled in both free church and radical critiques of its vacuous and spiritually empty organization. Einar Billing, who worked in Uppsala but was a son of the Lundensian high-churchman Gottfrid Billing, made a virtue of necessity and turned the criticism to the church's advantage. In a convincingly unobtrusive way, he promoted his view that God has a message for the Swedish people and that the church's present organization was best for the task. It encompassed practically all citizens and could permeate the entire society with law and gospel. He gave the folk church a religious motivation; its outer form was admirably suited for its inner task.

These views spread quickly. The introverted but brilliant scholar became the leading teaching father for the extroverted and activist students. He had a greater influence on their understanding of the church than either Eklund or Söderblom. The autonomous Student Christian Movement (SCM) was transformed into an expansive state church–anchored organization with the aim of awakening the parishes and thereby renewing Swedish culture. The discussions boiled over. How could the students reach out with their conviction that God has revealed himself in history and offers unconditional grace to all? How could educated youth, with the destiny of their native land and its church in their hands, best shape the future?

Within a year, a genuine student awakening began. The Young Church Movement, as it was called, was stamped with a new consciousness of the church that aroused enthusiasm and joy. It overflowed with energy, questions were brought to a head, and its enthusiasm was translated into action. The World Student Christian Federation's chairman John R. Mott visited Sweden. When Söderblom had first met him twenty years earlier, Mott was at the beginning of his journey. Now he was a wealthy American layman who, to the highest degree, belonged to "the age of energy." He had mobilized thousands of students for "the evangelization of the world in this generation" with his Christ-centered message of revival. His vision knew no sectarian boundaries and he had ignited an ecumenical process that was to permeate twentieth-century global Christianity. In Sweden, he met with Prince Oscar Bernadotte, the explorer Sven Hedin, Archbishop J. A. Ekman, and, of course, Nathan Söderblom. In Uppsala, he opened the eyes of students to the bright future of Christian mission. He had recently visited China and he urged the Church of Sweden to send missionaries to "the Middle Kingdom." Some who listened to him would, ten years later, make their way there, among them Knut B. Westman and Ingeborg Wikander.

Mott's Christianity of free evangelical associations blended together with the Young Church Movement's longing for a spiritual renewal in the old Lutheran state church. His global horizon encircled their nationalism and when, in 1909, the students gathered again in Huskvarna, the movement was at its highest point. Many students during that summer had gone out two-by-two on "crusades" to parishes throughout the country, preaching, debating with workers, and speaking of the folk church's tasks and possibilities. All the time they sang Eklund's spiritual national song, "Fädernas kyrka" ("The Fathers' Church"). Masses of people gathered with them and the students' confidence was never greater.

Söderblom was on his way to a Calvin Jubilee in Geneva where he was to receive his first honorary doctorate. He stopped in Huskvarna where, like Einar Billing, he gave one of the student meeting's main lectures. Söderblom has often been described as one of the "fathers" of the Young Church Movement, although in point of fact he took a "wait and see" attitude, staying in the background. He continued to be worn out from his illness. He had had more than enough to do in delivering the spring term's demanding lecture series on Catholic modernism, arranging the first Olaus Petri Foundation lectureship, and preparing for the visit of the delegation from the Church of England. He was not able to regularly participate in the meetings of the Student Christian Movement, but he had encouraged the awakening during the evening conversations at the Stabby rectory. Gustaf Aulén, who was then still Söderblom's docent, had reluctantly become vice-chairperson of the SCM. Manfred Björkquist, who was not a theology student but was working on his licentiate in pedagogy, organized the Young Church Movement with the intuition of a natural leader. A nearly feverish enthusiasm and a strong sense of common purpose marked the relations between the students and their teachers. The newly awakened feeling that the Church of Sweden, in spite of all its problems, was worth investing in created a contagious openness. When the Young Church Movement prepared its first crusade, it was experienced as a Pentecostal miracle. There was no Young Church Women movement, but, as it was often said, some of the Young Church Men were women. Billing's view of the religiously motivated folk church merged with the nationalistic ideology espoused by Eklund with the hope of counteracting the decay of society.

Söderblom's understanding of the church differed considerably from that of Billing and even more from that of Eklund. Their conceptual world stretched no further than the edges of parishes or the border of Sweden, while Söderblom's vision was universal. He distanced himself from Swedish self-sufficiency: "Above all the church does not mean Sweden's national life religiously understood and deepened by Christianity in contrast to the universal church; Sweden is, rather, a link in Christianity on earth" he would say. In direct reference to Björkquist he pointed out that there were many other countries with at least as valuable a spiritual legacy as Sweden's. If the Swedish people were "a people of God," that could be interpreted only as a task, namely, to allow God's spirit to reach and penetrate everyone in the country for their spiritual health and salvation. Other churches had the same task: to be the souls of their nations and to give life spiritual content. Söderblom's view of the church encompassed the whole of Christianity, but his universalism had an unmistakably spiritualizing element. The true, inner essence of the church revealed itself "in the unbroken succession of the contact of souls with revelation through a living spiritual stream," as he expressed it. The history of revelation took a step forward every time a soul penetrated by the spirit of Christ was incorporated into the holy and divine continuity of revelation. How the universal church should be formed concretely he did not say.

Many theologians shared Söderblom's view that Jesus lived in the expectation of the soon-to-arrive Kingdom of God and that he had no thoughts concerning a church of the future. Jesus came to rehabilitate and liberate individuals, making real "the ideal kingdom of personalities," not creating an organization. Söderblom did not deduce the church from Jesus, but neither did he underestimate the church's meaning for the continuation of revelation and as a means of continuing the mission of God. At the student conference in Huskvarna he spoke on "The Individual's Christianity and the Church." He praised the Young Church Movement, which was giving "an unanticipated life and pungency to the well-nigh forgotten question of the church," awakening enthusiasm and action. The student revival was not just a wave of church mysticism, as could be found in England; rather, it sprang from the inner life of the Church of Sweden. The movement joyously discovered hidden riches: parish involvement, ancient church buildings, worship, feast days, and the changes of the church year. All of this the Young Church Movement brought out of hiding. The movement had three elements that Söderblom especially valued: its religious understanding of the church, its moral power, and its evangelical freedom. He reminded them that the life of the Spirit was much more than the visible, temporary church. Only faith, hope, and love were lasting. Only the person had "never-ending value." The church should be used in a way that it was not now being used.

He described how the Church of Sweden was an integral part of human culture, impossible to limit to believing Christians and largely invisible to human eyes. Its confession, people, and order together constituted a historical and organic entity. It had hidden spaces for all who walk in faith. The visible church was like a mountaintop peeking out of the water; thus, it was impossible to set fast the true church's borders. People outside the church often had both deeper faith and better morals than active Christians. That could apply even to those within the labor movement, perhaps even those "who actually described themselves as hostile to Christianity and the church." The spirit of Christ could be more evident among those who lived an authentic personal life than in many model but loveless parishes. Even though he hailed Sweden's glorious history and loved the northern lights, folk music, and national literature, the Church of Sweden was — and must be — part of a supranational communion. Only in that way could it be a true church. Sweden had at one time rescued the Reformation for humanity. Now it once again had been given a world historical task, to unite the churches of the Reformation. But the Church of Sweden could not fulfill that task alone. It was no better than other churches.

In a hymn, which was published without attribution to an author, included in the first issue of the Young Church Movement's journal, *Vår Lösen* ("Our Watchword"), Söderblom, who was in fact the author, summarized his ecclesiology, his view of the church:

> Ring in the time of worship!
> Heart and hand, thoughts and tongues,
> people, our land, old and young,
> in work and calling, worship God.
> May the world as a whole
> Become God's church.

The final line is key to the hymn. If the church in past times often strived to sanctify itself and dominate and shape the world, Söderblom's thoughts and prayers were the direct opposite: from the hidden depths of the world would emerge a church without borders that, through humans' faith, creative work, and communion, would point toward the Kingdom of God. The church was not primarily institutional but spiritual. It was only partly visible, but it was active in history and through individuals who communicated Christ's life from generation to generation. Authoritarian guardianship of doctrine and every limitation of freedom of conscience were foreign to him. Both Eklund and Billing found his Huskvarna address on the invisible church and the inclusive spiritual context of life somewhat unclear, but many students welcomed Söderblom's universal, albeit elusive understanding of the church. Some of them were destined to be his close coworkers in ecumenical work.

It was not long before Söderblom became more outspokenly critical of the Young Church Movement's tendency to claim to operate in its own way while in every context using the word "church." They "indulged in the church renaissance" and threatened to talk the whole thing to death even before results had come about. It was a confession of poverty that they made so much of the fact that the church had begun to move. They ought to have been more reserved with their fanfares. Even though he sympathized with much that they were doing, his ecumenical inclinations would not allow him to accept the Young Church Movement's emphases on nationalism, confessionalism, and even clericalism.

In *Svenska kyrkans kropp och själ (The Church of Sweden's Body and Soul),* which he wrote while awaiting the naming of the archbishop in the spring of 1914, he described the relationship between the church as an external, concrete organization and the church as soul and spirit. In order to understand Söderblom's view of the church, it is worth quoting from the complicated and convoluted introduction to this work. This is a good example of how he thought and expressed himself at this time:

> In respect to the living, we distinguish between the soul and the body. One may ask, how deep into the hierarchy of things can a soul be traced? When does the inspiring influence of the spirit cease and when does 'dead' material take over? Is any body definitively dead? The goals of the spirit cannot sooner or later be claimed. The solid matter from which life has departed can yet again become the organ for a soul, like an old rusty horn which someone takes down from a wall. If he understands the technique he can release from it tones which a hundred years ago carried meaning from one person to another but then became silent. The lower limit of the body, organized matter, is undetermined. Corresponding to its intensity a spirit out of things and events creates organs and impressions far beyond the organism usually named its body. Even upwards the limit of the body is often impossible to locate. Where is the boundary between the soul and that which it inspires? Nevertheless, we draw a distinction between the form and the spirit which lives in the form. Even in that living organism which is the religious community, from its most primitive to its highest form, the church, the difference is apparent between the body with its fixed forms which in early stages included rites and structures and in later stages dogma and symbols, and the soul of emotions, ideas, faith and personal and communal experience, which to a greater or lesser degree is capable of forming a body for itself or making an already existing shape into its own organ, squeezed and inhibited in a difficult but still disciplining and testing envelope.

This complicated question concerning the dialectical relationship between body and soul, matter and spirit, was the starting point for Söderblom's ecclesiology, his understanding of the church. If society was the body, the church was its soul. If the church as an institution was the body, its spiritual life was its soul. But the boundaries remained blurred. Söderblom's concern was life, soul, spirit. External things were secondary. This concern could be expressed in many ways. The essential thing was "the inner." Auguste Sabatier had taught him that religion was a matter of the heart's encounter with God, who was not visible to human eyes but who could be found in one's "innermost being." Söderblom often spoke of preserving the inner, of keeping the most holy pure, and receiving God in life's innermost existence. As a direct consequence of Sabatier's views, Söderblom preached on "The Inner Guest," not just once but in Uppsala, Leipzig, New York, and Lausanne. He pursued this theme for a quarter of a century.

The church's "body" was not more than an outer shell. At times, however, he identified liturgical forms, dogma, symbols, and even the office of the bishop, which was so central to his ecumenical views, as that which belonged to the body. The church as an institution was a *provisorium*, but without it the "soul" would have no home. Body and soul were mutually dependent on each other, but the soul took priority, for the church's actual center was God, not as a theoretical construction or as a dogmatic paragraph but as a living spirit, the will and goal of all things. Söderblom held a theology of incarnation at a distance, since in its extension lay the threat of institutionalism.

Based on this distinction between body and soul, Söderblom was to formulate his spirituality, his episcopal vocation, and his ecumenical program. This connected all external forms; the churches could encounter each other in faith and service without encroaching on each other's orders. The primacy of the soul meant that no church could regard itself as superior to another church, and that every individual could preserve and defend the freedom of his or her conscience. To characterize the Church of Sweden he time and again cited the words of Gustavus Adolphus: "the majesty of our fatherland and the church of God that dwells therein." He could not find a better way to express that the nation was the body and the church its indispensable soul. It was thus consistent that Söderblom defended the state church as an organizational form, although he held that the church was more than a function of the state. It was animated with a life that could not be limited to one's own nation. In France, the separation of church and state in 1905 had split the nation and marginalized the church. Thus Söderblom's position was also pragmatic. Religiously seen there was no ideal form of church organization and the church's outer structure was not given once and for all, but every church must seek as effective an outer form as possible in order to fulfill its mission within its own context. For Sweden, the state church system had clear merit. It was a sign of historical continuity, it could reach out to all, and it guaranteed a high degree of personal freedom, even for its clergy. But it was no more than a local expression of the universal church.

To belong to, support, and renew the historic established Lutheran folk church and to develop its cooperation and communion with other churches were for Söderblom two sides of the same coin. Since the national churches in Europe were state churches that lived in symbiosis with national structures and values, the distinction between body and soul was a presupposition for unity. Unity could be developed only at the spiritual level. Thus, Söderblom never strived for an organizational unity among the churches, nor for any confessional or liturgical uniformity. Even as humans had a right to their individuality so did the churches, and as humans were a fellowship of different individuals, so must the universal church be a fellowship of communities with their own distinctive characteristics. Söderblom was generous and inclusive. His ecclesiology, together with his minimally normative theology, made his ecumenical work possible. He did not stand by institutional and confessional claims that required others to subordinate themselves or emphasized externals more than the inward dimension. He worked to bring the Swedish and English churches as well as other evangelical communities closer to each other, but he entertained little hope that the Roman Catholic Church would give up its institutional hegemony for the sake of Christian unity. The Orthodox Churches were not yet even within his horizon.

13

Institutional Coercion or Spiritual Freedom?

> Two forms of unity which threaten our culture are the Roman Jesuit system, a distorted image of genuine catholicity, and the tyranny of the masses, which is a distorted image of enlightened and responsible democracy.
>
> *Nathan Söderblom, 1912*

SÖDERBLOM SPENDS HOLY WEEK IN ROME. *On Wednesday he attends Pius X's audience. The Holy Father shuffles in in his white cassock, tired and friendly but lacking sincerity or brilliance in his disposition. In an unhealthy way he is bloated by the confinement in which he is forced to live and he is attended by a lackey who is like an angry house cat, but who attempts to be obliging. For the historian of religion, the pope appears as "the divine medicine man of primitive religion, whose secret flood of power people hope will rub off on their clothes and possessions." Söderblom's response is ironic and contemptuous. He speaks of skirted figures who arouse distaste. With hands on their breasts, they bow to their cardinals "with a greeting worthy of lovesick fools who happen to meet the one they worship."*

* * *

During his time in Paris Nathan Söderblom had seen up close how ultramontanism had gained ground in the Catholic Church at the cost of theological freedom. Around Leo XIII, who was Pope for a quarter of a century up to 1903, a comparatively permissive atmosphere had been allowed. He advanced a socially directed Catholicism that faced the problems of modern society. He supported a number of Catholic movements that included social justice in their programs and that often were marked by theologically open positions. When Pius X became Pope, opposing currents and reactionary forces took over. During the First Vatican

Council, 1869–1870, many bishops worked for deepened conciliation, but ultramontanism won a major victory. The church was centralized. The pope was declared infallible if he *ex cathedra* proclaimed new dogma. The Sacred Congregation of the Holy Office (so named in 1908, succeeding the Sacred Congregation of the Holy Inquisition, and since 1967, known as the Sacred Congregation for the Doctrine of the Faith) stood as an immovable safeguard against every deviation in life or teaching. A restrictive and submissive loyalty came to characterize the church. Söderblom often spoke of "Jesuitism." This described his view of the church's apparatus of control and its oppressive structure, not necessarily his view of the Society of Jesus as such, and surely not of individual Jesuits.

Pius X was not unambiguous. He came from simple circumstances, was personally warm and approachable, and had a strikingly emotional piety. In contrast to Leo XIII who attached great importance to scholastic philosophy, Pius X was nearly anti-intellectual. He struggled against the modern world and its values with a nearly apocalyptic mistrust of the future. Society was sick and the only available means of healing was to unerringly follow the church's decrees and traditional ordinances.

He carried out a number of administrative and legal reforms in order to make pastoral work easier. By lowering the age of confirmation to seven years and encouraging Sunday communion, he contributed to a renewal of congregational life. He reintroduced Gregorian chant, simplified the Daily Office, and reformed seminary education. But he allowed no laymen to assume leadership; on the contrary, he disbanded certain movements in which laity had played an independent role. For Pius X, the church consisted of just two kinds of people: shepherds and sheep. It was the duty of parishes to obediently follow their leaders along well-traveled and well-known paths. He was determined to ruthlessly shatter every attempt to liberalize theology and social thought. Everything that he arbitrarily called "modernism" was identified with heresy and treason. The book *Gospel and Church*, which Abbé Alfred Loisy had published in 1902, unleashed a direct confrontation between the pope and those who had other views.

In July 1907, the Congregation of the Holy Inquisition promulgated a listing of sixty-five heresies. This paralleled Pius IX's unsigned Syllabus of Errors of 1864, *Lamentabili sane exitu*. No fewer than thirty of these heresies were to be found in Loisy's writings. In September of that year, the pope issued the encyclical *Pascendi dominici gregis*, in which "modernism" was given its name. The encyclical was to a high degree an enumeration of dangerous tendencies in the work of a number of Catholic scholars. These modernists were condemned for the use of the historical-critical method, individualism, acceptance of the theory of evolution, questioning scholasticism as the absolute norm, and for the view that the Church must adapt to current political and social realities. On top of all that, they were accused of adopting the thinking and methods of Protestant theologians and of being influenced by the philosophy of Immanuel Kant. Those who were accused found the charges deeply unjust, but the Roman Catholic hierarchy was determined once and for all to crush all dissent. This was to be accomplished with the help of censors in every diocese, informers, and banishment from the church's communion. The encyclical was directed toward Catholic theologians, but Protestant theologians were equally indignant and the gulf between the churches became wider. Söderblom, who wholeheartedly numbered himself among the modern theologians without for that reason swallowing everything the Catholic modernists stood for, unambiguously chose sides in the controversy. The dispute did not disappear until the Second Vatican Council, which began in 1962. The struggle over modernism determined much of the ecumenical movement's early character and direction.

When Söderblom visited Loisy in 1908, he learned a great deal of that scholar's dismal view of the situation, but he also learned of the experience of others. He reacted strongly against the description by the Roman Curia of modernism as a unified system and took it upon himself to show how it could take different forms of expression. By presenting various theologians and streams of thought, he wanted to give an overall view of the many-faceted movement. Thus, in the spring of 1909, he took Catholic modernism as the topic for his Uppsala lectures. This topic was "hot" since the pope's encyclical had received extensive publicity even in Sweden. Never before had so many students, in theology and other fields, streamed to the lectures. Week after week at an early hour of the day, more than a hundred auditors filled the lecture hall. Söderblom demonstrated an impressively wide reading of the sources and competence in the history of ideas. His biographical descriptions and theological analyses contained incisive analyses of the papacy and "Jesuitism" as well as of the avatars of modernism. He described the basic differences between the Roman Catholic and Reformation traditions and came to the conclusion that any real rapprochement with the Catholic Church was out of the question.

One year later his book *Religionsproblemet inom katolicism och Protestantism* (*The Problem of Religion in Catholicism and Protestantism*), based on these lectures, was to be found in bookstores. It was dedicated to two of his benefactors, Harald Bildt and Hjalmar Wijk, who probably found it a bit difficult to get through the book's five hundred pages filled, as they were, with Latin references and complex theoretical reasoning. But at least Bildt read the book with considerable interest. He had called himself a theosophist, but now was coming closer to Christian mysticism, finding great joy in Anglican worship. He regretted that the esoteric side of Christianity had been kept secret and he wrestled with the question of how Christianity could be presented so as to attract modern, educated, and seriously inquisitive people. In a letter to Söderblom he described the Church of Sweden as lazy, hypocritical, sanctimonious, and bureaucratic — as "an old bag of a church for hypocrites and milksops." If anyone could infuse in the Swedish people strength, fearlessness, and an awareness of the church's treasure for the lives of souls it was Söderblom. Bildt, who was to spend a great deal of his life as a diplomat in Rome, could, like his good friend, do nothing other than to sympathize with the modernists.

Söderblom's book had two parts. The first was a historic and systematic description of modernism and its relation to Protestantism. The second was a more abstract illumination of central academic problems concerning religion. It was so theoretical and fundamental that many readers found it difficult to understand, but at the same time, it was the most systematic statement of his reflections on questions of religion that Söderblom ever published. *Religionsproblemet* was one of his most meaningful books, but it was never translated to other languages. Anna Söderblom, who was probably the only person who read everything that her husband wrote and who was always his chief critic, held that *Religionsproblemet* was his most vital book. In the volume, he not only wrote about a number of remarkable personalities of his time but also shared generously the riches of his own thinking.

Söderblom wrote constantly and in his own individual way. His bibliography, compiled after his death, included 667 titles, but was far from complete. Söderblom's books consisted for the most part of reworked lectures, articles, travel accounts, and sermons. He preserved his manuscripts even if they were only outlines scribbled down on scraps of paper. His books could include chapters from previous decades and he often repeated himself. Söderblom had brought many of his theologically important themes into focus even before he came to Uppsala in 1901. Most of what he subsequently published elaborated on and deepened those themes.

His books were largely collections of essays, coherent but not always with a clear line from beginning to end. He was passionately interested in language. His style varied from academic prose with an intricate structure of meaning filled with subordinate clauses to choppy journalistic speech composed with lively simplicity. His sermons were filled with metaphors and biblical citations. It was easier for him to describe people and report engagingly on his meetings and concrete experiences than it was to burrow into theoretical arguments. He was able to quickly combine differing phenomena, draw bold analogies, and make sharp distinctions. In spite of his rapid line of thought, he seldom lost its thread. He had a phenomenal memory and gathered material by constant, extensive, and careful reading of academic literature in French, German, English, and the Nordic languages. He even understood some Italian and made his own translations of Latin texts. He always carried his well-worn Greek New Testament, reading from it daily.

Just as the Young Church Movement was reaching its apex and students in Uppsala were afire with nationalistic and Lutheran enthusiasm, Söderblom chose to widen their field of vision by lecturing on Roman Catholic Christianity, helping them to see through both Catholic and evangelical propaganda. He wanted to show that the Catholic Church had room for much more than a quest for power, the worship of saints, and "Jesuitism." It possessed a warm spirit of piety that was more complete and methodically developed than in evangelical churches. The Franciscan ideal was alive and many struggled for freedom of thought. He dealt with theologians one at a time: the Englishman John Henry Newman, the American Isaac Thomas Hecker, the Frenchman Alfred Loisy, the Irishman George Tyrell, the German-Italian Friedrich von Hügel who emigrated to England. He continued with a broad analysis of variations of modernism in Great Britain, Italy, and Germany, concluding with a discussion of that movement's relationship to Protestantism.

Yet overall, Söderblom was not impressed with the leadership of the Roman Catholic Church. Its way of dealing with the modernists was a deep tragedy not only for them and for theological scholarship but for the whole Christian church. The Curia's overreaction to scientific development was a blow against all genuine religion. But Söderblom was also critical of the modernists. They certainly were headed in the right direction, but they did not go far enough since under no circumstances were they willing to break with their church. When they placed the church ahead of the individual person's responsibility, a troublesome gulf was created between the established life of piety and the free pursuit of truth. In their faithfulness to the church, the modernists at times became more Catholic than the pope himself. Even so, their ideal of the church they loved was rejected. The modernists were undoubtedly influenced by Schleiermacher, Kant, and Darwin, but also by Auguste Sabatier, Julius Wellhausen, and Adolf von Harnack, and many of them had personal contacts with Protestant theologians. But when accused of having Protestant tendencies, they quickly retreated. Their modernism was not "half-Protestantism" as some claimed. In Söderblom's view, modernism was at root "Arch-Catholic," for if Protestants such as Harnack found the essence of Christianity in the Gospels, Loisy and other Catholics continued to find that essence in the church's institutions, traditions, and sacraments. Even though biblical scholarship had come up with a new picture of Jesus, it was still the church's Christ who counted and who could give salvation. Their deeply held view that the church was given by God with the authority to determine what was true restrained the modernists. They came only halfway on the journey of critical scholarship, never risking their faith.

Things were harder for the Protestants. No pope limited their free search for truth. When questions arose there was no turning back. Biblical criticism could even call into question the actual existence of Jesus. The Protestant groups could shield no one from doubt. Did the historical Jesus suffer and die for humankind's sake and was he a necessary condition for salvation? Denials were always tempting. Evangelical Christians had nothing to hold on to other than the word of the Bible and human experience; the church did not help them. In this respect, the difference between the Roman Catholic and Reformation churches was fundamental. Söderblom held that in regard to Christian life and piety, the Catholics trusted too much in tradition, rites, and external means. Thus they lost an awareness of the variability of all things and did not understand that even religion must be renewed in accordance with the times. A proximity to Christ himself certainly made the liturgy and confession of the early church normative for all times, but, to cite an example from history, it must not be overlooked that Martin Luther in his time liberated the gospel's authentic content. In order to preserve its outer forms, the Catholic Church closed off the actual dynamics of life. With its basically reactionary attitude and exclusive praxis, it reduced itself to a sect.

Söderblom did not share the Catholic view that Jesus himself established the church and gave it a particular structure. The Christianity of the Gospels had no structure other than "life's concentration on itself in the revealed essence of Jesus." Jesus had no intention of creating a new religion. It was the experience of the presence of the Kingdom of God that convinced people to follow him and later to organize themselves into communities. Nor was salvation a monopoly of the church; it happened wherever humans were pardoned by God. The gospel was a seed that grew and bore fruit thanks to Christ. It had been preserved by confessors such as Paul, Augustine, Bernard of Clairvaux, Francis of Assisi, Luther, and Kierkegaard. It was thanks to such personalities that the Christian faith had been protected and transmitted through the centuries.

In actual practice, Söderblom had a high view of the church as an institution as long as it allowed scholars and believers full freedom and did not by police methods, coercion, or punishment attempt to hinder free choice and independent thought. The continuity of the church was for Söderblom just as evident in evangelical churches as in the Roman Catholic Church. In Sweden, he held that continuity with the early church was "purer" than in other quarters, but he also had a special love for the Anglican Church. No other national church body showed greater "theoretical liberality" than the Church of England.

The tension between personal and institutional religion determined both Söderblom's judgment of Christianity and his view of religion in its wider sense. The attitude of the Roman Catholic Church forced him to a definite ecumenical conclusion: to establish an official connection with Rome would be impossible for a long time. Even the value of such a connection was doubtful. According to him, the Curia in Rome no longer represented universal, catholic Christianity; rather, it represented a Tridentine and Vatican diminution of the essence of catholicism. The Anglican Church was sounder in its teaching and was actually more catholic than the Roman Church. But the Church of Sweden certainly also had a full measure of the most valuable thing any church could possess: a genuinely evangelical catholicity.

Söderblom developed his analysis of the Roman Catholic Church and its relationship to modernism without ever himself having been to Rome. An opportunity to visit Rome came in the spring of 1911 when Söderblom was invited to speak at a World Student Christian Federation conference in Constantinople. Oscar Ekman of Bjärka-Säby saw to it that the trip was paid for, and together with Anna, Söderblom spent two whole weeks in Rome and Athens on the way to Constantinople. On the journey they celebrated both Western and Eastern Easters, between which there was one week. He took notes on the journey, rewrote them, and published them in a booklet called *Tre heliga veckor* (*Three Holy Weeks*).

As always, he was curious, inquisitive, and attentive. He disregarded the tourist attractions. Instead, he went from church to church in Rome in order to take part in Holy Week's many worship services. In spite of his critical attitude toward the church's power structure and theological censorship, he was convinced that whoever sought the depth of Catholic piety would find a unity in faith that neither extravagance, compulsion, nor spiritual laxity could destroy. He recorded in detail how the priests conducted themselves, how the Psalms were sung, how the biblical texts were read, and how the atmosphere was altered by subtle changes in musical expression. He noted that Cardinal Vannutelli looked like a somewhat coarsened Gottfrid Billing and that another cardinal was chubby, well mannered, pious, and attractively clumsy. He described the history of the liturgical forms, indicated which publishers had released the orders of worship, and reflected over the different ways in which churches had preserved their common liturgical inheritance. During his visitations, he asked himself why Holy Week did not have the same importance in evangelical churches as in the Roman Catholic Church. Had the Protestants, with their dry, intellectual, and doctrinal interpretation of faith, lost too much of the ritual and experiential side of things? And why did the evangelical churches not observe Maundy Thursday, which was one of the few days in the life of Jesus that could be followed nearly hour by hour? He described Good Friday as an occasion for intercession for the pope, bishops, priests, deacons, subdeacons, acolytes, exorcists, lectors, doorkeepers, confessors, virgins, widows, and all of God's people, for catechumens, all who suffer, for heretics and sectarians, yes, also for Jews and heathens. These Solemn Prayers of Good Friday made an especially deep impression on him.

He scurried from church to church with notebook in hand, taking in all sorts of impressions. The suffering and death of Jesus had been the central motive in Söderblom's own faith ever since his own "conversion" when he discovered the meaning of the cross. Now he felt how the sufferings of Christ, interpreted in rites and texts, united all Christians. This feeling became so strong that he was nearly ready to reexamine his dismissal of the worship of relics and of what he interpreted as a popular mixture of Christian and heathen practices. He was so absorbed in all of this that he nearly missed noting that Emilia Fogelklou, who was also in Rome, wanted to see him. She found him to be oddly nervous, speaking of one thing after another without context, while his notes from the journey indicated that he was totally taken up with his research concerning Roman Catholic piety. Back in Uppsala, he was to emphasize his experience of the observance of Holy Week. Many customs and forms he had seen in Rome became, with time, integrated into the liturgical life of the Church of Sweden.

Söderblom would not have become the eager ecumenist he was had he not made contacts with leading Catholics. The pope's Wednesday audience was a disappointment to him, but not his meeting with the well-known church historian, Louis Marie Olivier Duchesne, who had survived the witch hunt of dissident thinkers carried on by Merry del Val, Vatican Secretary of State. He received Söderblom in the Palazzo Farnese. The two scholars had a conversation about both Zoroastrian eschatology and Swedish-English relations while Anna waited in a nearby salon. At just that time, an earthquake shook the building and the learned though cynical man's Angora cat disappeared. On the evening of Good Friday, Cardinal Mariano Rompolla received Söderblom. In 1903, he would have become pope instead of Pius X if the Austro-Hungarian emperor had not vetoed his candidacy. Now he was the archpriest of St. Peter's Basilica. The conversation with Rompolla, who was vastly more intelligent than Pius X, was the most interesting of Söderblom's time in Rome.

By the time Easter arrived and the resurrection of Christ was celebrated in the churches, the Söderbloms had left Rome in order to hike around Lake Nemi in the Alban Hills of Italy. They heard the Easter bells from a distance. On Easter Monday they were met by a procession of joyful women and sweaty men who carried a life-size picture of the resurrected one. Such a self-assertive and vulgar Easter celebration did not appeal to Söderblom. He felt that he had encountered the true Easter in the catacombs of Rome where inscriptions such as "You shall live in God" or "May God refresh your spirit" reminded him more of the rebirth of the soul than the resurrection of the body. That Christ in some historical and bodily sense became alive again had less meaning for Söderblom than his death on the cross. He did not deny the resurrection but, remarkably, he rarely preached on it. When he came to Constantinople, where according to their calendar the Orthodox celebrated the resurrection with such joy that the churches seemed to quake and when for the first time he could have participated in the Divine Liturgy, he chose instead to preach and lead an Easter service for twelve people in the chapel at the Swedish Embassy. He did not regret his choice for an instant.

On the way to Constantinople, he also took part in services in Athens where Holy Week had just begun. He compared the Orthodox Church's dramaturgy with what he had experienced in Rome. In Athens everything was more firmly anchored in the people. Liturgical dialogues about the woman who anointed Jesus's feet with precious nard and also about the betrayal by Judas who would not repent were sung by dark voices in crowded churches. For Söderblom, the exquisite pre-Christian grave reliefs he saw in the archeological museum served as background to Easter. The images were filled with hopeless sorrow and illustrated why the gospel was met with such a strong response in the world of antiquity. It changed grief into hope and trust.

More than 248 delegates, 70 of whom were women, gathered for the student conference at the American Robert College, an hour's boat trip from Constantinople up the Bosporus. John R. Mott was the conference leader. Karl Fries was serving as General Secretary of the World Student Christian Federation; he felt at home among the five Swedish delegates. Gathering in the conference hall, which was decorated with flags from many lands, were Russians in uniform, Swedes in white student caps, Turks and Arabs wearing white fezzes, bearded Greek priests in floor-length cassocks, Australians, Indians, Chinese, Japanese, and others. Söderblom already knew some of the delegates. Many of them, after the war, were to become his collaborators. One of these was Archemandrite Germanos Strenopoulos, who was to lead the Greek Orthodox into the ecumenical movement; another was the Scotch Presbyterian David Smith Cairns who shared Söderblom's vision of a united Christianity. Söderblom identified those who might possibly play a role in the future and maintained subsequent contact with them as far as possible. He always "gathered" people, noted something about their personalities, and saved those notes. When it came time to involve them in one project or another, this personal knowledge was of great value.

Constantinople was the gate to the Orient where all the founders of the great religions had lived: Jesus, of course, but also Zarathustra, Muhammed, Buddha, Lao-tse, and Confucius. When Söderblom was rowed over the Bosporus to visit the site of the Council of Chalcedon, A.D. 451, he spontaneously fell to his knees and kissed the soil of Asia where all of these holy people had walked. His ecumenical plans were still not well developed and until this point had been limited to the Western Reformation churches, but now they were enlarged to include not only Eastern and Oriental Orthodox Churches but also the young, forward-looking churches of India and China. Wang Chenting, who was later to become China's Foreign Minister, directed sharp criticism toward the Western missions in China that were carried on under the protection of foreign powers. He asked the students to support a necessary change, and for that he received the only applause of the conference. Söderblom was impressed by his audacious, self-confident attitude. One day, said Wang, the roles would be reversed and Westerners would come to China to learn what Christianity actually is. Söderblom listened attentively to what Wang had to say about the relations between Confucianism and Christianity and between mission and politics. The Church of Sweden had, at that time, no mission in China, but in the early 1920s, when Söderblom was chair of the board of the Church of Sweden Mission, the first missionaries were sent there. The directions of their work were colored more by what he learned from the culturally conscious Wang than from Mott, who was seeking to conquer the world for the gospel.

Christianity's history had only begun. God would reveal himself in land after land, to one people after the other. Mott had, as a chain in his global strategy, scheduled the conference for Constantinople. A previous conference had been held in Tokyo; now it was the intention to also include the Orthodox Churches in the world-encompassing student movement. Robert College was an American Protestant institution that was intended to convert Muslims to Christianity, but even the Orthodox minority in Turkey had reason to be uneasy at the Protestant intrusion. Nevertheless, the Ecumenical Patriarch Joachim III blessed the conference. For some of his younger priests, notably Germanos, who was Rector of the Seminary on the island of Halki, the conference was life changing. The student movement began to take root in Bulgaria, Serbia, and Romania, but only one Orthodox believer belonged to the movement's leadership, K. C. Chacko of the Malankara Syrian Church in India.

As usual, lectures were piled one on another. Söderblom was to answer the question: "Does God Continue to Reveal Himself to Humanity?" His thoughts concerning the role of geniuses, heroes, and saints in history were undoubtedly strange to many of those who listened, especially when he, as usual, brought up Jeanne d'Arc, Martin Luther, and Gustavus Adolphus. He had been asked to speak from a Nordic perspective and that he did. He did not limit himself to historical perspectives, but addressed the responsibility of the students to change the world. He concluded the lecture with a personal testimony concerning Jesus Christ as the decisive event in his own life. To that Mott and the other leaders could only say "Amen." The delegates ranked his lecture as the third best of the conference, after Mott's and Wang's.

After his experience of Roman Catholic and Orthodox worship, Söderblom was again confronted at Robert College with the Anglo-Saxon type of evangelical Christianity that had appealed so much to him when he was a student. Rome's, Athens's, and Constantinople's old churches stood where they had been for nearly two thousand years, overgrown, dusky, and full of memories, superstitions, poetry, and mystique. The contrast with the student movement's young, rational, prosaic organization with its optimistic concentration on activity and statistics could not have been greater. He could afford to be a bit ironic toward Mott who organized one conference after another, always the "biggest in the world" and the "most important" in the history of Christianity. Certainly, good organization was important, but personalities meant a great deal more, not to mention a sense of historic depth about which the student movement barely had a clue. Nevertheless, Söderblom hoped that the conference, which had taken a clear position for academic freedom, would prove itself meaningful on the journey toward the realization of Christian unity. To get the churches to cooperate with each other would require all the learning and diplomatic ability he possessed, along with the energy and enterprise that the students might be expected to mobilize. The new generation of Christian leaders — among them a number of Asians — made an impression on him, but it was his first encounter with the churches of the East that provided the great profit of his journey. His meeting with Germanos would have decisive importance for the ecumenical movement.

This was the only time in his life that Söderblom visited a Muslim country. His knowledge of other religions had been attained in university libraries or had come from Christian missionaries. Apart from some Jewish friends, he personally knew very few people who practiced a religion other than Christianity. He himself never took part in the cultic acts he described so vividly in his books. In Constantinople he had a glimpse of Islam. With his own eyes he saw how the mighty Hagia Sophia, started in the sixth century, had been ravaged and changed into a mosque. From some of his notes, which have been preserved, one can sense Söderblom's reaction. He considered how the temple of holy wisdom, Hagia Sophia, might have appeared in all its splendor, and he also considered the wisdom found in Islam. Contradicting that wisdom was the cubic Kaaba, in Mecca, nothing but "a black stone fetish" toward which all Islamic prayer is directed. Such primitivism was a stumbling block for Söderblom and perhaps why he never showed much interest in Islam. He also learned something of Constantinople's bloody history and experienced the motley life to be found in its streets and squares. The Muslims seemed in his eyes to be sorrowful and oppressed, but he never came in touch with them. On short notice he did give a lecture on science and salvation to some Greek and Turkish intellectuals, but he never came into closer contact with them than that.

While the other Nordic delegates to the conference made their way home through Greece, Italy, and Germany, Anna and Nathan boarded the Orient Express and traveled through one Balkan country after another. There was peace throughout Europe, even there. But war was not far off. Both in Germany and in England, there were many who fatefully believed that war was inevitable and unavoidable in the light of nationalism, imperialism, and the hunger for natural resources. All that was required was a spark.

14
With the Saints as Models

> A place of honor among the saints belongs to the genius of religion who in his soul determines to discern and serve the will of God in history.
>
> *Nathan Söderblom, 1911*

THE UNIVERSITY OF ST. ANDREWS celebrates its five hundredth anniversary in great style, a Scottish festival. Nathan Söderblom is one of many awarded an honorary doctorate. He describes the banquet in a witty article. He portrays the brilliant polymath, Andrew Lang, who glorified the gray city on the forbidding North Sea coast, and he also pictures the Moderator of the State Church of Scotland, an amusing type who looks like an old sea skipper dressed in a silk suit with ruffles. The students, whose right to clamor seems limitless, interrupt the ceremonies time after time with somewhat rude songs. From the platform there are streams of eloquence. When the Maharaja of Baroda holds forth about an enlightened march to the future, Söderblom makes his way out. The next day he is to visit the fourteenth Earl of Strathmore and his Lady in Macbeth's Glamis Castle.

* * *

On Wednesday, May 31, 1911, the awarding of doctorates in theology took place in the Uppsala Cathedral with Nathan Söderblom as the designated promoter. Einar Billing, Nils Johan Göransson, and Josef Bensow received their degrees. In addition, the professor of history Harald Hjärne and the linguistically talented missionary to India Anders Danielsson were awarded honorary doctorates. It was a great day for the faculty of theology since they had finally attained the right to award doctorates themselves on the basis of academic merit. Söderblom himself gave the principal address while the University Chancellor, the archbishop, the Provincial Governor, the mayor, and all the university professors, led by the Rector Magnificus, sat through the whole ceremony in the uncomfortable cathedral pews. Söderblom spoke on the subject, "Types of Saviours in the History of Religion." In his invitation to the celebration he had written on the interpretation of revelation, the same theme he had, in shortened form, developed in Constantinople a month earlier. The choice of this topic was a tribute to Hjärne whom he described as "the person who of all those alive has most directed my spirit" and who in his attention to Gustavus Adolphus and his views concerning the role of personalities in history had made a lasting impression on Söderblom. The famed historian had sometimes been so bold as to directly refer to Jesus. In the midst of the history of the world, a personality had appeared who was like no other, he had claimed. Jesus Christ pointed forward to the goal where all the straying ways of humanity would come together in a peace that transcended all plans and dreams. Söderblom referred to Hjärne generously. During the years around the turn of the century, great heroes and personalities were often elevated in an attempt to uplift the masses. Söderblom made a theology of this: the geniuses of art and science, the heroes of history, and the saints of the religions mediated God's continuing revelation and served an exemplary function. This happened not through teachings and dogma, but through the lives they lived.

Söderblom had, as we have seen, at an early stage questioned the widely held Protestant view that the revelation of God was finished once and for all in Jesus Christ and fully accounted for in the Bible, to which there was nothing to add. But, Söderblom asked rhetorically, how could it be maintained that God had once revealed himself to humankind but no longer did? Was heaven closed after the days of the Bible? Must not a living God who desires and works for salvation connect to humankind? This does not happen via promulgated dogma, but through the life and acts of humans. The witness of the church began with people reporting that they had seen and heard Jesus. The Bible was filled with such accounts. Before the Christian faith was theological, it was biographical. It had developed not from dogmatic teachings but from narratives, and this had continued through the centuries. That God continually reveals his will through individuals was a cornerstone in Söderblom's theological edifice. It was the basis for his view of history and his understanding of reality and morality.

In his invitation he chose, as he often did, three points of entry for his presentation: revelation through geniuses and saints, revelation through the historical process, and revelation through the conversion and moral life of individuals. The fact that time after time there appeared "geniuses" — trailblazing scientists or historically significant leaders, founders of religions or artists — proved that the creation of the world was steadily ongoing. In order to be called a genius, it was not enough to have received a rich if even puzzling genetic inheritance from one's parents. If someone suddenly appeared as a genius it was no coincidence, but rather a mysterious sign that exactly when needed, God had chosen that person for a decisive task. Then there appeared a kind of mutation that crossed the boundary between talent and genius. Geniuses had received the gift of interpreting God's creation and giving meaning to life not primarily through intellectual work but as heroes, martyrs and saints, artists, discoverers, and poets. They participated in the continuing creation and changed the presuppositions of life. From being "as bare as an empty sack or as sluggish as a full sack," life was awakened and renewed. It took on strength, vitality, and the will to reach a transcendent goal. Söderblom mentioned many examples from history: Jeanne d'Arc, Oliver Cromwell, Gustavus Adolphus, Peter the Great, George Washington, and even Otto von Bismarck. Their seriousness and spiritual strength had filled their times with purpose and a sacrificial attitude.

The same thing applied to heroes of the religions. The foremost of these was Martin Luther. With his uncommon learning and knowledge of languages, his good judgment and undaunted courage, his skill at translating Holy Scripture, his divine eloquence and evangelical proclamation of justification, and with his prophetic gifts, Luther must be counted among Christianity's true saints. In his spirit he was graced with something of God's own essence. His originality, freshness, strength, and rich personality witnessed profoundly to God's living presence.

When great geniuses wholeheartedly and single-mindedly serve God, they can be described as saints, even if they are not, as in Roman Catholic and Orthodox practice, made into objects of intercession. But clearly they are worthy of esteem. Within Protestantism, teachings concerning sainthood had been neglected as a consequence of its rejection of the cults of saints. Söderblom shared the Catholic Church's understanding that saints are Christians who completely submit themselves to the rule of God. But their holiness does not depend on their ability to perform miracles, but rather on the fact that the God who reigns and acts in the drama of history engenders personalities who by word and deed let his light radiate throughout the world. Söderblom repeated time and again the only definition of a saint he felt was valid: the saints are those who in life, character, and action clearly and unambiguously show that God lives.

That he was very much taken up with the thought of sainthood was totally consistent with his emphasis on the role of individual people in history. Through men and women who placed themselves at God's disposal and took on great and selfless tasks, the revelation of God continued through the centuries. The saints were not perfect, but they burned with the flame of tenderness and heartfelt experience. They had self-confidence but were not all cast in the same mold. Söderblom's own list of saints largely included European men, but he quite naturally also numbered the only canonized saint from Sweden, St. Birgitta, and even the nineteenth-century singer Jenny Lind among them. The saints were not primarily introverted and recognizably pious Christians but people of strong will who made a difference. He did not confine himself to the early church's calendar of saints with titles such as martyr, bishop, or virgin and he seldom named Mary, the mother of Jesus, the apostles, or the church fathers. But he included men who in twentieth-century Finland or the Baltics had struggled for freedom and placed them in the front rank of those who had suffered and died for their faith. There was also room for people of science, art, peace, and conscience in the great company of saints.

In the fall of 1911, he spent a month in England and Scotland together with Harald Hjärne. In the Salisbury Cathedral they presented a silver plaque in memory of Bishop John Wordsworth, who had played a leading role in Swedish-English church relations but who had recently died. In his speech, Söderblom remembered Sigfrid, David, Eskil, and Henrik, who had come to Sweden as missionaries nine hundred years before, and placed Wordsworth in that list of English saints. Söderblom had written his talk on a notepad where there were also two loose pages with his translation of a hymn, which the Bishop of Wakefield, William Walsham How, had written in 1864, the well-known "For All the Saints," later set to music by Ralph Vaughn Williams. Söderblom's translation was published in *Vår Lösen* (*Our Watchword*) just before All Saints Day. It soon became part of the All Saints observance in the Church of Sweden. The hymn's emphasis on the faithfulness, bravery, strength, and courage of saints corresponded to Söderblom's own understanding. His saints were not distant from the world; they belonged literally to *ecclesia militans*, the struggling church.

The second sign of God's continuing revelation that Söderblom offered in his invitation to the Academic Promotion could be read in the history of humanity. The servants of God had been given the ability to discern God's will in the events of history. The ones who first did this were Moses and the prophets, and in a certain way, also the Persian prophet Zarathustra. The idea that God leads humankind forward toward his ultimate victory was foreign to the Greeks and Romans but very much present for the Jews. God had rescued them from the Egyptians; their entire history was determined by the interventions of God. In many other religions, humans sought God by fleeing from history into a timeless, spiritual mysticism of infinity. Prophetic piety was quite different. It was characterized by God's actions both in the minute history of individuals and the great history of the world. Jesus, with his eschatological message, had entered the reality of Israel. The Kingdom was to come. God would show that he has the final power. History has a direction and every step along humanity's way was decisive. It was to God's power and will for the world that the great pioneers of Christianity bore witness.

When he wrote this, Nathan Söderblom had just returned from the only journey he ever made to Rome. He would not have been who he was if he had not taken the occasion to criticize the Roman Catholic Church. The evangelical and Roman churches agreed that God's revelation continued through history, but there was a decisive difference in their views: the Roman Catholics held that revelation continues through the church and its hierarchical structure with the pope at its apex, while evangelical Christians believed that God's continuing revelation occurred within the framework of general history. The church was certainly an instrument of God. It should be neither overestimated nor underestimated, and Protestants had good reason to value the church highly, conscientiously taking responsibility for the administration of Word and sacrament. But Roman Catholics must take care not to shield the church from the history of humanity and bury itself "in a mausoleum of obsolete ideas and conceptions" as modernity closed in. They confined revelation within institutions and theological systems and would not acknowledge that God communicates with humanity even outside the church. Söderblom presented two drastic but actual examples. It could happen that battleships in a certain historical situation had greater significance for God's kingdom than even a thousand sermons. It could also happen that the political changes in China, where the republican revolution was beginning to ferment and spiritual and intellectual forces were beginning to compete more on Western terms, might show themselves to be a more powerful revelation than the churches' extensive missionary enterprises.

The third sign of God's continuing revelation was God's ability to change individuals when they placed themselves into the history of revelation. In conversion and birth to new life, in the heights of moral and spiritual life, the power of God elevated the soul to an existence that was essentially similar to that of genius. Kierkegaard had said that life was a poem that humans wrote themselves but that a Christian allowed God to hold the pen. Söderblom agreed. The mark of answered prayer was not emotional rapture, but rather the power to overcome sin and difficulty and to take on an independent and principled ethical disposition. When believers, for whom faith itself and indeed the whole world were miracles, realize that the spirit of God permeates everything and that nothing is doomed to meaninglessness, it is a sign of the self-revelation of God.

Söderblom saw the difference between the general academic study of religion and theology as lying in the fact that revelation was essential to theology. In the general study of religion, the question of revelation was left open if not rejected outright. Theologians and historians of religion could have differing understandings of revelation, but that must not affect their research. The same was true for historical or psychological investigations; they must not be guided by any dogmatic considerations. A theologian could not, however, disregard that even the history of religion was a revelation of God. That was most clearly to be seen in prophetic religions.

It was one thing to lecture, write, and sing hymns as to how God communicates himself through the saints and geniuses of history, but Söderblom was not content with that. In Holy Trinity Church in Uppsala he had given visible form to his theology through sculpture and paintings. Perhaps on account of that, the architect Ferdinand Boberg invited him to work out the plan for the internal decoration of the Saltsjöbaden church just outside Stockholm, which he was designing. He asked for a total artistic program with pictures, texts, and symbols. The famed politician, banker, and financier Knut Wallenberg was committed to developing Saltsjöbaden, electrifying the train that went there, and building a Grand Hotel, a coeducational school, and other communal facilities that expressed modernity. He also wanted to erect a church where he and his wife Alice would be buried. For this, he engaged the time's most prominent architect and the well-known artists Carl Milles and Olle Hjortzberg. They were given a free hand and a generous budget. Söderblom gladly accepted the task, which he was to share with the art historian Johnny Roosval, and had a decisive influence over the iconography of the church interior and the symbolism of its bronze doors. He saw to it that people who came into the church would see the revelation of God roar throughout history, and he insisted that the church should be called The Church of Revelation.

At the time, a liturgical renewal had begun in Sweden, stimulated by the conversations with the Church of England and the revision of the 1894 order of worship. Söderblom was not only interested in art; he also wanted to beautify worship with eucharistic vestments and processions. There was an increasing interest in church design and furnishings, churches were being renovated, and several new churches were being built. It was a dream of his to set his mark on an entire church building that would reflect the new times to the highest degree. At Saltsjöbaden he was given a unique opportunity to proclaim the extent and richness of God's revelation in art and design. God, who was the true driving force of history, had brought forth personalities who radiated light. History was God's laboratory and God spoke even through people who did not know him or who denied him. In murals, mosaics, and sculpture, true prophets, geniuses, and saints would emerge. They would all turn toward the altar, the symbol of Christ, in whom all things are fulfilled.

To discern who God's witnesses were required a nearly prophetic vision and Söderblom felt that he possessed just that. With a certain tendency to glide between the religiously interpreted history of salvation and the secular events of history, he saw the entire world process as a coherent and ongoing event. The World War had not yet shattered the West's optimistic faith in its own continuing conquests in culture and civilization, nor had Söderblom's own dreams of the good world order intended in creation been lost. He cited Jesus's words, "My Father is still working, and I also am working" (John 5:17), and he believed in them.

His theology was more determined by the times than he himself understood. Whoever singled out people as "witnesses to God" risked exposing his or her own ideological preferences. This naturally also pertained to

Söderblom. His chosen witnesses all too often represented national and ecclesiastical authorities. Not seldom did he idealize Lutheran leaders. They appear in the Church of Revelation alongside biblical figures and Greek philosophers. On the walls of the nave are paintings of Abraham, Moses, Elijah, Isaiah, John the Baptist, and also Socrates and Plato. There is also an area with burial tablets, statues of five Swedish poets: Bishop Thomas, Olaus Petri, Haquin Spegel, Johan Olof Wallin, and Erik Gustaf Geijer. In the chancel, there is a triumph cross, of a type found in Gotland, on a beam with the inscription, "I believe in Jesus Christ, God's only-begotten son, our Lord." The beam is borne up by the Apostles Peter and Paul. In the narthex, Augustine and Monica his mother are depicted together with a long line of Swedish saints: Ansgar and Botvid, King Erik, Bishop Henrik, Birgitta and her confessor Mattias. Martin Luther in a monk's garment also appears, as does Gustavus Adolphus in knight's golden armor, both with halos. Bible verses and hymn lines appear in the pictures. In the dark church, the eye is directed to the freestanding altar of white Italian Carrara marble with four alabaster reliefs that summarize the message of the New Testament: Jesus's Sermon on the Mount, the sinful woman anointing Jesus in the house of Simon, Jesus in Gethsemane, and Jesus on the road to Emmaus.

The people portrayed were chosen by God. Their choice was shared by Söderblom himself. He often referred to feeling that his task had been "laid on him by a higher power." Nearly one year later to the day after the dedication of the Church of Revelation, he would be named archbishop and placed in a succession of witnesses going back to the days of Ansgar. In the modern Church of Revelation it was apparent that in large measure he shared the values of his own class in society. Those values were the result of the breakthrough of modernity and not a remnant of obsolete traditions, even if features of Sweden's historic mission in the world shone strongly. On the heavy bronze doors were described the contradictions of life — human need and divine assistance, the condemnation of guilt and the grace of forgiveness, mortality and immortality. But within the church, all was placed under the Father's protection and above the crucified Christ the heavens were open.

On the church's east wall was painted a throng of men with heads bowed before God. Among them, Söderblom himself was to be found. He had, along with Wallenberg and Boberg, created a church in which with great consistency he could convey his theological message in art. The basic theological edifice had materialized, not as a monument to the past but as a living, even if time-bound, witness. The Church of Revelation cost more than many rural churches together and could have raised highly critical voices. But only the best was sufficient when God was to be praised. That was also the case when Söderblom had his famous bishop's cope created for the 1925 ecumenical conference and when the Ansgar Chapel was built on Björkö.

The Church of Revelation was dedicated May 18, 1913, the same day that the opening of the new electric train from Stockholm was celebrated. A few days later, the Parliament approved a new law that gave 45 to 195 crowns in a yearly pension to everyone over the age of sixty-seven. This was the beginning of modern social legislation in Sweden. Söderblom was still a professor. He served partly in Uppsala and partly in Leipzig.

15

An Interval in Leipzig on the Way to the Archbishop's Palace

> The less attention one pays to luggage, the happier and easier the journey is. From many travelers one gets the impression that it is the suitcases that drag them around and not they carrying the suitcases.
>
> *Nathan Söderblom, 1913*

For a few April days in 1914 he lives with Anna and three of their children at Hotel Hohe Sonne am Rennsteig near Eisenach. They have a glorious view over Wartburg Castle. There Luther, excommunicated by his church and uncertain about the future, had hid under the name Junker Jörg while he translated the New Testament into German. Söderblom is third on the list of candidates to become archbishop. He feels that he will be named to the position, but that is far from certain. He writes a pamphlet called The Church of Sweden's Body and Soul. *It starts with a description of an ordination in the Uppsala Cathedral. The archbishop wears a golden cope, a miter, and carries a crozier from the twelfth century. Söderblom lives into the role.*

* * *

Ever since he had written his well-known article on the religion of revelation in 1903, Söderblom had consistently devoted himself to developing a Christian interpretation of the history of religion. In Germany, the study of *Religionswissenschaft* had been pursued for many decades, but in certain states where there was a widespread mistrust of the use of ordinary academic methods in relation to theology, some universities had gone their own way. The dispute over the relation of the history of religion to theology was vigorous. Adolf von Harnack opposed including the topic in the theological curriculum, but he had no objection to having the history of religion placed within the philosophical faculties. The nonconfessional "history of religion school" had, in one study after another, shown that the biblical accounts were related to alien, non-Hebraic cultures and conceptions of religion. At the University of Leipzig, which had a solid and relatively conservative Lutheran faculty, instruction in the history of religion was carried on in such a way that the doctrines and confessions of the church were not called into question. The university provided good academic conditions for the study of religion. Its theological faculty was impressive with such well-known scholars as Ludwig Ihmels, the dogmatician, Albert Hauck, the church historian, and Rudolf Kittel, the Old Testament exegete. Rector Karl Lamprecht was noted for his wide-ranging studies of universal history in its different aspects and a central area of research for him was the significance of the world religions.

The bold university, where Martin Luther had debated with Johan Eck in 1519, established a chair in the general history of religion, seeking a professor who was not an academic dilettante, a relativist in respect to religion, or a critic of the church. It was not easy to locate a qualified scholar who both valued the uniqueness of Christianity and was able to distinguish between methods of research and the content of faith. In the summer of 1911, Albert Hauck participated in a conference in Uppsala where he came to know and appreciate Söderblom. As soon as he returned to Leipzig he proposed that Söderblom be named to the professorship. Söderblom's name had also been suggested for a chair in Berlin, but his Danish friend Edvard Lehman, who a few years later would move to Lund, had been awarded that position. Söderblom was not sure what to do. He had no desire to leave his chair in Uppsala. Moreover, his health was uncertain and he had recently been forced to go to Karlsbad again for treatment, and with nine children, moving was no easy prospect. A compromise was reached whereby he was given a two-year appointment in Leipzig while retaining his position in Uppsala and teaching there when the German university was on holiday. Helge, the oldest son, remained in Uppsala where he was a student in the gymnasium, and Sven was in school in Malmö. Söderblom was allowed to retain his Swedish citizenship even when he was awarded German citizenship, which was necessary for a tenured professor. In October 1912, their goods left Uppsala for Leipzig. It was a short stay there with many trips between the two cities; shortly after the war broke out in August 1914, the family returned to Uppsala.

Leipzig was a growing industrial city of 600,000 people. It was a railroad hub with train connections in all directions. The empires had not yet been broken up into national states. The entire European continent had open borders and could be experienced as a common cultural sphere. This suited the mobile Söderblom. As a lover of Luther, his cup was filled to overflowing. He visited the places where Luther had been active, he remembered Gustavus Adolphus's death at Lützen a few miles away, and he led Swedish worship in Altranstädt where Charles XII had reached an agreement that had saved hundreds of evangelical churches and schools in nearby Silesia. In Söderblom's understanding of history the relationship among memory, materiality, and identity was important. He traveled in the imaginary geography of memory to places where there were vestiges of historic events. He invested his historical prototypes with symbolic attributes when he moved about in their space and territory.

Cultural life flourished in Leipzig and above all, he made the most of the music in the St. Thomas Church where Johann Sebastian Bach had been cantor from 1723 to 1750. When the choir so perfectly sang Bach's difficult motets or when his mighty fugues were played on the great Sauer organ, Söderblom experienced it as miraculous. The gate was opened to the holiness of music. Sometimes he hiked in the hills with Staffan, his son, and some of his comrades from Uppsala and there he recalled the meadow flowers from Norrala. He was well received and was immediately a full member of the faculty even though at 46 he was the youngest of them all. He attracted some ten students to his demanding seminars. Since the history of religion was not part of the basic curriculum, not many students came to his lectures. In spite of the fact that he handled German well, he stuck conscientiously to his manuscripts with all their references to original sources. He was careful to appear neither as an apologist for nor a challenger of the Christian faith.

Academically, the time in Leipzig was a fruitful period for him. First he wrote a small foundational book, *Naturlig religion och religionshistoria: en historik och ett program (Natural Religion and the History of Religion: A History and a Program)*. Theologians had long spoken of natural religion as the philosophical counterpart to faith in revelation. The book dealt with whether or not humans could attain knowledge of God aided only by reason. Had the time come for a general history of religion to assume the place earlier held by natural theology? Söderblom's answer was affirmative. Previously, Christian theology had been familiar only with the relatively decadent and religiously short-lived cultures and religions of the Greco-Roman world, but now theology had gained knowledge in depth of living and powerful religions. This had created a different picture of humanity's reactions to the holy than could be given by natural theology.

The question must also be raised as to the attitudes different religions should take toward each other. Is there a common core of truth in their myths, rites, and doctrines? Is there a common faith that a Creator God has given the world its basic constitution? For Söderblom, religion was at root something other than a rational cosmic and moral order. One cannot force *religion* into preconceived categories. Religion's innermost and distinctive feature is an unfathomable reverence for the holy and a nonrational encounter of a totally different kind than the spokespeople for natural religion presented. However wretched, primitive, or degenerate a religion was, it bore traces of truth and divine origin. If one took seriously religion's own testimony and development, one could not fail to discern how humanity at all times has stood in the presence of a simultaneously unapproachable and inescapable divine reality. The science of religion should organize this new knowledge around revelation as the organizing concept. It would then be the task of theology to interpret God's revelation wherever it is found and study how God has worked "until now."

Gudstrons uppkomst (*The Origin of Belief in God*) came to be Söderblom's internationally best-known work in the history of religion. It was published in Swedish in 1914 and then in a German translation; it was never published in English. It was a kind of summary of his research. Many historians of religion were preoccupied with finding a common source for all religion, but for Söderblom, it was an illusion to believe that one key could unlock the entire treasure chamber of religion and mythology. The reality of religion was too complex to be arranged in a single system and explained with a simple formula. No matter how remarkable academicians thought it to be, reality had not been construed in order to serve the goals of research, he remarked ironically.

In a way that was typical for him, Söderblom described not one but three parallel forms or hypotheses for the origins of belief in God: animism, mana or power, and high gods or "creator gods." Belief in God could have arisen when the spirits of the dead and of nature were given personal character and humans were gripped by fear of the supernatural, the alien, and the unexpected. Out of conceptions of destructive or beneficent powers, the experience of holiness could have arisen to become the basic category in all religion. Instead of speaking of a highest divine being as the world's creator and preserver, Söderblom spoke of *Frambringaren* (the Producer, the one who brings forth) as the source, explanation, and ground of all things. He did not accept unambiguous, absolute explanations or theoretical constructions that did violence to the diversity and richness of reality, but held fast to the view that reverence for the holy is the innermost essence of religion. In a well-known article of 1913 in the Hastings *Encyclopedia of Religion and Ethics*, he wrote that "Holiness is the great word in religion; it is even more essential than the notion of God. Real religion may exist without a definite conception of divinity, but there is no real religion without a distinction between holy and profane."

Clouds of anxiety floated over Europe, but Söderblom lengthened his appointment in Leipzig. Two years was altogether too short a time to establish his chair, attract doctoral candidates, and insure the status of his field within the university. He intended to return to Uppsala soon, but a great deal remained to be done before he could leave with a clear conscience. While he worried about how he could fulfill his task, something occurred that would turn all his plans upside down.

One day in November 1913, a group of Swedes gathered to celebrate the memory of Charles XII in Altranstädt. Söderblom led worship in the small castle chapel, Anna sang from the chancel, and in the castle yard a bonfire was ablaze. Smoke swept around the professor who stood in the winter wind with fluttering hair as he spoke of the warrior king and his soldiers, of the German fondness for weapons, and of the communion in faith between German and Swedish Protestants. That same day, Archbishop Johan August Ekman died in Uppsala. It was known that he was ill, but death came sooner than expected. Ekman was a pious, reserved, and retiring person without church political ambitions and without experience in leadership in larger contexts. That he had been named archbishop after the overbearing Anton Niklas Sundberg in 1900 had given rise to astonishment. He himself wrote to Gottfrid Billing, "A plant that is suited for the leeward side should not be transplanted to a stormy hill." The certain candidate for archbishop had been Billing himself, but even though he at first stood for election, he had ultimately withdrawn his name.

Ekman had been regarded as a weak archbishop, although he was known for his parish visitations. In twelve years he carried out no fewer than eighty-eight such visitations. He traveled most enthusiastically to Hälsingland where the people had not seen their bishop for a quarter of a century and where he wanted to support the clergy in their struggle against the "usual Hälsingland sins." But in the General Synod and in the Parliament, he gave free reign to Gottfrid Billing who was conservative and clever, had the ear of the king, and exercised significant influence. He had acquired so much power that he saw no reason to move to Uppsala. Thirteen years later, when he was 72, he continued to be politically active and was still determined not to stand for archbishop.

Speculation about who would be Ekman's successor started immediately. Anna was home in Uppsala during the first week in December and her friends told her how the discussions were going. She wrote to Nathan: "I cannot help but think that my generous, shining Nathan with your ability to see the good and capable and great in people and their relationships, and also with your love for the church without naïve faith in her saving power *per se*, and with your contacts and all, should have the call. But I am frightened at the thought." He had also noticed that his name was mentioned. There was no doubt that he wanted to become archbishop, but he felt that he had next to no chance. Thus he sought to hold the whole matter at a distance, although his final term in Leipzig was filled with anguish and unrest blended with hopes. He stood at the height of his career as a historian of religion and his future seemed well planned. The university in Uppsala wanted him back home, Berlin tempted him with a professorship, and he had duties in Leipzig. He attempted to hide his desire to become archbishop, just as he had once hidden his desire for a professor's chair. That he would be elected archbishop was not at all self-evident. If anything, it was, as Bengt Sundkler described it, a "providential paradox" that it happened.

The election of an archbishop was a matter of national importance, much more so then than now. It meant filling one of the kingdom's highest state offices and choosing the leader for a church that included almost all citizens and continued to have considerable influence in society. This election was uncommonly dramatic since there were no obvious candidates and the result was extremely uncertain. The list of potential candidates became longer every day. There were the bishops Lövgren, Danell, Bergquist, Lönegren, and Eklund, and also the professors Herman Lundström, Adolf Kolmodin, Einar Billing, and Nathan Söderblom. When the newspaper *Upsala Nya Tidning* put the question as to who university professors wanted to see in the post, Nils Johan Göransson answered that they would most like to see a man who had not yet worn a miter. In that answer one could see an impending showdown between church and university and between clergy and laity.

The practice then was that a diocesan bishop was chosen by diocesan clergy. A slate with the names of three candidates was given to the government and the king, who most often appointed the one who had received the most votes from the clergy. But the king was not bound to that; whoever was on the slate could be named. The same procedure pertained to the election of the archbishop, but since the archbishop was to represent the entire church and not only his diocese, there were no less than fifteen voting bodies involved: clergy in the archdiocese, the twelve diocesan chapters, and the Stockholm consistory. Since the archbishop *ex officio* was also Pro Chancellor of Uppsala University, its large consistory also had the right to vote. This meant that the votes of the clergy had comparatively less weight and that laypersons in the diocesan chapters and the university leadership could influence and even determine the outcome.

It was thought that the choice rested between two bishops: Hjalmar Danell of the Diocese of Skara and J. A. Eklund of the Diocese of Karlstad. The church paper *Svensk Kyrkotidning* (*Swedish Church Times*) waged an intensive campaign for both and suggested as the third name Herman Lundström. Söderblom was rarely mentioned. When a provisional election was held, Eklund, who had a high profile in both cultural and national matters, received many votes from clergy but none from the professors. The respected Gottfrid Billing had informed the other bishops that for his part he would vote for Eklund. He also made it clear that he did not want to see Söderblom as archbishop.

It was an extremely unsettled time in Sweden. When the Liberals, with the support of the Social Democrats, took the majority in the Second Chamber in 1911, Prime Minister Karl Staaff wanted to bring about a reform of the government, break the Conservative domination in the First Chamber, and stop all personal royal prerogatives. He had promised his voters to reduce expenditures on defense and inhibit the former right government's authorization of an armored ship, a so-called F-boat. This led to a conflict both with the king and the defense-friendly public, which in turn led to several initiatives to finance the building of armored ships. One such initiative was led by Manfred Björkquist. While Söderblom was in Leipzig, the temperature of the defense debate went up, anxiety grew, and agitation increased. On February 6, 1914, a farmers' march took place in Stockholm. This was the culmination of the defense movement. The king, in a most remarkable speech, sided with the demonstrators. Staaff's government fell. Hjalmar Hammarskjöld — the father of Dag Hammarskjöld — formed a caretaker government and a new election was called with only one question in its focus: the defense of Sweden.

When the decision on a new election was taken in Parliament on March 3, it received the king's full support. Gustaf V declared that, "every wish or attempt to exert personal royal power was, is, and always will be foreign to me." Söderblom was relieved and nearly euphoric over these words. They awakened a deep affection for the king. His clear reaction contributed to the good relations with the royal house that the archbishop and his wife were to develop. Söderblom had always been both a supporter of strong defense policies and a royalist. He believed that the constitutional monarchy had now been rescued even as the conflict over defense had been moderated. On the same day that the Parliamentary decision concerning a new election became official, Söderblom gave a substantial contribution to Björkquist's appeal for an armored boat.

Söderblom did not take part in the brutal attacks against Staaff that marked the election, but the question of defense was so crucial for him that he remained in Uppsala after his spring lectures so that he himself could cast a ballot. On Palm Sunday he added his vote to the petition, "Defense First." This was probably the first time — and certainly the last — that he participated in a political election. As archbishop, he would refrain from party politics, but he did not hide his sympathies. He was a political person from head to toe. With his faith in the individual's freedom and possibilities he stood ideologically close to liberalism, but he took such a determined distance from the anti-Christian values that the old student leftists — known as "Verdandister" after the radical student association — represented in governmental circles, that it was unthinkable for him to vote Liberal. In social questions he was most sympathetic with the Social Democrats and he respected Hjalmar Branting more than all other Swedish politicians, but he remained determined to defend the best in all political streams without binding himself to any particular party. His perspective extended far beyond Sweden, and with the churches as his base, he came to play a positive role in world politics.

Since he was in Uppsala, he was well informed about the discussions surrounding the election of the archbishop, which were held on March 18, a week before the election of the Parliament's Second Chamber. He became more and more certain that his own future would be as an academic rather than as a church leader. When the balloting took place, he cast his three votes as a member of the Diocesan Chapter. He voted for his old friend Sam Fries first, Einar Billing second, and — perhaps because it was not at all risky — Adolf Kolmodin third. He reported everything to Anna even as he attempted to appear unconcerned. As expected, Danell and Eklund received the most votes, 373 and 271 respectively. Only a few weeks had passed since the farmers' march took place and the heated political opposition between the conservative farmers, who had the king and the church on their side, and the Liberals and Social Democrats on the other side had not subsided. It was not surprising that Danell and Eklund, who were both outspokenly conservative, led the slate. But the third place on the list completely unexpectedly fell to Söderblom, although with only 106 votes. There were not many who believed that he would be one of the final three, but the professors at Uppsala had placed him first — which surely pleased him — as did the Diocesan Chapter in Lund, which was far from the events in Stockholm and also included modern theologians. Three other Diocesan Chapters had him in third place. In Västerås there was a three-way tie: Nils Lövgren, Einar Billing, and Nathan Söderblom each received three votes. The decision had to be made by drawing lots. A young gymnasium lector drew the lot and it fell to Söderblom. That one vote decided everything. If a different lot had been drawn, Söderblom would not have been on the final slate of three candidates and would never have become archbishop.

In a letter, Nathan reported to Anna how on the day of the election he had spent two hours wandering over the green frozen moss in an Uppsala forest. He sat on a tree stump and began to write *Svenska kyrkans kropp och själ (The Church of Sweden's Body and Soul)*. The Introduction included a detailed description of a Service of Ordination and how the bishop and the ordinand were vested. He clearly imagined himself in the role of the bishop. Anna, who was still in Leipzig, also gave vent to her feelings: "The night between the eighteenth and nineteenth I could not sleep. My thoughts of fear, joy, and wonderment were with you. You have made me — not just now but always — as proud and happy for you as a woman has ever been or ever will be. Should I not be pleased at the archbishop's election? The finest institution in the world has shown my beloved a great and high trust. . . . There came over me such a certainty that you would be named that I right away began to think of the one duty and activity after another that you and I would have." She deeply wanted him to become archbishop. Perhaps that had to do with the fact that the family had not found itself equally at home in Leipzig as he had. Anna was expecting another child, felt herself a stranger in Leipzig, and longed for home. Being named archbishop would offer Söderblom the possibility of breaking his agreement with the university while keeping his honor intact. He also dreamed: "Think about sitting in the most beautiful location in Sweden with the cathedral, Holy Trinity Church, Gustavianum, the University, the Vasa Castle, Odinslund, and the fields of Uppland in view. The sixtieth Archbishop of the Kingdom of Sweden. To speak with that authority words of peace and love." But he scarcely dared to believe that it would turn out like that. He was resigned, and so was Anna. In sorrow, he cited a letter to the editor of *Stockholms Dagblad* by Emil Liedgren: "Perhaps it will not happen again for a long time that the highest position in the Church of Sweden might be awarded to a spiritual leader with such deeply secured authority among younger clergy and churchly committed laity throughout the whole kingdom." Nathan thought aloud in a letter to Anna: "I am *episcopus in partibus* [titular bishop], not in power, praise, and glory. That calling I will with God's help fulfill. I will surely come, as will you, clearly to see and know how good this outcome is for me."

The king was free to name any one of the three candidates on the slate. Most people in the church felt that it would be both out of place and unwelcome to name Söderblom. The bishops had not voted for him. He did not receive one vote in the Uppsala Diocesan Chapter and the clergy of the archdiocese initially positioned him in fifth place. The campaign had been hair-raising, but the result was such that everyone who did not want Söderblom named could again breathe easily. It was becoming clear that even Söderblom was beginning to do that. A week after the election, he wrote to Tor Andrae that he was satisfied with the outcome. In spite of the obstacles, he had made it to the final slate of candidates and was thankful for the love that the church had demonstrated for him in the election. Now he was relieved of the heavy burdens that the archbishop's office would involve. For his part, he said, he preferred that Eklund and not Danell be named, but pointed out in the same breath and with a tone of disappointment that

Uppsala, along with Canterbury, was the most distinguished archbishop's seat in evangelical Christianity.

The farmers' march and the debate over defense had caused Karl Staaff's Liberal government to fall. On a wave of national and religious enthusiasm Hjalmar Hammarskjöld had formed a Conservative government supportive of the king. The country was deeply divided and the first task of the new leaders was to cool down the tensions. The Minister of Ecclesiastical Affairs, K. G. Westman, who was to handle the question of the archbishop, belonged to the circle around the historian Harald Hjärne and exerted every effort to have Söderblom named. Hjärne supported him in this. In the polarized situation of the time, it appeared urgent to name Söderblom who was positive toward defense and sympathetic toward the workers' movement. The Church of Sweden, with J. A. Eklund's blessing and Manfred Björkquist in the lead, seemed to be a "class church" while Söderblom had taken a more balanced view. King Gustaf V, who had to get himself out of the crisis to which he had contributed, had an understanding of Westman's proposal, but the matter was sensitive and it was necessary to proceed carefully. Westman accordingly asked Gottfrid Billing for advice. He responded at length and with candor. The gifted and charming Söderblom, according to Billing, would be the best of the candidates in respect to international contacts and in relation to Swedes who were alienated from the church. But with such weak support in the archdiocese and probably having received no votes at all from the bishops, he could not really be considered. To name him would be an offense to church people. Even though he showed great love for the church, no one really knew where he stood on theological and religious matters. He gave the impression of harboring divergent positions and could split the church. Billing thus recommended that Eklund be named archbishop.

The government gathered on May 20 behind closed doors to discuss the matter. At least three members of the cabinet spoke warmly for Söderblom, among them Knut A. Wallenberg, the Foreign Minister who had gotten to know Söderblom when the Church of Revelation was erected in Saltsjöbaden. The prime minister was hesitant, but the king was in agreement. Before evening, the government announced that the forty-eight-year-old professor in Leipzig was named Archbishop of Uppsala. When Söderblom received a telegram that he had been elected, he gathered his family in the apartment on Leipzig's Stallbaumstrasse for the singing of a hymn, but there was a fly in the ointment, most especially the distrust of the clergy in the archdiocese. That same day, his oldest son Helge graduated from the gymnasium; only Brita was there from the family.

The news spread quickly around Europe and words of congratulation streamed in. From Rome came a telegram: "*Gratiam vestram etiam — si heterodoxam gratia nostra salutat.* Pius." ("Our Grace greets Your Grace — even if your grace is heterodox. Pius X.") There was something suspicious about this papal greeting to a heretic. Henrik Schück, the Uppsala literary scholar, happened to be in the Eternal City at the time and it was he who pulled off this joke. Gottfrid Billing, who was regularly well informed about the government's doings, was completely taken by surprise. Others expressed considerable dismay. *Svensk kyrkotidning*, the clergy paper, criticized in bitter words the inexperienced government that did not take into account the church's clear will: "The naming of the third-ranked candidate demonstrates a ruthlessness toward the church . . . a bitter lack of respect which shocks the country's clergy and church people, that and nothing other. . . . Is such lack of respect justified? Certainly not."

Söderblom had no time to lose. Within a few weeks he had sent out his first circular letter to the archdiocese with the program for his consecration. At the same time he prepared to move home, back to Uppsala. On June 28, Archduke Franz Ferdinand was murdered in Sarajevo. A week later, Anna gave birth to their twelfth child who at his baptism was named after their old friends, Gustaf Göran Samuel Karl, but who came to be known as "Putte." There were complications with the birth and it took time for Anna to recover after the delivery. Nathan himself baptized the boy in their half-empty Leipzig apartment with only the family and nearest colleagues present. The general atmosphere was tense, nearly apocalyptic. On July 29, Austria invaded Serbia. Two days later, Söderblom delivered his farewell lecture in Leipzig; it dealt with Buddhism and Christianity. He took his leave from his students. Many of them would soon die in the trenches. One of them was Söderblom's amanuensis or *famulus* as he was called. He had brought the professor to his lectures, carried his books, and often eaten with the family.

In many ways the time in Germany had been good, although the final weeks were difficult. Söderblom marveled at the Germans for their willingness to sacrifice themselves for their native land and for what they regarded a just cause, but he felt that everything he himself regarded so highly would be trampled in blood, especially when England also declared war on Germany. Events developed quickly and every day seemed filled with drama. The "black week" was filled with mutual declarations of war. In despair, he wrote to the Archbishop of Canterbury that Germany and England together could save the peace in Europe. Davidson chose to wait and see. He perhaps shared the view that Germany would take over all of Europe if the British did not retaliate. Great Britain's role as a world power was under threat. But the war was driven by its own logic and humans had no power to control it.

Postal connections to Sweden were broken. It was necessary for Söderblom to leave before the Baltic Sea was blockaded. On August 8, he and his large family left Leipzig. They were fortunate to get places on a military train filled with intoxicated soldiers on their way to the front. The trip was long and extremely difficult. In Berlin, Söderblom was able to lead the Swedish congregation in worship before they traveled on to Sassnitz and Trelleborg on a ferry carrying many Russians and Balts who were trying to get home via Sweden and Finland. Finally, the family reached Uppsala. Anna was immediately taken to the hospital.

16

Archbishop of Sweden

> From beginning to end Christianity intends joy even if the journey has to go through distress.
>
> *Nathan Söderblom, 1914*

A FEW DAYS BEFORE HIS CONSECRATION, Söderblom receives a visit from a journalist. He wants to know the man who is about to step into the chain of Uppsala's ancient sacrificial priests and, later, church sovereigns. He finds a little man with a short-clipped mustache standing in the midst of boxes of books and mixed up furniture, the worst confusion he has ever seen. A little man with a broad, light forehead, blond hair, and the bluest eyes, a man of the world's purest Nordic blood, a little man in a black jacket with book dust on his collar, who will become the heir to all that has been Swedish culture through the centuries. The journalist writes: The spectacle is about to begin.

* * *

On the Western Front between Dixmande, Ypres, and La Bassee-Arras, the war raged on with undiminished strength. The Allies held the Germans in check. In the forests of Argonne, French troops were advancing and on the North Sea, the English fleet blockaded the German ships. Austria had invaded Serbia. In Rome, Benedict XV, who was more concerned with social matters, had just succeeded Pius X. In Sweden, there had been an election for the Second Chamber after vigorous debate over the question of defense. The right won a landslide victory and Hammarskjöld's government received continued confidence. It was a hard and fateful autumn, but in Uppsala things were festive.

On Sunday morning, November 8, 1914, while the city was still covered with haze and flags drooped, the streets were filled with well-dressed people. Many wanted to be sure of a place in the cathedral, others wanted to see the king and the crown prince pair, Prince Carl and Prince Eugen, arrive on the train from Stockholm. The royal cortege of stuttering autos puffed up Carolina Hill. In the university's main building, the Rector Magnificus and professors together received Hjalmar Hammarskjöld and his cabinet. The king made his way up the stairs. The university's male chorus sang and its director led them in hailing the "mighty, all gracious king," who nine months earlier, with the support of farmers and students, had brought about the fall of Karl Staaff's Liberal government. The cathedral bells sounded above the singers and everyone moved toward the cathedral. In the chancel, the German representatives in black robes and Danish and Norwegian bishops in ruffles jostled for places. The service was more than ordinarily festive. Two priests in magnificent chasubles led the liturgy at the altar before the Cathedral Dean Herman Lundström, vested in a black silk robe, ascended the pulpit and proclaimed the demand of genuine love to gather, convict, and give life.

When the parish announcements of marriages and an uncommonly large number of thanksgivings for the lives of those who had died had been read, the prayers of the church prayed, a hymn sung, and Hugo Alfvén's festive cantata sung from the balcony far in the back of the church, there was a short pause before the procession for the consecration was prepared to move down the chancel. The seventy-three-year-old Bishop of Lund, Gottfrid Billing, wearing a miter and with a crozier in his hand went first. His red and gold cope, characteristic of his province of Skåne, fluttered in the breeze. After him came the two oldest bishops, Knut Henning Gezelius von Schéele of Visby, who was seventy-six, and Edvard H. Rodhe from Gothenburg, who was sixty-nine. They were followed by Nathan Söderblom himself in a newly sewn white alb, adorned in lace with symbols made in Dalecarlia. He was pale and composed, short in stature, and in comparison with the others very young, only forty-eight years old. After him came the leaders of the Archdiocesan Chapter who were all ordained professors; then came six district deans and guests from Norway, Denmark, Germany, and the United States. Finally, six Swedish bishops came, all wearing chasubles. Only the three at the altar wore copes and miters and carried croziers. The disappointed J. A. Eklund from Karlstad and the aged Uddo Lechard Ullman from Strängnäs had chosen to stay at home. They were grey-haired men who had gathered to install the man whom none of them had voted to be archbishop. The word they used was "install."

Under Anglican influence, the language was later changed to "ordain" or "consecrate" a bishop.

Gottfrid Billing would certainly have preferred to install someone other than Söderblom. But now he was chosen and had been named and it would have been alien to Billing to question the government's and the king's decision. He gave a long speech that aroused attention. Actually, he had given the same talk at the installation of a rector for a parish in the Diocese of Lund. His starting point was the account in John's Gospel of Jesus's encounter with Nathanael, "an Israelite in whom there is no guile." But Billing made a mistake: Söderblom's actual given name was Jonathan not Nathanael. The old bishop called attention to the fact that the Master knew his disciples inside and out and discerned that which lay deepest in their personalities. Talent, brilliance, acuteness of thought, strong will, and the power of decisive action could be important attributes in the service of the Kingdom of God, but self-examination and seriousness were more crucial. The homily came to be regarded as prophetic. Its emphasis on the meaning of personality was in line with Söderblom's own thinking.

The letter of appointment was read, Bible verses were recited, and Söderblom in a high and resounding voice confessed the creed, answered the installation questions, and made his vows. Then he fell to his knees while Billing together with two other Swedish bishops, two deans, and the representative of the Augustana Synod from America, Lars Gustaf Abrahamson, shared the laying-on-of-hands and prayed the Our Father, thus "delivering up" the office of bishop to Söderblom. A gold pectoral cross was hung around his neck and he was vested in the magnificent golden cope, which Gustav III had once given to the archbishop. When he received the crozier, which according to him went back to the time of the first archbishop Stefan, he was moved to tears.

That Söderblom requested Abrahamson to participate in the laying-on-of-hands was a link in his efforts to deepen relations with the Augustana Synod, which he had initiated in 1909. The answer was not long in coming. In a written greeting, the Swedish descendents in America thanked the new archbishop: "Never before has our dear and beloved mother church expressed so powerfully to us its solidarity, so spontaneously its recognition, so freely and unrestrainedly its love. Doctor and Archbishop! You have captured the Augustana Synod. You have turned the children's heart to the fathers."

The service could have ended badly. When the procession was returning to the sacristy, old von Schéele stumbled on the choir steps and fell, but fortunately he did not hurt himself. After nearly three hours in church, the royal family and other distinguished guests gathered for lunch in the archbishop's residence with Professor Schück as host. In his talk, Söderblom is reported to have said, "We have today seen that Bishop Billing is a man who is able to wear the most splendid vestments in a way that one does not notice because of the beauty of the person who bears them." He noted also that the Archbishop of Lund in the twelfth century had wanted to retain his sovereignty over Uppsala. He himself would always listen to the Bishop of Lund. Billing answered: "If this young lad from Hälsingland who travels the skies will stick with this old fellow from Lund who holds back, I believe we will see things turn out well." The Uppsala student choirs, Orphei Drängar and Allmänna sången, celebrated the new archbishop who himself had been chairperson of the Student Union, a student singer, professor, and now also the University Pro-Chancellor. He was the true Uppsalian, as much the university's man as the church's man. That evening he returned to the cathedral for his first episcopal act. As part of a service of prayer for peace, he commissioned Pastor Paul Sandegren to be a missionary to South India. In the midst of flaming war, this was a reminder that the responsibilities of the Church of Sweden stretched far beyond the nation's borders. Before the parties at the student nations were over and the international guests could retire, it had become very late. Residents of Uppsala were talking with pride about a historic day.

The whole day had been directed from beginning to end by Nathan Söderblom himself. Ever since he had learned that he had been elected archbishop, he had devoted himself to planning everything, down to the last detail. The consecration was the first of its kind in a very long time; nearly all archbishops before him had already been consecrated bishops. Söderblom wanted to highlight three perspectives: the church's continuity, its universality, and its vocation in the present time.

He had begun by contacting the grand old man of the Bishops' Council, Gottfrid Billing, asking him to preside at the service. Twenty-one years earlier, in simple circumstances, Billing had ordained Söderblom to the priesthood in the Ersta Chapel. Now Söderblom asked that he install him as archbishop and to do so on November 8. That was Söderblom's father's birthday; if he had lived, he would have been ninety-one that day. But there were also other reasons for selecting that particular day. The installation

Uppsala students cheer Söderblom, 1914. As archbishop he was also pro-chancellor of the university.

would be framed by the observance of the death of Gustavus Adolphus at the battle of Lützen on November 6, 1632, and the birth of Martin Luther on November 10, 1483. For Söderblom, these were indispensable saints days; no other individuals in history had meant more for the freedom of the gospel and for him personally.

In order to mark the church's continuity, another person must be part of the picture: the first Archbishop of Uppsala, Stefan, a monk from Alvastra. Seven hundred fifty years had passed since he was consecrated in Sens in France by Archbishop Eskil of Lund. The year was 1164 and Pope Alexander III was present. This was the birth of the Kingdom of Sweden, for without an archbishop, no king could be crowned. No one could himself assume the power of king; that was power given only by God through the servants of the church. Söderblom may not have thought exactly that way, but he was convinced that it was good for the country if the legitimate power of the state and the church worked closely together, especially if the people were divided.

On the way from London to Leipzig on April 28, 1914, Söderblom had stopped in Sens, which was a few hours' train ride southeast of Paris, in order to see with his own eyes the cathedral where Stefan had been made archbishop. It was still improbable that Söderblom would be named archbishop, but he nevertheless took this detour to Sens and managed in one day to learn the cathedral's rich history and see its treasures. He especially noticed a relic case with enamel work from Limoges, which had a counterpart in his childhood church in Trönö. Both had pictures of martyr bishops — the case in Trönö of Thomas of Canterbury, the case in Sens of the Bishop of Paris Saint Denis who was beheaded at the end of the third century. Söderblom was not content with just a visit. He subsequently made a thorough academic study of the liturgy that was used at Stefan's consecration. He translated its prayers from Latin and discussed every detail in the formation of the rite. He paid special attention to the crozier that — even though restored many times — after 750 years was carried by the Swedish archbishops. At the consecration in Uppsala, a pamphlet was distributed describing Stefan and his consecration.

It was no coincidence that Söderblom paid such attention to Stefan. Nothing symbolized the continuity of the church from the time of the apostles in the same way as the office of the bishop. Söderblom's meeting with the Church of England had strengthened his faith in the meaning of that succession. Now he would himself perhaps be placed in the chain of bishops, and that would occur in Uppsala, which he regarded after Constantinople, Rome, and Canterbury as Christianity's foremost archbishopric. Anna had already in a clear dream seen him as archbishop, and for his own part, he could not deny how eagerly he wanted that to be the case. In spite of the fact that the odds were against him, he prepared himself for the possibility. He absolutely did not want to see Hjalmar Danell in the position, nor did he want to see the nationalistic grouch Eklund there. As usual, his Anna had it right: for the sake of the church he himself would be the best.

He was a historian of religion. The concrete manifestation of religion in Sweden was above all the Swedish state church with its historic attire and popular piety. Besides Christians and a handful of Jews, no other religious believers were to be found in the country. After years of having applied himself to the historical and global phenomena of other religions, he would now direct his undivided attention to the archdiocese, the Church of Sweden, the Reformation communion, and ultimately the whole of Christianity — in that order. He would unite his thorough understanding of history with the day's actual, current questions even as he would have the inner unity of the universal church in sight.

Before the Service of Consecration he sent letters of invitation in Latin to the primary church leaders in the Nordic countries, Great Britain, France, and Germany. He hoped that Anglican bishops would take part in the laying-on-of-hands. Archbishop Davidson, however, sent no bishops but instead asked Canons Mason of Canterbury and Bernhard of Salisbury to go to Uppsala; however, they were prevented from attending by the war. Nor could two invited French Lutherans come. Seven Germans, among them two of his colleagues from Leipzig, were invited. Three came, two from Saxony and one from Schleswig-Holstein. The Augustana Synod in the United States sent a representative. Just as during the discussions with the Church of England five years earlier, Söderblom paid special attention to the Swedish Americans. Those who belonged to the Augustana Synod were of Swedish language and blood and shared the same history. Thus, their representative was also to participate in the prayers of consecration and the laying-on-of-hands. It was noted that Söderblom invited church leaders who had taken office without the participation of any bishop. That pleased those who wanted to preserve for American church life the inherited tradition of the Swedish-American Lutheran spirit and order. Söderblom refrained from inviting anyone from the American Episcopal Church.

The guests from other countries participated in several memorable days, which in different ways conveyed the profile that Söderblom wanted to create for his ministry. He had hoped that the consecration would be a greater ecumenical event than it came to be, but nevertheless, the participation of church leaders from other countries was something totally new. The gold pectoral cross that the Archbishop of Canterbury sent to him was a visible sign of the Church of England's clear interest in communion with the Church of Sweden and with Söderblom personally.

The festivities actually began on Friday, November 6. Then it was that the Gustaf Adolf Society was established in Uppsala and three addresses concerning the hero king were delivered. On Saturday, a floral tribute was laid on Archbishop Ekman's grave in the cemetery and a portrait of him was unveiled. Later, the archdiocesan Bible Society gathered for an exegetical lecture on the social and political message of the Old Testament prophets. At evening prayer in the cathedral, Dr. Abrahamson from the Augustana

Synod preached both long and well before it was time for a concert of motets in Trinity Church led by Söderblom's old friend, the celebrated director of music for the university, Hugo Alfvén. The consecration of the Archbishop took place on Sunday and on Monday the Swedish bishops gathered for their first meeting under Söderblom's leadership. Even J. A. Eklund was there, although somewhat grudgingly. The agenda was lengthy: the new Swedish translation of the Bible, the use of Luther's *Small Catechism* in the public schools, the revision of the *Church Handbook* that contained the authorized liturgical orders, preparations for the Reformation Jubilee in 1917, pastoral care in the military, and a proposal from florists for a special day of remembrance for the dead. That evening, the medieval historian Knut B. Westman lectured on the origins and early development of the archdiocese. On Tuesday, it was Martin Luther's birthday and the Diocesan Chapter gathered to receive Söderblom's episcopal letter.

He had written that letter in brief periods of time in a dilapidated garden house that Justice Gustaf Ribbing had loaned him. In those days, all bishops wrote an episcopal letter as both a theological introduction to themselves and a statement of their intended program. These writings were often circulated widely, reviewed in the press, and read far beyond the circle of clergy. Söderblom's episcopal letter of eighty pages awakened great interest and parts of it were translated into other languages. His starting point was his father's injunction to him at the time of his death: "Not as lords over the congregation, but as helpers of your joy." *Joy* was the calling of the church and he wrote about that which interferes with joy: the accusations of a guilty conscience, natural anxiety and dread, the needs of the world, and the plight of workers. With the same social passion and the same ethical principles that marked some of his earlier writings, he asserted that it was not possible for the church to observe with equanimity how unbearably the present social and economic situation oppressed certain groups and classes in Swedish society.

Even though the church could not identify itself with particular economic theories, it lay in the nature of the case that its sympathy must be with the oppressed and with those political lines that took their situation as its own. Even as he emphasized that the church must stand free of all party politics, he expressed warm support for the workers' movement and a certain criticism of the Social Democrats. Democracy reflected the gospel only to the degree that it strengthened the value and responsibility of the individual. Because of his faith in the importance of individual personalities, Söderblom had some difficulty in accepting the view that society could be governed on the basis of the changing opinions of an uneducated majority. An occasional conglomeration of wills or individuals who united around this or that question was a caricature of democracy. He kept in mind the farmers' march and the workers' demonstrations that followed and allied himself wholeheartedly with Hammarskjöld's popularly elected government. In this episcopal letter he also dealt briefly with church doctrine, the life of prayer, music, and proclamation; he also discussed Christian education and the schools. But he wrote nothing concerning baptism and the eucharist.

When he wrote about the war, the text warmed up and took on a journalistic character. Within the episcopal letter were twenty-five pages of concrete reports from the first months of the war. The text burned with despair and an eagerness to act. The war had brought greater sorrow than anyone in his or her worst nightmare could have imagined and it threatened the joy of the Christian communion. Christianity, like other movements, had shown itself unable to protect peace. Preachers on the continent thundered against each other like canons and asserted the innocence of their own nations. Söderblom had experienced the war's outbreak in a mountain village in Bohemia and the tramp of military boots on cobbled streets continued to echo in his ears. In Leipzig, he had followed the German mobilization and was shaken by the British declaration of war. The two Protestant powers who could have preserved peace in the world stood instead on the verge of destroying each other. Chauvinism clothed itself in Christian garb and everyone believed they fought on God's side. Foreign missions, which were the churches' great work, suffered especially. But the war also brought greater crowds of people into the churches. Religion took on a new inwardness. Mercy and compassion revealed the presence of God. If Sweden were to be fortunate enough to be preserved from devastation, it would be the country's responsibility, together with other neutral states, to restore peace even if it would take decades.

Söderblom regarded nationalism as a force for both good and evil. It must be purified and deepened so that every people would come to realize their God-given calling. The same point of view had been expressed in the pre-war Young Church Movement. Even then, however, Söderblom had warned that nationalism could easily be distorted into self-righteousness.

Individual countries must fit their own interests into an international context where justice, not power or violence, was the guiding principle. "For religion no other standpoint is tenable than unconditionally and under all circumstances to assert the order of justice even in coexistence between the nations," he wrote. Thus he anticipated both the League of Nations and the intensive discussions concerning the universality of "justice given in creation" that Gustaf Aulén and others were to carry on during the 1930s. In other connections he had supported the idea of "a United States of Europe." The nations should come together, even while preserving their autonomy, in order to jointly protect the orders of justice and thus to prevent mutual destruction. Söderblom was not a pacifist and although he held that a strong defense was necessary to preserve the freedom and independence of Sweden, his program of peace dealt not with armaments but with an international order of justice.

He had returned to his diocese and home district and he gave his episcopal letter a very personal tone by reflecting on the Hälsingland of his childhood and memories of his father. The letter's description of his father's passionate restlessness, his blending of weakness and strength, his credulity, suspicion, and peculiarities, his struggle of faith and his steadfastness in service to the gospel, his biblical knowledge and serious care for souls, and his will's ascetic strictness — all of this was not only a presentation of his own background but a summons to the priests of the archdiocese. His father remained Söderblom's superego even as archbishop, constantly present. "If, as I believe," he wrote, "the departed have any sense of communion with the living, his glowing soul must now feel great unease. How shall it go! But yet he must feel joy that my calling is now attached more closely to the congregations which he loved and served to the best of his ability. Unrest and joy must for him lead to the certainty that all is possible through the mercy of God and that it is life's highest privilege to proclaim the message of joy." That Nathan Söderblom so consciously set his archbishop's consecration on his father's birthday was not simply a matter of piety; it signified both succession in service and that his father's strong will had finally conquered the son's reluctance.

17

Will and Sincerity

> In the soul's solitude with Jesus Christ and our God, something decisive occurs. Power is given. Then the battles in moral and cultural life are waged with positive results, with conquests for the Kingdom of God.
>
> *Nathan Söderblom, 1903*

In the evening, when from up near the castle Queen Gunilla's memorial bell from 1558 tolls 150 times to remind the people of the city that it is time to move on home for the night's rest, Nathan opens a window in the archbishop's residence to let in the sound of the castle bell. The family gathers for evening prayer: song, Bible readings, prayers introduced by the Sursum Corda — Habemus ad Dominum, benediction, and an evening hymn. The children form a choir with which he gladly practices in the evening. Guests are astonished and keep it all in their memories. Nathan has practiced such daily prayer since the rectory in Trönö in the 1860s.

* * *

Not many had thought that Nathan Söderblom would one day be archbishop. Now he stood, as he had dreamed he would, in the spacious library on the third floor of the archbishop's residence and looked out a window toward the cathedral. Beyond the train tracks and Old Uppsala, the flat countryside stretched out. He could see all the way to the twelfth-century Vaksala Church. His parents were both dead. His brother Svante was a military musician in California and Johan was an agricultural consultant in Västerbotten. His sister Elsa was a nurse and farmer's wife in Dalecarlia, while Hanna had remained in Uppsala after their mother's death. Only Nathan had followed in his father's footsteps and become a priest. He had now gone as far as anyone could on his priestly journey. Of his own ten children, the oldest was eighteen and a student; the youngest was only four months old. It was a large family, which with servants moved into the archbishop's home, perhaps the largest family since the house was erected in the early 1740s. Compared to Stabby it had many rooms, but each one was needed. The residence was like a little palace with no distinctions between private and official rooms. The archbishop always worked from home, his secretary living in the attic. In its position between the cathedral, the castle, and the university, the house symbolized the church's old connections with power and education. Söderblom was careful to preserve relations with the university, but he never sought political power, in contrast to many of his predecessors.

He had thought a great deal about what a bishop was and ought to be. His view concerning the office of the bishop was Lutheran, but with a special accent. In principle, he made no distinction between being a priest and being a bishop. At the same time, he regarded the office of the bishop as constitutional in an ideal sense and a necessity in a functional sense. In its external and formal aspects, the bishop was a governmental authority, but for him it was not essential to be a civil servant. The decisive aspect was that a bishop represented the church's continuity in confession and life stretching back to apostolic times. In his episcopal letter he had not mentioned apostolic succession, but the unbroken line of ordination was meaningful for him, not as a mechanical passing on of authority but as a living mediation of tradition. When he moved in circles where the question of apostolic succession was sensitive, he did not use the concept but rather pointed out that the service of being a shepherd and supervisor of the community had always existed and that through the centuries one bishop had followed another. The episcopal office was also a symbol and guarantee of the unity of the church. It was the task of every bishop to actively promote unity in the diocese, the country, and internationally. Söderblom was not significantly interested in the church's organization. Rather, he developed personal networks that, at least in the short term, gave him greater influence than more formal processes and in practice broadened his service to include much more than the archdiocese and the Church of Sweden.

In Sweden, the office of the bishop was maintained through the Reformation. It was not like that in other Lutheran churches. No other Lutheran church, except for Finland, appointed archbishops. In *Svenska kyrkans kropp och själ* (*The Church of Sweden's Body and Soul*), which Söderblom actually wrote for English-speaking readers, he described how this had come about. The first Lutheran bishop, Magnus Sommar in Strängnäs, together with two others had been consecrated as bishop by Petrus Magni who was himself consecrated in Rome. Later, in 1531, Sommar and Magni consecrated Laurentius Petri as Archbishop of Uppsala. Thus, apostolic succession was preserved even as, at the same time, a Swedish episcopate that was independent of Rome was introduced. The consecrations, to be sure, were not regarded as canonical by Rome, but without doubt they were valid. Söderblom was certain that succession had been saved despite the upheavals of the Reformation. He wrote: "As far back as there has been continuity, it has for our church been unbroken. Every possibility of doubting the continuity of the ritual for the consecration of bishops is for us excluded." This matter was particularly important in conversations with the Church of England. For high church Anglicans, the laying-on-of-hands with prayer to the Holy Spirit, from generation to generation, was a condition for church fellowship. While Söderblom was in agreement that succession in consecration is a great gift to the church, he did not regard it as a condition for church fellowship. According to *Confessio Augustana*, the Augsburg Confession of 1530, the office of the bishop belonged to an external order, which could be held or not held. History had shown that it was a good thing. Even if the succession of bishops was not unconditionally necessary, the office of the bishop definitely belonged to the *bene esse*, the well-being, of the church.

But what actually distinguished an archbishop from other bishops? He was not superior to them, nor did he have anything to say about matters in their dioceses. In Söderblom's time there was more emphasis on the independence of each diocese than there is now. The dioceses of the Church of Sweden were, practically speaking, twelve "local churches," which were held together by their bond with the state; by legal determinations concerning doctrine, worship, and organization; and by the General Synod, which used to meet only once every six years. The archbishop was the first among equals — *primus inter pares* — and internally and externally represented the church in all of its diversity. He represented the whole church when ordaining bishops, moderating the meetings of the General Synod, or officiating at royal baptisms, weddings, and funerals. "Foreign mission" and "Mission to Seamen" were, since 1874, the province of the Church of Sweden Mission Board. Voluntary work in the parishes, which had begun to flourish at the beginning of the twentieth century, was coordinated by the

Board of Diakonia. The archbishop was *ex officio* chairperson of both. Since the Middle Ages, the parishes, which he supervised, had been managed by democratically elected parish councils. The clergy were accountable to the diocesan chapter, but there was no diocesan administration in any current sense. Bishops were named by the government. Parliament had the last word in matters dealt with at the General Synod. There were jokes about the church being "the royal department of salvation" and there was a grain of truth in that expression. In spite of the old tradition of parishes maintaining their own affairs, parish life was strictly regulated by church law, led from above by the clergy, and supervised by the bishop. In reality, there was little democracy. This explained some of the growth of free churches since they offered members more possibilities for responsible participation. A uniform society, however, belonged to the past; the entire twentieth century would be a transitional time, during which Christianity's role and ecclesiastical organization in society was renegotiated. The old state church system was already a bit shaky when Söderblom took office as archbishop.

In most parishes, congregational life trotted along as it had for centuries. The Church of Sweden was an old-fashioned, tradition-bound institution, handling civil registration, gathering for worship according to the law, teaching the catechism, and supervising school education. Clergy cared for their small pastorates from the rectories, which were often centers of culture for the area. In parsonage gardens peonies and foxgloves bloomed. Pictures and memories of these peaceful homes were etched into people's consciousness. But in spite of its uniformity of structure and worship, the church had room for considerable diversity and there was often tension. There were many shades of revivalism: ecstatic Laestadianism, conservative Schartaunism, Lutheran confessionalism, and warm evangelicalism prospered within the established church and the free churches were at their peak. When the nineteenth-century revival movements cooled off, the spiritual temperature of the land was raised anew by the Pentecostal movement, which was imported directly from America. But with secularization, industrialization, and urbanization, religious indifference spread. When Söderblom returned to Sweden as a professor in 1901, he landed in the midst of the tense transition from traditional to modern theology. When he became archbishop thirteen years later, the rapidly changing society had overtaken the church. He knew this all too well, but he had little ability to do anything about it.

Söderblom adjusted to the prevailing conditions, but he did not let himself relax. His inclination to support change aroused anxiety among those who wanted the church to remain as it was. Criticism toward him was not long in coming. Even before he took office, he was counted out by *Svensk kyrkotidning* (*Swedish Church Times*) and rejected in *Göteborgs Stifts-Tidning* (*Gothenburg Diocese Times*). He was opposed in the church: the priests were guarded and the bishops were anxious. But the large daily newspapers and the cultural elite held him to be the right man at the right time. The professors at Uppsala and people like Harald Bildt and Knut A. Wallenberg with good reason supported him for his open and forward-looking attitude. Sweden needed a church leader like Söderblom if the oppositions between the state church and the free churches, between Christianity and the labor movement, and between theology and natural science were to be solved. Yet it was to be a long time before the people in the churches took him to heart.

There was no job description for the work of the archbishop, but there were a great many regular obligations. He should lead the diocesan chapter, ordain clergy, and exercise supervision over the parishes, just like the other bishops. As archbishop, he was also to chair the church synod and the commissions of the church, to consecrate other bishops, and to be Pro-Chancellor of Uppsala University. International organizations that were to demand his attention had not yet been formed, and there was no actual church administration. The archbishop himself, on the basis of his own qualifications and priorities, was allowed to determine how to carry out the work his position required. His predecessors had willingly assumed the role of powerful officeholders and on occasion had taken on sharp political profiles. They had moved in the ruling circles and served as national masters of ceremonies. Some had been leading cultural figures of their times, preoccupied with academies and the system of secret orders. Only in exceptional cases had an archbishop stood out as a renewer or spiritual leader of note. Some had concentrated on the archdiocese alone; others had primarily devoted themselves to concerns of the state, the royal house, or matters of public religion. The position became what the incumbents made of it.

Personality meant more than rules and regulations. Never had this been more the case than when Söderblom took office. With no mandate from the church, he selected his own arenas: peace work and ecumenism, cultural life, research, and the media. He became, as it were, a self-employed person who skillfully and unrestrainedly used his position in society and his office as archbishop to reach the goals he himself had established. For his international concerns he received almost no spiritual or moral support from the church and only rarely did he receive financial contributions from the state. An "ecumenical revival" grew around him, but this was maintained largely by interested financiers and self-appointed ecumenists. He had difficulty finding a home in the church for his movement for peace and social justice, and the bishops almost never backed him up. Thanks to women and men who were outside the church's decision-making process but who sponsored him, he could realize his visions. His warm liberality mobilized the financial, intellectual, and artistic elites to support him and he was well received in the royal house, but he never really gained the backing of the church.

Söderblom was a European with his heart in Uppsala. Prior to World War I, national boundaries were open and new railroads made it easy to travel between the cities of Europe. Few Swedes could match the archbishop in his knowledge of cultural, political, and spiritual currents on the continent and the British Isles. He mastered the major languages easily and with elegance, was formed by an extensive humanistic knowledge, and was equally at home in academic and artistic circles as he was among workers, merchants, and royalty. He aroused more admiration than some would tolerate. He was regarded as diffuse, imprecise, and complicated when he cited both Rosenius and Ritschl, Luther and Wesley, took delight in both the Salvation Army's brass music and the Quakers' silence, and nearly in the same breath expressed understanding for the rabidly radical young socialists. Many recognized Söderblom in what Torsten Fogelqvist wrote in *Dagens Nyheter*, a major Stockholm newspaper, just before his sixtieth birthday: "It is easy to point out the man's failings and it is at times necessary to react against them — a mobility which is easily seen as spinelessness, an impulsiveness which at times takes the form of whimsy, an eclecticism which in an inconsistent and scholastic manner seeks to tack together opposing things and which because of sympathy and good intentions easily rubs away necessary boundaries and distinctions, a propensity to appear on occasion as an almost ostentatious stage actor." In 1914, when he had just entered his service as archbishop, many wondered how he could keep so many balls in the air at the same time and if his many interests would distract from his attention to the ordinary daily matters of both the archdiocese and the whole Church of Sweden.

All Swedish bishops had an academic background. Those who had been professors had served in prebendary parishes and thus had some pastoral experience. Moreover, they had belonged to diocesan chapters. For Söderblom, however, to be archbishop required a considerable adjustment. In spite of the freedom to shape his own ministry, he was more restricted than he had been as a professor and his public exposure was significantly greater. He had ambitious plans, but time and time again they would be obstructed by more trivial duties that demanded his attention. His way of dealing with the tension between what he must do and what he wanted to do was to double his efforts. In 1922, he wrote to his wife: "I should with even greater conscientiousness take care of the direct and indirect responsibilities of my office and thereby pay for the international duties which have been laid on me by a higher power."

He was an odd figure among the bishops: theologically modern, politically farsighted, and socially engaged. Paradoxically, it was with steady references to history and tradition that he could exercise freedom in relation to established expectations. When he was criticized for going to extremes, he defended himself with what Martin Luther or the sixteenth-century archbishop Laurentius Petri had said or done. Some figures from the past were so alive for him that they could have been contemporaries. The church's long history from its origins was to be reflected in worship. He opposed attempts to modernize old hymns or to restore church buildings so that their original appearance was lost. He was not a traditionalist but he preserved the tradition and took theological and liturgical treasures from the closets of the past. History gave depth, context, and relevance to Christianity's contribution to the present time. It was a witness to God's continuing creation. It was by incorporation into the history of revelation that one became Christian. Revelation was the presupposition for life and life was the church's business. As a student at the beginning of the 1890s he wrote in his diary: "I read not to develop a view of life but to live." Studies, research, and pastoral work were designed to deepen the experience of life.

He was viewed as a radical person, liberated from bondage to what had been. Free he was, but he had won his freedom by acknowledging the heritage of Swedish culture in its spiritual expressions and by placing himself in the service of the will of God. He wanted to translate Luther's paradox into his own life: "A Christian is a perfectly free lord of all, subject to none" and "A Christian is a perfectly dutiful servant of all, subject to all" and he consciously trained himself in that set of relationships. His Swedishness had been strengthened during his years abroad. When he came home from Leipzig, he was totally dedicated to devoting all his strength to building up the Church of Sweden and opening it to the life of the Spirit so that it could fulfill anew its historic task in the world.

He had considerable self-confidence and seemed to lack the social inhibitions of most people. If he traveled by train, sat in a waiting room, or came to a meeting, it was not long before he had exchanged words with everyone, noted who they were, and tried to say something encouraging. His behavior was so unconventional that everyone noticed it. Was it something generally un-Swedish? How else could his spontaneity and restless eagerness to enter into conversation with those he met be explained? His presence filled the room and nobody was left untouched. He was at ease with himself and his values and felt no anxiety in encountering whatever was strange to him. He was prone to laughter and to making disarmingly humorous remarks and often had to check himself so as not spoil a formal atmosphere. When he spoke publicly, he sometimes named living persons by name, directly and sharply critical but without arrogance. He seldom let his critics go unanswered, but he avoided wasting time with polemics.

He was a visibly modest person. It took time for people to become used to an archbishop who traveled in third class, took a sandwich out of his pocket, did three things at the same time, talked to everyone, and tipped his hat as he walked through the city with half a dozen children in tow. There was a roguish character about him from his student years that never left him. But this did not at all mean that he was overly familiar with just anybody, letting himself be patted on the shoulder or drawn into trivial conversation. He was a controlled person who kept his distance and only revealed himself to others up to a certain point. No one entered fully into his life. In every conversation he maintained the initiative, perhaps to shield his innermost feelings. He possessed a fragile vulnerability, secrets that he rarely shared even with his wife but only with God in prayer.

Many spoke of his willpower and disciplined work habits. The mental legacy from his father, who at times lived a nearly ascetic life and rarely took time to eat with his family, shone through. In his father's eyes, idleness was a deadly sin. Nathan had learned to use every minute, live in the present, and never be careless in preparations. Even if his time seemed to stretch out, it was to be used well. He let his clergy know that they were expected to work themselves to death, but slowly and sensibly. That was precisely what he himself did. His capacity for work was united with an uncompromising will, but he was flexible and accommodating to others when necessary. He often used the picture of a race horse who ran fastest when whipped and given free rein by the jockey. Only under the hard but confident grip of duty could a person do his or her absolute best. To subordinate oneself without reservation to obedience to God is "blessedness" and nothing less is required of a Christian. With the dutifulness of heroes and saints as models, he continually practiced the self-discipline he was taught. He had little desire for comfort and did not spare himself even when illness struck.

The combination of an exceptional will to work with a strict sense of duty presupposed a capacity for organization. He had a fixed routine, even if he was often interrupted by visitors, unplanned meetings, travels, or the needs of his family. When he was in Uppsala, he began his days with morning prayer in the cathedral. Then he ate breakfast with those in his family who were not yet in school. Between bites he took his first look at the day's mail before he went upstairs to the library, which was his work room. Before lunch he dictated letters and wrote articles, reports, and sermons, continuing with that afterwards. When the Gunilla bell near the castle rang, it was time to gather everyone in the house for prayers. Then he continued his work for several more hours, at times late into the night. Anna and Nathan attempted to set time aside for the children every day, but they were clearly not able to be the parents they wanted to be. The children were, for the most part, cared for by servants and found themselves living in the public eye. They paid a high price for their parents' outgoing life, and having a whole crowd of teenagers in the house was, to say the least, demanding for the parents. To have the name Söderblom in Uppsala meant always being recognized and watched.

During weekends, the archbishop was often out on a visitation to a congregation. On Wednesday mornings the Diocesan Chapter met; on Thursday there were commission meetings in Stockholm. Thursday evenings were set aside for university matters. Guests came and went: lecturers from abroad, friends from his student days, professors and priests from the diocese. The kitchen staff was fully occupied; one never knew who would show up needing a meal and perhaps a bed. Around the dinner table, not only the children gathered, but also students and missionaries, artists and authors, Nobel Prize winners, and occasionally members of the royal family. After a few years as archbishop, Söderblom seemed to know everyone. Ever since he and Anna had arrived as a young couple in Paris and associated with the Swedish colony in the apartment on Rue Malleville, this was the way it had always been. Their home was always open, and that is what they wanted. If one was under "the grasp of the call," as he expressed it, one had no other choice than to give everything. Söderblom would hardly have been able to formulate job descriptions for servants of the church in later times.

Nathan Söderblom's great gift of grace was his ability to communicate with people and to reach out to them. Bengt Sundkler, as a result of his study of Söderblom's correspondence, commented, "We have never in this country had such a genius at communication as Nathan Söderblom." He became archbishop at a time when the state postal system functioned well, when letters within Europe — even during the war — usually reached their recipients within a few days and telegrams shortened the time for more important matters. In Söderblom's archives there were 38,000 letters from nearly 8,000 people. He kept all the letters he received, Swedish and foreign, short and long, casual greetings and analytical epistles. In order to get a glimpse of how extensive his correspondence was, Sundkler described one of Söderblom's ordinary working days. Söderblom had had a number of official duties out in the archdiocese before he could set aside a day for his correspondence — March 15, 1916. The young doctoral student Yngve Brilioth, who was later to become son-in-law and archbishop, was then his secretary. From his diary it can be seen that on that Wednesday, Söderblom dictated longer or shorter letters to twenty-nine people in Sweden and four to German clergymen, one letter to a professor in Leipzig, one to the rector of the English congregation in Stockholm, and one to the English ambassador there. He also sent a letter to the Red Cross in St. Petersburg and a letter of condolence, both in French; sent two letters to the Swedish government concerning school issues and church music; formulated an appeal for a social program in a working class area outside Stockholm; and sent a letter to Karl Fries concerning a conference. When Gerda Rosling in 1919, with financial support from the great philanthropist Oscar Ekman, became his full-time personal secretary, the volume of his correspondence increased considerably. He also dictated articles and entire books to her. How did he have the strength, day after day, year after year?

The first answer to that question, naturally, was that he had his large family around him and his wife's unfailing support. They were surrounded by a rich circle of private friends in Uppsala. Among them was the family of the provincial governor, the former prime minister, who lived in the Uppsala castle. Anna Söderblom and Agnes Hammarskjöld were very close to each other and their children went in and out of both homes. For Dag Hammarskjöld, who was a classmate of Jon Olov Söderblom, close contact with Nathan Söderblom had a decisive influence both on his religious development and his international perspective. He learned that a society without a religious compass would only drift, that faith and intellectual honesty must be held together, that each and every person must find his or her own path, and that everyone must take responsibility in the world. Through Söderblom, Dag Hammarskjöld came in contact with Thomas à Kempis, Pascal, Bergson, and Schweitzer, each of whom became for him an inspiring guide.

The Söderbloms at Christmas in the archbishop's residence, probably in 1917. Only Sven is missing — he is at war.

Music was an essential source of power for Söderblom. He counted Bach as the greatest of all composers, but he also sensed the mystery of existence in Beethoven's music. He wrote: "In Beethoven, especially in his later works, feeling and thought, hope, reconciliation, courage, resignation, and light piercing darkness are united in a nuanced yet coherent way which words cannot express or communicate but which those immersed in life's purgatory and in the soul's hell and heaven can understand." The most wonderful tones Söderblom knew were in the middle movement in A flat major of Beethoven's Fifth Symphony in C minor: "One sits and dreads its arrival, yet every time one hears it thoughts go toward the dream of St. Francis — the angels played the violin so beautifully that if one more stroke were taken the soul would have died from sensual pleasure."

His third source of strength was prayer. To his youngest daughter Yvonne he wrote: "Did I not say to you concerning prayer that I could not live for a day without ceaseless prayer?" When critics attacked him in connection with the archbishop's election, the pious Waldemar Rudin attempted to pour oil on the troubled waters. He reminded his critics, "But look, he is praying." Rudin was himself a mystic with roots in the same evangelical awakening as Söderblom. For both men it was the inner life that was an indispensable condition for fruitful work. As a child, Söderblom had learned often and simply to speak with God in prayer, and he did that throughout his whole life, naturally and spontaneously. Many have described how, when he showed them the cathedral, he would suggest that they kneel at the altar rail and pray together. In many circumstances he would take time for spontaneous, free, and confident prayer. In the midst of a meeting he could, to the surprise of others, leave the room in order to pray for a few moments in seclusion. When he was alone, he could easily sink into silent introspection.

Prayer was his life's most important activity. He distanced himself from Ritschl's unsympathetic and nearly sarcastic attitude toward everything associated with mysticism. In his cold intellectualism, Ritschl did not grasp the inwardness of religion, but for Söderblom inward silence was a necessity for life. At times he complained about how external concerns threatened to choke prayer instead of inspiring it, and he spoke often of the individual's rest and presence of mind in worship. In a sermon of 1898 he burst forth with: "O, you solitude, my sacred refuge where the motley pictures of the day no longer darken my eyes. You solitude, where my soul may rest, may see, may suffer, may repent, may hope. O, you solitude, you are not loneliness. That is what thoughtless people call you, people who do not know you, people who gaze at you and see only an infinite emptiness. No, you have a voice which is deeper and higher than all voices. For in solitude, behind all, over all, within all — there God lives."

When he preached on "the inner guest," he described how the soul draws itself back from its outer space, from the factory with its activities, into deep seclusion where things are still and no machines clatter, to the garden where life flourishes. There one could in conversation and prayer encounter the soul's inner guest. While this guest had changed and appeared in different ways in different religions, for Christians the guest is Christ, risen and glorified. His actual name is the "Spirit," the divine spirit of Christ. Söderblom distinguished inner communion with this Christ from what he called "the mysticism of infinity." This inner guest was the God of the prophets and the Father of Jesus Christ who made ethical demands which burned as "the fire of the zeal of the Lord." This was not the soul's or the personality's dissolution in divinity but an encounter between an "I" and a "thou." I know, said Söderblom, that the deeper I go, the more complete the concord becomes, the more intimately I am united with the inner guest, the clearer it becomes that this is an encounter, a refuge, a union, an attachment. The I that deals and speaks with the mysterious yet intimate guest, is my innermost self, to the degree that the encounter is true and sincere. "Then my clothes fall off, my being stands bare. Lord, have mercy on me, help me! I shrink back from total openness and attachment. But the inner guest is my friend. Before him my innermost being becomes still. O, let me always keep open the way to this refuge."

That the outgoing, energetic Söderblom was also a mystic can scarcely be questioned.

18
The Diplomat of Faith

> Love now requires efforts to make peace secure and diminish the lure of war. What we hope and believe is that Christian love's severe and miraculous power, which is God's power, will increasingly penetrate wills and at long last triumph over hate and hostility and the temptations to war of natural rivals.
>
> *Nathan Söderblom, 1914*

In the midst of preparations for the archbishop's consecration, Nathan Söderblom takes time to dedicate an addition to the Rosendal Folk School in Uppsala. It is surrounded by a military parade ground. The purpose of the school is to promote duty and self-discipline. He speaks to the children: Paris, the most beautiful of cities, is threatened by enemies. A deluge of words flows from politicians who have fled from the capital city. The quiet working people must pay for the extravagance of those idle talkers. The idealist, champion of peace, and leader of workers Jean Jaurès has been murdered. General Joseph Galliéni has been called home from Madagascar in order to lead the defense forces. He is no verbal hero, but rather a man of duty and competence. "This task I will fulfill to my uttermost," he promises. Söderblom points to Galliéni as a model for the boys who soon shall have the honor of wearing the military uniform and protecting peace in Sweden.

* * *

Nathan Söderblom had been elected and named archbishop in the midst of the political tumult that followed the farmers' march. He had moved from a Germany where "every muscle was stretched for the *Reich*," and he was quite certain that Sweden would be drawn into the war. He shared his countrymen's historic suspicion of Russia, the superpower that he believed to be the greatest threat. Even if he sometimes found German nationalism unsupportable, it could not be compared to "Russian wretchedness." He regretted his beloved France's "fornication with the Muscovites." The Russians' treatment of Finland hurt him deeply.

In his episcopal letter to the priests of the Uppsala Archdiocese, he pointed to the Church of Sweden's historic responsibility for peace and mutual understanding. Since Uppsala was, along with Canterbury, the leading center of Protestant Christianity, he proposed using his position to address the world. He was deeply shaken at the outbreak of war, but he was also aware that war could bring some positive outcomes. People could raise themselves from their moral decay, nonessentials could be swept away, and nationalism could lead to a deepening of religion. He spoke of a "contest" between people in which the best would win. There was also a struggle between the gods of nationalism and the God of Christianity. In a sermon in Uppsala a few weeks before his consecration, he had sharply attacked the distortion of the Christian picture of God that came in the wake of war. The gods of nationalism, choosing sides with different warring parties, were soon as numerous as were people and nations. Wartime religion, which in times of peace was commonly a religion of class, wounded authentic Christianity deeply. The God of Jesus Christ was mixed up with the false gods of self-interest. Every reference to God should be banished from the announcements of victory. Söderblom also warned that the "special god of Sweden," which borrowed elements of Christianity and gave rise to sincere and honorable feelings, actually could be an idol.

This was not the first time that he expressed himself on questions of politics and peace. During his time in Paris he had written in *Gefle-Posten* about the French-Russian alliance, which he then viewed as necessary if peace were to be preserved, and he also wrote about the Spanish-American War, which shattered the illusion that the United States was "the foremost defender and hope of peace." During the Boer War in South Africa he, unlike many Swedes, took the side of the Boers. In 1905, at the dissolution of the union between Sweden and Norway, he distanced himself from military intervention and spoke of Oscar II and the workers' movement as guarantors of the peaceful phasing out of the union. He followed the many turns of the question of defense and happily referred — as one friendly to defense — to Harald Hjärne: both defense and reform!

Against that background it was not surprising that while he worked on his episcopal letter, he also took the initiative to prepare an appeal for peace that he hoped all European churches would support. Already before he entered office, he thus prepared himself to address the world. He was, however, not the first to issue a call to peace. Pope Pius X on August 2, just a few weeks before his death, sent an admonition to peace to all the world's Catholics. Benedict XV, his successor, began his pontificate with a similar appeal. He was determined not to fail in using all in his power to bring an end to the war. Söderblom appreciated that. "This time the pope spoke on behalf of all Christianity," he wrote in his letter. Charles Babaut in Nimes had also turned to the churches with an appeal for peace but was rejected by both Germany and England. Söderblom decided to prepare his appeal without consulting either the Foreign Office of the government or the other bishops. Thus, he himself took responsibility for assuming for the Church of Sweden a mediating role in the present situation of war. He wanted to show that Christianity was supranational and that the churches that had escaped the devastation of war bore a special responsibility to work for peace and reconciliation. "If it is God's will that we should be spared, then we have, as clearly as such a dispensation can speak to a people and a church, a holy task for peace," he wrote in his episcopal letter. His own anguish, but above all, popular expectations of him as archbishop forced him to act. After many revisions, he was ready with his appeal. *For Peace and Christian Fellowship* reads, in its entirety:

> The War is causing untold distress. Christ's Body, the Church, suffers and mourns. Mankind in its need cries out: O Lord, how long? The tangle of underlying and active causes which have accumulated in the course of time, and the proximate events which have led to the breaking of peace, are left to history to unravel. God alone sees and judges the intents and thoughts of the heart. We, the servants of the Church, address to all those who have power or influence in the matter an earnest appeal seriously to keep peace before their eyes, in order that bloodshed soon may cease. We remind especially our Christian brethren of various nations that war cannot sunder the bond of internal union that Christ holds in us. Sure it is that every nation and every realm has its vocation in the divine plan of the world, and must, even in the face of heavy sacrifices, fulfill its duty, as far as the events indicate it and according to the dim conception of man. Our Faith perceives what the eye cannot always see: the strife of nations must finally serve the dispensation of the Almighty, and all the faithful in Christ are one. Let us therefore call upon God that he may destroy hate and enmity, and in mercy ordain peace for us. His will be done!

Two small words in this text became *leitmotivs* in his peace work in the next years: "soon" and "hate." In contrast to some others, Söderblom wanted to see a prompt end to the war. In his position there was a certain regard for Germany, but above all, there was a desire for an end to the slaughter of young people. Peace could not wait until Germany was crushed. The conflict had released an obstinate hate between the warring countries, and also between nonwarring countries. Their hate was often directed toward Germany, and Söderblom was consequently accused of partisanship when, on the basis of the gospel, he sought to tone down the hate. During the war years he constantly had to defend himself against those who saw him as being pro-German. He walked a difficult tightrope. Peace work required a strict neutrality, but his heart was with those who were hit the hardest and whom he considered to be the West's most important barrier against despised Bolshevism. England and France had joined with Russia to crush Germany. For Söderblom, the signs were ominous and they did not become better when in April 1917 the United States entered the war.

Söderblom sent his appeal for peace to church leaders in Denmark, Norway, Switzerland, the Netherlands, and the United States, and also to some select people in the warring countries in the hope that they would support him. It was a complicated process, with the aid of Swedish embassies, to get names and addresses and then to select representative individuals. It was especially difficult to find correct addresses within the diverse Christian landscape of the United States. He received help from the medieval historian Knut B. Westman who so eagerly had hoped to see him as archbishop. Westman would become an indispensable colleague in Söderblom's continuing international work.

Westman was from Härnösand and as a child, like Söderblom, he had seen ships in the harbor and had dreamed of the lands on the other side of the water. In Uppsala, he had also been deeply affected by Harald Hjärne, had been active in the Student Christian and Young Church Movements, and early on had developed contacts with future ecumenical leaders in England. He did his doctorate in 1911 with a dissertation on St. Birgitta. Söderblom bonded quickly with the young docent. Westman mastered German, English, and Latin and shared the archbishop's social and ecumenical vision. With a thorough and conscientious competence, he supported his old teacher when Söderblom needed a secretary who was prepared to work without salary.

Söderblom took on another of Hjärne's medieval historians as an assistant. This was the twenty-four-year-old Yngve Brilioth. He roomed in the archbishop's house and helped in his free time with the archbishop's correspondence. Brilioth was brilliantly gifted. He had good command of the European languages of culture, including Latin and Greek. After taking his doctorate in history, he moved on to theology and was ordained in 1918. The year after that he was married to Söderblom's oldest daughter Brita and in time became archbishop himself.

Söderblom's appeal became a signal to the churches that the new Archbishop of Uppsala was a leader to deal with. He hoped that the appeal would receive a positive response, but that did not happen. Rather, the answers exposed the deep splits between the churches caused by the war. Patriotism was so unrestrained — even from the pulpits — that every reminder that Christ united humankind across national borders fell on deaf ears. When the text, which was translated into seven languages, was published in both the Swedish and international press on November 27, only a handful of church leaders in neutral countries responded, chiefly the Finnish archbishop and the leader of the small Hungarian Unitarian Church. In contrast, recipients in Germany, Austria-Hungary, England, and France explained why they could not support this appeal. Two sections of the text caused their reservations. First, that history would one day reveal the actual causes of the war and that every nation that took part in the war saw itself as fulfilling its duty. They were all in agreement that their countries entered the war for the legitimate reason that they had to defend themselves. They could not agree that history would show any other reason than that peace was broken. Especially in Germany there was total unanimity: the country had been invaded and had to defend itself. Ninety-three leading academics — among them Adolf Deissmann, Rudolf Eucken, Adolf von Harnack, and Wilhelm Hermann, all of whom were close to Söderblom — published a manifesto in which they gave undivided support to Germany's actions. Second, to concede that all parties acted in fulfillment of their duties could be interpreted so that the actions of aggressors were to be accepted. A compromise could not lead to a just and moral peace, and thus the question was asked as to what kind of peace Söderblom pursued.

In Sweden, his appeal met with a positive response from some, while others found it completely naïve. Radical pacifists had expected more, while supporters of war found it to be a piece of unrealistic idealism. Söderblom was ahead of the times. But he had seen the German deployment with his own eyes and heard his colleague Professor Ludwig Ihmels's disturbing sermon in the University Church in Leipzig: "We lift our eyes upward. Where else? Around us are only enemies." He must do something. The combatants on both sides saw the war as a holy war and thus they deepened the divisions within Christianity. For Söderblom, unity between the churches and peace between the nations were two sides of the same coin. The war united churches and people in their respective countries, but internationally, walls were erected between them. The war was a setback for all the boundary-crossing cooperation that had just begun to take root, but Söderblom refused to give up his faith in the churches' spiritual fellowship as a power for peace to be reckoned with. The supranational communion between Christians must take precedence over any obligations toward national interests. European Christianity must be reconciled. To contribute to that was his calling.

He was least of all an unambiguous person. Even though he distanced himself from all forms of extreme nationalism, he was patriotic, a supporter of defense, faithful to the king, and a state church proponent. The people's and the church's moral and spiritual health were dependent on each other. In his own terminology, the nation was the body and the church its soul. Evangelical national churches had taken concrete form through their countries' histories and were therefore inseparably united with the people. There were no international ecumenical structures that could correct national perspectives, nor was there any established sacramental communion that transcended confessional boundaries. The boundary-crossing fellowship of which Söderblom spoke was both lofty and difficult to grasp. It lacked social anchorage, had no organizational form, and thus had no political influence. That he valued the history of Sweden so highly and that he emphasized the special task of Sweden to preserve evangelical freedom in Europe gave rise to the question of Sweden's own self-interest in the political process for peace.

Söderblom could not completely separate himself from what scholars called an organic or integrative nationalism. It was not totally beyond reason that he was accused of having German sympathies. However, with his French, English, and German experiences and his repudiation of national aggressiveness and self-satisfaction, there was good reason to listen to him regarding the European conflict. That he loved Germany did not mean that he valued France and England less. His warm and proud love for his homeland was something other than chauvinism and conceit. He wanted to be loyal both to Sweden and to his ecumenical commitments. Söderblom actualized the call that God had given to him by taking on the role of being a diplomat of faith. He wanted to make the church an informal third party that, on the basis of its spiritual communion, would mediate between the warring nations and thus contribute to a binding supranational order of justice.

Even if his appeal did not receive the response he hoped for, it was a starkly urgent summons to the churches to make concrete a Christian fellowship that transcended national boundaries, with himself as leader. He had for a long time been well known as a scholar of religion; now he appeared in a completely new role. He gave up research and took the first step on the ecumenical road he would follow for the rest of his life. Once he had launched the boat into the water, he had no choice but to row to the shore. He was soon captured by his own enterprise. It was a matter of honor for him to mobilize all of his strength to fulfill this project. He never doubted that God had given him this task. It was faith in combination with his uncompromising self-esteem that drove him, not his idealism.

In spite of all the media attention to the new archbishop, comments in the Swedish press concerning his peace appeal were scanty. The few papers that paid attention mirrored their own positions toward the war. The conservative *Göteborgs Aftonblad* totally rejected Söderblom's "papal" involvement in the question, while *Aftonbladet* and *Upsala Nya Tidning* were more positive. He could not promote his own position without taking into account opinion in the church and the government's foreign policy. The state church itself kept him within bounds, but he tested how far he could go within the prevailing political limits. Parliamentary democracy was still not well developed, a fact that allowed him personally, like other prominent leaders, comparatively ample elbow room. Sweden, together with Denmark and Norway, had declared itself neutral in order to keep out of the war and he approved of the Conservative government's neutrality, which obviously was somewhat biased in favor of Germany. A German victory over Russia would ward off the threat against Sweden, especially if it brought independence to Finland and the Baltic states. But the Social Democrats and Liberals tended to support the Allies even though they had no regard for the Russian Czar. Hjalmar Branting stood wholeheartedly on the side of the French.

Söderblom shared the fear of Russia and the aversion to Bolshevism. He interpreted the struggle between Germany and Russia as a decisive contest between Western civilization and Slavic barbarism, yet his chief interest was in having the war come to an end as quickly as possible. He was far from alone in seeking ways to peace. A number of associations, among them the Swedish Peace and Arbitration Society of which Branting was a member, organized a peace congress in 1915. New peace associations were formed and demonstrations were arranged throughout the country, many by women. In 1916, another conference issued an appeal for peace and invited the churches to support it, but Söderblom found it all too naïve and pacifist for him to sign. He had chosen his own way and continued on the basis of his own appeal to enlist the churches.

An organization that welcomed his appeal for peace was the World Alliance for Promoting International Friendship through the Churches. This group aimed originally to create good relations between German and British Christians. After a preparatory meeting — in which many participated who were to set the tone for the ecumenical movement, for example, Friedrich Siegmund-Schultze and Charles S. Macfarland — and with the help of a large donation from the American industrialist Andrew Carnegie, goals were broadened to include putting moral pressure on all the world's leaders to work for peace. The Alliance was established in Constanz on August 1, 1914, the same day that World War I broke out. Independent national sections were created and an international committee coordinated the work. The Alliance was an association of individuals, not of churches, and they hoped to enlist leaders from all the world's great religious organizations. No Swedish Lutheran was present in Constanz, but many of the delegates knew Söderblom. He was personally invited in 1915 to another conference of the Alliance in Bern, but in his place he sent Knut Westman along with a small Swedish delegation. He himself did not once travel outside Scandinavia during the war in order that his neutrality not be questioned. He maintained his international contacts by correspondence and through deputies, while he himself concentrated on tasks in the archdiocese and in the Church of Sweden as a whole. Yet he carefully followed the Alliance's development. Church cooperation was still totally dependent on individual enthusiasm and the Alliance had the potential of becoming one — albeit fragile — platform for Söderblom's peace work. He envisioned the possibility of using the Alliance to realize his plans and in 1917 took over the chairmanship of the Swedish section. Thus, at that time within the framework of the Alliance a limited Nordic cooperation had already begun.

The relations between the Nordic churches were surprisingly weak, confined mostly to areas of mission and diaconia. The Nordic student conferences held around the turn of the century had been disrupted by the dissolution of the Swedish-Norwegian union, but now the war again brought together people who had known each other as students. In September 1916, some thirty people gathered at a folk high school outside Gothenburg in order to deepen Nordic cooperation. Among them were Nils Widner who was to take special responsibility for Nordic contacts, Valdemar Ammundsen who was to play an important ecumenical role for Denmark and who would eventually become chairperson of the Alliance, and the liberal Norwegian theologian Lyder Brun. Söderblom himself could not be present, but his spirit hovered over the meeting. He was clearly oriented toward the goal of strengthening Nordic church fellowship. Prominent Norwegian and Danish bishops had been present at his consecration and many saw him already as the leading Nordic bishop, yes, as everyone's archbishop. The Norwegian Eivind Berggrav, at the time a young journalist and later Bishop of Oslo, had an immense admiration for Nathan Söderblom and later wrote: "He never took over the reins in our lands, he made suggestions and supported us. And he wished us all a place in the sun." Bishop Harald Ostenfeld in Copenhagen expressed the same feelings: "Söderblom actually became the Archbishop of Scandinavia, not because he pretended to be, but because with his spiritual standing and leadership, he really was just the one." Söderblom assumed leadership, but not until 1920 was he able to invite all the Nordic bishops to common discussions at Kulla Gunnarstorp Castle in Skåne.

In 1917, the war entered a new phase. Just at the time that the Russian Revolution weakened Russian involvement in the war, the United States entered on the side of the Allies. The American declaration of war against Germany also brought a number of other non-European countries into the conflict. The great European war was expanded into a world war. There was, however, on all sides a widespread fatigue over the war. The situation on both the Eastern and Western fronts was at a stalemate and more and more, there was talk of a solution based on mutual understanding. The Social Democrats, who like the churches had been swept into war fever and were deeply divided, attempted in different ways to take initiatives for peace. With great expectations, an international group of Social Democrats gathered in Stockholm, but things went nowhere. Peace overtures in Germany and England gave rise to internal political crises, but did not lead to a cease-fire. Pope Benedict XV made new attempts to break the deadlock with a number of concrete proposals for mutual disarmament and the establishment of an international legal system. These did not produce any immediate results, but they stimulated a desire for peace and provided direction for the peace negotiations that were to be led by the American president, Woodrow Wilson.

At the same time that the peace efforts grew, Söderblom was forced to deal with a personal issue that would haunt him for many years and actually threaten his own work for peace. In February 1917, his nineteen-year-old son Sven volunteered as an officer for the Fourth Prussian Artillery Regiment and after training was sent to the front. Söderblom had done everything in his power to have Sven remain in Sweden, but he could not prevent his son from leaving. This became public in Sweden and also in France and England. Söderblom was criticized for a lack of neutrality and had a hard time looking his French and English friends in the eye. Even six years later, in times of depression he would refer to Sven's war adventure as "an unhelpful obstacle in the way of the task that during my short life and in my miserable way I was promoting. Overall I was faced by this, privately and publicly." His son's military career was no more than an episode. In 1923, Sven emigrated to the United States. Nathan Söderblom's trustworthiness had, however, taken a blow and many felt that his son's actions confirmed the suspicion that Söderblom was actually on the side of the Germans.

When the political initiatives for peace had broken down and the warring countries armed themselves for what would be decisive battles, it became even more urgent than before to keep the churches' peace movement alive. The Reformation Jubilee of October 1917 offered an opportunity for the Nordic churches to follow up on the peace appeal of three years earlier. Söderblom proposed to Bishops Harald Ostenfeld of Copenhagen and Jens Frølich Tandberg of Oslo that together they should invite church leaders from the neutral countries to a conference. Ostenfeld was an energetic, theologically liberal person with international experience and explicit socialist sympathies, in many ways similar to Söderblom. Tandberg was older and more conservative. Together with Dutch and

Swiss church leaders they would gather to issue a call for both prayer and efforts for a durable and just peace even as they called to mind the Reformation and faithfulness to the evangelical legacy. The conference had to be postponed, but at Pentecost 1917 they were nevertheless able to issue a new manifesto referred to as the "Whitsuntide Appeal." It was signed by Söderblom, Ostenfeld, Tandberg, two Dutch pastors, and Professor Henri DuBois of Switzerland. They desired to "keep the hope of peace living" and "bless all efforts for a righteous and durable peace." The latter formulation could not be made more precise if all signatories were to identify with it. Söderblom explained later that the phrase "efforts for a righteous and durable peace" alluded to the workers' movement's efforts for peace and the Social Democrats' conference, which was held in Stockholm at the same time. In the leftist press, the manifesto was greeted with gratification that the church and the Social Democrats were taking the same position in regard to "the burning question of the day." For the churches it was most urgent both to strengthen their internal fellowship and to work to heal the wounds caused by the war. As before, however, the appeal received a mixed reception. It was welcomed by those who wished to bring the churches closer to one another, but criticized by others who held that it was treasonous toward Christianity to speak of peace before the struggle of their own people was brought to victory. In France the appeal was completely rejected since it lacked any reference to the crime that they held lay in the German instigation of the war.

Söderblom had proposed that the Nordic churches should observe the peoples' desire for peace at worship on Pentecost. Ostenfeld, however, did not support this idea. The Allies had just started a spring offensive designed to bring things to a conclusion. While this was going on it was not, according to the Bishop of Copenhagen, proper to be speaking of peace. In Sweden, however, the free churches, the theological faculties, and peace organizations of all kinds cast their lot for a more vigorous Christian contribution to peace efforts. A Day of Prayer for Peace was announced for August 26 and Söderblom gave voice to all who held that the time for bloodshed had long passed. He had Swedish Christians with him as he moved ahead with plans for a great international peace conference. In cooperation with the Nordic representatives of the Alliance he began to plan such an event for Uppsala. It was postponed twice before it was finally held in the middle of December 1917. Invitations were sent to a long list of church leaders in Europe and the United States, but nearly all found reasons to reject the offer. The most common reason was that the time was too short and that travels were too risky. Söderblom should, many thought, wait with the conference until there was peace. Only thirty-four delegates came to Uppsala, two from the Netherlands and Switzerland and the rest from Scandinavia, sixteen of whom were from Sweden. Twenty-four of the delegates belonged to national committees of the Alliance.

It was a great disappointment to Söderblom that no one from the warring countries was present. However, instead of giving up, he used the meeting to work out guidelines for a future international conference of church leaders, which he was determined to hold in spite of the war. The time was used to the fullest. Taking into account services of worship, including an ordination to the priesthood in which the Reformed professors from the Netherlands and Switzerland participated in the laying-on-of-hands, it was remarkable how much was accomplished in three days. No fewer than eleven sessions were devoted to questions such as the supranational unity of Christians in Christ, the internal and reciprocal duties of nations and Christians, the sanctity of justice and the international legal system, and what the church could do to combat hate and distrust, together with the supranational character of mission and its actual problems. The conversations resulted in many resolutions, which paved the way for the international conference that actually occurred — but not until 1925. They talked of the unity of all Christians in the cross of Christ and of the diversity within the Christian tradition that together should, in a fashion better than in the past, be proclaimed in word and deeds. They considered also whether or not Christians were prepared to take responsibility after the war when a new world order would be formed. Söderblom was mandated to send a new and more thoroughly worked out invitation to the churches.

The report from this meeting of neutrals was worked into its final form by Söderblom, Westman, and Berggrav. Berggrav reported how Söderblom would pace back and forth across the floor of his library, gesticulating and talking. He came across "marvelous" formulations, for he was a master at that, and the others would loyally write down these "pearls of wisdom." But these gems did not always agree either with what the conference delegates had proposed or with their own wishes. The formulations were both unclear and biased. Time after time the others had to say, "No, archbishop, that won't work." He smiled when he heard their arguments and responded, "No, that won't work!" and began again.

He stuck to the thought of calling an international conference around the question of peace. He began again, time after time, and finally against all odds it came to be. Until then, it was his work as bishop of the Uppsala diocese that mostly occupied him. Paradoxically, the war gave him good opportunity to spend his time visiting parish after parish in Uppland, Gästrikland, and Häsingland instead of traveling to other countries.

19

Bishop of the Diocese of Uppsala

> Personal proclamation is and will be the most important part of our vocation. The sermon, which is able to comfort, teach, exhort, and admonish, is superior to every other pastoral task.
>
> *Nathan Söderblom, 1914*

THE ARCHBISHOP CELEBRATES MASS *in Hagby church. It is a neo-classic, square, whitewashed church with a large copy of Thorvaldsen's statue of Christ over the altar. The church is not to Söderblom's taste. In the sacristy he instructs the local musician. He goes back and forth with slow, dignified steps and says, "Now, I pretend that I walk in a procession. The Introit, the 'Holy, Holy, Holy,' should be played at this tempo and pace. This is what I call 'Bjuråker Holy,' and I want it to be played just like the old organist played it when I was a child in Bjuråker." The well-known German organist Georg Kempff, who is serving as a priest in the diocese, is with him. He begins the service with a half-hour long improvisation on Bach's Fugue in E Major and weaves into it Söderblom's melody to "In This Pleasing Summertime." The congregation learns the summer hymn. At the tenth verse it seems that the thin roof of the church will lift away. The Cantor Anders Hilding is so moved that tears make it difficult for him to see the words. The sun streams in through the large, Romanesque windows.*

* * *

Nathan Söderblom threw himself into his work as bishop in the Diocese of Uppsala with heart and soul. This involved, first, the creation of trust among the clergy who had not chosen to have him as their bishop. With their help he hoped that he could lead the parishes into the modern world and the new thinking that the times required. With no written guidelines, there were basically four tools at his disposal: visitations, the clergy conference, ordinations, and the diocesan chapter. He had no diocesan office, not even a secretary. The twenty-eight district deans could, at his instruction, accomplish a good deal, but in actual practice he had to do most things himself. For over a decade he had lived in the academic world, moved among European intellectuals, and accounted for most of his own time. Now the situation was totally different. His days were filled with travels to the parishes, local matters, and, not seldom, pure trivialities. He had made it clear to himself and others that now it was the diocese that mattered. Everything else was to be secondary. He knew from the beginning, of course, that things would not be quite that way. He had many personal plans that were both more attractive and promising than anything the small rural parishes could offer. In reality, the structures of the state church were intractable and there was not much that an individual bishop could do about them. The inertia of tradition and the shortage of coworkers inhibited quick changes. But a goal-oriented bishop could, in spite of everything, make a difference. Söderblom used his charisma, but he did not focus on organizational reforms. He exercised leadership by encouragement and thoughtfulness, not by rules or the formulation of objectives. He lent luster and joy to the parishes he visited, but when he left, most continued in the same old ruts.

The archdiocese had a long history, stretching back to the eleventh century, and it was extremely large. It stretched from Stockholm to Hälsingland and included coastal islands, flat country, and wooded areas. For impoverished small farmers far away on the border with Härjedalen, Uppsala seemed infinitely distant; for blasé Stockholmers, Uppsala was a complacent and out-of-the-way spot. Intellectual and spiritual resources streamed as on a slope down toward Uppsala and Sigtuna where the Sigtuna Foundation was being built. Söderblom often compared the diocese to the Holy Land. Delightful and blooming Galilee was, of course, his beloved Hälsingland where the Dellen lakes sparkled like Gennesaret. Gästrikland was well-traveled Samaria with the seaport Gävle as a modern Caesarea Philippi. Judea was Uppland and Uppsala Jerusalem. There the ancient cult was thriving and there the battle about the future was going on.

In Söderblom's time, the Diocese of Uppsala had 260 parishes for a population of 610,000. The shortage of clergy in the large cities was difficult to deal with since few new appointments were being created by the government and the ecclesiastical organization was rigid to the point of immobility. Parishes in Stockholm were led by a consistorium with the pastor primarius as leader. Stockholm did not become a diocese of its own until 1942. From Uppsala to the diocese's northernmost parish it was over 180 miles of dusty and crooked dirt roads. A train stuttered slowly on the main northern line. A trip from Uppsala to Bollnäs took the better part of a day. Söderblom was accustomed to planning his own trips. He searched in his well-thumbed copy of *Sweden's Communications* for convenient trains and busses, ferries and archipelago boats. There were many stations along the railroad lines and he took opportunities at the stops to send a postcard, meet someone he knew, or get a bite to eat. If his predecessor Ekman had a name as a frequent visitor, he was nothing in comparison to Söderblom. He quickly figured out that it would take fourteen years for him to visit all of the diocese's parishes. In order that the intervals between episcopal visitations not be too long, he instructed the rural deans to visit the parishes in their deaneries every seventh year. In order to accomplish what he saw to be his primary tasks, he often declined invitations to lecture or preach in other parts of the country. He actually did manage to visit all the pastorates in the diocese; in 1916 alone he carried out at least seventeen visitations. That meant an equal number of weekends away from Uppsala and his family. After his long trip to America in 1923, he visited at least thirteen parishes in the following year even though he was then mostly taken up with preparations for his major ecumenical conference. He was totally committed to carrying out his original program and he was able to do just that.

Episcopal visitations were a longstanding practice. They occurred as early as the fourth century in the eastern sections of the church and subsequently became an important element in the whole life of Christianity. The archdiocese was for a long time sparsely populated, and up to 1647 it even included upper Norrland. Distances within it were considerable and clearly there were often long intervals between visitations. Because of the archbishop's many other tasks, visitations were often neglected. Söderblom wanted to remedy this situation. At the clergy conference of 1927 he repeated what he had said when he was named: "The Bishop of Uppsala's proper call centers first and last around the diocese. Everything else is secondary. This must be expressed publically and emphatically in light of the many distractions of various kinds." His apologetic tone was warranted. But the truth nevertheless remained: he devoted himself more to diocesan concerns and was more visible in its parishes than most archbishops before and after him.

When any of the parishes received the solemn notification that by virtue of the episcopal office with which he was vested, Söderblom intended to carry out a visitation, preparations began. The visitations nearly always followed the same order. Beginning with the children in the school or in the church, he examined them in their knowledge of Christianity, telling them something of the community's and the church's history and then singing with them. They learned the well-known prayers of Ansgar, Birgitta, and Gustavus Adolphus by heart: Lord, give me grace to be a good person; Lord, show me your way and make me willing to follow it; Lord, teach me today to live to the praise of your holy name.

The visitation would continue with a gathering of the parish council. He would take an inventory of the church's silver, vestments, organ, and other property while at the same time instructing the church wardens in the history of the objects and how they should be cared for. He would also interpret historic parish documents. He would review the report of the parish rector, lead an examination of confirmands, which regularly expanded into an examination of the congregation, celebrate high mass, and finally, summarize his overall impressions at a parish assembly. If he had international guests with him, they would participate in different ways. Those who met the theologian Nikolai Glubokovski from St. Petersburg; the theologian, physician, and organist Albert Schweitzer from Lambaréné; the Orthodox Bishop Ireneos from Novi Sad; or the Anglican Bishop Herbert Hensley Henson from Durham never forgot it. As soon as Söderblom returned home to Uppsala, he would personally write a lengthy and detailed report with a literary quality that made it a culturally historic document.

In one such report, he described how a professor from Athens visited the ninety-five-year-old Anna Andersson and heard a good deal of her life story. In another, he mentioned "five conversations under the seal of confession." He told how a blind man in Ljusdal talked about the first time he heard a musical instrument: an old soldier from Järvsö had played a single-stringed psalmodikon. In another report, he described both laying a wreath at the grave of the American Augustana pastor Lars Paul Esbjörn in Östervåla and praying for persecuted Christians in Russia. He wrote about chiming bells after the service and meetings with free churches, but also about difficult parish disputes, which he sought to solve during late evenings. One can read how he encouraged abstinence work within the parishes and protested against unjust social conditions, especially against the miserable circumstances of agricultural workers. In Vaxholm he happened to criticize what he considered women's all-too-short skirts, which in turn caused the Stockholm newspapers to make fun of him, but he also expressed himself against Sunday labor, extravagant parties, inadequate poorhouses, and the growing number of divorces. It was sometimes said that he swept conflicts and unsatisfactory situations in the parishes under the rug and concentrated on positive judgments, but some also noted the irony when he either congratulated a parish on its fine rector or a rector on his fine parish.

In Hälsingland, the neo-evangelical revival continued while many churches in Uppland were nearly empty on Sundays. In Gästrikland, he encountered problems that went with industrialization. At times there was open conflict between the church and the workers' movement. Söderblom conducted visitations to all the parishes in the diocese. In the fall of 1929 he came to the last one: Söderby-Karl in Lyhundra north of Norrtälje. He began his visitation report with the words: "I can truly make mine the apostle's word: 'I have longed for you.'" He had been ill and was not at all certain that he could fulfill his commitment to visit all the parishes in the diocese. He succeeded, however — and immediately began a second round.

Söderblom had a traditional view of the parish, but he shared the desire of the Young Church Movement to increase the participation of laity. He defended the state church system as long as the freedom of the gospel was not constrained. The borders of the church should be wide enough to include both difference and diversity. Renewal should come from within; it was the church's "soul" that was important, not the church's "body." Every form of church organization was, for him, provisional. If spirit and life were to be found within a parish, its outer form was of less importance. He had established his own goals for congregational life: the first was a renewal of the proclamation of the gospel, the second a richer liturgical and musical life, and the third a conscientious care for the parish's spiritual and material cultural heritage. He also wanted to see an opening up of the Lutheran tradition toward a more ecumenical outlook. His own low church and undogmatic view of the church allowed him to show great generosity toward the free church communities. And his aesthetic inclinations allowed him to welcome the growing high church liturgical renewal, provided it was not excessive.

There was, however, an inherited culture in the church over which he had no control and that he could not fundamentally challenge. People were regarded not only as incurable sinners but also as weak and dependent. In the domestic world, the husband had responsibility for his family and all dependents. In the parish, everyone was dependent on the priest who through ordination was entrusted with the administration of Word and sacrament, which were essential to salvation. The priest was to care for his sheep and the individual's own responsibility was limited. A protest against this traditional ordering of things was in progress. The free churches resisted the control of the state church, and the labor movement resisted capitalist power. By emphasizing the role of the individual person, the individual's responsibility for his or her faith, and by his opposition to all forms of religious institutionalism, Söderblom entered the protest via a different path. This appealed to the urban elites, but did not awaken the response he wished for in the old parishes or among the clergy who remained content in their role as spiritual guardians, which was, in turn, strengthened by their responsibility for civil and church registration.

During visitations Söderblom devoted himself almost exclusively to parishes and schools that were still under the diocesan chapter's jurisdiction. He seldom made visits to industries or factories. Agriculture supported most of the people and he felt himself very much at home among farmers and workers of the soil. When he met such people, he blossomed, sat down and talked with a farmer's wife or a field hand and reminisced about his own childhood in Hälsingland. He had a genuine interest in people and listened attentively to matters great and small in their lives. They remembered his concern, warmth, and humor. For him, the diocese was not an administrative structure but a territory for personal and pastoral responsibility. The parish community became visible around the bishop. His was a ministry of encouragement. There was joy and festivity when the bishop came.

For the first five years, Söderblom was constantly on the go in the diocese, not only on official visitations but also to preach and lecture; dedicate churches, cemeteries, and parish halls; install clergy; and take part in youth meetings or choir festivals. He was then healthy and possessed the strength to do as much as he liked. The clergy experienced this explosion of energy with mixed feelings. If he passed by a rectory, he would knock on the door no matter how late the hour. His urgent appeals could bother the conscience of any priest. Not everyone possessed his stamina, nor were they all prepared to work until their strength was exhausted. To have a leader who wanted, could, and did do more than all the others was not always for the best. For some it could lead to a weakening of self-confidence; for others it could even lead to resignation.

Three times he convened a convocation of the clergy in Uppsala. The church law prescribed, as it had for centuries, that every sixth year the bishop was to assemble all the diocesan clergy. On this occasion, the bishop was to report on his ministry, deliver a lecture, and celebrate worship. A "clergy convocation dissertation" was to be presented and the remembrance of deceased brother priests was given major attention. On these three occasions, Söderblom lectured on Christian education, Christian unity, and the nature of the sermon. In his episcopal report he summarized the answers that the rectors had provided to a questionnaire. In 1915, it was necessary for him to indicate that the celebration of the eucharist had nearly disappeared in many places, but that the disuse of the altar was not as great in parishes where the youth movement had made inroads. In many places the eucharist was celebrated only in connection with confirmation; it was on its way to becoming a "one-time sacrament." In some exceptional cases, however, a service of holy communion was held once a month on Sunday afternoon, and it had begun to be more generally observed on Maundy Thursdays. Söderblom acknowledged the weakening of eucharistic observance as a fact, but he had no strategy for returning it to a central place in church life. In 1927, he could, however, report a certain improvement. He pointed out to the clergy that the situation in England had become better under the influence of Anglo-Catholicism and that in the Church of Denmark the eucharist was celebrated every Sunday. Holy communion should be a part of the high mass, but the prevailing order of worship made it difficult. People had many reasons not to receive the sacrament. One was the demand of the revival movements for a "pure" table of holy communion intended for "worthy" Christians alone. "We do not come because of indifference but because of reverence" was a common answer given when people were asked why they stayed away from communion. Another reason communicants were so few was the fact that the clergy were not allowed to commune themselves without special approval. It was prescribed that another clergyman had to be present to offer the sacrament to them.

Söderblom recalled how the then Bishop of Västerås Nils Lövgren once came to Paris and both absolved him in confession and gave him communion. In a letter to Sam Fries in the spring of 1900, he made the comment that communion was received only once a year, on Maundy Thursday or Good Friday. "The old adoration, the timeless sacrament, seems to me doomed slowly to disappear. For many of our church people holy communion is in every respect already dead. Yet all attempts at repristination will fail. Instead: forward, draw nearer to the spirit of Jesus." He was convinced that it would not work to turn back the clock. The past could not be repeated, but nevertheless, he sensed a loss. A quarter of a century later he would see slight signs of a return to eucharistic practice. He himself had contributed to this by often celebrating holy communion in connection with visitations and ordinations. By that time, the practice of requiring people to make an advance announcement of participation in holy communion had been stopped, as had the prohibition against the priest communing himself. Yet he was not especially hopeful, even though he would have welcomed a return to eucharistic worship. It was not until after his death that the high church movement seriously began to leave its mark on the Church of Sweden. This was stimulated not least by the book of his son-in-law Yngve Brilioth, *Nattvarden i evangeliskt gudstjänstliv*, 1926 (*Eucharistic Faith and Practice Evangelical and Catholic,* 1930). Actually, Söderblom did not press the question of the eucharist. For him it was the sermon that stood in the center.

Nothing could be more urgent than to witness to the presence of the living God. Without that, all is meaningless. When Söderblom, in an impressionistic and personal way, summarized his view of preaching at the clergy convocation in 1927, he exclaimed: "The living God is nearer to us than anything else. In him we live, we move, and we have our being. How could we live even one day without God? How could we keep going without continually praying to him, calling to him, and invoking him, *Kyrie eleison*? Thanking him, worshiping him, feeling his presence as a light which shines over our journey and which pierces even the blackest darkness, believing in him in spite of everything even when he hides his fatherly hand from us?" Blessedness for Söderblom was the certainty of God's presence, nothing more and nothing less. This certainty had come out of deep tribulation. His own experience had taught him that faith in a living God was anything but self-evident. But if God was present, not even the hell of suffering could take away blessedness.

For those who would proclaim the gospel, it was not sufficient to say *abracadabra*. Söderblom reminded the clergy of the Hebrew onomatopoetic tone in the word of the prophet: kit sav latsav tsav latsav kav lakav kab lakav zeir sjam geir sjam, "For it is precept upon precept, precept upon precept, line upon line, line upon line, here a little, there a little" (Isaiah 28:10). The sermon easily becomes mere words, and in reality nothing had ever been more difficult than to preach. Nothing was more futile than to attempt to fill up rows of narrow-necked bottles by emptying a bucket of water over them. Nothing was more painful for a preacher than to "whip an empty brain in order to produce a stillborn thought." Söderblom wanted shorter sermons even as he wanted celebrations of holy communion without lengthy expository messages, but if people went to church to hear the sermon, then it was best that they heard something worth listening to. If a sermon is to be called Christian, it must confine itself to the central questions of faith, contain both law and gospel, and not allow contact with God to degenerate to trivialities.

Preaching had, according to Söderblom, three conditions: first, a focus on God's revelation centered on redemption through Christ; second, the preacher's outer, moral discipline and inner, spiritual life; and third, a close relationship between the preacher and the congregation. The sermon demanded all the preacher's talents: acuteness of thought, beauty and clarity of language, engaging illustrations, and an intimate knowledge of Scripture in combination with both contemporary ways of thinking and the classical literature of humanity. A voice of the Savior could — like the riches of spiritual experience, the warmth of love, and the power of the Spirit — easily be drowned in a tepid flood of characterless, shaggy, and careless sermonizing or be lost in the piles of dry and powerless fodder that had always been offered to Christianity. The message of the cross must be the center of the sermon, but a gospel without ethical demand was nothing less than blasphemy and immorality.

Not all priests have the gift of preaching, but what one cannot produce himself, he can borrow from others. A priest should not be afraid to repeat himself if he really has something to say; a sermon is often better if it is delivered three or four times. During his last year, Söderblom developed long-term plans to have the best preachers in the diocese travel around the parishes for a number of weeks in order day after day, evening after evening in a "heart capturing" way to proclaim the gospel. In a communication from the diocesan chapter, which he wrote a few days before his death, he made this proposal. In it, he referred indirectly to his father who for many years was an itinerant revival preacher who showed many people the way to heaven. What prevented this plan from being realized was not a lack of spiritual resources but the fact that the church organization was so "terribly and rigidly democratic that often one must wonder about our Lord's governance."

The sermon was the weightiest element in the service of worship, but the liturgy itself with its hymns, prayers, and readings was also in need of restoration after the decay of the nineteenth century. Well into that century there were neither flowers nor candles on the altars, the hymn singing was absurdly slow, and hour-long sermons were more the rule than the exception. Eucharistic vestments were used only rarely. The music of the liturgy was the same throughout the year and most of it was in a minor key. If the eucharist was celebrated in the main service, it was preceded by a special confessional service. After that service, the high mass followed with yet another confession of sin at the altar and another from the pulpit and finally an admonition during the holy communion itself just before the elements were distributed. Everything took place under the sign of somber seriousness and repentance. The free churches stood for light music, personal communication, and joy over salvation.

Söderblom wanted to give freedom and beauty to worship, make the most of the musical possibilities, and express continuity with the early church. He put considerable stress on such things but was continually criticized for introducing theatricality and frills, which according to his critics would have been alien to both Martin Luther and the Swedish reformer Olaus Petri. From his first day as archbishop and nearly to his last, he was attacked in newspapers for processions, vestments, gestures, and the liturgical pomp with which he surrounded himself. He undoubtedly possessed a touch of being a Protestant church prince and that was provocative. Söderblom, who according to a journalist was the pious master of festival forms, was time after time put on the defensive. Polemics, however, did not suit him and he often limited himself to emphasizing that he was only following church law and the officially approved church handbook. After the dedication of the open-air church at the Sigtuna Foundation in 1918, when priests in vestments and the archbishop in his shimmering gold cope walked through the arcades surrounding what resembled a monastery garden, the Stockholm *Aftontidningen* was highly critical. Söderblom responded: "To take offense that the church, with its centuries old traditions, seeks to give dignified form to its acts, points to a sad prejudice that is incapable of understanding the claims of both ancient traditions and the sensibilities of religious art." As late as 1930, when the Abbey Church in Vadstena celebrated its five hundredth jubilee, he commented from the pulpit with good-natured irony about the attention given to the vestments that were being worn: "When one speaks of the legacy of the early church one commonly thinks of such simple things as church vestments. These relics from early church practice have been used in all dioceses in all ages and if they are now given more attention than before, perhaps at my instigation, it shows that journalists are going to church more than before — which in and of itself is a cause for joy."

No one, however, believed that Söderblom defended the use of vestments and other external practices only because of loyalty to ancient tradition. He was an artist and something of a dramatic actor. He had a high view of the office of both priest and bishop. It was this office — not the bishop's own person — that was made visible by vestments and other symbols. If Uppsala stood on the same level as Constantinople and Canterbury, it was important that the archbishop appear with the same splendor as his counterparts. His practices gave legitimacy to the ceremonial interests of the budding high church movement. Soon, eucharistic vestments in the colors of the church year were to be found even in small parishes. Even in the 1960s, however, it was still the custom in many places that the priest preached while wearing a long black cape.

Music belonged to liturgy. In Leipzig, with its great tradition of church music, Söderblom basked in the organ music of Johann Sebastian Bach, music that illuminated the word of God and proclaimed the gospel in melody. That pertained above all to Bach's fugues, in which a mighty theme was placed against its counterpoint and was confronted with differing voices before the fugue was completed, everything summed up, and darkness overcome. Nathan Söderblom was in love with the fugues of Bach. He always listened as if for the first time. On occasion Söderblom offered his own "unprofessional" interpretation of the music. He treasured the B-minor Mass above all else and he gave it a detailed interpretation. Its starting point was the Nicene Creed's powerful hymn of praise to the Creator. In an artful G-major duet, this hymn moved into the second article's description of the Son being eternally begotten of the Father, "God from God, Light from Light," and then to the innermost secret of the mass, which places the soul in prayerful dread before the tragedy of life and the mystery of salvation. Thus far the incarnation is central, that God became man through the Holy Spirit by the Virgin Mary. The Christmas idyll with the child in a crib is described, and here the mass gives reason for its name: "Above the bases' heavy, muffled B-minor strokes in triple time, which later wander down toward an even deeper depth, the violins finally — half against their own will, as it were — start a higher expressively sorrowful melody which reminds one of sobs and dropping tears and then the alto begins to sing a theme in minor key which pierces through marrow and bone, placing the beginning of Christ's sufferings not at Golgotha but at his very birth." To Söderblom, Bach's understanding of humanity, however, was not at all one of aching pessimism. The wonderful chorus *Crucifixus* allows the listeners to have a feeling of salvation. After the death on the cross, the chorus in a quiet D-major chord sings of Jesus's rest in the grave before the trumpets sound. New life and the new world order of the resurrected one break forth.

Georg Kempff, a well-known German interpreter of Bach who was also a clergyman, organized a Bach festival in Gävle and Sandviken. Two mixed choruses from the two cities took part. More than six thousand people came to the eight concerts and there were also a number of lectures given during the festival. Söderblom, naturally, was among the lecturers. He spoke of music causing the chords of the soul to vibrate and having its home in the supernatural; yes, it belonged to what is called religion. Bach, more than all others, had the gift to convey this heavenly music. Especially his Passions merited the title of "the fifth Gospel." Bach, however, was not yet heard very often in Sweden, although Söderblom contributed to his growing importance for Swedish church music.

When Söderblom fell miserably ill in 1908 and went to Karlsbad for rest and recuperation, he happened, while traveling, to go into the Thomaskirche in Leipzig. There, beginning in 1723, Bach had served as cantor for twenty-seven years. At dusk, Söderblom crouched in a choir stall while the church was filled with music sung by a choir of angelic voices. It was the famed boys' choir, and he would hear it many times when he later moved to Leipzig. It awakened dreams of also having a boys' choir in the Uppsala cathedral, but how could that dream become reality? It happened in a way as surprising as the donation that allowed him to establish the Olaus Petri Foundation.

In September 1917, a boys' choir from Berlin sang in Uppsala and a few days later Söderblom received a visit from a woman who was so taken by what she had heard that she wanted to give an initial contribution of one thousand crowns for the establishment of such a choir. The gift was multiplied rapidly and quickly became one of the most substantial donations ever given in modern times to the Uppsala cathedral. Gifts were not only large enough to start a boys' choir on a solid financial base but also to build a special gallery for the choir with its own organ. The donor, Sally von Bahr, was the wife of a high-ranking military officer. When invited to choose the inscription over the gallery, she suggested: "The Glory of the Lord filled the Temple." The choir started in 1921 under the leadership of Fredrik Mellander. In Uppsala, free tuition and lodging could not be supplied for the boys as was done in Germany and England, but Söderblom's dream had come true and Bach had yet another interpreter in Sweden.

Priests did not bring about the election of Nathan Söderblom as bishop and thus the atmosphere at his first clergy convocation was reserved. Some priests held on to their negative picture of him, but it actually took only a few years before most clergy proudly spoke of "our Nathan." In spite of the fact that the Young Church Movement gave rise to many vocations, the shortage of priests was serious. The "diocesan bond" meant that in principle one could be ordained only in the diocese where he was born and moving to another diocese without special permission was not allowed. But there were many candidates for the ministry who wanted to be ordained by the inspiring archbishop in Uppsala. To the great annoyance of the other bishops, he did not abstain from inviting them to the archdiocese. Altogether he ordained 198 priests for Uppsala and no fewer than 79 of them were born in other dioceses. To begin with, ordinations took place during Söderblom's first year in connection with evening prayer, but he soon changed that. Ordinations were to take place in direct relation to high mass and were to include communion, just as in the Anglican Church. He created an atmosphere of sanctity and festivity around the ordination service so that each priest would remember the event with joy. His homilies were simple, sincere, and seemingly improvised.

He demanded much of himself, but also of his priests. He did not have much tolerance for stupidity, and even less for laziness. He did not hide either his sympathies or his antipathies. He wanted his clergy to excel in at least some area and he very much appreciated those who were devoted to research, virtually regardless of the field. He valued the younger priests, many of whom he had come to know as a professor. Some clergy he picked out for international tasks.

The diocesan chapter was a regular feature of his working week. He set aside time to counsel members concerning various problems in the parishes, but he took formal matters lightly and did not always involve himself in routine affairs, such as hiring an instructor in a primary school or even minor doctrinal questions. On the other hand, he did a great deal of work on comprehensive questions such as the rights of dissenters, instruction in Christianity, or organizational reforms. He knew his diocese inside and out and maintained contact with the clergy as much as possible. In the diocesan chapter, he held all the threads together.

As archbishop, however, he had to take responsibility for the future of the entire church. When the war came to a close, the bond between church and state in Sweden began to be questioned by radical leftists. They threatened to hold the church hostage for their socialist politics.

20

The Freedom of the Church

> To deny the ideals guiding the labor movement would be to deny the Bible.
>
> *Nathan Söderblom, 1918*

ALREADY IN PARIS Nathan Söderblom becomes known as a great fund-raiser. In one way or another he always finds the money he needs. He steps into the office of a businessman in Stockholm, tells him about a diaconic training center that needs to be built, and asks for a hundred thousand crowns. Caught by surprise, the man promises to give him what he asked for. The appeal for war casualties brings in millions. In America he receives many thousands of dollars to transmit to clergy and academics in post-war Europe. As the great Stockholm Conference approaches, he asks clergy in the various dioceses to identify wealthy individuals who might consider contributing. He writes to one person after another and raises the money he needs. He does not underestimate the desire of people to do good and he offers them the satisfaction of giving. His own family economy, however, is fragile; he has many mouths to feed. Without the extra income he receives from writing, it would be impossible.

* * *

For Nathan Söderblom, the church was an indispensible and integrated part of the life of Swedish culture. He aimed at also making it an international actor for justice, peace, and unity. Even if, as Bishop of Uppsala, he put the concerns of the diocese before everything else, he still felt called to far greater tasks. He described them in four concentric circles. The innermost circle was made up of the Church of Sweden itself with its General Synod, Bishops' Conference, General Church Assembly, and a long list of boards and committees. The next circle consisted of Swedish descendants in other countries. They had lived for hundreds of years in Finland, the

Baltic nations, and Russia. In the United States, the Augustana Synod had 600,000 members who still used the Swedish language in worship. For all of these, the Swedish archbishop felt a certain responsibility. The third circle included other Lutherans in Scandinavia, Germany, and France, minority churches in Eastern Europe, and other Lutheran churches in the United States. In this circle there were also Lutheran congregations in Latin America, Africa, and Asia. The fourth and largest circle was that of the whole of Christianity. This was divided into Evangelical (Protestant), Roman Catholic, and Orthodox churches. In Söderblom's church geography, the Catholic and Orthodox churches lay far away and he did not take into account the growing Pentecostal movement or the African Independent Churches. In his Christian universe, Wittenberg had a privileged place as the home of the Reformation. Moreover, Constantinople, Canterbury, and Uppsala were not to be seen as second to Rome in respect to a meaningful and living catholic tradition.

He was convinced that precisely in his capacity as the Archbishop of Uppsala he had a historically determined call to symbolize and to work actively for the unity of the church, not only in Sweden but also among other Christians of Swedish heritage, in the churches of the Reformation, and ultimately in all of Christianity. The universal church contained a nearly limitless diversity of local churches. He avoided speaking of "the Church of Sweden," "the Swedish church," or "our church." Instead, he used expressions like "the church and congregations of Christ in Sweden" or "Christianity in Sweden." This included all organized religious enterprises, both the state church and the free churches, and all true believers. The congregation of Christ in Sweden was greater than the Church of Sweden and it was a "side chapel" in the universal church.

He attributed to the archbishop's seat in Uppsala a position comparable to the leading patriarchates in Christendom. This was, to say the least, presumptuous. When it came down to it, Sweden was an out-of-the-way part of the world and in recent times had scarcely distinguished itself in respect either to theology or spiritual life. The role of Gustavus Adolphus in the seventeenth century had not strengthened Sweden's international position as much as Söderblom thought, with the possible exception of its estimation in Germany and Austria. The Church of Sweden was actually, at the start of the twentieth century, a largely decaying provincial church that lived on the gracious conditions established by the state and borrowed most of its theology and church music from other parts of the world. The spiritual power of the church had been drained by emigration and the rise of the free churches. Even if the Young Church Movement and a number of voluntary organizations had sparked new enthusiasm and had laid the groundwork for a democratization of the church, as an institution it was bound both hand and foot and people had low expectations of it. The church was not an independent social "body" within society, but appeared more like a child's drawing of a person with a large head and spindly arms and legs. The priests had responsibility for just about everything. They distributed the Word and sacraments to rather passive residents of the parish who had little to say about the congregation's inner life.

Söderblom needed a concrete basis for his work, especially when his tasks brought him beyond Sweden's borders. The state church with its underdeveloped democratic structure did not offer him the organization his mission required. In spite of the fact that he was archbishop, he never had at his disposal anything other than an extremely small secretariat. He was like a lonely St. George struggling against the social injustices of the time — unbridled capitalism, militarism, and nationalism — in order to save the church's credibility and its desire for unity. At the beginning he could not even count on the support of the bishops.

The Lutheran distinction between the earthly and the spiritual kingdoms had marked Sweden for four hundred years. The church was not accustomed to criticizing the government, much less confronting it. As an established church, it was expected neither to carry on a critique of society nor to engage in shaping opinion. Its task was to preach law and gospel and by the example of individuals to influence families and society. The church's highest representative organ was the General Synod, but from that body Söderblom did not expect much. It had come into being in connection with the constitutional reform of Parliament in 1866. With sixty elected members — half clergy, half laity — it was approximately the same size as the old ecclesiastical estate. The bishops were all members of the Synod and dominated the discussions. Among the laity in the Synod there was a clear overrepresentation of high government officials, landowners, and industrial leaders. They represented their dioceses but with no political mandate. The Church Assembly was, as Tor Andrae described it, "a most pure gerontocracy, a peculiar relic in that youthful century." It was convened at several-year intervals in order to deal with the issues delegated to it by the government, chiefly changes in the church law or the liturgical books. All such matters required the synodical consent, but the Parliament made the final decisions. In practice this meant that the General Synod had a kind of veto right but not much authority of its own. It was a formalistic, circumscribed, and sluggish institution that did not appeal to Söderblom and never became his forum. In contrast to some of his predecessors who were political thoroughbreds, Söderblom preferred to express his concerns in speeches and writings and in more informal contexts. Although he was chairman of the General Synod, he allowed the astute and experienced Gottfrid Billing to handle most things unchallenged up to his death in 1925.

The Bishops Conference appeared to be a more suitable arena for Söderblom. It had no official status but it offered the possibility of regular discussions between the bishops. It had been instituted in 1902 with the aim of preparing for meetings of the General Synod. Söderblom convened a meeting of the bishops in connection with his consecration and immediately assumed leadership. The bishops had not voted for him, but when he was officially named, they had acknowledged the situation and sent telegrams of congratulation. Most of them had known Söderblom for a long time. His friendly consideration quickly put them in a better mood, but they were determined to use the Bishops Conference to exercise a "moderating, supporting, and binding influence" on him. They considered whether the Bishops Conference should become a permanent committee of the General Synod but in light of the fragile relationship between church and state, they did not pursue the matter. The Conference took on new tasks and established a working procedure, but it remained an independent grouping. That it regularly held its meetings in Stockholm and not in Uppsala de-emphasized the archbishop's importance even though he set its agenda. After a few years, Söderblom was able to gather the bishops around a joint episcopal letter that dealt with the war. In this letter, they together formulated the church's global responsibility in line with Söderblom's vision of a church that was united and without borders. Some of the bishops gradually became involved in his international program, but it went slowly. Their knowledge of foreign languages was poor, there was never enough time, and the bishops had little understanding of contacts beyond the Lutheran churches. The only one of them who had any international experience to speak of was von Schéele in Visby, but he was already elderly. Like the General Synod, the Bishops Conference also lacked qualifications for serving as a base for Söderblom's detailed ecumenical program. Seen organizationally, it really hung in the air, totally dependent on him and a handful of individual supporters. But the ecumenical program itself took on legitimacy by virtue of the fact that Söderblom acted in his capacity as archbishop of one of the world's largest churches.

The bishops were nervous that Söderblom would help himself to all too much freedom. Even if they attempted to hold him back, the attention of the media on him meant that he personally always landed in the spotlight. In practice, this made the archbishop more than *primus inter pares*, first among equals. The general public's positive expectations of the young and unpredictable Söderblom encouraged him to interpret his mission in his own way.

He was an experienced communicator and took every occasion to reach out. One such occasion was, for later generations of Swedes, almost incomprehensible: to prepare the royal edict for the annual Days of Prayer. In his time, these yearly proclamations awakened great interest. They were an obvious expression of the connection between church and state. King Gustav Vasa initiated four special Days of Prayer each year, which later received the names Penitential Day, Reformation Day, Mission Day, and Thanksgiving Day. Since the king determined when these days were to be observed and confirmed the appeals, they took on national character. The royal edict was read from all the pulpits on New Year's Day. This filled the churches with people who wanted to hear the king's appeal as well as annual statistical information about the community. At the government's request, Söderblom prepared the texts for the Days of Prayer. He gave them such provocative content that on occasion the government felt forced to censor him, but even when the texts were made milder they gave rise to public debate.

It was well known that on social questions Söderblom took positions friendly to the workers. Ever since he had spoken in 1897 to the History of Religions Congress in Stockholm and called the students at Skokloster to give a cheer for the workers, "our land's true nobility who bear the burden and the heat of the day," people knew where they had him on the political scale of right and left. The year before he became archbishop, the Minister of Ecclesiastical Affairs in the Liberal government, Fridtjuv Berg, for the first time asked him to write the proclamation for the Days of Prayer, which in the king's name would be read in the churches. He chose to criticize the lack of communal responsibility so evident in society: "There still are in Sweden families who in spite of honest efforts cannot give their children sufficient bread or secure for them a good home." He called for a zeal that set fellow human beings above all else. In his sermons and lectures he emphasized issues of solidarity and justice, injustice, and lovelessness. His text for 1915 was also colored by his social view of Christianity: "From the distress of Swedish homes and their hopeless battle against need, come cries, perhaps unspoken yet heard by God, against a society in which others have won a secure place. Woe to the unconcealed yet specious self-interest of individuals or classes that indifferently close their eyes to their brothers' suffering and thereby make themselves unworthy of society's protection."

The Conservative government had appointed an archbishop who was not afraid ideologically to take sides with the opposition, even if he kept out of party politics. The Minister was forced to heavily edit the text before it was handed over to the king for his signature. The next year the cabinet, for safety's sake, and without informing Söderblom, turned to J. A. Eklund, the Bishop of Karlstad, in order to obtain a more acceptable proposal. Nevertheless, it was still Söderblom who stood for the final text to the Swedish people. He admonished them to social justice in solidarity with those in need, and to peace and reconciliation in the world. These were the same issues that occupied him in both his diocesan episcopal letter and his appeal for peace. At a Service of Prayer in the Uppsala Cathedral on May 1, 1917, when four thousand workers demonstrated in Uppsala, he sharpened his tone and attacked the exorbitant profits made in the economies of industrialism and financial speculation. He demanded that the state intervene: "This ruthless desire for profit must be kept in check. It must not prevail by trading on the sweat and pain, yes, on the health and life of the workers." He was thoroughly skeptical of liberalism and stood close to the labor movement, but he insisted that the church not identify itself with one or another political program. The Social Democrat Värner Rydén took over the post of Minister of Ecclesiastical Affairs in November 1917. He made a few additions to the text for the Days of Prayer, but he eliminated nothing from Söderblom's draft. Even in 1919 he allowed the remark to be retained that "gold piles up excessively for a few, while there are still Swedish homes where in spite of their loyal fulfillment of duty people live in drudgery and insecurity." The following year, when Olof Olsson was the responsible state official, a few of Söderblom's sentences aroused considerable attention:

"Rightly distributed, there is enough daily bread for everyone. Rightly distributed, work does not need to oppress anyone."

The war had finally come to an end, but political and social unrest spread. Bolshevism took power in Russia in November 1917, introducing a violent campaign against the church. This resulted in a complete divorce between the state and the church, from which all privileges and property were taken. Bishops and priests were imprisoned and executed. Education was completely secularized. The Russian government undertook a severe purging of everything connected with religion. In Germany too there was political radicalization and both Social Democrats and Communists demanded a divorce between church and state. This was carried out in 1919 by the Weimar Republic, but in a more favorable way for the church than in Russia. The church was allowed to retain both property and income by taxation.

In Sweden, developments in Germany were followed with great interest, but even more so developments in Finland. At New Year 1918, the "Red Terror" was let loose in Helsinki, leading to civil war between "Reds" and "Whites." In Sweden, highly vocal opinion was expressed in favor of supporting the Whites with weapons. The loudest wanted direct military intervention from the Swedish side. A volunteer battalion was formed but mobilization in support of the Whites was vigorously opposed by the political left. During February, more than five hundred rallies were held around Sweden in opposition to armed action in Finland. This conflict of views created a nervous and dangerous atmosphere in Sweden, perhaps the worst during World War I, and violence lurked on both sides. At a large rally of workers held on February 11 in Sandviken, Söderblom entered the debate directly, warning of revolution. He maintained that Sweden's civil order could develop toward greater social justice. Söderblom appealed for confidence in the newly elected Swedish government.

In the fall 1917 election, the left had increased and this resulted for the first time in a coalition government of Liberals and Social Democrats. Arthur Engberg had been elected to the Second Chamber of Parliament. Together with a group of young Social Democrats — Per Albin Hansson, Gustav Möller, Per Edvin Sköld, and others — he immediately assumed a leading role. He was twenty-two years younger than Söderblom and also came from Hälsingland. Söderblom had been his examiner when he graduated from gymnasium and had encouraged him to become a priest. That did not happen; in the choice between a humanistic education and politics, politics won out. As editor-in-chief of *Arbetet* from 1918 and of *Social Demokraten* from 1924, he came to be seen as the party's great cultural personality. Engberg not only had a comprehensive classical education and a lively interest in religion, but he also came to accept the moral nihilism and negative view of religion held by the philosopher Axel Hägerström. As a student he had taken part in many of the then popular debates regarding religion, Einar Billing often having been his opponent.

When the radical left wave swept over Europe, Engberg began his campaign against the state church system. He distanced himself from Söderblom's attempt to anchor the church in the labor movement. Christianity and socialism were, according to Engberg, irreconcilable, a view that in 1918 he expressed in Parliament in connection with a motion to separate the church from the state. He conceded, however, that the state church system had its positive sides. It offered the possibility of both controlling religious life and of combating superstition and obscurantism. In the Parliamentary debate, Engberg's fellow Social Democrat Harald Hallén — a priest from Arvika on whom Söderblom would rely during the debate — became his chief opponent.

Tension continued and in 1920, Söderblom's text for the Days of Prayer brought about an acute crisis. Olof Olsson had become Minister of Ecclesiastical Affairs. He was a "heathen" who took Engberg's side and refused to support the Christian message that was imbedded in the text. The rules were then altered so that the archbishop alone would take full responsibility for the text. This gave rise to an indignant debate. That the king and the government would no longer sanction the text was interpreted by J. A. Eklund and the right as a blow against the state church and the first step toward its dissolution. But for Engberg, it was a sign that the archbishop had further strengthened his position, which did not please him.

Söderblom was exposed to repeated attacks from Engberg's side but for a long time met them with humor. The archbishop jokingly recalled a person whose temperament went berserk in old Hälsingland: "I see before me a shouting, noisy person who hops around and strikes from one side and then the other. So contradictory were the arguments of this gifted, warmhearted, and mightily ambitious young countryman." Soon, however, the tone became more serious between them. In spite of a certain respect for Söderblom, Engberg did not believe that the gulf between them could ever be bridged: "Our understandings toward life are so different. Therefore, an open conflict between us is unavoidable." Söderblom represented an alternative ideology that attracted the bourgeois non-socialists. He combined cultural conservatism with worker-friendly anti-socialism and anticipated a socially conservative solution to the problems of inequality. This was more in line with the kind of Christian democratic welfare politics that he had seen in Germany than with leftist Swedish socialism, which was tinted with Marxism. The newspapers were filled with editorials and columns. Matters concerning the state church added grist to Engberg's mill. Söderblom's attempt to harmoniously integrate church and culture within a preserved state church system had, according to Engberg, no chance at all of being realized. Nevertheless, he did not propose an immediate divorce. First, the church should be neutralized by being placed totally under the control of the state. Property should be confiscated, the General Synod abolished, and the clergy appointed by the government as common civil servants. Only when the church was completely domesticated should it be done away with.

Attacks against the church did not come only from the left. A number of Liberals like Torsten Fogelqvist and Torgny Segerstedt, who were not known as defenders of orthodox Christianity, warned that modern theology was beginning to hollow out the traditional conceptions of faith, with the consequence that the teachings of the church were crumbling away. Söderblom understood the criticism as being basically the same from both sides. Neither free thinkers nor "old church" traditionalists were able to grasp the freedom that genuine trust in God gave, but rather ended up, in different ways, in a kind of fundamentalism. Such a literalistic Christianity was not evangelical, wrote Söderblom, and it was not at all the case that an undogmatic Christianity lacked backbone. True confidence in God set people free from being slavishly bound to dogma. The presupposition for true confidence was subordination to the living God, not fixation on words.

The debate regarding church and state intensified. The church's proponents recognized the seriousness of the whole matter and began to prepare themselves for a change in relationships. Has the time come, wrote the coming Bishop of Härnösand Torsten Bohlin in *Vår Lösen* (*Our Watchword*), for the church to take the initiative toward breaking up its alliance with the state? If the state made the situation of the church untenable, the church must go its own way even if its property were expropriated. It was necessary to be prepared for conflict. Many from the Young Church Movement wanted to see a more activistic church that demanded greater freedom. The Union of Clergy and the Diocese of Gothenburg, in contrast, defended the old system. For them, the whole matter involved nothing less than Christianity's position in society and its influence on the lives of people. Most of the debaters were in agreement that a continued connection to the state was advantageous for the church; it was above all the members of the free churches who believed that it would be best for the church if it broke that connection. They thus tended to make common cause with Engberg. Söderblom chose to lie low. He was of the opinion that it was not in the church's interest to destroy the bridges to the state and he sought a solution that would avoid confrontation.

In what amounted to a programmatic lecture given at the newly built Engelbrekt Church in Stockholm on December 8, 1918, Söderblom spoke in opposition to Engberg and made a proposal as to how the alienation between clergy and the workers movement could be overcome. He pointed out that the patriarchal attitude toward social and economic questions that had prevailed among the clergy had inhibited the church, but was now being overcome. In his view, priests could take whatever political position they wanted, but that position must not block them from people who had a special need of consideration and care. The church endorsed the demand for social justice because it was in agreement with the spirit of the Old Testament prophets and the spirit of Christ. It would, he added, be a denial of the Bible to deny the ideals that guided the labor movement. He himself had stood up for those ideals as early as 1897 when the Social Democrats did not yet have much influence. Now he wanted to awaken a spiritual unrest among clergy and fellow Christians that would help call the church to fulfill its task in the service of people and society.

The same day that he gave this speech to a fully crowded church, a special committee of Parliament reached an agreement concerning the right to vote in local elections. Under threat of a revolution, King Gustaf V and the political right were forced to approve a democratization of government proposed by the Liberal and Social Democratic parties. Söderblom stood on the government's side and personally attempted to persuade the leaders of the political right to listen to reason. When the democratic breakthrough became a fact, Söderblom wrote to the Minister of Ecclesiastical Affairs and congratulated him. But Bishop J. A. Eklund did not welcome the change, which would, according to him, cause Sweden's constitution to collapse and guarantee the complete victory of the left. While neither belonged to any party, Eklund and Söderblom represented the extremes within the Swedish episcopate. The antagonism that had existed between them since they came to Uppsala was now to be seen in the light of day. Söderblom adopted a positive view of the growing democratization; Eklund lamented "the unchristian march of democracy." Engberg opposed both. In the spring of 1919 things really heated up.

Then it was that Rydén drove legislation through Parliament that would take catechetical instruction out of the public schools and reduce the study of Christianity to two hours per week with an emphasis on the Sermon on the Mount and ethics. The Bishops Conference, as one would expect, went to the defense of school-based catechetical instruction. There was also a motion placed before the 1920 congress of the Social Democratic Party that the state church should be done away with and all church property should be placed under the ownership of the general public. In this debate, Arthur Engberg and Harald Hallén again opposed each other. Hallén, using France as an example, warned that there would be a conservative reaction if the church began to be dismantled, but he suggested, along with other compromises, that there could be free withdrawal from — that is, membership in — the church. The congress adopted Engberg's proposal, but Hallén succeeded in having passed "an opinion in defense of religious values" that dampened the effect of the proposal. Even with complete religious freedom, the state should offer a legal framework and economic means for a preserved folk church. Engberg saw otherwise. For him, the state church was an aspect of state activity, similar to schools or defense. Therefore, it should be placed totally under the control of the state so that when the time was right, it could be discarded. He began by offering a motion in Parliament to abolish the right of the General Synod to veto proposals from the government on church matters.

Agitation against the folk church also increased within the free churches. After a crisis in the Student Christian Movement in 1912 when the free church students chose to go their own way, those churches were radicalized under the leadership of Axel Andersson of the Mission Covenant Church, the Baptist N. J. Nordström, and the Methodist August Strömstedt. The paper *Frikyrklig Tidskrift* covered everything Söderblom did with a critical eye. The Baptist Gunnar Westin, who was later to become professor, under the pseudonym of Per Gune wrote one critical article after another about Söderblom in the daily newspaper *Svenska Morgonbladet*. The distrust of Söderblom among free church leaders was increased by Söderblom's own low estimate of the liberal Prime Minister Nils Edén. When the Young Church Movement acted to support the conservatives, Söderblom defended democracy and universal suffrage even though he also expressed anxiety about what might happen if power were given into the hands of the uneducated masses. In 1912, his wife Anna had actively participated in a campaign against women's suffrage, but was vigorously opposed by her husband's old friend Lydia Wahlström. But now universal suffrage was on its way — the Parliament's decision was made on May 24, 1919. Thus one disagreement between Social Democrats, the free churches, and established church could be put aside. Söderblom wanted to direct attention forward.

On the Second Day of Easter 1919 he again spoke in the large Engelbrekt Church, which was completely filled with people, among them the crown prince and his wife. His theme was: "Are We Going toward the Rebirth of Religion?" After the war there were some signs of such a development and Söderblom, for his part, was convinced that humankind, after such suffering, would move toward the central mystery of Christianity: the cross of Christ. Reconciliation was necessary and where could it be found other than in Christ? He was not speaking about church growth but rather about the deepening of the inner life. If the churches did not reconcile with each other, how could the nations? The rebirth of religion, therefore, was a condition for peace. The cross was humanity's hope. Much in Christianity had lost its power and should be left behind as relics of history. That applied to ideas and formulations that had hardened into dogma even though they did not have their origin in the biblical prophets and evangelists, being products rather of Hellenistic and Near Eastern culture.

The first volume of the anthology *Det andliga nutidsläget och kyrkan* (*The Present Spiritual Situation and the Church*) had just been published. An essay by the liberal theologian Emanuel Linderholm, "From Dogma to the Gospel," proved to be its most controversial contribution, but Linderholm was not the only author pleading for a radical reformation of the Church of Sweden, for a new process of training clergy, and also for a church more in tune with current culture. The volume had a short introduction by Söderblom. In his lecture, he mentioned the book in passing without taking a position regarding its contents. That he even made a reference to the book resulted in him being violently criticized by both conservative and politically liberal free church people. The anthology, whose second and third volumes soon appeared, was described as a coordinated attack by modern theology against free church and conservative Christians. That Manfred Björkquist was the editor and the conservative bishops J. A. Eklund and Hjalmar Danell both had essays in the book did not help. Some regarded the book as a concession offered by theologians who wanted to retain the state church. They were accused of being prepared to make whatever compromises of faith were necessary to get the general public on their side.

Söderblom became the scapegoat for all of this. That *Svenska Morgonbladet* would accuse him was foreseeable. Arthur Engberg's vile attack bothered him more. He described Söderblom as a chameleon and a master at saying yes and no simultaneously. He could in the same breath dismiss dogmas as "shells and mythology" and also swear that he would not touch hard-won formulations. He was a dramatic actor who sat in several chairs at the same time. Now Engberg wanted an answer: Did or did not Söderblom agree with Linderholm's essay? Would the state religion in the future need to carry with it all its dogmatic rubbish? Engberg did not get a clear answer. He found Söderblom's reply to his question a dazzling pyrotechnics of words that said everything yet nothing. Therefore, Engberg had only contempt for the archbishop's "tightrope walking" and for hiding the fact that he himself was waving farewell to dogma. The culturally radical Social Democrat Martin Koch was even stronger: Söderblom's conduct was nothing other than dishonesty and church political calculation. He had come out as a new little Luther in order, under false pretenses, to bring about a new reformation. But in reality, he had nothing to offer to those in spiritual need other than historical delicacies, aesthetic drivel, theatrical jokes, and emotional feelings.

Under attack from radical Social Democrats, liberals, and free church leaders, all of whom questioned the state church, Söderblom attempted to win over forces in the labor movement who were not hostile toward the church and used the splits in the party to his advantage. The Social Democrat priest Harald Hallén, who had been a member of Parliament since 1912, kept Söderblom well informed concerning developments in the party. Söderblom's special friend was the unskilled laborer and agitator Fabian Månsson whose novel *Rättfärdiggörelsen genom tron* (*Justification by Faith*) had many readers. For him, socialism and Christianity were the two foundation stones of life and the church was an indispensable moral force in society. Söderblom had appointed him to the hymnal committee. Things moved slowly, but finally Söderblom had to stand up openly against Engberg, "the country's specialist in hostility to the church." In a number of lectures in different places the archbishop described his own position regarding the church-state question, but he kept most of his ammunition for the General Church Assembly in Stockholm in March 1920.

He was tired of everything, nearly ready to resign. He wanted to return to his research in the history of religions. In the middle of February he wrote to Manfred Björkquist: "Inept as I am in everything political, I heartily wish that I could turn to a more spiritual way of serving the church and the Kingdom of God." It was painful to him that he was forced to waste his energy on an endless variety of tasks for the sake of church institutions and interests. He would rather have devoted the years he had left to that which he knew better than anything else, the study of religion, but he had no choice other than to do the best he could in his present position. He was torn between research and the public role that demanded all his time and strength, but he was nevertheless able to rejoice that religion captured its place "among people of depth even in the labor movement."

The General Church Assembly was a major event. It offered a chance for common church people to meet, especially around questions of diaconia and mission. In contrast to the General Synod, it had a broad democratic foundation. Of the six hundred delegates from the whole country most were laypeople. Altogether, two thousand people gathered in Stockholm's Blasieholmen Church. It had been built for revivals in 1868 and had three balconies with the pulpit as the center of attention. In the midst of Stockholm — not far from the House of Parliament — Söderblom took the occasion to demonstrate the church's democratic will and popular roots. Well aware of his lack of support in the General Synod and the Bishops Conference, he turned the General Church Assembly into an opinion-shaping organ that he controlled himself and where he was not bound by legislation and rules of procedure. It became his most important ecclesial base for international work for peace, ecumenical relations, social engagement, and now also for a showdown with the political wing of the Social Democratic Party that was most radically against the church. In addition to Fabian Månsson, he saw to it that the Social Democratic member of Parliament P. H. Sjöblom had a place on the program. Both could seriously lay claim to representing the working class.

He himself spoke on "The Church's Claim for Freedom." The speech later came to be regarded as the high point of his church political career. The theme was occasioned by Engberg's motion in Parliament to do away with the Church Assembly's right to veto. Söderblom found it repugnant to refute an individual's hatred of Christianity, but it was now necessary. The matter concerned nothing less than the integrity and freedom of the church. Arthur Engberg's plan was that Parliament should be given unrestricted power over the life, teaching, and organization of the congregations. But if the church were to serve the Kingdom of God in the world, Söderblom said, it needed *both* a material base *and* freedom to fulfill its task on its own terms. The archbishop called the threat to give church property to the state "murder with intent to rob" and found it "refreshing" that such a proposal was met with opposition even within the Social Democratic Party. He underlined the church's right to handle its own affairs and proposed both a modernized General Synod and a centralized church administration. Both of these things could be brought about by strengthening the existing voluntary diocesan councils. There was also a need for permanent church management structures on the diocesan level. All coercion from the state must cease. Those who desire it should have full freedom to leave the church. The clergy needed assistance with civil record keeping in order that they could devote themselves to their central task. The church buildings should not be profaned by civil burials. The church-state question should be made the subject of a popular referendum. Since the state could not do without religion without injuring itself, it should listen to reason and give the church its full support.

The General Church Assembly had the church and the labor movement as its overall theme. Söderblom was eager to demonstrate how democratization and economic equality emanated from Christianity and therefore should not only be accepted but promoted by the church. For several decades he had been greatly preoccupied with social questions, but he had never developed a fully well thought out economic and social program. He focused on one social issue after another: inequality, poverty, the housing shortage, abuse, and unemployment. In lectures, newspaper articles, and sermons, he offered concrete and immediate local examples of need and misery and emphasized the special responsibility of Christians to take action. At times he would point directly to individuals who were guilty of causing distress, as he did in Solna in 1921 when he singled out by name a property owner in Huvudsta who was directly responsible for miserable living conditions. The media paid a great deal of attention and "the greedy troll," as Söderblom called him, attempted to bring him to court. "Too bad that I did not receive a summons," he wrote to his daughter Lucie. "That would have been the finishing touch and perhaps done the trick in Huvudsta."

Söderblom insisted that salvation was something other and more than social justice. That he counted Fabian Månsson among his friends caused many to raise their eyebrows and he took every occasion to support the priests who sat on the Social Democrat bench in Parliament, Harald Hallén and Ernst Klefbeck. But he kept himself out of party politics.

At the Assembly, P. H. Sjöblom spoke on "The Labor Movement's Materialism" and Fabian Månsson on "The Gospel and the Renewal of Society." Söderblom noticed that Hjalmar Branting had sneaked into one of the balconies in order to hear what was being said. Branting, "the father of socialism in Sweden," served as prime minister. Söderblom called him to the podium and welcomed him with hearty admiration: "You dedicated your life to the labor movement at a time when this did not bring power, honor, or glory, rather the opposite," said the archbishop. Those who look beneath the surface have long known the spirit of idealism and sacrifice, which, under different theories, constitutes the essence of the workers' movement. What does the church stand for? An unselfish mercy, a zeal of righteousness, and a faith that is far beyond measure. In our time, we cannot afford unnecessary antagonisms and unnecessary divisions. Rather, we need "ever greater common understanding between all honest wills, between all upright idealisms which possess an unselfish desire for good and which can work for the blessing of our youth and for the spiritual and moral life of Sweden."

Söderblom's and Branting's handshake in the Blasieholmen Church can be interpreted as a turning point in relations between the church and the Social Democrats. The acute crisis was over. The church began to discover a new role in the modern, democratic society. But Söderblom came to be regarded as a "situational theologian" who sought to satisfy everyone — both the state church and the free church, both the faithful and the agnostics, both the conservatives and the Social Democrats. Just a few months after the General Church Assembly, the Social Democrats lost their coveted power of government.

21
Practical Christianity

> Never before in world history has it happened that a nation, which above most others is characterized by industry, order, and care for society's poor, has been brought to such nameless suffering as the now blockaded and afflicted German people. Hundreds of thousands perish from hunger. Innocent children suffer the most.
>
> *Nathan Söderblom, 1919*

In April 1921, Nathan Söderblom comes to Berlin. The needs continue to dismay. He has a long list of children who are living under miserable conditions and need help. Spontaneously, he turns to the priests of the archdiocese: "Are there any homes in your parishes that can receive some of these children, in addition to what you already have done with willing love?" The children come. The archbishop's wife, Anna Söderblom, the wife of a bank director, Svea Ameln, the mayor's wife, Ellen von Bahr, and Thyra Quensel, the wife of a professor, find homes for them for several months.

* * *

When the delegates to the small conference on peace held in Uppsala in 1917 traveled home just eight days before Christmas, they had drawn up an outline for a larger conference. They hoped that it would take place within six months, but the reality of the war did not allow it. It was unrealistic to think that an international conference could be convened in April 1918. Those who were invited must first make the delicate decision as to whether or not they would even come. That required careful consideration. To make such a journey through war-torn Europe or across the North Sea, not to speak of crossing the Atlantic, was for many a practical impossibility. The project seemed dead even before it began, but Söderblom did not allow himself to be stopped. He got Bishops Hans Ostenfeld of Copenhagen and

Jens Tandberg of Oslo to send out invitations in every direction. The objective was unclearly formulated, but the bishops pointed out that it would be an irreparable loss and a scandal for the church if it failed to show the cross of Christ as a uniting power, stronger than all national antagonisms. The motivation for the conference was religious. The actual encounter of Christians from both sides of the conflict was what was essential, not this or that resolution. If they only came together, the result would speak for itself. The agenda should be based on the six points that were discussed at the December meeting: the spiritual unity of Christians, Christianity and war, ways to peace, the inviolability of justice, the international legal system, and also practical problems such as the practice of missions in each other's colonies. Everything was imprecise and very general. A definite date for the conference was not set, nor was it decided whether it would be held in Uppsala; Switzerland and Norway were also suggested. Much had been built on wishful thinking and already in February Söderblom found it necessary to move the conference ahead to September. His attempt to bring church leaders together in 1918 demonstrated both a nearly desperate desire to break deadlocked positions and an astounding overconfidence in the possibility of bringing about something decisive.

The September conference would, Söderblom hoped, be large and representative. Since no one from the warring countries desired or was allowed to encounter enemies, he planned an arrangement in which delegates from neutral countries, the Central Powers, and the Allies would work in different sections so they would not meet each other. Common discussions would be held only if everyone desired them and only if there were conditions allowing such discussion. The deliberations would be strictly confidential. In the invitations it was promised that no one would be at risk for unanticipated encounters with enemies, inside or outside the facilities. Such a guarantee was necessary if the conference were actually to take place. Above all, it was the French who refused to have the slightest contact with the Germans. Only an irrepressibly optimistic and strong-willed person like Nathan Söderblom could dream that under such circumstances a constructive conversation could take place.

In the archbishop's residence, Knut Westman and Yngve Brilioth worked day and night. They wrote letters and sent telegrams with invitations to evangelical churches and Christian organizations in Germany, France, Great Britain, Austria, Hungary, the Netherlands, Switzerland, and the United States, and also to the Old Catholic Church and the Orthodox Churches and, not to be forgotten, the Roman Catholic Church. In every sort of positive reaction, Söderblom saw his dreams coming true and he looked forward to a major ecumenical gathering.

He had collaborators who spoke for the event. The Swedish priests in Paris, London, Berlin, and Copenhagen supported him wholeheartedly, as did the diplomat Harald Bildt in Rome and above all, Johannes Kolmodin in Constantinople. He was a son of the conservative professor in exegetics Adolf Kolmodin who, in spite of his involvement in mission work, never fully understood Söderblom's extensive ecumenism. Johannes Kolmodin was a docent in Semitic languages and also one of Harald Hjärne's students. He traveled to Constantinople in 1917 in order to study Turkish sources relevant to the history of Charles XII. He remained there for many years, holding a modest position in the Swedish legation, and he became Söderblom's indispensable contact person in the Near East. With nearly inexhaustible knowledge and diplomatic finesse, he succeeded in getting Patriarch Germanos V to consider sending a bishop to Uppsala when he was assured that Archbishop Söderblom was independent in relation to Rome and the only archbishop among twelve to fifteen million Christians. Germanos perhaps believed Uppsala to be a kind of Nordic-Baltic patriarchate and Söderblom had nothing against that. Ever since he himself visited Constantinople in 1911, he had sought to include the Orthodox world in his work for Christian unity. With the help of Kolmodin, it appeared that he might succeed. But in order to get the Patriarchate on board it was necessary to have the cooperation of both the *Sublime Porte* — the Ottomanic government — and the Foreign Ministry of Sweden.

Everyone who was invited from the warring countries found reasons not to come. Some felt that the conference should have been held in Switzerland, others found it impossible to meet before the war was over. The Vatican, which at the time did not even recognize Protestants as authentically Christian, formulated a diplomatic but definite *non possumus*. The Patriarch in Constantinople was sympathetic, but in the end named no one. In Germany, there were some theologians who were prepared to travel, but only as private individuals. They preferred, moreover, that the conference be limited to Protestant participants. In England, the Archbishop of Canterbury consulted carefully with the government before he replied that the Anglicans could participate only if Orthodox and Roman Catholic bishops were also there. There were, however, others in Great Britain who gave Söderblom their full support. The French firmly rejected all invitations. To participate in a conference with Germans also present would be treason toward the heroic French soldiers. Any spiritual fellowship with German Christians would not be possible before the Germans officially acknowledged their responsibility for the war. Moreover, in France Söderblom was viewed as clearly German-friendly. The Americans were impressed by the French and also declined to participate, holding the Swedish archbishop to be decidedly "pro-German."

There was nothing that could be done. The planned conference was canceled. All efforts had been in vain. The European community was fragmented and the churches were so deeply split that they were not able to look beyond the hostilities to remind themselves of what they had in common in spite of the war: the Christian heritage. Christian leaders around the world, however, understood that the Archbishop of Uppsala was prepared to gather the churches to work together for peace as soon as it was possible. By means of copious correspondence, Söderblom kept the idea of a conference alive. He looked forward to the day when "Germany, the people of industry, scholarship, dreams, and passionate music, France, the nation with style and taste, brilliance and burnished energy, and the British Empire with maturely realistic wisdom and practiced in the art of government, with its mystics and with our civilization's most excellent type of humanity" would reach understanding. That was a dream, but with God, nothing was impossible.

When the conference plans came to a standstill, Söderblom soon struck out in another direction. He decided to make use of the flexible rules of the Olaus Petri Foundation and invite lecturers from different countries to come to Uppsala to speak on the theme, "The Unity of the Church." The lectures were to illuminate the churches' positions vis-à-vis each other, dealing with various aspects of Christian unity. As long as the war continued, it was difficult to hold these lectures as planned, but as soon as the weapons were silent, it became easier. In spite of the difficulties of travel, church leaders and academics made their way to Uppsala where they were received with the archbishop's hospitality, the cathedral's festive worship, and the students' eagerness to hear from the churches that had been separated from them during the war but that now were coming into a changed world.

For Söderblom himself, these lectures put him in direct contact with people he would work with later. The lecturers came one at a time and did not risk running into their enemies. Nevertheless, Pastor Edouard Soulier's participation caused an outcry in the French press, which made the mistake of confusing the lectures with the earlier planned conference. Professor Nikolai Glubokovski from Petrograd, or St. Petersburg as the city is now known, had even worse problems. When he, to his complete surprise, received a telegram inviting him to lecture in Uppsala, the Bolsheviks had already unleashed their political terror. They showed open hostility toward all academics, and especially theologians. Hunger was rampant and it was practically impossible to leave Russia. Glubokovski succeeded, with Söderblom's help, and against all odds made it to Sweden. The archbishop received him with effusive warmth, arranged for a Russian interpreter, and saw to it that he could rest for a whole month with a family outside Uppsala. After having given his lecture, he worked for a while in the university library classifying early Slavic books and handwritten documents.

After a few months he returned to Petrograd. The Bolshevik reality was then far worse than he had realized. Ten years later he reported: "They convicted and executed by firing squad without a trial. The animals in the zoo were fed with human bodies. There was no possibility of obtaining the most insignificant kind of work, of living tolerably, or of dying in peace. We found ourselves on a raging volcano or in the midst of a howling pack of wolves." Through his contacts — this time the young Estonian foreign minister and people in Finland with good Russian connections — Söderblom was able once again to get the theologian out of Russia to Viborg in Finnish Karelia. From there, he gradually made his way via Czechoslovakia and Serbia to Bulgaria. He took part in ecumenical work as long as he could, thanks to Söderblom, who in all respects seemed to him to be like a saint.

With lecturers from Great Britain, Russia, France, Holland, Switzerland, Hungary, Denmark, Norway, Finland, Iceland, and Sweden, Söderblom arranged regular academic events with international and ecclesial overtones, creating an active network for continued ecumenical work. What that would actually lead to was still unclear. For Söderblom, encounters between outstanding people from differing places was always important, since everything was dependent on committed individuals and their communication with each other. Only by learning to know the other could suspicion be overcome. As long as there were no established international church structures, the ecumenical movement had to be supported by independent individuals.

In spite of the fact that he devoted so much time and energy to his attempts to hold a conference and then to the Olaus Petri lectures, he also tirelessly continued his ordinary work as archbishop. He could not accomplish everything he wanted, and at times he was dispirited and overworked. It was obviously difficult to unite diocesan tasks with all of his other undertakings. Since he lacked personal resources, he was unable to pay a salary for an assistant. If he asked the Diocesan Chapter for help, they would censure him for taking on far too much. He compared himself to counterpart bishops in the Church of England and even to Swedish free church leaders who had administrative personnel at their disposal. With a bit of envy, he sighed that he felt "somewhat like I am drowning. Life is short. The night comes soon and with it God's merciful rest for the weary. I need time for purely spiritual work. I cannot get rid of the practical duties which I have not assumed but have been piled on me." The tone shows how worn out he was. Above all, his growing correspondence took his time. Then, Manfred Björkquist approached the landowner Oscar Ekman about providing a full-time secretary for the archbishop. As usual, Ekman came to the rescue and Söderblom was able to engage Gerda Rodling. She was the niece of his old friend Sam Fries, which for Söderblom was in itself an important "qualification." She took dictation in many languages and made quick and correct transcriptions. She moved into a small apartment in the archbishop's residence and was largely available twenty-four hours a day. At times she traveled with him and was able to take dictation anyplace — on the train, on a street corner, or even when he was chairing a meeting. He also dictated his sermons to her, as well as lectures and articles, which he later reviewed. He even ventured to dictate whole books to her. She would describe how he walked around in his library, rattling a bunch of keys, sometimes taking a short rest on the sofa, but always continuing to dictate in an even, monotonous voice. Thanks to Gerda Rodling, who remained his secretary up to the time of his death, he was able to accomplish so much.

During the first years of the war, Söderblom could do no more for peace than continuously speak about it and as far as possible maintain his contacts in the warring lands. He sent money and necessities to individual academic and clergy families in Dorpat, Königsberg, and Petrograd — now known as Tartu, Kaliningrad, and St. Petersburg — and soon became involved in more extensive aid and relief efforts. Practical Christianity was the theme of his life and he was an innovative and capable organizer. The New Year's Collection in the archdiocese in 1914 was a modest beginning. The money that was given went to Lutheran congregations in East Prussia, Belgium, and France. Soon much larger contributions were to be sent through the Gustaf Adolf Foundation to war-torn congregations. The government set the purposes for national collections; Söderblom was able to obtain many annual contributions for the Gustaf Adolf Foundation. Large sums were donated to Lutheran congregations, chiefly in Germany and later also in France, Austria, and Romania.

When John R. Mott turned to Söderblom in 1915 for support for work among prisoners of war, work that had been started by the Student Christian Movement in Germany, he was ready to respond. From German sources he had learned of unbearable situations in the prison camps. Aid to prisoners of war was to engage him for many years. His attention was directed to spiritual care and the possibility of worship in the camps, but also to securing books for the prisoners to read and to improving the conditions of hygiene. He quickly found a young man who was willing to take up these tasks, the linguistically gifted associate priest in Ockelbo, Herman Neander. As a newly ordained priest in 1909, he had received one of the first Olaus Petri Foundation scholarships for the study of Greek and Russian and for building up contacts with the Orthodox Churches. He spent two years in Greece and Russia, traveling also to the monastic republic of Athos and Palestine. Shortly before the outbreak of war, he had also visited the old Swedish village — "Gammalsvenskby" — in southern Ukraine in order to give money for a school building. Söderblom now called upon him to visit Russian prisoners in Germany and Poland and then — together with the "angel of Siberia," Elsa Brändström — German prisoners in Russia and Siberia in order to help them in various ways and to celebrate worship with them. He was also to assist Catholic priests in visiting camps in Russia and Orthodox priests in visiting camps of the Central Powers. It became clear that Neander was an outstanding choice. He did exceptional work and was greatly admired. Söderblom supported him in matters both great and small, gathered money, and saw to it that Neander was able to distribute a quarter of a million books among prisoners of war.

Söderblom himself compiled a German prayer book with biblical passages, hymns, and prayers that was widely distributed. He frequently wrote encouraging letters to Neander and to his family in Ockelbo: "Dear Fru Neander! You surely merit a place in the history of relief work during this war, so bravely have you endured your loneliness. I think often of you in my prayers." In letters to Herman Neander he sometimes referred to people he knew in various places. When Neander, on the way home from Siberia, was imprisoned for three months in Korea under suspicion of espionage and finally came to Tokyo, he received a letter from Söderblom: "Greet Dr. Ishibashi whom I know from Leipzig and ask him if he has finished his dissertation, written under my supervision, concerning Kitabatake [a fourteenth-century Japanese statesman and author]." Söderblom cooperated with the Deutsche Kriegsgefangenenhilfe (German Aid to Prisoners of War) and above all with the Swedish Red Cross, whose president was Prince Carl.

Differing forms of aid and relief work placed more and more of a claim on his time. Work among German and Russian prisoners of war required resources. The need in war-struck Lutheran congregations was indescribable and when the war was over, the Allies continued their blockade of the Central Powers. In Germany, millions starved and that especially affected children. Söderblom took the initiative for a nationwide relief action that was carried out by the Swedish Red Cross. There was a major collection of money, clothes, and food. Thousands of undernourished German, Austrian, Estonian, and Latvian children came to Sweden for periods of time in order to recover their health. Many Swedish parsonages were opened to these children. Administering this program required major voluntary contributions. The Uppsala district of the Red Cross set up an office in the archbishop's palace under the leadership of Anna Söderblom. The archbishop was able to organize a national collection for the Red Cross and another for Save the Children, and he was personally engaged in finding families willing to receive children. In Uppsala, one could see long lines of children marching from the railroad station to the archbishop's palace in order to be fed, registered, and sent along to other parts of the diocese. Everything required the most detailed attention and cooperation between various parties was not always easy. It was especially difficult to get money for train tickets, but Söderblom succeeded with that too. All told, he gathered in many millions of Swedish crowns for aid and relief work.

Help to prisoners of war, Lutheran congregations, and starving children gave the archbishop and his wife a remarkable celebrity in the affected countries. Pictures spread and Söderblom was given the title "apostle of reconciliation." On two occasions he was awarded the German Red Cross's most significant medal of honor and his work received the attention of the German government. Since the blockade was the initiative of the Allies, his action was quite naturally interpreted as a political stand for Germany. That did not make his work to bring France and England into his continuing search for peace and unity any easier.

The cease-fire of November 1918 let loose a long list of activities aimed at influencing the conditions for peace. Within two days, the archbishop sent out his first circular letter to the parishes of the archdiocese with the prayer that "the justice of love" would guide the peace negotiations. In every sermon he spoke of peace and its conditions. The goal must be "a renewed humanity, a society of justice for all people." He considered calling a peace conference in Paris in order to influence the negotiations, but was directly dissuaded from this by Archbishop Davidson. He had to be content doing what was possible at home in Sweden. In the Blasieholmen Church 3,500 people signed a manifesto for a peace built on "the basic teachings of Jesus concerning reconciliation, justice, and brotherhood." It was studiously noticed in Germany that Söderblom's name stood at the top. One month later, the Uppsala Cathedral was filled with Christians from all communions. They concurred with the same manifesto for a reconciling peace. Across the country three hundred thousand Christians from all communions supported the appeal. Söderblom summed it up: "Never, as long as the world has been, have prayers from the burning hearts of so many Christians been raised for statesmen and their activities as during these weeks. Never have deliberations been followed by so many eyes, never has there been recorded so many people's honest longing for and hope of a better and more satisfactory formation of humanity's great kingdom."

The manifesto was addressed to the American president Woodrow Wilson who led the peace negotiations at Versailles. He was hailed as the savior of Europe and many wanted to believe that his personal rectitude would characterize the peace process. Thus, the disappointment was all the greater when the conditions for peace became known at the beginning of May 1919. The German Empire had collapsed and the representatives of the newly established Weimar Republic were the ones who signed the Treaty of Versailles. Germany was forced to accept entire blame for the Great War and was burdened with an enormous debt of reparations. The Swedish committee of the World Alliance for Promoting International Friendship through the Churches and many others protested this "peace of violence," which could lead to a new world war, and pleaded that the conditions imposed on Germany be lessened. People were urged to support the relief and aid work that was going on and to pray for those who had suffered such heavy loss. Söderblom was more convinced than ever that the churches must speak directly and together to the authors of the treaty and the leaders of the nations. He wrote articles on this for both the German and English press. Plans to gather church leaders from the whole world and to create a vehicle for practical cooperation matured. Life and Work was conceived in his thoughts and feelings. It was the war, but also and equally the unjust peace, which drove the ecumenical movement forward.

22

The Love of God Unites Enemies

> When the Spirit of the Lord pervades our sundered, materialized, and crippled Christendom, then the dividing walls which have arisen in the course of time will hold no longer. They shall be torn asunder, not by well-meaning strivings for unity, but by the Lord's own might. And in its single great flow, the flood of God's love shall unite us all who are moved by the Spirit of our Lord.
>
> *Nathan Söderblom, 1923*

ON SEPTEMBER 24, 1920, ANNA TURNS FIFTY YEARS OLD. Gifts and words of congratulation come streaming in. The same day, Nathan baptizes his first grandchild, Brita and Yngve Brilioth's daughter. This happens in Holy Trinity Church. The archbishop is vested in a black gown, the girl screams, and her six-year-old Uncle Putte plays the organ. At dinner, Anna sits with four children lined up on each side. They talk, read, and sing. A visiting English bishop is amazed at this intensive family life in a bishop's home. The next morning he travels by boat to Stockholm. The sun shines; luncheon on board is magnificent. When he arrives in Stockholm, the bishop learns that the king himself wants to receive him.

* * *

Faith and Order was the second ecumenical movement of the time. It was largely Anglicans and the American Episcopal Church with Bishop Charles Brent in the lead who stood behind this attempt to gather the churches around matters of church order and doctrine. This movement had come a little further along than Life and Work, which Söderblom was working to establish. In June 1919, an American Faith and Order delegation came to Uppsala in order to see if their plans could be coordinated with Söderblom's. This was the first time the two initiatives encountered each other.

The meeting took place in the session chamber in Uppsala where the same old bishops stared down from the walls as they had during the Swedish-English deliberations in 1909. They discussed the possibility of uniting the two movements, but Söderblom was not in favor of that. Instinctively he felt that one stood for institutional and the other for personal religion, one for the churches' established orders and the other for free but coordinated action in the world. He did not have the patience to wait for the churches to come to agreement over doctrinal questions. The needs of the time were altogether too pressing and doctrinal differences did not need to hinder the churches from acting together. Merger with Faith and Order had to wait. It was not until the 1930s that the two movements together formed the World Council of Churches.

When the World Alliance for Promoting International Friendship through the Churches could finally gather some sixty delegates from fourteen countries in an old hotel in Oud Wassenaar near The Hague in September 1919, Söderblom himself attended. He had not been present when the Alliance was established, nor had he been part of its first conference in Bern in 1915. Local committees had since been formed in many countries, Söderblom being chair of the Swedish group. The organization was still small, created by a handful of people who at the beginning did not represent anything more than themselves. He knew many of the delegates from the past and very much wanted to meet them again. After having failed so completely at organizing conferences but having considerable success with the Olaus Petri Lectures, and after his conversations with Faith and Order, his plans had become clearer. Oud Wassenaar offered him the opportunity to anchor his vision of an ecumenical conference and an ecumenical council within the Alliance. "Evangelical catholicity" would be the theological basis for cooperation and unity.

The difficulties seemed nearly insurmountable. The bishops in Sweden had not given much support for his plans. His son Sven's military adventure in Germany had damaged his reputation as a mediator. That he spoke bluntly and acted for Germany's cause after the armistice had led to both the French and the English turning a deaf ear. He was exhausted and had difficulty summoning his normal enthusiasm. He kept mostly in the background and sat quietly while the other delegates heatedly debated the politically unsolvable question of guilt. The French and Belgian delegates maintained that blame for the war lay completely with Germany. The war had been fought on French and Belgian territory and at the end, the Germans had burned down industrial plants, flooded mines, and devastated fruit farms in order to destroy the countries' means of support. Thus, reparations were required. Wilfred Monod, who was not able to be at Oud Wassenaar, demanded by letter that if the Germans desired to be in the Alliance, they at least had to acknowledge that the invasion of Belgium was morally indefensible. Such a condition had not been included in the invitation to the conference, but the Germans nevertheless issued a personal declaration distancing themselves from that invasion. That made an impression. The conference could continue its work, but the Germans' declaration by no means meant that the question of guilt, *la Schuldfrage* as it was referred to, was solved. It would haunt the provisional ecumenical movement for a long time and be discussed by historians for nearly a century.

There was a great deal on the agenda. One point dealt with the freedom to carry on missions in all countries. This was seen to be a fundamental question of religious freedom. When a common agreement was finally reached, Söderblom spontaneously began to sing the hymn *Nun danket Alle Gott*, "Now Thank We All Our God." The conference also welcomed the formation of the League of Nations, taking the position that Germany too should be included in the organization. Nathan Söderblom in Uppsala, Wilfred Monod in Paris, Friedrich Siegmund-Schultze in Berlin, and Edward Talbot in Winchester all — in different ways — had spoken in their native countries about the League of Nations as a body in need of the soul and moral backbone that could be supplied by the churches. Söderblom had even said that "the people's league must be religion" and that the realization of a supranational order of society "must be a religious idea, if it is not to be either a caricature or an institution upheld only by external force." Another question discussed had to do with protection for Protestant minorities. When new national boundaries were established, small religious communities could get caught between the large Orthodox and Catholic churches. But the Alliance's most urgent concern was to contribute to an international legal system. Consciousness of law was God's gift to humanity and Christians must promote the maintenance of law's sovereignty in opposition to all glorification of violence. This corresponded completely with Söderblom's way of thinking and he took the occasion to set forth his ideas for an international conference and the formation of an ecumenical council.

What was needed was such a council to provide a common Christian voice in the world community. Similar thoughts were being expressed in the Patriarchate at Constantinople where an encyclical was being prepared proposing the establishment of a league of churches parallel to the League of Nations. An ecumenical council would not infringe on the independence of individual churches but would rather exert influence by the weight of its religious, moral, and social positions. The powerlessness of the churches during the war had shown how absolutely necessary it was to create a common forum for international questions. Reconciliation and solidarity must have an important place in the churches' *credo* equal to the three articles of the Creed. Söderblom did not anticipate that the Roman Catholic Church would commit itself to the council, but he proposed that the Ecumenical Patriarch and the Archbishop of Canterbury would be members by virtue of their office. He surely counted on the Archbishop of Uppsala also being a member, but he did not say that. He thought that the council should be governed by a democratically elected body. In order that a council could be established, for the fourth time he suggested that a conference be held in Scandinavia. If it were to be located in Uppsala he could already pledge to guarantee the financing. As usual, he was impatient; he proposed that the conference take place the following year.

The war was over and now many were prepared to support his proposal, especially Charles Macfarland who led the Federal Council of the Churches of Christ in America. Ever since that council was formed in 1908, it had become a model for other ecumenical councils. The Alliance itself had neither the resources nor the competence to organize a conference of this kind and decided to send the proposal on to its national committees. This incurred the obvious risk that everything would come to nothing. Thus, some of the delegates in Oud Wassenaar took the matter into their own hands and appointed a three-person group to move ahead: Söderblom, Macfarland, and Otto Herold of Switzerland. If Söderblom's idea were to be realized, it now depended on these three. They immediately agreed to invite ten people to Paris within a few months to begin planning. Söderblom appointed the rector of the Swedish congregation in London, Albert Hellerström, and Yngve Brilioth, who was then studying in Oxford, as his representatives. Even though there were many Englishmen at Oud Wassenaar, Archbishop Davidson sent no one to Paris. His excuse was the same as before: if the Catholics and Orthodox did not participate, neither would the Anglican Church.

The seventy-one-year-old Davidson both harbored a certain distrust of

Söderblom, who he thought moved too fast, and had to take church political considerations at home into account. The Anglo-Catholic movement had wind in its sails and wanted the Anglican Church to orient itself toward Rome rather than toward continental and American Protestantism. Söderblom had reason to be anxious. Along with the hopelessly reactionary pope, the Archbishop of Canterbury was the most influential leader in Christendom. The British Empire stretched over half the world and the Anglican Church was stronger than ever. If Davidson spoke he was listened to, but now, when ecumenical cooperation should begin to be organized, he had doubts. If he backed out, the whole project would collapse. Lutheranism in Germany had been weakened by the war, American Christianity was badly fragmented, and the Orthodox were in a life and death struggle to survive the attacks of the Bolsheviks in Russia and the Young Turks in the Ottoman Empire. Only the churches in Scandinavia and Great Britain were in relatively good condition. Together, they had to take responsibility if things were to move forward. It was in consultation with Davidson that Söderblom had begun his ecumenical work ten years earlier. Even prior to the meeting of the Swedes and British in 1909, he had visited Davidson at Lambeth Palace, a meeting that confirmed his view that differing forms of organization and ordained ministry did not stand in the way of the church's universality or prevent deeper fellowship between the churches. For Söderblom, "catholicity" was unity's key concept. It was the Anglicans who led him to think along such lines.

Was not the worldwide church like a tree with three large branches: one Roman, one Orthodox, and one Evangelical? According to the Nicene Creed, which Christians adopted before they divided, the church has four distinctive marks: unity, holiness, catholicity, and apostolicity. No church has greater right to claim these marks than others. There is Roman catholicity, Greek catholicity, and Evangelical catholicity. They grow from the same root, historically possess the same stem, and one is not superior to the others. All church families possess rich diversity. There are both Oriental and Byzantine Orthodox churches, and between them, the Orthodox national churches have differing characteristics. In the Roman Catholic Church, monastic orders differ so widely from each other that one is reminded of disorderly Protestantism. One can scarcely count the evangelical communities, which even carry on missions in each other's territories, but their catholicity cannot be questioned. Catholicity is a fact of the history of religion since all churches have their origin in the biblical revelation. In the West, evangelical catholicity existed as a hidden undercurrent long before the Reformation. With Martin Luther it came into the daylight, and since then has been carried from generation to generation.

The church did not come down from heaven ready-made, but was more like a deep-rooted old oak tree that grew slowly as it put forth new shoots. The diversity of the churches reflected people's historic, cultural, and other distinctive differences. Söderblom had a deep respect for every church's individuality. No church could replace another and all received nourishment from the same earth. That there were state churches and free churches presented no problem as long as they complemented each other, but if a church in self-sufficiency separated itself from others, it should be described as a sect no matter how large it was. National churches had an ideal structure for permeating a whole people with Christian values. That Söderblom's religious fatherland was the Lutheran confession did not contradict his view of the church universal. Converts in one direction or another often do not understand that the greatest treasure and deepest unity of the church lies not in outer forms or in doctrines but in the gospel itself.

"Evangelical catholicity" was thus the key word in both his ecclesiology and his ecumenical program. The concept had been used in a somewhat different way in Germany during the latter part of the nineteenth century, and in England it was understood in a way that regarded the Anglican Church, thanks to its continuity in liturgy and the episcopal office, as a bridge church between the Roman Catholic and Orthodox churches, on the one side, and the reformed churches, on the other. For Söderblom, "evangelical catholicity" was applied to the Church of Sweden with its unbroken history, its medieval churches, and popular traditions. He possessed a great and romantic passion for the Middle Ages, proudly emphasizing his church's liturgical and structural heritage and its episcopal office as signs of its continuity through the sixteenth-century upheavals. His goal was to bring together the churches that had arisen during the Reformation into a supranational spiritual communion with evangelical catholicity as its distinguishing mark. Their solidarity should be deepened and transformed by practical cooperation, but confessional, cultural, and organizational distinctiveness should be preserved, at least for a time. Söderblom never ceased speaking of unity in preserved diversity.

When he began to use the concept of evangelical catholicity in 1911, it had a cutting touch of anti-Catholic polemics. It intended to uncover a free alternative to a papism that claimed infallibility and strove for uniformity. The rigidity of Rome made all ecumenical gains impossible. There the church's "body" had suffocated its "spirit" and this was seen at its worst among the Jesuits. For Söderblom, this was a caricature of authentic Christianity. Instead of offering the freedom of the gospel, they schooled people to become obedient machines. The Roman Church's ecumenical method was to absorb other churches solely on its own terms. Other churches endeavored, in contrast, through dialogue and study to attain concord in doctrine and liturgy. For his own part, Söderblom wanted to use "the method of love," which on the basis of the catholicity possessed by all would make it possible to meet the great challenges of the present time. After the war, when the emphasis in his commitments shifted from emergency work for peace to the question of church unity and cooperation, he took the opportunity in lectures and publications to deepen his thoughts around evangelical catholicity.

Ecumenism was intended to uncover the inherent catholicity of all the churches. Söderblom's language about the church's body and soul could be confused with the New Testament picture of the church as the body of Christ, but he never held that the church as an institution represents Christ's continued existence on earth as an extension of the incarnation. On the contrary, he was instinctively doubtful of incarnational theology, especially in its Anglican form. The church's external form was for him like a provisional house in which the spiritual life lived. Without spirit nothing, no matter how well organized, could be the church. Spiritual life, conviction, inwardness, and personal experience of God were primary, but the soul needs a body. This was provided by the church's external organization and institutions. While the soul remains one and the same everywhere and in all times, the body takes different forms. The "invisible" and the "visible" church must not be allowed to drift apart. The church is never simply a spiritual phenomenon, but must be made manifest in historical, concrete forms. The church of the future certainly might appear in many different ways, but it must be united in common faith and service. It should be a dogmatically tolerant community of worship in which different traditions are like "side chapels" united in the one holy, catholic, and apostolic church of Christ.

On the basis of evangelical catholicity, it follows that the churches are mutually to acknowledge one another, show a genuine interest in each other's traditions, and share each other's Communion Table, and on the same basis, their own traditions and faithfulness are to be deepened. Every tradition is a binding gift of God. No tradition should elevate itself to be the norm for others. If the churches were united in social work, their common confession should also be visible. When they come with their varied gifts of grace to the ecumenical communion, "the glory of gathered Christianity" is revealed.

God is not dogma or ideas but living Spirit, and as much as the church is filled by the Spirit of Christ, it should reach unity in instruction, proclamation, and social action. Catholicity has no borders. To realize it in a movement like Life and Work is an immediate possibility, but it could also permeate the League of Nations and the international order of justice.

Söderblom certainly agreed that the unity of the church also required working on doctrinal issues, but in the emergency situation that prevailed after the war, practical social ethics must take priority over dogmatic matters. Christian unity could take different forms, but everything must grow from within. Unity could not be imposed but must rather come as an answer to the prayers of Christians and their longing for peace and salvation. Jesus did not ask about dogma but called humans to live in imitation of him. Evangelical catholicity was, therefore, best expressed in unconditional service to fellow human beings. It was not a program of liturgical reform and did not involve a movement toward the Roman Catholic Church. Söderblom was perpetually criticized for ritualism, but most things in the high church movement were alien to him; he was unreservedly grateful for having been born and raised as an evangelical Lutheran Christian. He scarcely ever wondered if there might be a richer and more authentic church in the world than the Church of Sweden.

The years after the end of the war were filled to the brim with work, more than at any other time in his life. At the same time as the church political crisis went on, receiving great attention in the Swedish media, and his relief work demanded so much, the archbishop had to take on his international tasks with full energy. One task, as we have seen, was to pursue the question of an international conference. Another was to complete the agreement with the Church of England.

The visit of the English delegation to Uppsala in 1909 had been epochmaking, but ecumenical mills grind slowly. Since the Lambeth Conference convenes only every tenth year and the war had intervened, the report from 1909 could not be acted on before 1920. Then the Anglican bishops acknowledged the Swedish succession of ordination and indicated that the Church of Sweden had a correct understanding of the office of bishop. In consequence, they recommended that members of the Church of Sweden should have full right to receive Holy Communion in Anglican churches and that Swedish priests could preach there. They also recommended that bishops from one church should be invited to participate in the other's consecration of bishops. The Swedish bishops responded to this affirmatively in 1922 and eucharistic fellowship became a fact. Already in September 1920, however, when Einar Billing and Viktor Rundgren were consecrated Bishops of Västerås and Visby, Söderblom had invited the Archbishop of Canterbury to send a bishop to participate in the consecration. He sent the Bishop of Peterborough, Frank Theodore Woods, who belonged to the low church wing of the Church of England. Woods was an old-fashioned gentleman who easily united the culture of the upper class with the culture of the church. Inspired by Söderblom, he became extremely active in the ecumenical movement and ultimately received the important assignment of being the opening preacher at the Stockholm Meeting of 1925.

One more Anglican bishop participated in the service of consecration — Herbert Hensley Henson from Durham, whom Söderblom had invited to give the Olaus Petri Lectures. Of the English bishops, he was the one who stood closest to Söderblom in theological matters, but to invite him to participate in the consecration was a bit risky. He was controversial, outspoken, and a bit sarcastic. He took a decided distance from both the Anglo-Catholic and Evangelical movements and kept himself in the middle, broad church where the educated upper class with its watered-down form of culture religion felt at home. Theologically, Henson was so liberal that in 1916 Archbishop Davidson had considered leaving office rather than having to consecrate him bishop. In spite of the fact that Davidson had become more skeptical toward the many ideas of the Swedish archbishop and refused to send delegates to the ecumenical conference in Geneva that same year, Söderblom took the risk of having Henson participate. The church political stakes were high. In the absolutely worst case, the whole agreement concerning eucharistic fellowship could collapse and the Church of England would have stayed outside the ecumenical movement. But it was Woods who was the official representative of Canterbury. His participation confirmed the Swedish-English relationship and he cooperated significantly in seeing that the Church of England supported Life and Work.

For the English bishops, the journey to exotic Sweden was memorable. Söderblom, who was conscious that he was writing history, prepared everything in the most minute detail. The king and crown prince received the bishops and one dinner party followed the other. Söderblom himself did have some difficulties in dealing with two such differing representatives of English church life. When he put in a good word for Woods, Henson objected, and when Henson agreed, Woods raised his eyebrows. In his memoirs, Henson described how Söderblom displayed a conventional churchly liberalism, sympathized with socialism, had a strong feeling for democracy, and demonstrated his abhorrence of all kinds of clericalism. He gave Henson the impression of being an ambitious and power-conscious person who enjoyed playing the role of an important prelate. He had a good bit in common with Henson's own archbishop, whom he did not regard especially highly. Söderblom did not hide his apparent sympathy for Germany even as, in American style, he fraternized with everybody. Henson was rather ironic in describing the Swedes' confidence in the reunion of the churches. The Orthodox Metropolitan Germanos was also in Uppsala. Henson found it annoying to see how his hosts strutted about for him, even seeing to it that he was awarded a royal order.

Bishop Theodore Woods of Peterborough, Metropolitan Germanos of Thyateira, Archbishop Söderblom, and Bishop Herbert Hensley Henson of Durham. Uppsala, 1920.

Nevertheless, Henson was fond of the Church of Sweden. It reminded him of his own church before the Anglo-Catholics took over and when the established church was still intact. He treasured the naturalness of its worship without all of the self-conscious peculiarities that marked ceremonial events in England. For his own part, Henson on principle never wore a miter and he was pleased that this peculiar kind of headgear was not widely appreciated in Sweden. But he did notice that the high church movement often sneaked in with retreats, rites and vestments, and had a tendency to look down even on Lutheran churches that did not have bishops. That made him nervous, but what else could one expect? Low church people were intellectually so underdeveloped that one could disregard their influence. For Henson, Söderblom represented the best: a broad churchmanship that was firmly rooted in history. But politically he leaned too much to the left. Around Henson's own episcopal palace, which was located in the midst of coal mining territory, a strike was going on during his journey. He sympathized with the workers in their hard conditions, but for his part was not prepared to budge an inch from the hard line of the mine owners.

That Henson was strongly opposed to liturgical excess and that Woods was a low churchman did not help Söderblom when something like a modern media campaign rose up against the catholicizing tendencies that he demonstrated in connection with the bishops' consecration. He had followed the rubrics of the *Handbook* to the letter, but for a long time, a bitter mood had developed among free church members, Social Democrats, and some clergy against his magnificent public appearances, and now that really exploded. The presence of two English bishops and a Greek metropolitan fortified this reaction. In the newspaper *Dagens Nyheter* one read: "All the glittering, futuristic, slovenly bright colors surely awakened in many the thought that here was play-acting and not worship in spirit and in truth. One felt in any case convinced that this matchless pomp stood in direct contrast to what in daily life traditional Lutheranism demands and teaches."

Söderblom at first took all this rather lightly. In the newspaper *Upsala Nya Tidning* he wrote that, "although Good Templars go in procession and professors and union leaders, and members of Parliament and students and others do the same, there are many who wonder whether one gives Catholicism an airing if in church the clergy go in orderly procession instead of running over each other." That was not adequate as an answer, nor were his customary references to the 1571 *Church Order* of Laurentius Petri. If only he could, he would avoid polemics and limit himself to explanations. He had never learned the media's playing rules, preferring always to encounter people face to face. But the campaign did not stop. Thus, in the middle of October, he gave a lecture to the Uppsala Student Christian Union in order to basically explain and clarify the differences between "Roman" and "catholic." He talked about how control and freedom, supervision and trust, institution and spirit, collective and individual, religion of the law and religion of the spirit were contrary to each other. Evangelical Christians have complete freedom to employ all liturgical forms that are not in conflict with the gospel. If the programmatically low churchman and liberal theologian Emanuel Linderholm had, in the midst of the war, succeeded in obtaining a remarkably beautiful, meticulously decorated surplice for his own use, so must others be free to do the same. With that ironic observation, the debate came to an end, but it would return many times. The press learned to overlook many of Söderblom's passing fancies and behaviors, but the line was drawn at the slightest whiff of papism.

Einar Billing and Viktor Rundgren were the first Swedish bishops to be consecrated with participation from the Church of England. Söderblom was assisted at the altar by the nearly eighty-year-old Gottfrid Billing, Hjalmar Danell, and the two English bishops. Metropolitan Germanos of Seleukeia, later Metropolitan of Thyateira, was also present, clad in liturgical vestments. The ecumenical contributions that Söderblom had made before the war were beginning to bear fruit. It was Einar Billing who laid the theological groundwork for the Swedish folk church during the first decades of an actually democratic government. He did that in his episcopal letter to the Diocese of Västerås.

Before we proceed to Söderblom's plans for the conference, we must devote some chapters to his relations with Luther and Lutheranism, to the Swedish Academy, and to foreign mission. For Söderblom, it was difficult to separate one from the other. During the hugely eventful years at the beginning of the 1920s, only God knew where he was to be found and what occupied his thoughts. He seemed to be everywhere and had so many irons in the fire that people in his presence constantly expressed both astonishment and admiration. He played a leading role, not least in Germany, even as he became one of the most well-known people in the cultural life of Sweden.

23
Luther and Lutheranism

> If we leave out of consideration Christianity's own relation to Christ himself, I know of no event in world history more closely connected to one personality than the Reformation with Martin Luther.
>
> *Nathan Söderblom, 1919*

In the Castle Church in Wittenberg on the First Sunday in Lent 1922 there is a celebration of Martin Luther's return from the Wartburg four hundred years earlier. He had with him the New Testament, which he had translated into German, and he restored order after the ravages of the Anabaptists and iconoclasts. Nathan Söderblom lays a large laurel wreath on Luther's grave. On the wreath's ribbon one can read: Memoriæ Benedictæ Martini Lutheri Wittembergiam reducis Arch.Ups. De propheta Wittembergensi, quo major post Paulum ecclesiæ catholicæ et apostolicæ non est missus, DEUM æterno cum gaudio laudant in Suecia Fideles. In translation this means: "From the Archbishop of Uppsala in the blessed memory of Martin Luther's return to Wittenberg. The faithful in Sweden praise God with everlasting joy for the prophet from Wittenberg, the greatest since Paul to be sent to the universal catholic church." Söderblom gives a short speech. Everyone stands and listens breathlessly. Who has ever spoken like this about the one who has given the city its fame?

* * *

In the parsonage at Norrala Martin Luther's portrait hung in the salon. That was not uncommon. Lukas Cranach the Elder's painting of 1521 was an icon that was revered and loved. Every Swede had plowed through the catechism. "A Mighty Fortress Is Our God" was engraved on their hearts. Söderblom had grown up with Luther's *Postilla*, biblical commentaries, and hymns as his daily spiritual bread. During his student years, he identified himself with the young Luther, who in his eyes was not a teacher of dogmatics or the founder of a church, but a young, coarse-grained, and zestful rebel who fought a life-and-death struggle for unconditional grace in his own life and who stood free in respect to both the letters of the Bible and the authority of the church. Söderblom had continued to study Luther. He was of the opinion that the key to the Reformation was more Luther's personality than Lutheran doctrine. As professor, Söderblom twice devoted a term's lectures to the reformer, and in speeches and sermons, he often returned to Luther as the chief example of the religious genius that influences the history of humanity.

Söderblom had a rich supply of material to use when, in connection with the four hundredth anniversary of the Reformation in 1917, he held a series of lectures on Martin Luther's humor and melancholy in the new Engelbrekt Church in Stockholm. The church was packed for the lectures. He had developed his approach to the issue at a summer course with the artist Anders Zorn in Mora some ten years earlier. He asserted that *trust* is Lutheranism's most characteristic element, the element that gives universality to its understanding of faith. People who had difficulty with the dogmatism of orthodox Lutheranism or with the inwardness and moralism of pietism were able to respond to Söderblom's view of trust in God as the basis for Christian freedom. His analysis of Luther's personality was his most original contribution to Luther research.

Söderblom painted a personal and audacious picture of a reformer with whom he felt so close that the word "identified" could be used. He was not, however, reluctant to make critical observations. In the lectures there were echoes of Söderblom's own frame of mind, his apprehension of faith, his relationship to his father, self-discipline, and consciousness of duty. Even though there were four hundred years between them, Söderblom described Luther in terms taken from the psychology of religion that made them seem contemporaries. With the word of God as their only weapon, both struggled against a church that limited the individual's freedom and responsibility. They desired to liberate Christianity's central religious content: unconditional grace. The placid Söderblom certainly never had the uncontrolled outbursts of wrath that Luther had and he possessed nothing of the latter's coarse, sarcastic, and ironic language. Nor did he lay the blame for his illnesses, adversities, and personal weaknesses on the devil, whom he never heard padding around the archbishop's residence. But he did know from experience how it felt when the darkness of melancholy and despair poured in. More than once death had breathed hard on him, and he thanked his friends who saw to it that he received care and survived. Just like Luther, he saw the finger of God in whatever happened and tried to take each day with confident trust. When Söderblom — albeit less vividly than Luther — was afflicted with depression and despondency, he protected himself with studies, work, friendships, and not least, music. By a nearly inhuman self-discipline, Söderblom hid his darker sides from others. Luther and Söderblom were both charged by the Bible, quick witted, and humorous and they did not take themselves too seriously. They did not doubt that God had called them to renew the Christian church.

In six of the lectures, Söderblom was able to tactfully describe with repelling realism for his sensitive listeners Luther's swings between comic exhilaration and darkest depression and how those swings influenced him and his theology. Söderblom was not the first to notice that Luther, in the language of our time, had a bipolar personality. His contribution was to take into consideration Luther's manic depressive condition in interpreting his theology. Luther's fluctuating mental condition became a mirror of condemnation and grace, law and gospel. Humor, which was often both coarse and repulsive, was for Luther both a safety valve for pent up anger and an expression of inner freedom. He was known as a lively and cheerful person who bluntly challenged his opponents' self-confident pretensions. An example of this was when he came to the decisive Leipzig debate with Johann Eck in 1519 concerning indulgences carrying a bouquet of flowers and now and again, like Ferdinand the bull, smelled them while his opponent thundered at his worst. At times, his coarse jokes could be purely abusive and he did not spare invective. To call his opponents swine and asses was perhaps all right, but to speak of them as possessed by the devil and as "children of Satan" was too much even for Söderblom his admirer, who was, however, able to make up excuses for most of these expressions. He valued Luther's sincerity and self-esteem. No one else could write about himself: "The fame and praise I have by the grace of God may or may not please the devil and all his followers, but since the time of the apostles no doctor or author, no theologian or lawyer has so gloriously and clearly strengthened, instructed, and comforted the conscience of worldly leaders as through God's special grace have I. I am certain of that. For even St. Augustine and St. Ambrose who are the best of their kind, are not comparable to me." Concerning words such as these, Söderblom was of the opinion that to praise oneself for one's gifts was not the same as to boast about one's self.

Humor sheltered Luther from both self-righteousness and conceit. It was an expression of the freedom he had obtained through the forgiveness of sin. It unmasked artificial holiness and self-assumed piety. Holiness — true sanctity — must come from within a heart that unreservedly belongs to God. Hypocrisy and humor could not be united, while, in contrast, confidence and trust were the native soil of freedom and humor. But there was a limit. In the soul's existential battle with sin and death, there was no place for humor. When one stands before the holy stripped of all self-righteousness, no arguments, no matter how splendid, will do; then, only grace counts.

In order to understand Luther, one must also grasp his dark side, the melancholy that periodically plagued him throughout his whole life. Söderblom had no psychiatric training, but during his time as chaplain at the hospital in Ulleråker, he had learned to recognize symptoms of depression or of melancholy, the term then in use. Even though he left diagnoses to medical science, he was eager to distinguish between depression in a clinical sense and the anxiety and self-reproach that often struck Luther. Theologically, these latter feelings dealt with "the law of God," which drove Luther to doubt and to a sense of having been forsaken by God. This feeling could be so stark that it awakened suicidal thoughts. There was only one way out: to hold fast to the gospel of God's mercy through Christ. When things were at their most difficult, no external means were of help, only communion with the tempted, suffering, and risen Lord in whom the love of God was active. It was the actual heart of evangelical faith that a person in his or her most ultimate struggle and deepest darkness meets a God who shared that anguish.

Söderblom showed that Luther's mental depressions and spiritual tribulations did not coincide in time and should not be mixed together, although they were not without connections. The religious problem was not only a question of the distress of conscience and guilt; it was also related to sufferings and misfortunes for which Luther could not be held morally responsible. He had feelings of guilt for genuine offenses. For these, there was forgiveness. But he was also afflicted by anxiety and torments of conscience that had their roots in his melancholy. Luther himself could not distinguish one from the other and thus felt more distressed and condemned than was within reason. Sin consisted in a lack of trust, but when melancholy struck, his confidence was replaced by deceit. The confidence that the church extended in its sacraments was not sufficient; he felt that he must find his own inner certainty and he was not content with less.

He was possessed by his own quest for unshakeable confidence. Life was either heaven or hell, either grace or damnation. He saw no nuance. He lacked every ounce of an ability to save himself. Faith and grace alone — nothing else held. The unrest in his heart drove him time after time into a great solitude, there to struggle with the devil. And finally he found ground for his confidence: justification by grace through faith.

Söderblom continued his series of lectures with three quite independent presentations in which his rich storytelling gifts were on display. He spoke about Luther's journey to Worms, a story enshrouded in myth, when people reportedly hailed him along the highway and when in the presence of the Emperor, he refused to recant his writings. Söderblom also reported on Luther's encounter with the learned humanist Erasmus of Rotterdam and devoted his final lecture to Luther's position regarding the Peasants' Revolt of 1524 and 1525. If there was anything Luther wrote that Söderblom wanted to wish away, it was his short and shameful treatise of 1525, *Against the Robbing and Murdering Hordes of Peasants*. In his eagerness to restore the order of law, Luther with all the fury he could summon urged the authorities to crush the rebellion. It was their holy duty to strike down the rebels with every means at their disposal. It was, then, no surprise that the people turned against Luther. He had been the hero of the whole nation, but in no time at all, he became the most unpopular person in Germany. He did not understand the connection between social conditions and the gospel, nor did he understand that God stood on the side of the oppressed in their struggle for justice. Luther was convinced that it was the duty of those in power to maintain society's fragile order in defense of security and freedom at any price. They believed that the gospel must be preserved in its purity and not be mixed up with politics. Society's needs and the soul's needs should be kept separate. This led to disaster.

When four hundred years had passed since Martin Luther nailed up his theses on the door of the Castle Church in Wittenberg in 1517, a great Reformation Festival took place in the Uppsala Cathedral on October 31, 1917 and the Swedish people received a new translation of the Bible, the first since the time of Charles XII. The war raged on. Great Britain was engaged in an offensive against the Germans and against Turkey in the Holy Land. Soon the Balfour Declaration would declare that Palestine would provide a homeland for the Jewish people. Events came in quick succession. On November 7, Lenin seized power in Russia. One month later, Finland declared itself independent. In Sweden, the socialists and liberals won the election to the Second Chamber. For the first time, Hjalmar Branting entered the government. The availability of food was barely sufficient and unrest spread over Sweden.

At the festival, Söderblom gave a rhetorically well-crafted speech, tender hearted and free from any bombastic metaphors. It dealt with confidence in God as the innermost foundation for the heart. Freedom through trusting in God was "the signature of religion." There were three ways to react to the demand for righteousness: to trust in one's own ability to live according to God's law; to rely on one's own personal experience of God; or to live in trust and faith in Christ. Morality, no matter how fine, was not sufficient since the holiness of God was more demanding than anything humans, even in their best moments, could imagine. There were people who reached out to God via the way of mysticism, sincere souls who "sought for themselves a spiritual corner distant from the worldliness of the church." Among such people Luther felt at home since the mystic's fragile theology of the cross resonated in him. But he did not stay there; his longing for freedom drove him still further until he found "a purer blessedness than in the mystics' shuddering intoxication." He reached into Christianity's holiest of holies. There, the entire religion was encompassed in one word: trust. The religion of law could at its best awaken penitence and mysticism could awaken deep delight in God, but it was the gospel of trust that gave the children of God their freedom. Trust was not affected if one's picture of the world changed, since under the veneer of culture, humans remain the same in all times. As catastrophic as world conditions were, trust was needed more than ever and this was, at a deep level, also the starting point for Christian unity. From a human point of view, God had given Sweden a special responsibility: to defend evangelical freedom. After three years of doubt, opposition, and isolation, Söderblom in this talk opened the door to new duties and possibilities.

He gathered much of the material he had used in lectures in Helsinki, Åbo, and Copenhagen and published it in the well-known book *Humor och melankoli och andra Lutherstudier* (*Humor and Melancholy and Other Luther Studies*). The book came out in 1919 and became an immediate sales success. Ten years later in 1929, he published another Luther study, *Mar-*

tin Luthers lilla katekes belyst (*Martin Luther's Small Catechism Illuminated*). This book, however, really presented no new research; it was a handbook for students, teachers, and clergy.

That he had a lifelong interest in Luther and devoted trailblazing research to him did not mean that Söderblom was universally regarded as an authentic Lutheran. Both the other-worldly pietists and the dogmatically orthodox had difficulty in accepting this socially engaged and doctrinally flexible archbishop. Elements of quietism and dogmatism were especially strong in some of the Central European minority churches that lived with the memory of the Counter-Reformation. Such traits also marked many of the immigrant Lutheran churches in North America and Australia. In the Nordic countries the situation was different, but even there Söderblom up to the time of his death was criticized as a modern and liberal theologian who was not to be trusted. Yet he was Lutheran and wanted to be Lutheran, and he believed that he had set free anew the kernel of Luther's theology: unconditional grace and its universal scope.

The Lutheran churches in Northern Europe had had some contact with each other, above all through the universities. In Germany, the Allgemeine Evangelisch-Lutherische Konferenz (AELK), the General Evangelical Lutheran Conference, had been formed in 1867 and had expanded to include some Nordic church leaders. The Bishop of Visby, K. H. G. von Schéele, was involved at an early point. After the Jubilee in Uppsala in 1893, where German princes were present and the chairman of the student body, Nathan Söderblom, gave a much-acclaimed speech, King Oscar II urged the Nordic churches to be more actively involved in Lutheran cooperation. He acted in the same manner as Kaiser Wilhelm who eagerly stepped forward as the leader of German Protestantism. For Oscar II, the idea of the king as the church's highest leader, *summus episcopus*, was not at all foreign. In 1901, the AELK met in Malmö. Lutheran fellowship was established. Nearly all the Swedish bishops participated. Bishop von Schéele had tried in vain to secure the presence of some Americans. With 1,000 Nordic and 250 German participants, this event became a remarkable demonstration of confessional solidarity.

At just that time, Nathan Söderblom was occupied with moving into the rectory at Stabby and preparing his inaugural lecture as professor, but from afar he learned what had occurred in Malmö. Most of those who had gathered there were conservative and kept their distance from "modern" and "rationalistic" theology, but there was no unanimity. It was significant that the Lutherans, like the Anglicans, had begun to organize themselves internationally. In time, the AELK would be part of the development of the Lutheran World Convention and later the Lutheran World Federation.

Söderblom, who moved in much larger ecumenical contexts, would always be constrained in these Lutheran organizations, which were home to many of his critics. In Sweden, the General Union of Clergy was the home base for the confessionalistic forces. Its publication *Svensk Kyrkotidning* (*Swedish Church Times*) had done what it could to prevent Söderblom from becoming archbishop. The Union of Clergy reluctantly followed his ecumenical work, but became more engaged in the International Union for the Protection of Protestantism, which was formed in Berlin in 1923. It had a branch in Sweden where the Union of Clergy instituted a special committee to oppose the growing influence of Catholicism. For Söderblom, it became a major church diplomatic challenge to get the Lutheran churches on board the ecumenical boat. In certain circles in Germany he was certainly suspect as a theologian, but his contributions and understanding of Germany's situation had given him a good name and reputation. In the Church of Sweden, his most bitter opposition was to be found among the conservatives and the pietists in the tradition of Henrik Schartau. Since most of the church's priests belonged to the Union of Clergy, it was unsettling to him that the gulf between the "ecumenists" and the leadership of the Union under Sam Stadener, later Bishop of Strängnäs and of Växjö, grew. Söderblom had his strongest support among educated middle-class laity who, influenced by the Young Church Movement and modern theology, developed a "folk church" variant of culture Protestantism.

In the summer of 1911, the thirteenth meeting of the General Evangelical Lutheran Conference was held in Uppsala. Söderblom participated for the first time. He had just returned from his journey to Rome and Constantinople, in which he renewed his contact with the Student Christian Movement and its form of Anglo-Saxon revival Christianity. He had spoken to the students about his heroes of faith, Martin Luther and Gustavus Adolphus, and reminded them that the Reformation was not a historical rupture but a reconnection with the early church after the degenerations of the late Middle Ages. During the meeting in Uppsala he continued along the same line. He spoke of the Lutheran church's legitimate claim to be a branch of the universal church even as he pointed to its continuity with and special calling within Christianity. He emphasized the church's independence and pointed to the episcopal office as a kind of guarantee of that independence, especially in countries with state churches.

Even at this point, he occasionally used the concept of "evangelical catholicity" in order to emphasize the equivalence of the Protestant churches with Rome. In a speech in Lützen in 1912, he said he looked forward to the day "when evangelical self-esteem, with inviolable respect toward everyone's spiritual heritage and distinctiveness, has grown so strong and even in external things attained such expression compared with this evangelical catholicity even the worst ecclesial hardness of heart must be judged to be sectarian." In contrast to Roman Catholicism, this evangelical catholicity grows from beneath. No hierarchical power structure or unchangeable dogma should dictate the conditions of or be allowed to limit the freedom of the faithful.

When he moved to Leipzig, Söderblom landed right in the midst of the conflict between traditional and modern theology and the tension surrounding the purely Lutheran provincial churches and the United Churches, which combined both Lutheran and Reformed heritages. The General Superintendents often went in different directions but step by step, the churches drew nearer to each other. There was a growing dissatisfaction with the churches' out-of-date structure and constitution. The bureaucracy and state church system were paralyzing. Some of Söderblom's friends were in favor of a freer folk church possessing its own authority to make decisions. But Germany was imbued with monarchism and the evangelical churches had lived since the Reformation with the prince as their *summus episcopus*. The kaiser had the final power and he was not prepared to let it go.

After Söderblom became archbishop, it was his goal to win the German church leaders to his ecumenical program, which included the office of ordained bishop. For a number of years he had been of the opinion that the German superintendents should be bishops. Encouraged by the church historian Adolf von Harnack, who in a journal article had mentioned the value of the episcopal office, Söderblom at the time of the Reformation Jubilee wrote directly to Wilhelm II, the kaiser of Germany and king of Prussia, and pointed out how important the office of bishop was both for the unity of the church and as an expression of the church's loyal independence in relation to the power of the state. To have bishops would also place Protestantism more on an equal footing with the Roman Catholic Church. The letter gave rise to exhaustive discussions among the kaiser's ecclesiastical advisors. The two arguments concerning ecumenism and the relationship between church and state were turned down, but the question of a symbolic equality with the Roman Catholic Church was deemed relevant. It could be dealt with in such a way that the kaiser gave the title and dignity of bishop to leading persons in the Evangelical Church, but an episcopal office in the ecclesial sense of the word was out of the question. The kaiser responded cordially to Söderblom's letter. He rejected the proposal to introduce the episcopal office, but left open the possibility of conferring the title of bishop on deserving persons. Söderblom overinterpreted the kaiser's answer and suggested that the discussions be continued. He wanted to see ordained bishops, not simply a change in the title of the General Superintendents. But the kaiser would not introduce an independent episcopate that, he felt, would give the church too much freedom and reduce his own influence. When Germany surrendered and the Republic proclaimed, the kaiser went into exile, the state church was discontinued, and the title of bishop began to be used in one provincial church after the other.

The first evangelical assembly held in the time of the Weimar Republic took place in Dresden in 1919. It was a kind of farewell to the kaiser, although the atmosphere in the church was quite hostile to the Republic. German Christians wanted to hold on to the monarchy even if they did not want Kaiser Wilhelm back. A *Vernuftsrepublikaner*, a republican by reason, could at the same time be a *Herzenmonarchist*, a monarchist at heart. But there was no returning: the church must leave its past, reorganize, and look forward. Söderblom, who had so much of his heart in Germany and who — thanks to the aid given to congregations, prisoners of war, and children — was highly regarded in the country, wanted to contribute to positive developments. He took part in Lutheran church conferences in Stuttgart in 1921, Wittenberg in 1922, and Eisenach in 1923. In Stuttgart, the decision was made to form a federation of twenty-eight independent provincial churches. This was a decisive step and the churches pledged to take part in international ecumenical work. For Söderblom this was immensely pleasing. Now he knew the direction the German churches would take even though the question of war guilt cast such a dark shadow over their international relations. He felt it was especially urgent to bring along the Germans. With their Lutheran tradition, the Germans would balance the strong Anglo-American elements in the ecumenical movement. People who independently and of their own interest were already involved — for example, Adolf Deissmann, F. A. Spiecker, and Friedrich Siegmund-Schultze — would now have a more official role in ecumenical contexts.

As a former professor in Leipzig and with *Humor och melankoli* in his baggage, he felt he had credentials as a Luther scholar to enter discussions concerning the history of the Reformation as well as the Lutheran confessions. It was in Germany that the great reformer had carried on his work and it was from there that Söderblom expected that the renewal of Lutheranism would come. He insistently repeated his claim that no one had had a greater, deeper, and more enduring influence on the history of the West than Martin Luther, the monk who stood alone before the emperor and the entire Parliament in Worms but did not budge an inch from his convictions. Thus, asserted Söderblom, scarcely a week had passed since his ordination without him giving thanks to God that he was born on Lutheran ground. Since the time of the New Testament, a greater evangelist than Dr. Martin Luther had not appeared in the church of Christ.

Söderblom understood the potential of international Lutheranism and was convinced that it would come to fruition within the Life and Work movement. At its meeting in Eisenach in 1923, the General Conference formed the Lutheran World Convention. Söderblom had gone to the meeting on behalf of Life and Work, but as it turned out, he was not especially welcome. He was not offered a place on the program even though he was archbishop of the world's largest Lutheran church. Outspoken conservative participants determined the tone of the meeting and his fundamental social ethical position conflicted with their interpretation of the teaching concerning God's two kingdoms. Nor could they accept his relativistic view of traditional dogma and they wondered, given his points of departure, if Söderblom actually was orthodox. Even in Germany the doctrine of the two kingdoms had many nuances, but the dominating view was one of a theology of orders that preserved present society. This was combined with a quietism that separated the Kingdom of God from everything associated with worldly progress. Scandinavian Lutherans embraced a more dynamic theology of creation, which made it possible even with an eschatological view of the Kingdom of God to draw certain conclusions as to how the world should be organized.

Ludwig Ihmels personally invited Söderblom to deliver a meditation at the opening Service of Worship and he ultimately also gave a lecture. Again, he pointed to Luther's universal significance and emphasized that the German Reformation belonged to all of Christianity. His universalism meant less suspicion, denial, caution, or fear but more genuine trust in God. It was to the credit of Ihmels and some American friends that he was received among these staunchly confessionalistic Lutherans, but he never reached their inner circle. It did not even help that as soon as he learned that Hainstein — a sanitarium between Eisenach and the Wartburg — was perhaps going to be sold to the Jesuits, he raised funds so that the Lutheran church could buy it and thus save the Wartburg from landing in the shadow of Catholic propaganda. With the help of Queen Victoria of Sweden, with whom he was on very good terms, and his wealthy friend Alfred "Alle" Ekström, he was able to raise enough money so that Hainstein could become a Lutheran folk high school and a conference center in the style of the Sigtuna Foundation in Sweden.

Söderblom thus at several points became involved directly in German church life, first by urging the institution of the episcopal office to mark the church's freedom and its evangelical catholicity, and then to save Hainstein. The office of the bishop was certainly not absolutely necessary, but that it would strengthen the churches' "ecumenicity" was reason enough to reestablish it in the Reformation's homeland. During 1917, the Luther year, it had become especially urgent for him to unite the Reformation parts of Christianity "along other lines than the ecclesiastical power of Rome" and thus support a church grounded in a deep and evangelical understanding of the creeds. Gustavus Adolphus had not been able to form a *corpus evangelicorum* and now it was time for a new attempt. The office of the bishop would be the sign of an international Lutheran communion. He himself was archbishop in a land that for nearly two hundred years had been a protective power for Protestant Christianity and for freedom of faith in Europe. He acted with history on his side. In his speech in the Uppsala Cathedral during the Reformation Jubilee of 1917, he had formulated the Swedish vocation and prayed with his whole heart: "May no weakness, no good but shortsighted intention, betray the responsibility which, to judge humanly, has been laid on Sweden by God himself, to be a home and a defense for evangelical trust and freedom in the world."

24

The Swedish Academy

One never betrays high ideals unpunished. A literary lapse is no religious merit.

Nathan Söderblom, 1920

The eighteen members of the Swedish Academy sit down around the table in the session chamber. Verner von Heidenstam has come from Övralid. Across from him sits Hjalmar Hammarskjöld. Albert Engström takes the minutes. Heidenstam asks: "Where is Söderblom?" Hammarskjöld answers: "He is in Stuttgart." Heidenstam leaves the chamber on a short errand. He comes back and says: "Yes, but Söderblom is sitting out in the hall!" Hammarskjöld: "So, is he there too?"

* * *

At 11:00 A.M. on Friday, December 3, 1920, members of the General Synod were seated in the hall of the First Chamber of Parliament. It was an illustrious assemblage of bishops, deans, judges, members of Parliament, businessmen, and provincial governors. An academy bursar, a general, and a wholesale dealer were also there. They were to make decisions about matters that affected the church's future. Both the Minister of Ecclesiastical Affairs and the Minister of Justice were in their places and the public gallery was filled. There was tension in the air, for now the question of the *Psalmbok*, the Hymnal, was to be decided. The General Synod was expected to make a proposal to the Parliament and in the state church system it was Parliament's decision to make. The discussion in the Synod had drawn on interminably — for decades — and it had been debated in newspapers and in parish meetings for as long as anyone could remember. The Hymnal was a folk book and a standard for language. It was to be found in every home, and every school day began with a hymn. The Hymnal authorized in 1819 was still in use. It contained more than five hundred hymns, more than half written by the celebrated poet Johan Olof Wallin, who was later to become archbishop. It was a splendid national monument, but after one hundred years it was antiquated in both language and content. The gospel songs of the revival movements, which could not match the hymns in the *Psalmbok* in either poetry or music, threatened to take the book's place in the peoples' consciousness. When church choirs formed a national organization at the end of the nineteenth century, the demand for a revised *Psalmbok* was sharpened. Bishop J. A. Eklund of Karlstad, who was a fine hymn writer and translator, made an attempt at revision in 1911. It received a mixed reception and in yet another form was proposed again in 1914. Many old hymns had been eliminated and new ones added, but the popular gospel songs were still excluded. That proposal also did not fall on fertile soil. The Swedish Academy rejected the new texts and defended the legacy of Wallin.

Another attempt was made and another provisional hymnal was published in 1917. When even that attempt met the same fate, a new committee, the fourth, was formed. It proposed a supplement to the 1819 book that would include both revival songs and contemporary hymns. A number of new texts were written by Emil Liedgren, Siri Dalquist, Jenny Holmåsen, Sam Gabrielson, and other young authors. Söderblom had reluctantly participated in the committee's work. Several times he urged his friend, the highly esteemed poet Erik Axel Karlfeldt, who served as permanent secretary of the Swedish Academy, to contribute hymns, but in vain. The closest he came to success was when Karlfeldt wrote the text to Hugo Alfvén's cantata, composed for the Reformation Jubilee of 1917. That gave rise to Söderblom's spontaneous admiration: "Just think, there is a poet still alive!" Together, Karlfeldt and Söderblom were given honorary doctorates that year.

Now the General Synod was to take positions on two proposals. The first was for a fundamental revision of the old *Psalmbok*. Supporting this proposal were the two bishops, J. A. Eklund and Gottfrid Billing. The second was for a supplement, which was prepared by Söderblom and others. When the debate began, Söderblom — who was chair of the Synod — did something that awakened great attention and was regarded by some as an outright coup. Contrary to the Synod's agenda and established practice, he himself took the floor and spoke for more than two hours against the proposed revision and in favor of the supplement. Previously he had supported a revision of the 1819 hymnal, but now he was convinced that the Synod should adopt the proposed supplement. In the revision, Wallin's texts had been edited so drastically that they, according to Söderblom, lacked "heart and soul" and gave the impression of being "domesticated and leveled out." Moreover, a number of worthwhile hymns had been dropped and some inferior texts of later dates had been added. Hymns can certainly die, said Söderblom, but it did not help to replace dead hymns with stillborn ones. Both belong in the cemetery. "Over the deceased hymns a tombstone could be erected. But stillborn hymns would at best be mourned by the ones who believed that their lifeless fetus should find a place in the land of the living." He could not support violating old poems and agreed with the warning of the Swedish Academy to let things alone. When the Academy has something to say, one should listen. His long address was a defeat for Eklund who had led the work of revision.

Söderblom argued convincingly for the supplement that he felt should be used along with a nearly unchanged Wallin *Psalmbok*. He wanted to include the best of his beloved gospel songs and he also spoke warmly in favor of newly written hymns. He dared to compare Emil Liedgren with Wallin, but the "deepest" of all new hymns was Natanael Beskow's "Tränger i dolda djupen ned, tanken som söker och spanar" ("My thoughts to secret depths may strive, thoughts of seeking and searching"). This was a poem speaking of God as both hidden and revealed, and of a seeker being led from a vague sense of God's love to seeing and possessing, from the experience of being carried by God to a final recognition of God's revelation. It was a hymn that made God great and the world small, picturing faith as trust and hope. It was like an echo of Söderblom's own theology and faith.

The Synod was required to make a choice between the past and the present. With new hymns, a modern worldview and a corresponding picture of God would be conveyed in every parish. It was a crucial issue. More than forty of the sixty members of the Synod took to the floor. The discussion continued until 2:30 in the morning. Then the Synod in principle approved of Söderblom's proposal for a supplement to the *Psalmbok*. He had ventured boldly and was fortunate to have the Swedish Academy and other cautious traditionalists on his side. The ultimate result in practice should have been a new hymnal, but the Parliament had the last word and there the question got stuck. Not until 1937 was a new *Psalmbok* approved.

The one who brought this decision about was, ironically, Arthur Engberg who by that time had ceased in his own opposition to the church.

The Swedish Academy, "The Eighteen," now knew where the archbishop stood on what was for them an important question. No one was surprised when in 1921, Söderblom was elected to occupy chair number sixteen after Waldemar Rudin who died that year. There were not many within the cultural life of Sweden who could compete with him for that honor. The editor of the Norwegian journal *Kirke og Kultur (Church and Culture),* Eivind Berggrav, who was Söderblom's devoted admirer and who would step into his shoes as the Nordic countries' foremost church leader, wrote: "Everyone knows that he not only loves culture, but *practices* it, nurtures and shares it with artists, authors, diplomats, social democrats. The heartbeat of the era vibrates within him and expands with the day. He runs — like Olav Tryggvason — outside the bounds, on the blades of the oars while his men row; with virility he practices the sports of culture and exceeds the accomplishments of everyone else."

Söderblom was an attentive reader of literature already as a student. In the group Free from the Heart, poetry from the 1880s and 1890s was analyzed. In the Stabby rectory, Anna and Nathan read aloud to each other. In Paris, newly published Swedish books had been an essential link to the homeland. He had written significant essays on authors from both past and present, and even as archbishop he was able to keep up to date. In his homily at the burial of Gustaf Fröding in 1911, he had carefully taken the hand of the poet who had been trampled down by both small-minded middle-class convention and by mental illness and led him to the land of the living. "Three small books were published and a whole language is in grief" was one of his compelling formulations. Fröding had unmasked human shame and honor and left no one unmoved. What more could one ask of him?

Only a few days later, Söderblom wrote to the Academy and suggested that August Strindberg should receive the Nobel Prize. "No author has more grippingly, artistically, and effectively than Strindberg described the reaction of the spirit against the suffocating dogmatism of materialism," he wrote. But it was too late. Controversy over Strindberg raged. A year later, when Söderblom buried Strindberg, he did not preach; he only read Bible verses and a hymn of death by the seventeenth-century Swedish baroque poet, Lasse Lucidor (Lars Johansson). Strindberg had underlined the poem, which appeared in its original version in his *Psalmbok*:

Death does not astound me
even though it seems dreadful.
For he has been crushed by Christ
and cannot wound me.
Judgment I fear greatly
for I have done ill.
But the trust I do not forget
is that Jesus is my brother.

Notably, Strindberg had gone on attack against the literature of the 1890s and Heidenstam reacted violently in its defense. He described Strindberg's admirers as "partisans and rodents who look up at life through a rat hole. They are cynical and coarse-natured, broken in mind, self-betrayers, envious, unhappy, and woeful." Then a national fundraising campaign to honor Strindberg was organized and on the list of contributors was, among others, Professor Söderblom. People asked if he could really be so one-sided. No, replied Söderblom in the newspaper *Dagens Nyheter,* he had a more nuanced view of the matter. Much of Strindberg's writing was inferior, he admitted, but within his work was also the very best. In the most common of Swedish words and in daily events he could "bring out the deepest destitutions in the sublime drama of human life." His greatness was not only Swedish but international and human.

Heidenstam wrote to Söderblom and asked if he was so superior to all others that he could objectively judge the current cultural scandal. "Strindbergism," wrote Heidenstam, was a corrupting process, which was on its way to making Sweden a madhouse for riff-raff. For him, Strindberg was a sign of "the revolutionary opposition's final decadence and dissolution into chaos" and his philosophy of religion was a collection of muddy attacks aimed here and there. To purchase a Hebew lexicon or throw the word "God" around toward tiresome compatriots did not qualify one as "profound." Söderblom replied that in spite of the vulgarity, baseness, drivel, and nonsense in Strindberg there were tones from the human heart that would find an echo for eternity. He lacked moral courage, to be sure, but he possessed a kind of desperate demand for freedom that was in contrast to all dogmatism and self-righteousness. Söderblom reminded Heidenstam that in 1888 when he took the poet's *Vallfart och vandringsår* (*Pilgrimage: The Wander Years*) into his hands, he greedily drank "this sun-fed wine after the weak beer and vinegar of the '80s." He stood fast in his belief that Strindberg belonged to Sweden's few universal literary names. "He is our Dostoevsky or Kierkegaard."

One year later, Söderblom congratulated Heidenstam on his entry into the Swedish Academy, but when Heidenstam wrote the Academy's evaluation of the *Psalmbok* proposal of 1914 and rejected all linguistic modernization, Söderblom answered with a touch of irony: "The mellowness of age grants a certain sanctity even to extremely worthless goods. But I thank you for this important contribution regarding a serious question." Nearer than that these two never came.

When Söderblom himself took his place among "The Eighteen" and his lamp was lit at chair sixteen on the table of the magnificent session room, he did not come as a stranger to anyone. There sat Henrik Schück, the professor of literature who belonged to his nearest circle of friends; Harald Hjärne, the influential historian and teacher who for a long time had been his confidant; Erik Axel Karlfeldt, the poet with whom he had been friends since student days and whom he admired immensely; the linguist Adolf Noreen, who in the 1880s had convinced him to write "new Swedish"; and the provincial governor Hjalmar Hammarskjöld, who was his neighbor in the nearby Uppsala castle; not to forget Gottfrid Billing, who was the Academy's director and who now greeted the new member with great warmth. Billing had officiated at his ordinations as both priest and bishop and had always kept a watchful eye on him. A few weeks after the formal event, Söderblom wrote: "Yes, since old Billing has now initiated me three times, there is hardly any other mystery into which he can introduce me. It is remarkable that it should have fallen to his lot to have so much to do with this troublemaker. He has been unfailingly friendly." Among the members there were also others whom he knew. He was himself known by them all.

To be elected to the Swedish Academy was confirmation of the fact that he clearly belonged to the nation's cultural elite. The election did not come as a surprise. The outcome was known as early as March 1921 when it was written in *Svenska Dagbladet* that, "He is one of the time's foremost intellectuals and both as an author and a spiritual orator he always has style. He is not only a genuine representative of the church but also an uncommonly many-sided cultural figure and his broad international connections bring to the Academy a benefit which, given the mandate of the Nobel Prize, is greatly to be treasured." That Söderblom that same week received an additional large donation for the Olaus Petri Foundation, thus making possible its impressive list of famous lecturers over the years, did not lessen his satisfaction.

While he was at work on his inaugural address he wrote to Karlfeldt, the Permanent Secretary of the Academy: "I dread this like a schoolboy, a student with an overdue essay." An address it was, long and rich in content, and Karlfeldt said that he had never heard such an inaugural address at the Academy. It was a memorial depiction of Waldemar Rudin — mystic and pietist, theologian and poet — and who could have given that with deeper knowledge of this striking personality than Söderblom? Rudin had been like a father to him when he first came to Uppsala and they had been close for nearly forty years. Rudin had belonged to the Academy for a quarter of a century. Yet there were few in that brilliant society of letters who really knew what ideas moved that gentle prophetic figure. With his shaggy white head on an angle and his eyes staring into the distance, Rudin whispered his message. With the trembling hands of an old man he gave force to his words. Söderblom wrote a spiritual biography of Rudin. He described him as the epitome of a pious person. If one were to have asked average Swedes who in the world they would identify as a true Christian — believers, agnostics and atheists, free church and established church people, children of the world and people of conscience, specialists in religion and middle-class God-fearers, academics and manual laborers, nobodies and celebrities — they all would have named Waldemar Rudin. He was a John-like figure whom many would call a saint, a Swedish Kierkegaard whose spiritual journey Söderblom traced into the depths of the soul and out to the boundaries of thought and earth. They had so much in common.

Waldemar Rudin's Inner Life grew to a manuscript of 130 pages and in a certain way also became a report on Söderblom's own inner life. His inaugural address was an uncommon testimony to be delivered under the crystal chandeliers of the Swedish Academy. It appeared to be more than a coincidence that Söderblom succeeded one who was his first mentor and spiritual guide in Uppsala. Chair number sixteen represented a line from Rydberg through Rudin to Söderblom and it would be continued by Söderblom's student Tor Andrae. Living spirituality belonged to the principal expressions of culture and for thousands of years had left its mark in the greatest works of world literature. It must have its place in the Swedish Academy.

Söderblom always attempted to attend the Academy's Thursday meetings. He enjoyed belonging to this chosen circle. The Academy's motto was "Genius and Taste." Genius implied "talented, gifted" and taste stood for a kind of aesthetic ability to interpret things or make judgments. Those words could, without difficulty, be applied to geniuses who, according to Söderblom, played special roles in history. That an archbishop belonged to the Swedish Academy was natural. Christianity was "simply the truth" and represented the highest in life, even in contemporary culture. According to Söderblom, God could reveal himself in time through the work of great authors, but one would need to have perceptivity, a *sensorium* for religion, and an openness to culture to discover this. Söderblom possessed all of these traits.

The ambitious son of a clergyman had now come as close to the most outstanding people in society as anyone could wish. He admired successful and educated people of good lineage and looked for "distinction" in everyone he met. In spite of the fact that he was so welcome among outstanding scholars, wealthy landowners, and energetic entrepreneurs and easily got along with them, his heart, paradoxically, remained with the most disadvantaged people. As archbishop he certainly belonged among the well-educated and established classes. The royal family, high nobility, and major people of finance supported him while the church and the labor movement had a more ambiguous relationship. In Paris, it used to be said that Anders Zorn the artist landed "high on the gravy train." What was one then to say of Söderblom? Unlike Zorn, though, he put on no false pretenses. He was himself and he was proud of his background.

In addition to the members of the Swedish Academy, whom he met daily in Uppsala, he kept especially close contact with Erik Axel Karlfeldt and Selma Lagerlöf, both of whom he regarded highly. Letters to Karlfeldt, the poet who was to be awarded the Nobel Prize for Literature in 1931, opened with salutations such as "Poet, brother" and "Poet, dear Permanent Secretary" or "Favored fellow human being." Selma Lagerlöf, the novelist and in 1909 the first woman awarded the Nobel Prize for Literature, was greeted in a crescendo: "Noble dear friend, Dear noble Selma, Selma *optima, Selmissima.*" In 1923, Söderblom delivered the director's address at the Academy's annual solemn celebration. He had just returned from his journey to America and he asserted that Europe no longer had a monopoly on the future of civilization. It was, rather, the Americans who could rescue civilization. He reminded the members of the Academy of the urgency of paying attention to those on the other side of the ocean who spoke Swedish and who had great interest in preserving Swedish in the United States even though the language was both changed and distorted.

Since his time in Paris Söderblom had always been at home in the world of culture, largely because he was himself an artist who by scholarship, religion, and music strove to uncover and interpret the innermost essence of existence. Of the authors of his generation he stood closest to Karlfeldt, and of the painters it was Anders Zorn. Even after Zorn died and was buried by Söderblom in 1920, Emma Zorn, the Söderbloms, and the Karlfeldts continued their social contacts. They made long visits to churches in Uppland, celebrated the annual spring festival on April 30 in Uppsala, and had dinners together. Söderblom was known for his joyous exclamations that were embellished with superlatives. When it came to Karlfeldt's poetry no words were adequate. *Hösthorn* (*The Horn of Autumn*) was published in 1927 and Söderblom wrote to Karlfeldt in his characteristic way: "The day when the bookstore window shined with *Hösthorn*, and quickly disappeared since it was sold out, I was able to get a copy which I immediately devoured. But one cannot do that. The soul is not able to digest it. One should not try to devour it, and I have already begun to read and reflect and read again and smile and admire and turn on to the path where one forgets himself and is led to the One, the Only, the Great, the Eternal, the Necessary." For Söderblom, Karlfeldt was matchless as a poet and he was also a speaker who could cover poets and the entire Academy with a vault, "a surely reliable Nordic heaven," which gives the certainty that God reigns over them. During his last years, Söderblom always had a photograph of Karlfeldt on his desk.

What influence did Söderblom have in respect to the Academy's two major tasks: to designate recipients of the Nobel Prizes and to choose new members? That the French philosopher Henri Bergson — who meant so much to Söderblom's own reflections on the mystery of life, creative development, and the prophetic dimension of history — was awarded the Nobel Prize for Literature in 1927 must have been extremely satisfying to the archbishop. He had dealt seriously with Bergson's thought in *Religionsproblemet* (*The Problem of Religion*), 1910, and had asked him to present the Olaus Petri Lectures. Sadly, his rheumatism prevented Bergson from making a December journey to frigid Sweden in order to receive the Nobel

Prize. When Gottfrid Billing died in 1925, Söderblom was at first unsuccessful in his attempt to have Bishop J. A. Eklund named in his place. As an alternative, he proposed the name of Natanael Beskow, whom he regarded as Sweden's most outstanding hymn writer since Johan Olof Wallin. He received support from Selma Lagerlöf, but a majority chose instead the philosopher Hans Larsson, whose way of thinking was far removed from that of Söderblom. It was also Söderblom who first proposed that Karlfeldt should receive the Nobel Prize. The Academy had observed the one hundred fiftieth anniversary of Johan Olof Wallin and Söderblom had finally gotten a hymn from the hand of Karlfeldt: "Nu jagar stormen våra år" ("When storms are chasing our days as skies above the sea"). Karlfeldt, however, died and the prize was given posthumously. Söderblom officiated at his funeral on April 12, 1931, in Stockholm. An old newsreel shows how the catafalque, drawn by horses, went amidst trolley cars and Model T Fords across Skeppsbron, the Ships Bridge, up to Storkyrkan, followed by throngs of black-clothed people, among them Söderblom. He gave no funeral address; he rather read some verses from the Bible and Karlfeldt's own prayer:

> Give us a hearth for our course
> of due and daily bread.
> Give us a breast as safe resource
> when dangers are ahead.
> Give us a faith as our force
> before we once are dead.

At the burial at the Folkärna Church, the air was filled with sleet. Three months later, Söderblom was also dead.

25

Mission Is Dialogue

> China's classics will form a kind of Old Testament which acquires its full meaning only when the New is joined to it.
>
> *Nathan Söderblom, 1911*

At the Kronstadt Fortress in Petrograd the final battle begins. The revolt of the Communist workers and seamen against the deceit and terror of the Soviet state is crushed. Their dream is self-determination, bread, and freedom. The same evening, the first Lutheran bishop is consecrated in the New Jerusalem Church in Tranquebar, a stone's throw from the shore of the Indian Ocean. For a long time, the city had been a Danish colony and King Frederick IV in Copenhagen's Amalienborg Palace had sent missionaries there. Now, for more than two hundred years, Bartholomew Ziegenbalg had rested under a gravestone in front of the pulpit. In order to share Christian faith, he had studied Hinduism. At last the Indian church attains independence. Christian farm workers stand erect and hope for the future. In Uppsala, Nathan Söderblom prays for both the Russians and the Tamils.

* * *

As archbishop, Nathan Söderblom was chairperson *ex officio* of the Church of Sweden Mission. That task interested him greatly. Here he could put into practice his knowledge of the history of religions and also bring Africa and Asia into his ecumenical program. His view of mission was not common at the time. For him, Christianity was a distinctly unique religion with universal claims and with Jesus Christ as Savior. Söderblom had personally experienced both God's mercy and his consuming fire and he had a firmly rooted trust in God's grace. In his academic policy statement of 1907, *Studiet av religionerna* (*The Study of Religions*), he maintained that Christianity does not understand itself as one of the religions of the world "but in its essence, in Christ, in its ideal possibilities, as the religion *par préférence*, the object to which all hearts in need of salvation and all who seek the divine finally aim." On that point, all "friends of mission" could agree with him. Indeed, since his childhood and his student years he had been one of those friends. But his studies of the history of religion and his ecumenical experiences had subsequently expanded his perspective. God's entire revelation had certainly taken place in Christ, but it had not there been brought to an end; God could also communicate himself through all religions. Söderblom, therefore, wished to approach all who worshiped God with openness, with curiosity, and with respect for their experiences in encountering the holy. A serious study of other religions could only advance Christianity and in the best of cases provide it with new insights.

Like most others of his generation he had an evolutionary view that placed Christianity at the pinnacle. When scholars and advocates of religion constructed a theory of evolution, it was usually their own culture that landed at the top step of the development. That pertained to Christians as well as to Buddhists, to Europeans as well as to Chinese. Söderblom belonged to a Western culture that up until World War I claimed superiority and the privilege of evaluating and interpreting other civilizations. This had determined the self-understanding of both Christian missions and Western natural science. But Söderblom was neither a determinist who believed that history must follow a predetermined course, nor a programmatic evolutionist for whom everything went in one direction. Different actors could enter history and unexpectedly alter the direction of developments. In the Judeo-Christian tradition, Moses and Jesus were the great examples of that. Religions also developed under differing historical and cultural conditions, which affected both personal and institutional encounters with the holy. That encounter was, for Söderblom, the core of all religion.

Mission had its starting point in the revelation of Christ, but its task was not simply to convert people to Christian faith but to spread the Kingdom of God, which was an entity greater than Christianity. In the complex history of humankind, into which so many religions were woven, there was a dynamic movement that could be identified as the will of God, a movement that aimed at God's dominion. That movement was to be acknowledged by all Christians since mission was by definition participation in it. The different threads in general revelation converged and were united in Christ.

He was the sign that God seeks all people, and this was the deepest meaning of the incarnation. The task of mission was to bring all people of other faiths to participation in Christ without forcing them to give up their own cultural and spiritual treasures.

Söderblom's view of mission was Christocentric, but he steered clear of all simple historicism. Revelation had not come to a chronological end with the death and resurrection of Jesus but continued wherever humans explored the secrets of history and perceived the address of God. Söderblom contributed to the formation of fully recognized and independent churches with bishops and other classical marks. But Asian and African churches had to assume forms other than those of the West, not becoming like imported plants in a foreign milieu. They must have a deep knowledge of the local religions in order to find points of contact and thus develop their awareness of what is essential to Christianity. In the midst of the multifaceted world of religion, they should make manifest the living God.

When Söderblom became chairperson of the Church of Sweden Mission, it had been in existence for forty years. The Church of Sweden carried on extensive work in South Africa, in Zimbabwe, which was then called Southern Rhodesia, and in South India. Seamen's churches in different places in Europe were also the Mission's responsibility. To a high degree, he contributed to giving the Swedish foreign mission its own character. From the beginning it was organized as a church mission borne by every parish in the Church of Sweden, and not as an independent missionary society. When Söderblom came into the picture, the Young Church Movement began to put its stamp on the work, even if the economic support came from conservative parishes, largely on the west coast. Thanks to Söderblom, the Church of Sweden Mission came to be characterized by an openness in respect to theologies of religion, culture, and ecumenism; by far-sighted social activity; and by productive contacts with the university and scholarship. The first thing he did as archbishop was to ordain a missionary, Paul Sandegren, for service in South India. With his experience and knowledge of languages, Sandegren later became one of Söderblom's closest colleagues in the ecumenical movement.

As a result of meetings, mission conferences, and conversations with the approximately 130 missionaries, Söderblom was given a concrete picture of the work. It was an expansive period, contributions were up fourfold, and activities increased. After a long period of hesitancy, the

Board at the beginning of the 1920s broadened its work to China where so many other missionaries were already active. Asia was Söderblom's special field of interest. He was not equally engaged in Africa. Apart from Albert Schweitzer's Lambaréné and Haile Selassie's Ethiopia, that continent was pretty much absent from his mental map; Asia concerned him. There, all the great world religions had their origins and there blossomed the millennia-rich cultures he had attempted to understand through his scholarship.

The outbreak of war in 1914 paralyzed many mission organizations. Uncertain economic conditions and travel difficulties combined to put a halt to things for many. The Church of Sweden Mission, which shared work in the Leipzig Mission's "field" in Tamil Nadu in South India, took responsibility there for German congregations, schools, and medical work since the British authorities expelled nearly all the German missionaries and forbade economic dealings with Germany. The Swedes could manage the work, but only with considerable difficulties. Moreover, the boards in Leipzig and Uppsala had differing positions in respect to vital and strategic matters. Söderblom, who was fully familiar with the Leipzig Mission's conservative confessional position, energetically pursued his own line. He wanted to give the Tamil Church greater independence within the constitutional limits that he himself had drawn up. At his first meeting with the Mission board, he proposed that the Indian church should have its own bishop. The Germans had no interest in such a proposal, but Söderblom stood his ground. The church needed, he felt, an episcopal order for the sake of both continuity and ordered governance. This was a link in his desire to manifest evangelical catholicity and he thus engaged himself, perhaps more than was reasonable, in working out statutes for the Tamil Evangelical Lutheran Church. There was a need for speed. If the church did not have its own constitution, there was a risk that the German property would be confiscated by the British. His proposal was sent to India, but when the Tamil Church ratified it in January 1919, all stipulations about episcopacy had been removed.

The Mission then decided to send a delegation to India to visit the church and conclude negotiations about the church's governance. Söderblom wanted to make the trip himself but this was not possible since he had to lead the General Synod in Sweden. The Bishop of Skara, Hjalmar Danell, led the delegation, which also included K. B. Westman who was to represent Söderblom's position. Before they traveled, Söderblom wrote an episcopal letter to the Indian church and recommended that the office of the bishop be instituted. This was reluctantly accepted and Hjalmar Danell consecrated Ernst Heuman as "Bishop of Tranquebar." This happened on March 7, 1921, the evening of the day that the new church order was adopted. The first Lutheran missionaries had landed in Tamil Nadu in 1706, having been supported by King Frederick IV of Denmark. It had taken a great while before the church had become independent.

The discussion about missionary bishops was not new. It was necessary for the supervision of local parishes and as a guarantee that the clergy would be ordained in proper orders. Söderblom had made the suggestion and now he had gotten his way even sooner than expected. Even if the bishop was a Swedish missionary, he was nevertheless chosen and consecrated in the local church. Heuman's most difficult task was to unite the church. Not unexpectedly, there was considerable tension between the many "German" and the few "Swedish" congregations, and the German opposition to the episcopal office remained. Heuman, with his pastoral and unpretentious emphases and his humble devotional piety, won the respect of virtually everyone. In the 1880s, he had been chairperson of the Student Mission Association and subsequently followed Lars Skrefsrud to the Norwegian Santal Mission in India. After a few years, he moved to the Church of Sweden Mission in South India where many regarded him as a spiritual teacher, a "sadhu" or holy man. He died in 1926.

As chairman of the Church of Sweden Mission, Söderblom was also concerned with China. The Student Volunteer Movement, which had been started by John R. Mott and which Söderblom encountered in the United States in 1890, had devoted itself to the recruitment of well-educated academics for service in China. During his visit to Uppsala in 1909, Mott had encouraged students to go to China where a number of universities had already been established by English and American missionaries. He sowed this seed especially among some in the Young Church Movement. At the time of the Reformation Jubilee in 1917, the question of starting a Swedish mission in China was under serious consideration. Söderblom was eager for Swedish academics to travel to China, not least with the thought in his mind of the discoveries in the history of religion they could bring back home. One who had already made her way there was the versatile and far-sighted Ingeborg Wikander who was responsible for the work of the YWCA in Changsha in the province of Hunan. But when the question was raised whether the Church of Sweden should seriously begin its own mission work in China, Söderblom was initially dubious. Because of Mott's imperialistic way of thinking and his anti-German views, his reputation among Europeans had somewhat diminished. Söderblom instead made contact with Erik Folke who had traveled to China in 1887 and worked in Henan with the China Inland Mission. When it became clear to Söderblom that the Church of Sweden should concentrate its work on higher education and he had gotten approval from the experienced Folke, he went ahead with the same energy he had devoted to so many other projects.

That Ruth Nathorst, daughter of the well-known professor and Arctic explorer Alfred Nathorst, and the gifted young priest Fritz Holmgren would be the first to go made his decision easier. Holmgren had summarized his understanding of mission in the journal *Svensk Missionstidskrift*: "There can be no question of some kind of imposition of European ways of thinking and European theology, but rather what is needed is necessary participation in the riches of Christian intellectual life so that it might stimulate an indigenous theology that will arise when the people of the East themselves begin to consider the substance of their Christian faith." This was completely in line with what Söderblom had heard Wang Chenting say in Constantinople in 1911 and it agreed with his own view of mission.

The request of these two people to be the Church of Sweden's first missionaries in China reached the mission board in October of 1917. Preparations for the celebration of the Reformation Jubilee were then fully under way. It was to include the Day of Gustavus Adolphus, November 6, and in good Söderblom style not only be a celebration of Luther but also of the hero king's rescue of the Reformation. At that time it was Germany; now it was China that awaited a contribution from Sweden. In this connection, Adolf Kolmodin proposed that the Church of Sweden Mission establish a Swedish university in China. In connection with the Reformation Jubilee a number of academics gathered in Uppsala to discuss that proposal. One of the principal speakers was the engineer and geologist Erik Nyström who, together with Timothy Richards, had taken part in building a university in Shansi. His experience in uniting Chinese culture with Western science aroused Söderblom's enthusiasm. That he had also worked with the world-famous Arctic explorer, paleontologist, and archaeologist Gunnar Andersson, who discovered the "Peking man," made things even better. Nyström, however, had had no contact with missionaries; on the contrary, he looked at them in mostly negative terms. The Mission's grandiose plans for a full-scale modern university in Sun Yat-sen's Republic of China matured in the encounter between Nyström and Söderblom.

The path from ideas to action was short. Through the Export Association, Söderblom thought he could find industrialists with special interest in China that would be willing to bear part of the costs. The university should be situated in the middle of China, in Hankou in Hubei Province, and the Church of Sweden Mission should be the university's Board of Trustees. Nyström was asked to develop concrete plans. He sought support from the Chinese authorities, but he did not consult any missionaries. After just one year, in December 1918, the Mission made the decision to establish the university. For Söderblom it was a historic moment. He thanked God "who endowed our Swedish church with the wonderful task of bringing something of the light of his revelation into the darkness of the world," and in sincere prayer he asked God for his blessing over the steps now being taken and over the enterprise that, through this action, was expected to be realized.

The entire Mission stood behind this decision and Söderblom quickly took things further. He formed a special committee with Crown Prince Gustaf Adolf as chairman. The crown prince had developed a great interest in East Asian culture and had carefully followed Nyström's and Andersson's activities. The Export Association was represented by the chairperson of its board, Herman Lagercrantz, who himself had been a missionary for the Salvation Army. Professors from the Karolinska Medical Institute and the Stockholm Technical University were part of the group, along with Söderblom with his theological expertise. In January 1919, the committee met in the Stockholm Royal Castle. Söderblom reviewed in detail the plans of the Mission. It was to be a university with at least three faculties: a faculty of ethics and religious studies, a faculty of medicine, and a faculty of natural sciences and technology. Knowing the special interests of the crown prince, he pointed out that areas such as archaeology, art history, and philology would be added later. He realized that it might cause problems for other interested parties if the university were to be controlled by the Church of Sweden Mission and thus he emphasized that by no means would any kind of spiritual coercion be involved. The university should "fulfill its vocation with full respect for the inherent power of truth." The students, in accord with their own interests, would "immerse themselves partly in Western and partly in Chinese religious and ethical histories and fundamental world views." The university should be viewed as a contribution from all the people of Sweden to China, and in his role as the nation's archbishop, he took responsibility for that. He had introduced his address with the following words: "The World War is over. How can our people show their thankfulness for the extraordinary benefit we have received by not being dragged into that bloody devastation?" Yes, by accepting international obligations. The war had given rise to a great deal of sacrifice; now it was crucial not to avoid but even more to accept the Swedish vocation in and for the world.

To Söderblom's considerable amazement, the industrialists and the representatives of the medical and technical sciences immediately rejected the entire project. They judged that the economic resources were lacking and also felt that the Swedish universities should not support such an ecclesiastical enterprise. In the end, only the crown prince and the archbishop wanted to proceed. For Söderblom, the entire thing was a fiasco. He had staked his prestige on the fulfillment of these plans, plans that were in fact already well known to the public. He was defeated at the committee's first meeting and those who opposed him were not insignificant personages. He had to give up. The audacious plan for a university was nothing more than a spectacular episode.

Things were made more complicated by the fact that the project did not have the support of the Lutheran missionaries who had been working in China for a few decades, and by the fact that the Church of Sweden Mission had already begun to hire teachers. When the plans for a university went down, the Mission decided to explore the establishment of a college. This required cooperation with other Lutheran missionaries who themselves already had well-advanced plans for such an institution. Those missionaries insisted not only on negotiations regarding the Swedish plans but also that the Swedish missionaries should not only work in education but should also participate in the regular work of evangelization and the building of congregations. The Mission had to start again from the beginning. In order to meet this request, K. B. Westman and Gustaf Österlin were sent first to America and then to China in order to consult with a long list of Lutheran mission organizations. Österlin was to stay in China to lead the work, so before they left, he was formally commissioned as a missionary. Westman was to travel from China to India to take part in negotiations there regarding the church structure and the episcopal office.

In the United States, the two Swedes were met with deep suspicion on the part of the conservative American Lutherans and they were subjected to a thorough examination concerning the faith and confession of the Church of Sweden. If not before, they now learned that the Swedish church was not particularly welcome to participate in Lutheran collaborative efforts. With the liberal Söderblom as its leader, it had a poor reputation among right-wing Lutherans. They had little understanding of historical-critical biblical studies, even less for the study of the phenomenology of religion, and least of all for ecumenical cooperation. In Midwest America, Westman and Österlin were met with "iciness."

When the roughly treated men arrived in China — where Mao Zedong was just beginning to form the Chinese Communist Party — it went somewhat better. They visited a large number of Christian and state institutions of higher education and Westman traveled to Beijing in order to meet the university chancellor Cai Yuanpei. In the midst of the summer heat, when hundreds of missionaries gathered in Kikungshan, they had the chance to meet the leaders of nearly all the Lutheran missions. The examination regarding "sound doctrine" was repeated, the Swedes explained and defended themselves, and finally a decision was reached that the Church of Sweden could start a college. Assurances regarding the financing of the college played a large part in leading to that decision. What at the beginning was thought of as an independent university was in effect reduced so much that at the end it was not even a college but something like a small high school in Taohwalun near the city of Yueyang in the province of Hunan. Söderblom had difficulty giving up the original idea, but was forced to recognize that it could not be realized. The elaborate plans of the Church of Sweden were transformed into a rather insignificant venture confined within a confessional Lutheran framework. It was then that Söderblom found a totally different way to carry on missionary work in China, one that was more compatible with his personal view.

A missionary of the Norwegian Mission Society, Karl Ludvig Reichelt, who had arrived in China in 1903, had an interest in the thought world and religious praxis of Buddhism. He was deeply impressed with the spirituality he encountered in monasteries and he attempted to approach Buddhists with the Christian gospel without violating their spiritual traditions. He studied the Chinese form of Mahayana and especially Pure Land Buddhism. In 1919, while he was still teaching at the Lutheran Theological Seminary in Shekow, he met a young Buddhist monk, Kuan-tu, who as a result of his teaching came to the certainty that Christ was the fulfillment of Buddhism. After he was baptized, he joined Reichelt in establishing a special mission to reach Buddhist monks.

Reichelt's way of approaching Buddhism was based partly on his reading of Söderblom. He wholeheartedly shared Söderblom's notion that God reveals himself in all religions, even if that revelation has its superior expression in Jesus Christ. After he had met the Swedish delegation that came to discuss plans for a college, Reichelt made direct contact with Söderblom. The latter responded by inviting Reichelt to Uppsala to give the Olaus Petri Lectures on Chinese religion. There would be four lectures, two on Mahayana Buddhism, one on Kuan-tu and his personal story, and one on the new mission among Buddhist monks.

Reichelt could not have come at a more opportune time. The plans for a university had come to nothing and Söderblom least of all wanted the Swedish China mission to become entangled in the concerns of conservative, anti-ecumenical Lutherans. To Ruth Nathorst he wrote that, "besides the unique Old Testament we must have as many 'Old Testaments' as there are religions, for all religions include a longing for and a prophecy of Christ." Reichelt had noticed especially that Söderblom described traditional Chinese culture as an Old Testament and that he also held that the early church interpreted Hellenistic culture as preparation for the gospel.

The archbishop and the missionary to the Buddhists were in their best years and they had a great deal in common. The background of each was in a low church and strict pietism, but they had left that behind as they matured into progressive, although in certain respects conservative, theologians. Both had spent a couple of years in Leipzig. They had bold visions and were not at all reluctant to take risks and to argue their case even in the face of opposition. They knew what their vocation was and their families often had to adjust themselves to that calling. Söderblom was deeply interested in Buddhism and was impressed by Reichelt's insights into the history of religions and his determination to create a church adapted to Chinese Buddhism. Such a church would certainly be viewed as liberal, but Reichelt was anxious that also it be rooted in Lutheran tradition.

When Reichelt had given his lectures, he published them in a book entitled *Fra Østens Religiøse Liv* (*From the Religious Life of the East*), which he dedicated to Söderblom. He described Mahayana Buddhism and even more, Pure Land Buddhism, as religions of salvation that had partly developed in the eighth century under the influence of the Assyrian Church of the East or "Nestorianism." Reichelt also believed that some of the roots of Buddhism could be found in Christianity, so the church he established was embellished with a Nestorian cross growing out of a lotus blossom. The Church of Sweden Mission, with Söderblom as its chairman, decided to support Reichelt's enterprise.

The Church of Sweden Mission had an ecumenical basis and was open to dialogue and enculturation to a degree that was foreign to most mission organizations. That Söderblom received Karl Ludvig Reichelt with such warmth was confirmation of a theology of mission that did not have much in common with the great watchword of the 1920s, "The Christian Occupation of China."

26

Mare Lutheranum

The Baltic is Lutheranism's inland sea.
Nathan Söderblom, 1917

After a stormy night at sea, when even the archbishop had taken a turn at the helm, Alle Ekström's motorboat Polar II, with ten men on board, reaches the Baltic coast. Outside the island of Hiiumaa the boat's motor stops. It careens and rolls violently. That's the way it is with humans, Söderblom writes: temptations are much more dangerous when the will, effort, and a goal do not drive one forward. Without power and movement, one helplessly falls prey to the influence of others. Mechanics get the motor started. For two weeks the group travels between islands and port cities. When the journey's finest day comes toward evening, they arrive in Tallinn. In the red light of the setting sun, the city with its high and thorny profile lies before their eyes. To his son Jan Olof, Nathan starts singing a hymn, "Our eyes the Holy Mountain see."

* * *

Lutheranism had its strongest foothold in the lands around the Baltic Sea. In northern Germany as well as in Denmark, Sweden, Finland, Estonia, and Latvia, most of the inhabitants belonged to national Lutheran churches. In Lithuania and Poland there were significant Lutheran minorities. For more than a millennium those who lived alongside the inland sea had had contact with each other since it was easier to travel over water than over land.

Early on, Söderblom set up his strategy. He would bring the Lutheran churches on the Baltic closer to each other so that they would become the core of a European *corpus Christianum* and, having ordained bishops, become a stronghold of evangelical catholicity. He began by approaching the churches in Denmark and Norway where the history differed a great deal from that of the Swedes and Finns. The Nordic churches had much in common. The languages were closely related, all were state churches, and all had experienced similar popular awakenings or revivals. At mid-nineteenth century, a considerable amount of contact had developed between the Scandinavian churches, often around mission and diaconal service, and an increasing consciousness of a common Lutheran heritage had strengthened the feeling of solidarity. When the war broke out, the bishops in Copenhagen, Oslo, and Åbo had signed Söderblom's appeal for peace. An interest in deepening cooperation grew. Nils Widner had been the Swedish priest in Copenhagen and he became Söderblom's indispensable partner in the development of Nordic relations. In the fall of 1916 he organized a Nordic clergy conference at the folk high school in Nääs, outside Gothenburg. Many of the participants had known each other since student meetings at the turn of the century, among them Eivind Berggrav from Norway, Valdemar Ammundsen from Denmark, and Manfred Björkquist from Sweden. A committee was formed for continued cooperation and when the group gathered again a year later, a number of bishops were also present. Söderblom was elected chairman and assumed the role of undisputed spokesperson for Christians of the North. And only he had a well-considered plan for what needed to be done.

Essays that he had written often showed up in the most unexpected contexts. It had been that way with his short but groundbreaking 1903 article on the religion of revelation. It had been published in a *Festschrift* for an old professor. In a celebratory volume for the tenth anniversary of Gustaf V's reign in 1917, Söderblom's essay "The Jubilee Year and the Unity of the Church" appeared. This was an ecumenical program in which he developed the idea of Christian unity built not on institutional merger but rather on the churches' common evangelical confession. Its principle of freedom would allow each church to remain faithful to its own spiritual heritage and culturally formed uniqueness, but at the same time to live in unity with the others. He surveyed the world's evangelical communions and came to the conclusion that the evangelical faith and its ideals had, in the Nordic countries, "an abode which in unbroken freedom from Roman ecclesiastical power had no counterpart in the world." Thus, cooperation between the Nordic churches was a divine vocation. In no other locale did evangelical catholicity, which could overcome the divisions in Christianity, have a better prospect of being expressed. The Nordic churches belonged together and that was best shown in that each possessed "the biblical and universal ministry of the bishop." It was natural that the bishops took on themselves the responsibility of deepening the churches' fellowship. The question of apostolic succession was delicate in both Denmark and Norway, so he did not bring it up.

In 1919, he took the initiative in calling a meeting of the Nordic bishops. He was then in the midst of preparing the proposal for an international conference and an ecumenical council, which he was to set forth in Oud Wassenaar. Since it was uncertain that Sweden alone would receive a place in the contemplated council, but the Nordic churches together would certainly have such a place, especially if they included the Baltic churches, he wanted to create grounds for a common international initiative. The bishops of Copenhagen and Oslo had already worked with him. Now he invited all of the Nordic bishops to a week together at the Kulla Gunnarstorp castle in Skåne in July 1920. He had convinced Count Axel Wachtmeister to serve as host and pay for the expenses of the entire event. Other castle owners would follow suit. For a few more decades, counts and barons were to host the Nordic bishops and in that way support church cooperation. Söderblom had, as we have seen, a phenomenal ability to persuade people to open both their homes and their wallets for his projects. He had the reputation of being, alongside Manfred Björkquist, Sweden's greatest fund-raiser.

At Kulla Gunnarstorp, the Swedish, Danish, Norwegian, and Icelandic bishops met for the first time since the days of the Kalmar Union in the fifteenth century, although the Finnish bishops stayed at home. The question as to whether the islands of Åland should belong to Finland or Sweden had given rise to such great political tension between the countries that the Finnish bishops felt unable to attend. And they also had other reasons for staying away. Finland's biblicistic Archbishop Gustav Johansson was coldly unsympathetic to both Söderblom's liberal theology and his ecumenical initiatives, and thus even to a Nordic bishops' meeting.

Since the conference took place within the Diocese of Lund, Söderblom asked Gottfrid Billing to be chairperson, although in practice most things were in his own hands. The participants themselves proposed themes for the discussions that were immediate and predictable: "the danger of Rome," an issue throughout Protestant Europe; the state–church question, which was immediate in both Finland and Sweden; social justice and the churches' relationship to the working class; the office of the bishop; and how solidarity between the Nordic churches could be strengthened. The bishops wrote a short pastoral letter to "the congregations in the North" and admonished them to remain confident in the midst of the social and political upheavals that were going on "for the Lord lives. He lives in our midst in his gospel." The meeting was monitored by the press. They expressed a certain disappointment that the bishops spoke in such generalities. When they were all gathered together, more was expected, "something powerful and urgent."

The most important thing, though, was that the meeting took place. If the Nordic churches had a special "place and task" in the newly awakened ecumenical movement and were possibly to show the way toward unity within evangelical Christianity, they must get to know one another. Söderblom dreamed that they would constitute "the core" of a communion of faith that would also include the Church of England and the German Evangelical Church Union, which was then being formed. Together with Estonia and Latvia, the North had all that was necessary to be a "church block" with special ecumenical weight. Söderblom had broadened his perspective; from the beginning he had spoken of the historically given ecumenical calling of the Church of Sweden. Now he included all of the Nordic and Baltic churches in that calling. He carried on a goal-conscious foreign policy for the churches and was on the way to creating an alliance among the churches around the Baltic.

Still, however, Finland, Estonia, and Latvia remained outside. This was a great concern for Söderblom. He had often expressed a special love for Finland and he held on to that love in spite of all the difficulties his colleague, the Archbishop of Åbo, caused him. "Finland is for us an educator in much that is good. Above all in love for our native land," he wrote in his diary in 1892 when his own patriotism had awakened. Finland was then ruled by the Russian Czars, but the country stood closer to Sweden "than any other nation on earth." Even though the Finnish church had been forced to break with the Swedish church, they had belonged inseparably together for seven hundred years. Since Finland had gained independence when Czar Nikolaus abdicated in 1917, Söderblom was eager that the Finnish Lutheran church, after its long isolation, should again be fully incorporated into the Nordic church fellowship. When the "Red" uprising broke out in Helsinki at the end of January 1918, the entire nation was soon involved in civil war. The Finnish church did not hesitate in taking a stand on the side of the "Whites," nor did Söderblom. At a workers' meeting in Sandviken, he warned of the possibility of revolution in Sweden. In a letter to Manfred Björkquist, he called for Swedish volunteers to fight with the Whites, but he strongly opposed any military intervention from Sweden. The bloody battle in Finland and the opposing positions to which it gave rise even in Sweden slowed down cooperation between the two churches.

The crisis became worse when the problem concerning Åland sharpened. A great majority of the island's inhabitants, in connection with the liberation of Finland, had expressed their wish that the province should become part of Sweden. A strong public opinion in Sweden, including Söderblom's, welcomed that. In Finland, considerable bitterness arose toward both Ålanders and Swedes. When Söderblom traveled to Finland for the first time in 1919, he felt the hostile atmosphere. He concluded that a good relationship between Finland and Sweden as independent nations must take precedence over everything in spite of the expectations of the residents of the archipelago of Åland. Söderblom clarified his position both for Archbishop Johansson and Carl Gustaf Mannerheim, who was the head of state in Finland, and subsequently acted consistently with this political position. What he really thought of the whole situation remained hidden from everyone. In a letter to Immanuel Colliander, Bishop of Mikkeli in Finland, he wrote: "I understand myself as a servant of Christ and the church, and I cannot in this capacity of responsibility identify myself with any national political position." But emotions continued to run high in respect to Åland. When the Finnish bishops chose to stay away from the Nordic bishops' conference, every attempt to persuade them to come failed. Söderblom was distressed over the fact that the conflict had reached such dimensions and he was critical of himself. As the bishops gathered in Kulla Gunnarstorp, he prayed at evening prayer: "Disperse, Lord, the discord which now prevails with our brother nation Finland; take individual and national pride from us and from others; cleanse, gather, and strengthen us for common and holy tasks."

He had two especially intimate contacts in Finland, Professor Arthur Hjelt whom he had met in his student movement days, and Jaako Gummerus, who in 1920 became Bishop of Borgå (Porvoo), and would later move to Tammerfors. Thanks to them, he got Finland involved in the work of the World Alliance. The stubborn old Archbishop of Åbo could not prevent the ecumenical idea from taking root even in Finland.

In Poland, the situation was also extremely complicated. Ethnic and cultural strife between Lutheran Christians was so strong that all unity appeared to be far beyond reach. Contributing to a solution of this problem became the first common challenge for the Nordic bishops. There were approximately 800,000 Lutheran Christians in Poland and there almost was a civil war between the German speakers, who still had ties to Prussia, and the Polish speakers, who were determined that the whole church be loyal to the government and use Polish as the language of worship. The situation was further complicated by the fact that the Polish-speaking part of the church was united with Reformed Christians while the German speakers held fast to "the pure Augsburg Confession." Moreover, there was a significant group of Lutherans in the region of Galicia who lived surrounded by the Roman Catholic majority and were themselves anxious about the preservation of their own cultural traditions.

After the Treaty of Versailles, many churches in Europe were beset by similar problems. It went into Söderblom's ecumenical strategy to strengthen solidarity between evangelical minority churches, creating some kind of body to hold them together. Further, he was anxious that all should be able to hear the gospel in their own languages. The office of the bishop symbolized a unity that transcends ethnic and linguistic barriers and affirms the churches' common roots. When cultural and historical differences threatened to divide churches, he was determined to strengthen whatever united them. It would be best, he felt, if the episcopal office were instituted in all Lutheran churches and Uppsala were to become the center for all Lutheranism, just as all the world's Anglicans gathered around the Archbishop of Canterbury. But these were thoughts that, for the most part, he kept to himself.

In an attempt to solve the problems in Poland, he convened a conference of reconciliation in Uppsala in the spring of 1921. Eivind Berggrav had taken the initiative and the bishops of Oslo and Copenhagen supported the endeavor. From Poland, seven representatives of the differing groups came. The other participants were from Norway, Denmark, Finland, Estonia, and the United States. Sweden had the most delegates, including no fewer than seven bishops. The expert on international law and former prime minister Hjalmar Hammarskjöld and the jurist Gustaf Ribbing were called on to contribute to the formation of a durable church order. The negotiations had three elements: language, ethnicity, and confession. Discussions went on for a whole week, but no agreement was reached. The conflicts, however, were considerably lessened.

As a consequence of the Russian Revolution, Estonia, Latvia, and Lithuania received national independence. Since the twelfth century, Swedes had lived along the coast of Estonia and on its large islands. The Swedish royal power had supported the settlements since they contributed to pacifying the territory, which often was a refuge for pirates who endangered the Baltic and even came into Sweden's own Lake Mälaren. The settlements were also stimulated by the Teutonic Order, which saw them as part of Estonia's becoming Christian. But the fate of the Swedish immigrants in Estonia changed. For a long time they felt deserted both by Sweden and by the Teutonic Order, even though the old Swedish villages survived. At the time of the Reformation, as many Swedes lived in the present Tallinn as in Uppsala. When Sweden, toward the end of the sixteenth century, took power in Estonia, 10 percent of the inhabitants spoke Swedish. They were chiefly fishermen, small farmers, and laborers who did not have much in common with the new Swedish upper class that was emerging. In 1710, the country was conquered by Russia, and at least a quarter of the Swedes died from war, famine, and plague. The situation became so miserable that thousands of Swedes left in order to find a living somewhere else within the Russian Empire. Nearly a thousand inhabitants of the island of Dagö (Hiiumaa) snatched up the offer of land in the Ukraine. In May 1782, those who survived the hardships arrived in the Ukraine at what would come to be called Gammalsvenskby, "Old Swedish Village."

The low-water mark for Estonian Swedes was reached in the 1880s. Of the approximately six thousand who remained in Estonia, most lived in pure misery. Not a few of them had joined the Russian Orthodox Church. A few preachers sent there by the Swedish Evangelical Mission reported on the dreadful circumstances: sickness, alcoholism, filth, illiteracy, a religion that approached heathenism, and a language that was a mixture of Swedish, German, Estonian, and Russian. The "apostles" from Sweden made certain advances. Literacy and abstinence both increased, and that made for some economic improvement. At the time of the outbreak of World War I, there were fourteen Swedish schools in Estonia. When Russia withdrew from the war in 1918, the kaiser's German army took power in the country. The Swedes welcomed the Germans, which led to a breach between Estonians and Swedes that would not heal. Germany collapsed and the Red Estonians proclaimed a socialist republic. This unleashed a bloody civil war in the spring of 1919. The Whites were victorious.

While all of this was going on, Sweden scarcely lifted a finger to assist or defend the Swedish population in Estonia. Söderblom, however, kept himself well informed concerning the struggle for freedom and followed developments with the greatest interest. His sense of history was awakened when the small Baltic countries received the freedom for which they had longed for centuries. He was encouraged from an unexpected direction, namely, from a well-known revolutionary and Estonian nationalist, Alexander Kesküla. He had fled to Sweden, where he developed great plans for a Swedish–Finnish–Estonian federation that would be a bulwark against Russia. Since the Swedish government was not inclined to agree to any kind of involvement in the Baltic countries, Kesküla was pleased that there was at least one person who carried on an active foreign policy, even if it was for the sake of the church. And for Söderblom it was, indeed, a matter of politics. He was well informed concerning the German power play. In view of the Catholic Church's strength in Lithuania and Poland, he endeavored to strengthen Protestant power in Estonia and Latvia. His actions were a reminder of the time when there was political and ecclesiastical unity under Swedish rule. Gustav II Adolf, Carl X Gustav, and King Charles XII had sailed their warships across what was then a Swedish inland sea. The Archbishop of Uppsala had exercised ecclesial supervision. Thus, the idea that the Archbishop of Uppsala had a certain responsibility for the Baltic churches was not alien to Söderblom. He felt united with the Baltic people in their national struggle. Their aversion to the German presence caused them to turn toward Sweden and they were in agreement with his vision of a *mare lutheranum*.

The Lutheran leaders in free Estonia and Latvia soon turned to Söderblom, asking if he would consecrate them as bishops. He was willing to do this, but the matter had to be handled with care since the strong German congregations were not prepared to simply allow their superintendents to become bishops. On June 5, 1921, Söderblom consecrated Jacob Kukk as Bishop of Estonia. To lessen German criticism of this act, he invited Jaako Gummerus from German-friendly Finland to assist him.

The service was a great celebration, an affirmation of the nation's and the church's freedom. Söderblom and Gummerus were housed in the magnificent country residence built by Peter the Great in Kathrinenthal.

Nearly twenty thousand people filled the streets to watch as the procession with the two bishops, twelve priests from the Estonian and German congregations, representatives of the churches in Latvia and Ingria, and the theological faculty of the University of Tartu passed slowly to the Charles Church. In his consecratory address, Söderblom reminded his hearers of the time when Estonia, Finland, Latvia, and Sweden belonged to one and the same kingdom. "Are we dreaming or are we awake?" he asked. Now the four were again together as in former days, not in a political sense but in a much deeper fellowship symbolized by Uppsala and Borgå (Porvoo), Reval (Talinn) and Riga. He led the service, partly in Estonian. He had practiced the language a great deal in order to be understood and also in order not to dislocate his tongue, but his symbolic acts spoke a far more distinct language. He followed the Swedish order for a bishop's consecration. Instead of a miter, he handed a Bible to the bishop and he hung on Kukk a cross that he himself had worn around his neck. This was a way of showing that Estonia's bishop was now incorporated into the Swedish succession, but it was above all a gesture that pointed to something else. Several Lutheran and Orthodox priests, including the Orthodox Bishop Platon, were murdered on January 14, 1919 by the Reds, only hours before the city was liberated by the Estonian army. When Bishop Platon's body was later found, he still wore his bishop's cross. It was passed on to his successor. Söderblom knew about this and Kukk understood.

There were tensions between the Estonians and the Germans, but in Latvia the situation was even more critical. The leader of the Latvian church was Kãrlis Irbe. He was somewhat older than Söderblom and for many years had worked among Latvian refugees in Russia and Siberia before he could return to Riga in 1920. There it became his task to develop a polity for the church in free Latvia. He made contact with Söderblom in order to seek guidance. Irbe was of the view that the bishop's office was a requisite for unity between the Protestant national churches and believed that he would gain greater influence if he were consecrated bishop. He adopted Söderblom's view of the episcopacy and suggested not only that the Latvians get their own bishop, but also the German minority. So it came to pass that on a Sunday in July 1922, Söderblom conducted two bishop's ordinations in Riga. In the morning he consecrated General Superintendent Kãrlis Irbe in the Church of St. James, and in the afternoon, the German priest P. H. Poelchau in the Church of St. Peter. The conflicts between the

Latvians and the Germans were too great to make a common service of consecration possible, but Söderblom took the position that the Latvian-born bishop should be superior to the German immigrant. In his consecration address, he proposed, without having discussed the matter earlier, that Irbe should be called archbishop, a proposal that Irbe refused. In Riga too Söderblom gave his consecratory address in the nation's language.

The journey to Riga had been an adventure. Söderblom's very good friend Alfred "Alle" Ekström was an engineer who had made a fortune in the electrification of the Swedish and English countryside. He had a large motor yacht, Polar II, and suggested to Söderblom that they should take some of their sons and travel by yacht first to Estonia, where Söderblom was to visit some old Swedish congregations, and then to Riga. With ten men on board, they took off from Stockholm and returned a few weeks later. On Wormsi Island, Söderblom installed a new rector and officiated at a traditional wedding. He visited the church of Noarootsi, and when he arrived on the island of Ruhnu, he remarked: "The most beautiful race I have ever seen, especially the men, tall, muscular, straight, powerful profiles." The entire population of the island had their roots in Sweden and they worshiped in the St. Magdalene Church, which was Estonia's oldest preserved timber building. The people of Ruhnu knelt when they entered the church as well as during prayers and the benediction. They had never been subjected to serfdom and they had preserved their dignity.

These three bishops' consecrations could be interpreted as meaning that the Lutheran national churches in Estonia and Latvia were in some sense subordinate to Uppsala. Some voices were also raised in saying that the churches in Sweden, Finland, and the Baltic lands should be united under common leadership. Söderblom had no such plans, but his reading of Swedish history, his high estimation of the Uppsala archbishopric, and his ecumenical program made the priority he gave to the churches around the Baltic easy to understand. He recognized the significance of the churches in the liberation of their nations and in the struggle against Bolshevism, and he attributed to them a role parallel to his own political convictions.

In the Estonian coastal city of Haapsalu, where the Russian aristocracy and the czars themselves at one point came to bathe, the bishop's castle and the imposing church towered over the settlement of wooden houses. Since the thirteenth century, the city had been the central place for Estonia's Swedish colony. One evening, Nathan Söderblom and Alle Ekström sat there in a heart-to-heart conversation. They were very close and their families, with many children, were often together at an estate in Hemsjö in the south of Sweden where the Ekströms spent the summers. But a shadow had fallen over their friendship. Two of their children, nineteen-year-olds, had fallen in love with each other. Anna Söderblom had set her foot down on this "hard and cold": they must meet no more, nor could they correspond with each other. In the archbishop's palace there was a stricter view of what young people were allowed to do than at Hemsjö and in a letter from Söderblom, there was a tone of accusation concerning Ekström's well-meant invitations to the young people for ski trips, car outings, and boat rides. The friendship between the families was strained. It was then that the engineer got the idea of inviting the archbishop for a few adventurous days in eastern waters. Söderblom could restore his strength and, as was common, devote nearly every day to his commitments. This was the background to the 1922 motorboat trip in the Baltic. The boat had a seventy-five horse power diesel motor and a two-man crew. A couple of crowded weeks on board and a few colorful adventures brought the two men closer to each other.

In the conversation that July evening, Ekström emphasized that a man must first and foremost think of himself and his own. He felt great satisfaction at everything he had accomplished and the fortune he had acquired. Söderblom disagreed. No person could, in the long run, feel content if he did not find himself in a larger context. To live authentically, one must participate in God's life; otherwise one did not fully live. It was, said Söderblom, an uncommon happiness and an unmerited gift to create something, regardless of what it was, that then lived by its own power and was a part of God's ongoing creation. He thought to himself: perhaps one needed the eyes of an artist to recognize that there was a history to what one had set in motion. The fascination was no less if others did not know where the initiative and human guidance came from. Perhaps others even derided and fought against what was new but only later found it to be so good that they wanted to participate. Perhaps one could have a creative capacity even without seeking God. But when creativity reached its highest point, a feeling of humility took over, together with an experience of being led by a higher power. Thus it was that creative activity should be exercised: in a flexible feeling of accomplishing nothing yourself, but in the consciousness of carrying out another's work.

In the light of that July evening, the two men sat together and thought aloud. The one was a practical builder of electrical networks and a man of investments; the other was filled with the network of friendships he had created on the Baltic coast. Both wanted to believe that their activities contributed to a higher plan. They shared each other's material and spiritual assets. In his notebook, Söderblom scrawled some thoughts concerning how the uncommon gifts of creativity and fellowship with God could both be experienced. It did not depend on any special human equipment but came from the needs of the heart. "It happens in prayer, in the encounter with God."

27

Tagore, Heiler, Schweitzer, Sundar Singh, and Ras Teferi

C'est Dieu même qui parle par votre bouche.

Nathan Söderblom, 1924

At the end of May 1921, the world-famous philosopher and poet Rabindranath Tagore comes to Uppsala. He is the first non-European poet to receive the Nobel Prize. Many read the collection of poetry Gitanjali, *written in Bengali and translated from English to Swedish. Tagore is a friend to Gandhi and a bridge builder between East and West, between Hinduism and Christianity. The visit is unexpected and preparations take place hurriedly the night before. Söderblom shows him the cathedral. OD, the chorus, sings, and the university's auditorium, known as the aula, is filled to overflowing. Tagore's address is banal and says nothing and is given with a peculiar rhythm in which every second or third syllable is overemphasized. Great crowds of people gather outside. A picture shows Söderblom walking vigorously toward the archbishop's palace dressed in a cassock and with his doctor's hat on. By his side goes Tagore, five years older than Söderblom, tall and stately with billowing grey hair and a large beard. The long, buttoned-up overcoat flutters. Women in hats and with parasols crowd in to catch a glimpse of him. Well into the archbishop's palace, he is crowned with a garland of lilies-of-the-valley before he is seated at the table.*

* * *

Söderblom's many guests from abroad brightened Uppsala. During the war there had not been many visitors, but now they came in a never-ceasing stream. Some were refugees, others bishops, academics, or royalty. The isolation had been broken, but it was still remarkable that so many found their way to this little northern land. One of them was a young and highly gifted German historian of religion named Friedrich Heiler. He was a Roman Catholic, but sought out the Church of Sweden where he felt more at home. He became a close confidant to Söderblom and influenced his ecumenical theology.

During the war, Heiler had been a medical orderly. For long hours at night he read everything he could find by Söderblom. He knew C. P. Tiele's *Kompendium der Religionsgeschichte* (*Compendium of the History of Religion*) in the edition revised by Söderblom virtually by heart. He learned Swedish in order to pick up whatever had not been translated. His studies had inspired him to write a doctoral dissertation on prayer, which he sent to Söderblom in 1918. Söderblom answered immediately, expressing the hope that Heiler, with untiring diligence, critical love of truth, and a soul and mind close to Söderblom's own, would continue his study of religion. Söderblom reviewed his book the same week in the newspaper *Stockholms Dagblad*.

There really was a similarity of mind, and a lively correspondence followed. By age, Söderblom could have been Heiler's father. He developed a warm affection for the sensitive and intellectually brilliant young docent, who at the age of thirty became a professor at Marburg. With his dissertation, Heiler had come to cross-purposes with the Roman Catholic Church. He had difficulty enduring its restrictions on freedom of scholarship and its inner contradictions and thus decided to convert to the evangelical faith. In the Church of Sweden he found the realization of his understanding of the church. That summer, 1919, Söderblom invited Heiler to Sweden. It had been a terrible winter in Munich, with a socialist revolution followed by a communist coup d'état and violent conflicts between "Whites" and "Reds." In contrast, Sweden was like paradise. His personal contact with Söderblom was decisive for Heiler's future.

He arrived on one of the last days of July 1919 at Alle Ekström's estate at Hemsjö where the Söderblom family was visiting. They were staying in a cabin by the river, but there were also other guests. Wilhelm and Georg Kempf and their parents were staying in the "white house." At the estate there were horses, cars, and boats, and paths lent themselves to long promenades. At mealtimes everyone gathered in the mansion under the generous hospitality of Signe and Alle Ekström. The evenings were filled with music. The elderly Georg Kulenkampff-Post, who was regarded as Germany's greatest violinist, played Bach's Partita No. 2 in D-Minor with its concluding Chaconne, one of the most technically and musically demanding works for solo violin ever composed. Son Georg talked of Schubert and sang his *Die schöne Müllerin*, but when he came to *Der Neugierige*, "The Questioner," Söderblom took over. With his eyes fixed on his beloved Anna he sang sincerely and directly: "*Ja* heisst das eine Wörtchen, das andre heist *Nein*, die beiden Wörtchen schliessen die ganze Welt mir ein" ("*Yes*, is the one little word, the other is *No*. The two words together make up my entire world").

Heiler had been asked to give a lecture at the General Church Assembly when it met in Vadstena. He understood and wrote Swedish tolerably well, but now he had to learn in a few days how to speak the language well enough to be understood. Söderblom had decided to give the meeting new substance. Accordingly, he had invited representatives of Lutheran sister churches in Estonia, Norway, Finland, Denmark, and the United States to attend, and he was also bold enough to call on the young German Catholic to speak on evangelical Christianity and mysticism. Social Democrat Harald Hallén spoke on Christian social responsibility. These controversial innovations were balanced by the three main lectures delivered by J. A. Eklund, Gustaf Aulén, and Söderblom himself. In the garden at Kvissberg, where they were staying, Heiler spoke with Söderblom about conversion to the Lutheran church. Söderblom advised him against requesting separation from the Roman Catholic Church. When he received the eucharist in its two forms, bread and wine, at the Assembly's final Mass in the Church of St. Birgitta, it would mark his conversion to the Lutheran faith since according to canon law, he would be excommunicating himself. Heiler followed Söderblom's advice, but he had a kind of religious dual citizenship in that he neither formally left his old church nor was he formally received in his new church.

Heiler stayed in Sweden for the fall term, accompanying the archbishop on his visitations and becoming familiar with the university. He grew to know Herman Neander and Einar Billing; they both became his friends. Söderblom then persuaded him to return to Germany. They continued to correspond in letters that were, in the best sense, expressions of pastoral care and for Söderblom uncommonly personal. After his motor boat journey to Riga in 1922, he wrote to Heiler: "At home again, thankful, tired, pressed by unspeakable worries, troubles, responsibilities, and joys, gladdened in my soul by signs of a new friendship with a dear, faithful young friend." A few years later, on the day before Christmas Eve 1924, he communicated to Heiler, who was torn between catholic and evangelical allegiances and was disappointed in both churches: "Pilgrimage can be burdensome for a disciple of the Savior who has the painful, although for his fellow Christians infinitely valuable, lot to personally break down the dividing wall in order to unite the best in evangelical and Roman mysticism." Heiler had to pay for his conversion with criticism from both sides, and thus he felt a kind of spiritual homelessness. For Söderblom, that price was not too high. He continued: "Myself, I used to say when I have been attacked from both sides, that the one who has been knocked down by both right and left, will have to walk straight ahead. At times it is rather bitter, but — where there is a truly evangelical spirit — through this experience the communion of the heart becomes more sincere."

Heiler maintained contact with Söderblom through the years even though their personal meetings were few. He searched for identity as an evangelical catholic, practiced Franciscan spirituality, and led the high church movement in the German Lutheran church. His writings were translated into Swedish and influenced the Swedish picture of the Roman Catholic Church. In dialogue with Heiler, Söderblom refined and made more precise what he meant by "evangelical catholicity." He remarked that he was the one who laid stress on "evangelical" and it was Heiler who emphasized "catholic." They had a great deal in common, including a great admiration for Sadhu Sundar Singh, who came to Uppsala in April 1922 and stayed for some days in the archbishop's home.

If there was a guru who captured attention in Europe, it was this mysterious Indian mystic. Interest in India and Indian religions was at this time widespread even in Sweden. Rabindranath Tagore had shared the best of Bengali culture with the Western world. Mahatma Gandhi had started his nonviolent campaign against the British authorities and was gaining ever greater influence. Hinduism showed many signs of a new life. Swami Vivikananda, who had played a central role at the Parliament of World Religions in Chicago in 1893, stood as a symbol of the neo-Hinduism that was spreading throughout the world. Its holy scriptures were read by students at Western universities and there was widespread hope that Christianity and Hinduism would enrich one another.

Then, Sadhu Sundar Singh appeared. He had assumed for himself, or possibly was awarded, the honorific title "sadhu." This implied that he had found the correct path to enlightenment. He was an Indian Sikh who was baptized on his sixteenth birthday and subsequently traveled far and wide as a legendary Christian evangelist. In 1920, he came to Europe for the first time. A book of interviews, *The Sadhu: A Study in Mysticism and Practical Religion,* had given him legitimacy as a Christian mystic. He had fasted, spent long periods of time in prayer and meditation, and had visions and heard voices, but his message was clearly evangelical. Was he proof that Christianity had genuinely taken root in India's spiritual soil and assumed an authentically Indian form? Many wanted to believe that this was the case. Söderblom was one of them. He described Sundar Singh as being simultaneously a genuine Hindu and a wholehearted evangelical Christian, a person who both demonstrated the universality and adaptability of the Christian confession and witnessed to a purified Christianity that, in its essence, revealed what had been eclipsed in the West.

During his European tour, Sundar Singh spent a month in Sweden at Söderblom's invitation. He received considerable attention within Swedish Christianity. Siri Dahlquist translated his book into Swedish and her encounter with the Indian mystic inspired her to write a mission hymn that captured some of the atmosphere surrounding him. In the first printed version of the hymn, the first and third stanzas read:

> May other peoples learn the law of Christ
> and other souls by him be set aflame.
> May other voices praise the God of Christ
> in other tongues in many foreign lands.
>
> O Christ, you are immensely rich
> yet after centuries we only saw
> of all your truth but a little glimpse.
> The fullness of God's gift we do not know.

Sundar Singh preached in the Cathedral and spoke in the university aula. This was the only time he and Söderblom met each other. One can see them in a picture from the archbishop's library: Söderblom in his frock and cross, Sundar Singh with short hair and dark beard, dressed in a fluttering white cloak. He reminded people of popular pictures of Jesus and was met with the greatest veneration. His visit in Uppsala was written about a great deal, but judgments were varied. *Upsala Nya Tidning* wrote that the Sadhu's presentation in the aula was remarkably simplistic and lacked both ethical and aesthetic pathos. If the apostle from India did not have more to offer, it was disturbing that the church used him in this way. The newspaper protested that the aula was made available to a charlatan, and also noted that few students or faculty were present. It was suggested that an archbishop who allowed such a guest to speak in the aula was perhaps not especially suited to be university chancellor. The debate went on for a few weeks and other papers also found fault. There were many disappointed and critical interventions. Would it not have been better if Sundar Singh had stayed at home in India rather than showing up as a curiosity in the Western world? Many asked, was not the whole thing humbug?

Others defended him, including the conservative Adolf Kolmodin. Söderblom, uncharacteristically, kept his silence. During the three days he was in Uppsala, the archbishop had spent a great deal of time with the exotic mystic and genuinely attempted to understand him. With his uncontrollable desire to report on what he had been involved in, Söderblom published a little book, *Sundar Singhs budskap utgivet och belyst* (*Sundar Singh's Message Brought Out and Explained*), which in addition to some of Sundar Singh's own writings and his sermon in the cathedral also contained notes from their conversations and a chapter on the three great men of modern India: Tagore, Gandhi, and Sundar Singh. Söderblom did not offer a closer evaluation of the visit, but did admit that the lecture in the university aula was something of a miscalculation. The Sadhu had, of course, not shown any bleeding feet, and there was nothing particularly remarkable or exotic in his appearance or talk either.

When Söderblom showed him the cathedral, Sundar Singh stopped at the grave of Emanuel Swedenborg. He had heard about Swedenborg and studied his writings. He was convinced that he himself had been in contact with Swedenborg's heavenly spirit, which instructed him to perform as a guru. When Söderblom wrote a short foreword to a small book by Sundar Singh in 1926, he noted certain similarities to Swedenborg, but it was not until 1928 that he learned from the Sadhu about his communication with the Swedish mystic. Even if Söderblom, like so many others, was strongly taken by "the Lord's Indian apostle," he really did not know how he should deal with what he had come to know. But Friedrich Heiler, who had defended him before he came to Sweden and continued to do so, almost desperately sought to prove that Sundar Singh was an authentic mystic. That was shortly before Sadhu Sundar Singh went off to Tibet in 1929 and, without a trace, lost himself in the Himalayas.

For many years, Söderblom was taken by Sadhu Sundar Singh's life and teachings. Did not this mystic confirm that Christ was the fulfillment of all religion?

The encounter with this living Indian visionary was important and virtually unique for Söderblom. In his study of unfamiliar religions, he had been completely bound to texts and other documents. He overestimated both the literary and normative significance of scriptures in non-European cultures. His only meeting with a living and sincerely religious person who had grown up within Hinduism but had become a Christian gave rise to many questions. Söderblom received different answers to his questions from the Sadhu than from the holy texts of Hinduism. Since Söderblom did not wish to compare the "mountaintops" in Christianity with "the lowland of the general history of religion," he focused rather on outstanding personalities. The saintly, mendicant monk Sadhu Sundar Singh was one. He was surrounded by enthusiasm from the West, but Söderblom remained uncertain how to interpret the integration of Christianity and Bhakti piety as represented by the Sadhu.

It was, however, far easier for Söderblom to estimate another visitor, Albert Schweitzer. During the war he, as a German citizen, had been able to continue his work as a missionary doctor in French Gabon. But in 1917 he was taken, a French prisoner of war, and brought first to Bordeaux and then to Provence. Söderblom wished to help him by inviting him to give the Olaus Petri Lectures in Uppsala. He secured the help of the Archbishop of Canterbury in tracking him down. The invitation reached Schweitzer in Strasbourg at the end of 1919. By that time, he had received French citizenship and had been set free, but he was ill and depressed and did not know if he could secure permission to travel to Sweden.

Schweitzer had heard of Nathan Söderblom as a scholar of religion, but he did not know that he had become archbishop. They had both lived in Paris at the end of the 1890s, heard the same renowned organists, and taken their doctorates at the Sorbonne, but they had never met. Schweitzer was even more famous in Europe than Söderblom.

His career was without parallel. As the son of a clergyman in German Alsace, he had learned to play the organ and became so proficient that the renowned organist Charles-Marie Widor in Saint-Sulpice in Paris took him as a free student and introduced him to the organ music of Johann Sebastian Bach. Schweitzer was familiar with the German chorales and could show how Bach, in his chorale preludes, allowed tone and rhythm to illustrate the text. This led to the first of Schweitzer's studies of Bach's descriptive music, a study with which Söderblom was familiar. Schweitzer became celebrated as an organist and led an organ movement that turned away from romanticism and revived the baroque.

Schweitzer, however, was equally as well known as a New Testament scholar. He had immersed himself in the enormous research concerning the life of Jesus, which had been going on for decades, and he questioned most of what had been produced concerning the "historical" Jesus. The theologians' picture of Jesus had been changing continually and to a high degree reflected the moral values of the late nineteenth century. Schweitzer, in contrast, interpreted the figure of Jesus in the light of Jesus's own words and deeds and in relation to late Jewish eschatology. He concluded that the "historical" Jesus who affirmed the nineteenth-century bourgeois ethical ideal had never in reality existed. Instead, Schweitzer set forth the figure of a prophet who proclaimed that the last times were near. After a large number of well-noticed studies on this theme, Schweitzer received his doctorate in theology in 1911.

But he had greater plans than to be an organist and a theologian. Even as a teenager he felt that he must repay something of the great debt that Christian Europe had incurred as a consequence of barbaric colonialism. When he was thirty years old, he thus began a medical education and in 1913, traveled with his family to Gabon, taking a fourteen-day journey from the coast, to build a small hospital in Lambaréné. It was extraordinarily primitive. Besides his wife, Helene, he was the only doctor to serve a never-ending stream of patients. The war prohibited contact with the outside world. Completely exhausted, Schweitzer made it to France. After a time in prisoner of war camps he was able to resume his studies, at the same time serving as a pastor in Strasbourg. He wrote yet another dissertation, this time on the philosophy of civilization. When he finally came to Uppsala in April 1920, he held doctorates in theology, medicine, and philosophy and was also a renowned organist. It is not difficult to imagine Söderblom's amazement at the man. Together with his wife, he settled in the archbishop's residence. He gave his lectures and remained for several months.

He described his precarious situation to Söderblom. He had built and operated the hospital in Lambaréné at his own expense. When the war broke out, all contributions dried up and he was forced to borrow money to keep the hospital going and now there was no possibility that he could cover his debts. Söderblom, who was no less energetic than his guest, arranged for Schweitzer to travel around Sweden giving lectures and organ concerts in order to raise money for his hospital. In parish after parish, people received the learned and humble man. When he left Sweden after a few months, he had raised enough money to pay his debts. He came back to Sweden the next year and continued his tour. Then he traveled back to Africa and built up the hospital; it was now as large as a whole village and he had a full team of coworkers. Swedish generosity had assured the hospital's continued existence and Lambaréné became well known throughout the country.

In his book, *On the Edge of the Primeval Forest* (English, 1922), Schweitzer gave an account of his work. It was translated into Swedish by his most important sponsor, Baroness Greta Lagerfelt, who, like Anna Söderblom, had been confirmed by Fredrik Fehr and was part of the Söderbloms' circle of friends. She first met Schweitzer at the archbishop's residence, received him as a guest in her own home, and through fund-raising and her own generosity contributed to Lambaréné as long as she lived. Not many realized that the entire proceeds from the sale of eggs at the Duseborg Manor went to Schweitzer's mission. Inspired by Schweitzer, Greta Lagerfelt also took considerable responsibility for the preservation of old organs in Sweden. When the organ in her own parish, Gammalkil in the county of Östergötland, was restored in 1951, the seventy-six-year old Albert Schweitzer gave the dedicatory concert. This received a great deal of attention and it has often been noted that it was in large measure due to Greta Lagerfelt that, in 1952, he received the Nobel Peace Prize.

Schweitzer and Söderblom were Lutheran theologians, wide-ranging academicians who longed for more time for research and writing. Both were artists who excelled at mastering the language of music. Both viewed the way from thought to action as short; they set practical Christianity first. They were affected by the Great War and subsequently dedicated their lives to reconciliation between peoples and nations. In many ways they were related souls, two universal geniuses whose paths crossed.

Before Schweitzer returned to Gabon in 1923, he wrote his most influential book, *Civilization and Ethics.* Since Descartes and Kant, Western philosophy had sought to account for objective reality and the unique position of the human being in the world. They were not successful and now scientific materialism, with Charles Darwin and Herbert Spencer as its two chief architects, had created a picture of the world's development that was completely devoid of ethics, centering only on the question of survival. Schweitzer had another interpretation. His starting point was that life desires to live and that everything living lives among others who also share the desire to live. One form of life must live off others, but human consciousness knows and understands the desire of other beings to live. An ethical person, therefore, attempts so far as possible to protect and respect the lives of others. The will to live is constantly being renewed. This was both an evolutionary necessity and a spiritual phenomenon. Life and love are rooted in a personal spiritual relation to the entire universe. Ethics proceeds from respect for the lives of others. A human being should behave toward others as he or she wishes others to behave toward him- or herself. Objective reality is ethically neutral, but humans stand free to create civilization's ethical structure based on respect for the life of all that is living. Only such respect can lead to unselfish service for others and all creation. Reverence for life is the highest of ethical principles, and humanity's final task and meaning.

Söderblom's ethical perspective was universal, but it scarcely included the world of nature and all that is alive. He was a social ethicist influenced by idealism. His Stockholm Conference included nothing that tended toward environmental or biological ethics. In that respect, Schweitzer was ahead of him. Söderblom was also more interested in Asia and its religions than in Africa. As chair of the Church of Sweden Mission, he naturally had contact with and followed the work of the church's missionaries in South Africa and Southern Rhodesia, but with Schweitzer it was another matter. He was no ordinary missionary, but an intellectual giant who for reasons of morality gave up his career in order to assist poor communities living along a river in the heart of Africa. He was driven by his abhorrence of colonialism. His reverence for life was more than the title of a book; it was a way of living for which he paid a high price. Söderblom was perhaps more deeply impressed with his interpretation of Bach than with his ethical mysticism. He did not live long enough to rejoice at Schweitzer's zealous opposition to atomic weapons, nor his Nobel Peace Prize.

One of the rare African guests at the archbishop's palace would leave lasting marks. This was Ras Teferi who, in 1930, was to be crowned emperor with the title Haile Selassie I, Lion of Judah, Elect of God, King of Kings of Ethiopia. The Ethiopian crown prince, together with his wife Menen Asfaw, and some of his courtiers traveled through many European countries including Sweden, where the Swedish Evangelical Mission had its home base. Its missionaries had traveled to Addis Ababa in 1904 and won his confidence. He wanted to see the country from which they came. On Pentecost 1924, he visited Uppsala. The county governor, archbishop, university rector, and mayor were his hosts, showing him the university and answering the crown prince's many questions. At solemn vespers in the cathedral, the pews were filled with enthusiastic mission supporters. Söderblom showed his respect for these evangelicals by wearing only a simple black priest's cape. For once, he was taller than his eminent guest who came to the church in a light broad-brimmed hat with a cape slung over his shoulders and white gaiters. The text for evening prayer from the Acts of the Apostles was the account of the miracle on Pentecost when the people "from every nation under heaven" who were gathered in Jerusalem could understand each other's speech and were united in the Spirit. In his sermon, Söderblom lifted up other biblical citations concerning the Queen of Sheba and the Ethiopian eunuch being baptized by Philip on his way from Jerusalem. Then he turned toward Ras Teferi and addressed him in French. He reminded him that Christianity had already arrived in Ethiopia in the time of the apostles. The great Christian people on the horn of Africa had adopted the Christian message many hundreds of years before the Swedes. It was a privilege now to receive the wise and learned crown prince and regent over Ethiopia with a greeting filled with love. He mentioned the crown prince's work for education, health care, the abolition of slavery, and the development of a just society, and presented him with gifts. He took the opportunity also to invite the Ethiopian Orthodox Church to the forthcoming ecumenical conference.

The crown prince in his response affirmed that all of the world's Christians had Christ as their foundation, even if there were some differences between them. He was extremely pleased to come to Sweden to see the

Archbishop Söderblom, Crown Prince Ras Teferi, and Governor Hjalmar Hammarskjöld on their way to the Uppsala Cathedral, Pentecost 1924.

country and its people. In the past, Swedes and Ethiopians did not know each other because of the distance, but when the Swedes came to Ethiopia and told of their land's beauty and its people's friendliness, the Ethiopian people began to want to visit Sweden. He hoped that the friendship between Ethiopia and Sweden would grow even stronger in the future and presented a gift to the cathedral: money, which a silversmith in Stockholm formed into a silver lamp that hung under the boy choir's balcony up to the time of the cathedral's most recent restoration. Beeswax candles, which had been specially blessed, were sent to Uppsala every year as long as Haile Selassie lived. In the vespers, Söderblom pronounced both the invocation and the benediction in Amharic.

The archbishop's wife was never to forget Ras Teferi's dark-hued visage with fine Semitic features and beautiful, soulful eyes, his expressive gestures and his slow, lively, and thoughtful speech. She felt that she had found herself at an opera where he sang the tenor part and his courtiers sang the bass parts.

Ras Teferi and Söderblom won each other's confidence and the crown prince asked for a private conversation. They met at the Grand Hotel in Stockholm together with the future foreign minister of Ethiopia, Blata Hiruy Wolde-Selassie who was an evangelical Christian. The conversation dealt with the divisions among Christians. Söderblom explained why things were as they were, and when Ras Teferi asked: "Why do not evangelical Christians unite?" he eagerly reported on the coming ecumenical conference. He repeated the invitation already given to the crown prince. Söderblom described the crown prince's reaction: "He listened and his expressive eyes told me, even if his mouth did not acknowledge it and even as he retained his eastern dignity, that he scarcely believed his ears. Is such a thing really in the works?" Their trustful relationship continued in correspondence to the time of the archbishop's death. Söderblom expressed gratitude for the silver lamp and sent a photograph of the emperor and the archbishop in a silver frame. Söderblom also sent a personal message reporting on the ecumenical conference, which had initiated a process of uniting the evangelical churches in a way that was "prophetic and inspired by the Most Holy. " He also described the celebration of All Saints Day in Sweden and reminded the Ethiopian ruler that the blessed ones are those who, in world history or among small groups of people, have shown that they hunger and thirst for justice. Among these blessed persons, Ras Teferi would also be numbered when he would be crowned emperor. Many of Söderblom's letters dealt with Johannes Kolmodin, his emissary to the Orthodox churches, whom he convinced the crown prince to employ as his advisor. He also reminded him of their conversation in Stockholm, when God himself had spoken through the crown prince's mouth, and informed him that an international ecumenical council had been formed. He hoped that the Ethiopian Orthodox Church would be a member. The tone of the correspondence became more intimate. In one of his last letters, Söderblom reported that on one of his travels in Switzerland he had met the emperor's charming daughter.

Söderblom was a self-conscious European, but he never expressed what was common in the colonial times, namely, the disparagement of other peoples. He received his visitors in a totally unprejudiced way, sometimes carrying their luggage from the station himself, prayed with them before a picture of the Crucified One, and listened in order to learn. After his death, they all remembered his boundless generosity, which they seldom encountered in any other place.

28
The Road to Stockholm

> This has become for me a holy and necessary obligation. I perhaps owe my episcopacy and my fellow Christians an explanation, an apologia pro vita mea.
>
> *Nathan Söderblom, 1926*

In the evening darkness Nathan Söderblom walks up the steep path above the Hôtel des Alpes. He is in the Berner Oberland, in the midst of nature's own cathedral. The long narrow valley above Lauterbrunnen is the nave. Grindelwald and Wengen on one side and Mürren and Gimmelwald on the other are rows of pews; the walls are the peaks of the surrounding Alps. The many-voiced murmurings from the Alpine streams are an organ that does not become silent. As he walks, he thinks of Sir Henry Lunn who was the first to introduce skiing in the Alps and who now with magnificent hospitality has invited some fifty clergy and laity to his luxurious tourist hotel. As early as 1892 he had provided his great resources for the start of an ecumenical movement and the journal Review of Churches. *Now Söderblom's ecumenical dreams are being realized. There is only one year remaining before the Stockholm Conference. But in spite of the hotel's comfort, the beauty of the surroundings, and kindred souls, the strong personalities have difficulty reaching agreement. An avalanche tumbles down the hillside, a thunderstorm drowns out the streams with its thirty-two-foot trombone.*

* * *

When the representatives of the World Alliance for Promoting International Friendship through the Churches met in Oud Wassenaar in 1919 they gave responsibility for the ecumenical conference that Nathan Söderblom had proposed to a three-person committee with the authority to bring the ship into harbor. For all practical purposes, this meant that the conference became its own project under the leadership of Söderblom,

Charles Macfarland, and Otto Herold. Thus, the Life and Work movement was born. In time, it would grow even to the point of absorbing the World Alliance. These three people quickly called together a small working group in Paris, which endorsed Söderblom's plan and commissioned Frederick Lynch of the Federal Council of the Churches of Christ in America to organize a larger meeting in Geneva in 1920 to discuss how the plan should be developed. The ball was now in New York, but Söderblom did not let it go.

Those who were invited to Geneva were all Protestants. The American delegation was the largest, officially appointed by the Federal Council. The next largest group came from Sweden, handpicked by Söderblom himself and approved by the General Church Assembly. Canterbury sent no one in light of the fact that neither the Roman Catholic Church nor the Orthodox churches were invited. The Evangelical Church Committee in Germany did not receive an invitation, but some Germans participated on their own initiative. People from France, Belgium, Denmark, Norway, Italy, and Switzerland were also among the seventy delegates.

The nine Swedish delegates met on August 5 on the ferry to Germany. The energetic and youthful Nathan Söderblom was filled with expectations. Major Anders Sjöstedt, who had promised to finance the ecumenical conference if it was located in Uppsala, handled the travel arrangements. The group included, among others, the professor of systematic theology Gustaf Aulén, Söderblom's son-in-law Yngve Brilioth who was doing research in Oxford, the high church priest from Malmö Albert Lysander, and the internationally experienced Karl Fries. After a day in Berlin, the group took the night train south, through a country that was still severely marked by the war. They saw that third class was overcrowded, peoples' faces were furrowed by hardships, coins were replaced with small notes in local values, and stamps did not stick to letters. But the train was on time. Even though soap and towels were missing, the second-class compartments in which they stayed were comfortable. Between Frankfurt and Basel, Söderblom led a Swedish high mass with Gustaf Aulén as hymn conductor and other travelers as astonished onlookers. In Basel, the German foreign minister Walter Simons left the train. Söderblom did not miss the opportunity to step forward and introduce himself. Their conversation on the railroad platform led to Simons's participation in the Stockholm Conference. Arriving in Geneva, the Swedes checked in at the Hotel Beau Séjour on the edge of the city, stunned by the beauty around them, with the rushing river Arve in the long valley below and the Alps in the distance.

Before others arrived, the Swedes, under Söderblom's direction, decided how the conference should be run. Lynch had made the external arrangements, but he presumed that Söderblom would have responsibility for the substance of the meeting. Dissatisfaction arose as the meeting was so poorly organized, but since many participants had only a vague understanding of what the issues really were, Söderblom, in his excellent fashion, was able to take the stage and bring everything together. He resolutely assumed leadership, saw to it that the meeting had structure, and let nothing out of his control. It would now be decided if his conference was to take place and if the Life and Work movement would set sail. In Oud Wassenaar he had laid low, but now it was precisely the reverse. Everything revolved around "his" conference and at every point his will prevailed.

He began by reviewing his plans. During the international crisis that still had not come to an end, a common Christian voice was missing. Christians in many nations had certainly made significant contributions in healing wounds and fostering peace, but in order to achieve genuine results, they must work together. An international conference of church leaders should, in clear terms, formulate the Christian understanding of different social structures, ideologies, and systems of law. To prevent this from being an isolated event, a permanent ecumenical council should be created. With a purely spiritual authority and with no right to involve itself in the affairs of individual churches, such a council should continually and closely follow developments and, guided by conscience and Christian principle, take positions on specific issues in order to lead the way for the churches. Söderblom referred to the encyclical of the Patriarch of Constantinople, proposing that an ecclesial counterpart to the League of Nations should be formed. Söderblom's ideas met with a response, but as he had feared, the Geneva conference proved stormy and difficult to manage.

Once again, nationalism and *la Schuldfrage*, the question of guilt, swelled up and threatened to bring his efforts to naught. American clergy appeared in uniforms bedecked with war medals. From France, one delegate came with an official document setting an acknowledgment of Germany's war guilt as a condition for the participation of the French. The Belgians took their side. But what could the Germans do? They had not been appointed by their churches and, moreover, were not in agreement among themselves. Thus, a moral problem loomed large and decisively right through the meeting and the atmosphere became rancorous. Then the Italian Ernesto Giampiccoli, who had lost a son in the war, and certain Americans brought the conference forward; the war was over, all governments had sins on their consciences, and now it was necessary to move ahead. The fact that the Germans were not official delegates saved the conference. They had no authority and therefore, the French document had to remain unanswered. For Söderblom, the situation was nearly unbearable. Later he described how Giampiccoli — like a Christ-figure and out of the sorrow of his fatherly heart — had spoken the word of Christian reconciliation. Arthur Brown, who was chairperson of this critical session, led in the singing of a hymn.

Disagreements also arose concerning who should participate in the planned conference. For many, especially the Swiss Protestants, it was unthinkable that Roman Catholics would be involved. That view had to be weighed against the fact that the Anglicans were determined not to participate if the Catholic and Orthodox churches were not invited. Söderblom insisted that all the churches of Christianity should be treated equally. How they might answer was their own decision, but to set up an ecumenical meeting that in advance excluded some churches was for him a contradiction. He doubted, however, that the Curia in Rome would accept.

In the midst of this discussion, Söderblom made a spectacular maneuver, to say the least. He had, in great secrecy, seen to it that some Orthodox church leaders, who were in Geneva for other reasons, would appear completely unexpectedly. He had directed all of this in detail. Suddenly, Metropolitan Germanos of Seleukia, the Archbishop of Nubia, and the Greek professor Chrysostomos Papadopoulos showed up in the hall. It was August 11, 1920 at 10:00 A.M. when these Orthodox leaders made their entry into the scarcely established ecumenical movement of Western Protestantism. The entire conference was amazed. Herman Neander, who was Söderblom's personal ambassador to the Eastern churches, greeted the guests in fluent modern Greek and the Swedes swelled with pride. Metropolitan Germanos spoke warmly about the coming conference and promised to keep the patriarch informed. Germanos prayed in Greek for the unity of the church before they left the assembly hall. Söderblom's initiative, an artistic coup, decisively changed the presuppositions for Life and Work. Without the cooperation of the Orthodox, the movement would have become a purely Protestant and thus a rather marginal undertaking, but now the conference concluded that all churches should be invited. The voting, by acclamation, was a victory for Söderblom. He wished to have an authentically ecumenical conference and now that could be a reality.

The third question that gave rise to heated debate was where the conference should take place. Söderblom's position was extremely clear: it was to be in Uppsala and no place else. Nevertheless, he developed his argument in detail. The conference should be held in a place where there was genuine involvement and interest. In that respect, the United States would be the best location. It was, however, a long distance to America and serious crises were still going on in Europe. Thus the conference could not take place there. London and Paris were not possible, but Oxford or Cambridge would be fine meeting places. As long as the wounds from the war were not completely healed, however, another country would be more appropriate. He praised Switzerland and Holland but dismissed them as possible locations and finally arrived at Uppsala, or possibly Stockholm, as the best venue. The only thing needed for full agreement was Anders Sjösted's promise to cover all costs. He was the director of public transportation in Uppsala and had financial interests in a number of hydroelectric power plants in Sweden. He was one of Söderblom's enthusiastic supporters and declared himself ready to come up with a large amount of money if Uppsala became the conference city. That, however, did not happen. Uppsala clearly could not be host to such a large event. The conference site had to be shifted to Stockholm, but Söderblom saw to it that the Uppsala Cathedral and the university would be the location of its ceremonial conclusion.

A provisional committee of twenty-five people, with Söderblom, Macfarland, and Lynch as leaders, was charged with carrying out what had been agreed on in Geneva. The foundation was laid and the Universal Christian Conference on Life and Work had begun to take shape. Söderblom had already dedicated six years of work to its realization. He was unflinchingly convinced that God himself had specifically called him to unify the Christian churches around the cause of peace. Despite all opposition, he had not given up and now the boat had finally set sail. The week in Geneva had been the most stressful he had experienced up until then. "We have, during a few days, carried out difficult, extremely demanding work," he wrote to Anna. But Geneva was only the beginning. Five more years of preparations awaited him. They would claim his strength and will to the last drop.

Directly after Söderblom's conference in Geneva there followed another, Faith and Order. Life and Work was directed toward social ethics and practical Christianity; Faith and Order's intention was to unite the churches in faith and doctrine. Gustaf Aulén and Yngve Brilioth remained in Geneva for the second conference, which took on a totally different character. Many Anglicans participated, as did a number of Orthodox dignitaries. The rosy-cheeked Protestants in business suits viewed these people as extremely exotic with their long beards, black silk robes, peculiar cylindrical hats, and holy "amulets" mounted in precious stones hanging on golden neck chains. While the deliberations of Life and Work had been overheated and driven by Söderblom's nervous haste, Faith and Order gave the impression of serene calm. No Frenchmen were present to constantly attack the Germans, which contributed to the relaxed atmosphere. The American Episcopalian bishop Charles Brent, who was a missionary bishop in the Philippines, led the deliberations, but the American layman Robert Gardiner, who was the meeting's driving force and also covered the costs, made an equally deep impression on the Swedes. The socially radical high church English bishop Charles Gore, who had left the Diocese of Oxford in order to devote more time to research and writing, also drew attention from the Swedish delegation. They also reported that the Quaker Lucy Gardner, the only female participant, sat and knitted and sewed as she listened attentively and at times intervened. She would soon be one of Söderblom's critically openhearted colleagues.

The discussions dealt with the Nicene Creed as the ground of unity, the office of the bishop, and apostolic succession. Gustaf Aulén reported on the English-Swedish discussions that were under way, as well as on the position of the Church of Sweden that episcopal succession was a positive asset but not a requirement for the unity of the church. Both he and Brilioth were Anglophiles who came to feel more at home in Faith and Order than in Life and Work. Step by step, they distanced themselves from Söderblom. Each developed his own position in respect to ecclesiological questions and abandoned their archbishop's more liberal theological starting points. Söderblom, on the other hand, maintained his distinction between Life and Work and Faith and Order but was grateful for all the support he received from Brent and Gardiner. For Söderblom, dogmatic differences must not hinder practical cooperation and he simply did not have the time to wait for the results of Faith and Order's intricate discussions on doctrine. Without embarrassment he celebrated the eucharist with all friends of Jesus, regardless of their theological views concerning sacrament and ministry.

What about the World Alliance for Promoting International Friendship through the Churches? It also gathered in Geneva during the eventful summer of 1920. Tension had arisen between those who wished to elect the Archbishop of Canterbury as chairperson and those who were in favor of Söderblom. Since he had already been assured about his conference, he was content to become one of the Alliance's many vice presidents. In 1920, then, the ecumenical movement continued to consist of loose and overlapping groups of more or less self-appointed people who felt a commitment to cooperation. Many of them were active in all of the provisional organizations. Söderblom could handpick his colleagues from among those who inspired confidence.

During the first year of the 1920s, Söderblom traveled incessantly on behalf of Life and Work. He did not neglect his parishes or the Diocesan Chapter, but his focus was on the forthcoming ecumenical conference, which he had dreamed of for so long. He confirmed youth from the royal house, participated in meetings of the Swedish Academy, deepened ecclesial relations around the Baltic, debated and commented in the newspapers, preached nearly every Sunday, received a stream of visitors, socialized at castles and manor houses, led countless meetings, and even spent time with his children. But he also had to establish his conference among reluctant German superintendents, in the suspicious French Protestant Federation, among doubting Orthodox bishops, with the somewhat skeptical Archbishop of Canterbury, and not least, among brothers in the faith on the other side of the Atlantic. He had personal emissaries throughout the world, all of whom did invaluable work in persuading and convincing church leaders of every differing view. The diplomat in Rome, Harald Bildt, developed contacts with the Vatican and later with the Oriental churches. Johannes Kolmodin, who served as a translator at the Swedish General Consulate in Istanbul, held the door open to the Ecumenical Patriarchate and thereby to other Byzantine churches. Herman Neander, who for a long time had worked among prisoners of war and refugees in Russia, played an important part. The rector of the Swedish church in London, Albert Hellerström, had personal contacts with the Church of England and was indispensable, as were the Swedish priests in Paris and Berlin. Paul Sandegren, who had come home after serving as a missionary in India, was also included within his closest circle of colleagues. But Söderblom himself held all the threads in his hand and followed everything down to the most minute detail; when the conference concluded on an August Sunday in 1925, he even decided the seating at the luncheon table in the Uppsala University auditorium, the aula.

The provisional committee that had been named in Geneva held its first meeting with Bishop Frank Woods, then of Peterborough, as host; Söderblom had won his allegiance at the bishop's consecration in Uppsala a year earlier. The Bishop of Oxford, Hubert Burge, whom Söderblom regarded especially highly, was also present. He was "the most spiritual personality" in the bishops' row in the House of Lords and also more discerning than most English bishops. That could not be said of Herbert Hensley Henson of Durham, whom Söderblom had struck from his list. Nor did William Temple, who was then Bishop of Manchester, participate, although he would soon step up as the ecumenical movement's most driving force.

The provisional committee was replaced by one more formally chosen. It had thirty-eight members and an executive committee with a flexible mandate. To Söderblom's disappointment, this new committee moved the date for the Stockholm conference forward to 1925. This was necessary for adequate planning, but Söderblom had difficulty agreeing. He was impatient and underestimated the difficulties, but the committee gave him no choice. It also moved the most controversial issues concerning peace to the side and proposed many other social ethical questions for action that gave Söderblom no end of difficulty.

When the committee gathered in Helsingborg in Sweden in 1922 it began to find its feet. During the days before, the Alliance had held a large conference in Copenhagen in which even Orthodox leaders participated. As in Oud Wassenaar, the situation of religious minorities was discussed, as were disarmament and the church's role in the reconciliation and restoration of Europe. Söderblom struck the tone: "Never has the call for unity sounded more strongly, more deeply, more extensively in Christendom." The political situation was uncertain and dangerous; disarmament negotiations in Washington were blocked by France, which now was Europe's superpower and had the world's strongest army; in its antipathy toward Germany it would make no concessions whatsoever. Söderblom was deeply disappointed over the position of the superpowers and he made no attempt to hide it. This received considerable attention in the press. "He is the Temperament of the Nordic Church," wrote one. In his address on the last day of the meeting, he disclosed his dream of a triple alliance among England, France, and Germany as the basis for European security since the League of Nations had not yet achieved sufficient strength and authority. This was not the first time Söderblom had spoken in terms that much later led to the European Union. Even before World War I, he had advocated for the formation of a European federation for peace. Nationalism must be rejected. Binding supranational structures and international law were the absolute presuppositions for lasting peace.

In Helsingborg he was on his home terrain, and he took over the entire meeting. Together with K. B. Westman, he had prepared the agenda in detail and he led every session himself. He welcomed the delegates in Greek, English, German, French, and the Nordic tongues and the meeting started with prayer in many languages. His forty-year-old friend and admirer Crown Prince Gustaf Adolf, who was becoming more and more involved in Söderblom's plans, spoke. In the Maria Church, the Dean of Worcester Cathedral, Moore Ede, "who during a long life emphasized the gospel's social content," preached, and in the Gustaf Adolf Church, Adolf Deissmann delivered the proclamation. He had never "separated his fiery and bloody love for his homeland from the living and more essential fellowship around the Savior," wrote Söderblom. Together they gave a foretaste of what was to come. In Helsingborg, the Stockholm conference took form.

Söderblom attempted to limit the issues that were to be considered. But the pressure was too great. Everything should be taken up and the whole issue of peace risked being relegated to the background. Finally, there was unity concerning six main themes: (1) the church's general responsibility in light of God's plan for the world; (2) the church and economic and industrial problems; (3) the church and social and moral problems; (4) the church and international relations; (5) the church and education; and, (6) different ways of strengthening cooperation between the churches and bringing them together on a federated base. How these themes should be approached was to be hammered out in a number of local, national, and regional meetings. In this process, Life and Work would become a movement rooted in the churches and societies of the entire Western world.

The ongoing preparatory work took on a fixed structure with an active executive committee and Henry Atkinson as general secretary. He lived in the United States. Since letters took a long time, the transatlantic cable was overloaded, and there were no international telephone connections, much of the administrative work stayed with Söderblom's colleagues in Uppsala with K. B. Westman at the helm.

Faith and Order also planned to hold its first world conference in 1925. It was to take place in Washington. Brent and Gardiner, who were eager to strengthen connections between the two movements, also wanted Life and Work to hold its conference there. The proposal was discussed in Helsingborg, but for Söderblom the matter was clear. The two movements should be kept separate and his meeting should be in Sweden. The difficulty was to give as positive an answer as possible to the two eager Americans. During the discussion, Hermann Kapler, who was chairperson of the Evangelischen Kirchenausschuss, the Evangelical Church Committee, in Berlin, formulated the expression "doctrine divides, service unites." Söderblom would continually repeat this formula without having a clue that eighty years later the relationship would be nearly the precise opposite. Social ethical questions, from atomic weapons to same-sex marriage, would clearly become greater issues of conflict than dogmatic theology.

Kapler was a pragmatic layperson who was more interested in practical cooperation than in doctrinal discussion. Neither long-term organizational considerations nor comparative ecclesiology should be allowed to put a spoke in the wheel of a project that, when all was said and done, chiefly concerned Europe. Söderblom spoke explicitly: "Faith and Order's far-off goal must not delay the pressing necessity of immediately affirming our fellowship in clearly conceived principles and joint action in the imitation of our Savior, in the service which he carried out and which he commissioned us to continue." He received wholehearted support from Bishop Burge, who was representing the Archbishop of Canterbury. Together with Burge, Söderblom took a long walk to the Sofiero Castle, which was the summer residence of the crown prince. Burge had been headmaster of Winchester College — the oldest school in Britain — "which by strict training in self-discipline and presence of mind contributed to the creation of the manly type of Englishman." This appealed to Söderblom and he counted these hours together with him as genuinely important in the preparation for the conference. With Burge as Canterbury's spokesperson, he knew that he again had the full support of the English church. That would be evident when not only the Church of England but also the free churches held a major conference on social ethical matters in Birmingham in 1924. This gave root to Söderblom's vision in Great Britain where Miss Gardner, the Quaker, "was the balance wheel in the clock's work."

Söderblom managed everything. He had to develop a special interest in church statistics since it was important to have as balanced and fair representation as possible. It was not simply a matter of a church's size, however, since spiritual character and significance for the whole of Christianity were also factors to be taken into account. A young researcher in Uppsala developed a statistical key for deciding how many delegates each church was entitled to. Thus, Söderblom anticipated decades of heated discussion about how ecumenical decision-making bodies should be composed in respect to church members, confessions, and cultures, but at the time of the Stockholm conference, what would come to be the most difficult question was not yet actual: the balance between women and men.

The pieces began to fall into place, but the last stretch of the road to Stockholm became extremely rough. In 1921, Anders Sjöstedt lost most of his fortune and Söderblom was forced to find other financiers to back the conference. That did not mean that Sjöstedt disappeared from the picture. He was secretary-treasurer of the Swedish chapter of the Alliance, and he financed the operation of "the ecumenical office" in Uppsala, led the logistical preparations for Stockholm, paid fees to assistants, directed the bookkeeping, and saw to it that a thorough review and audit took place after the Stockholm Conference was over. Toward the end, it remained uncertain both that the economic calculations would prove correct and that a sufficient number of sponsors would be found. Nevertheless, these were perhaps not the most difficult problems.

During a conference on inner mission and *diakonia* in Munich in September 1922, Söderblom showed serious signs of vascular disease. Genuine concern for his health began to spread widely. Then, Nils Widner — as others had done in the past — initiated a collection of funds so that Söderblom could have a long period of recovery outside Sweden. Alle Ekström, the prosperous engineer who owned the motor yacht Polar II, also participated in this. He turned to the crown prince and other concerned individuals to make sure that the archbishop received the help he needed, especially since the Stockholm Conference was approaching. Together with Oscar Ekman, he also saw to it that the archbishop was given his own secretariat.

For ten years Söderblom had been well, but now he was suddenly subject to severe heart problems and was at times forced to rest. An uneasy Anna traveled with him on as many of his journeys as possible, with nitroglycerin pills in her purse. He had received a warning, but he continued to work at almost the same pace as before. The great conference must take precedence over everything else, even over his own health. The situation was made more difficult when his closest colleague, K. B. Westman, who was not appointed to the Uppsala chair in church history he had hoped for, decided in 1923 to return to China to become headmaster of the college that the Church of Sweden Mission was building in Hunan. This was not an easy decision in light of the fundamentalism Westman had encountered among Lutheran missionaries in China, and for Söderblom it felt as though everything was falling apart. He tried to convince Westman to stay at home, and in the board of the Mission, he voted against his appointment to China. When Westman had arrived in China, he appealed to him to return home at least through the Stockholm Conference. But Westman was deaf to all persuasion. Yngve Brilioth had to bear the heavy burden with the small secretariat.

Then something else happened that rocked Söderblom's plans to their foundations. In January 1923, French and Belgian troops occupied the Ruhr. They wanted both to pressure Germany to pay war reparations and to secure the border. It was a brutal occupation with a great deal of violence and Söderblom reacted immediately and emotionally. "Day and night the thought of the French outrage hangs over me like a nightmare," he wrote to a German friend. Encouraged by Gottfrid Billing, he formulated an appeal for peace and reconciliation directed to Christians throughout the world, to responsible political leaders, and especially to the American president Warren Harding. "We judge no one, for humans see only in part. But we condemn the methods of violence," his letter stated. All of the Swedish bishops signed the message. He did not often receive their support, but since Billing had taken the initiative they were convinced. Söderblom did not consult with the Foreign Ministry in spite of the fact that his action was politically sensitive. That the archbishop involved himself in various issues was not uncommon, but never before had the entire Swedish episcopate meddled in foreign politics.

The statement received a great deal of attention both in Sweden and in other countries and it unleashed an avalanche of virulent comments from the side of the Allies. In Germany, however, the appeal was welcomed up to the highest political level and two universities paid tribute to Söderblom by awarding him honorary doctorates, one in Berlin, three in Greifswald, and later also in Bonn. The University of Halle-Wittenberg named him an honorary citizen, hailing him as "friend of the Germans." Söderblom was not especially impressed by these distinctions, which were not only academically motivated but according to one diploma, awarded to a "defender of our cause." For a long time he had been accused of being all too friendly toward the Germans. Now his credibility again suffered. That at the same time he also received Oxford's finest honor, Doctor of Laws, to a certain degree lessened his conflicted feelings, but it was not England that was the problem. It was France.

There the uproar was the greatest. The French Premier Raymond Poincaré telegraphed a six-page defense to Söderblom and the leaders of the French churches kept a sharp distance from their Swedish colleagues. Söderblom attempted to explain the Swedish bishops' position both to Poincaré and to the Roman Catholic Archbishop of Paris, but to no avail. His Protestant friends, who knew his strong feelings for France, also turned against him. There were, however, some French priests and laypeople who sympathized with the appeal of the Swedish bishops. This was a consolation to Söderblom who was very upset at the French reaction. He was prepared to expend himself in restoring good relations, declaring his love for France and the world's most beautiful language, and recalling the French influence on Swedish Christianity throughout history. He devised a whole strategy to win back the confidence of the French; it hurt the most that a crisis had arisen in his relations with his old friend Wilfred Monod. The two had been close spiritually and personally since they had resumed contact at the beginning of the 1920s.

Many questioned how the diplomatically experienced Söderblom could act so naïvely and thoughtlessly that it actually placed his conference in jeopardy. But it turned out that his controversial position actually strengthened confidence in him, not only in the eyes of the Germans. His actions were consistent with his view of the supremacy of international law. For him, the letter was above all an appeal to the U.S. president to break America's isolation and give France a talking-to. When the controversy over the Swedish bishops' letter nearly reached gale force, Nathan Söderblom, together with his wife Anna and his son, Jon Olof, who had just graduated from secondary school, went off on a three-month trip to the United States. There he had the chance to express his wish for more active American involvement in Europe both to leaders of Congress and to the president himself.

29

A Detour to America

Were not our hearts at times burning within us?

Nathan Söderblom, 1924

NATHAN SÖDERBLOM'S ONLY DAY IN WASHINGTON is cold and wet. The capitol shines in the dirty grey air. There, Congress is holding rowdy ballots. Calvin Coolidge receives him in the White House. He has been president for four months; he speaks in such few words that he is called "the sphinx on the Potomac." Söderblom notices that he has a small nose, a pinched-up mouth, small lips, and friendly eyes. He is not impressive. The opposite is the case with Herbert Hoover, the Secretary of Commerce: "Not simply an economic genius but a serious Christian soul. One of the few great people in our ragged times. One who dares to look and think. And he can. And speaks and acts in the ways he considers right. With more politics in his performance he would have been president." He did become that, although he ended with a worse reputation than Coolidge. To the members of Congress, Söderblom speaks about restoring the international relations torn apart by the war. After dinner with the Swedish ambassador, he takes the night train back to New York. A journey to America, which was beginning to seem like a state visit, comes to its end. In a few days, the Swedish-American Line's Drottningholm *sets out and steams toward Gothenburg in the midst of a tremendous storm.*

* * *

Nearly all of the large Protestant churches in the United States except the Lutherans were members of the Federal Council of Churches. In 1920, the council had assumed major responsibility for carrying out the plans for Söderblom's conference. Charles Macfarland and Frederick Lynch were thus eager to have Söderblom come to the United States to speak on behalf of his project. They invited him twice, but he could not fit a long journey into his schedule and his heart problems also placed obstacles in his way. In the fall of 1923, however, the trip became possible. For nearly three months he traveled back and forth across the American continent, together with his wife Anna. Their seventeen-year-old son Jon Olof came along as his secretary. He had on occasion been with his father on parish visitations and knew what was required. Now he had an experience that would be of great value, since in a few years he would become the private secretary of Prime Minister Per Albin Hansson.

Henry Atkinson, who was General Secretary of the Alliance and its well-financed American branch, the Church Peace Union, had in Helsingborg also been chosen General Secretary of Life and Work. He had already invited Söderblom to visit the United States. But at the Reformation Jubilee in 1917, the archbishop held out the prospect of visiting the Augustana Synod. When his old friend Lars G. Abrahamson, at approximately the same time as Atkinson, sent a formal invitation, Söderblom could only accept the invitation with thanks. Thus it was that the ecumenists felt that he deceived them. That he gave priority to the Lutheran churches gave rise to irritation, caused friction, and raised legitimate questions as to Söderblom's ecumenical strategy. However, after the initial confusions were laid to rest, Atkinson and Abrahamson agreed that the Church Peace Union and the Augustana Synod would share costs. These were not insignificant since it was first class all the way — ship, trains, and hotels. Söderblom had no choice but to do what was expected of him. His schedule would have been overwhelming even for a younger and fully healthy person. In ten weeks Söderblom spoke, lectured, and preached 120 times — "two months with voice intact, one without," as he described it all. Traveling by train he went from New York to San Francisco, San Diego, and Los Angeles and then to Chicago, Duluth, Minneapolis and Rock Island, then to Philadelphia and back to Minnesota, to Boston and New Haven, ending in Washington and New York.

After ten days of seasickness and fog, the Swedish travelers landed in Manhattan where they were met by the U.S. Marine Band, before being taken with a police escort to City Hall. The mayor of New York City received them, speeches were exchanged, and the flashes from many press photographers warned them of what awaited them in every place they would visit. They were installed in the legendary and luxurious Vanderbilt Hotel on Park Avenue. The program in New York culminated in a banquet given by the Lutheran churches in the Hotel Astoria, which occupied a whole block on Times Square. Fourteen hundred people found places in the large ballroom and an adjacent room. The most honored guests were seated on a dais at the very front. The food was served with a precision that amazed the archbishop's wife. When dessert was finished, everyone turned their chairs toward the podium, galleries were filled, and Söderblom was greeted with expressions of praise and applause even before he himself could utter a word. He had an hour to speak while the banquet guests leaned back — satisfied, and smoking — and listened to the famed archbishop. He told how as a twenty-four-year-old he had participated in a student conference in Northfield, Massachusetts, and heard Ira Sankey sing of the shepherd who left the ninety-nine sheep in order to find the hundredth. That song had followed him through the years and he had even attempted to have it included in the Swedish hymnal. Now he wanted to remind the Americans of their spiritual heritage. There was not a sound in the large ballroom and Anna stared down at the table when Söderblom began to sing, "There were ninety and nine." He sang all verses in his clear tenor voice. The speech and the song were live on radio, which was then something quite new. As far away as Chicago, people would report that they had heard him. His informal and personable touch struck home. Immediately he became popular.

The journey became a long triumphal march through the Swedish communities in America. In Chicago, where there were more Swedes than in Gothenburg, a squadron of mounted police escorted the archbishop's car to City Hall. Söderblom reminded people — as he did wherever he appeared — that the best thing Swedish immigrants could do to honor Sweden was to live as good American citizens. And the best they could do for the United States was to share all they have brought from Sweden: Lutheranism's faith and ideals, a passion for self-government, honesty, openness, conscientiousness, and diligence in work. Söderblom enthusiastically compared Chicago with Jerusalem, the holy city, citing Psalm 122: "May they prosper who love you. Peace be within your walls."

All of the positive pictures of the United States that he had harbored within him from childhood were confirmed. He expressed measureless wonderment at what the Americans had accomplished. This multicultural society pointed forward and he hoped that the United States would play an ever greater role in the world. But he was not uncritical. He made note of glaring injustices and widespread poverty. He saw that Native Americans were practically on their way to extinction, and distressed, he spoke with Anna about racism and the situation of the "negroes." He was deeply affected as he sang their spirituals. On the train to Buffalo, he wrote: "The train whistle's anxious, trembling noise sounds like the saxophone in their orchestra, a kind of primitive *vox humanus*, sucking, quivering, with a bit of wildness." But these were no more than marginal notes as he moved from city to city, from church to church, from university to university and was hailed and interviewed, as he preached, lectured, and gave after-dinner speeches week after week. In Minneapolis, ten thousand people came to hear him; at Augustana College in Rock Island, the students gathered with torches to meet him on November 6, the day of Gustavus Adolphus's death — just as in Uppsala. He enjoyed standing in the limelight and he did just that, unchallenged, day after day. Rhetoric was at a premium and Söderblom made maximum use of his gift of communication, although with humility and without demagoguery. No one could miss his satisfaction when an audience shouted, whistled, and gave thunderous applause. One could compare his way of capturing an audience with Desmond Tutu's, to choose a later church leader. He radiated humor, warmth, intelligence, and a deep personal spirituality. The journey to America was like a parish visitation writ large. The archbishop listened, observed, taught, encouraged, and advised. When he came home, he edited the "protocol" of his trip into a book of nearly four hundred pages, *Från Uppsala till Rock Island: En predikofärd i nya världen (From Uppsala to Rock Island: A Preaching Journey in the New World).*

The trip was highly official and he was received as "patriarch of the evangelical church." He dressed in clergy attire and his Swedish doctor's hat; at worship he carried Uppsala's medieval crozier, the episcopal shepherd's crook. But at the same time, the journey had a deeply personal character. He often said that mentally the United States was Sweden's nearest neighbor, for relatives lived there and from there came letters to Småland or Hälsingland. He had his own relatives in America — an uncle, a brother, and a son. In San Francisco he met Sven, who had moved there after his unfortunate military career. There, Söderblom also met, for the first time, his mother's eighty-seven-year-old brother who had fought in the American Civil War. A student comrade from Hudiksvall, a person with whom he had done his military service, an Uppsala student, and a fruit grower with roots in Bjuråker appeared. In Rockford, his godfather from Trönö sought him out. He had left Hälsingland in 1888 and was now eighty. In Bishop Hill, an early Swedish settlement in Illinois, Anna met a second cousin to Nathan.

It was also easy to feel at home among the clergy of the Augustana Synod. There were some who had received the star of the Order of the North from the King of Sweden, and there were some very learned men. Conversations could unexpectedly change into pure Latin. Old Swedish revival songs were heard in the new and splendid institutions that these energetic immigrants had built to preserve and develop their Swedish heritage. Söderblom, who himself had been involved in the establishment of both the Samaritan Deaconess Home and the Sigtuna Foundation, visited high schools and colleges, seminaries and hospitals, old people's homes, clubs, and churches. And he also visited a Lutheran publishing house, newspapers, insurance agencies, and pension boards. To be sure, he was himself an entrepreneur, but the dynamism he found in the American congregations was something he had never observed in the Swedish state church. For its part, the Swedish church had a long history, a richer liturgy, and — not to be forgotten — the office of the bishop. The churches had a great deal to learn from each other.

As early as at the negotiations with the Church of England in Uppsala in 1909, it had been important for Söderblom to argue for the independence of the Augustana Synod. He had stood up for the synod's interests against the proposals of the American Episcopal Church. As archbishop, he felt that he had a personal responsibility for all Lutherans of Swedish descent regardless of where they lived; moreover, as a former priest in Paris, he instinctively felt a pastoral responsibility for Swedes in foreign lands. The Augustana Synod was the largest Swedish-speaking church outside Sweden. It had grown to be larger than the Swedish-speaking minority in Finland. It was only in 1923 that it decided to adopt English as its chief language, both in worship and administration. Söderblom welcomed that decision wholeheartedly, but it also made caring for the synod's relations with the mother church in Sweden even more urgent.

The Augustana Synod had resisted being absorbed by the Episcopal Church and also, like the other American Lutheran churches, had remained outside the Federal Council of Churches and ecumenical cooperation. Accordingly, Söderblom had three goals for his American journey: to strengthen the Swedish synod's integrity as its own community, to work for the inclusion of the American Lutheran churches in national and international ecumenical collaborations, and to reinforce Augustana's relations with the Church of Sweden, if possible by adopting an episcopacy consecrated in the Swedish order. Additionally, he wanted to encourage major American universities to pay greater attention to Swedish theology and research. That his visit provided great encouragement to the leaders of Augustana is clear without doubt. He also succeeded in getting three American Lutheran churches to participate in his upcoming Stockholm Conference. As far as the matter of the episcopacy was concerned, however, he chose to lay low. He avoided the question in spite of the fact that one East Coast conference of the Augustana Synod had already expressed its desire to have a bishop and in spite of the fact that he participated in the laying-on-of-hands when Gustaf Brandelle was installed to a second term as president of Augustana. The bishops of the Church of Sweden subsequently sent a bishop's pectoral cross to him, but Brandelle did not really know what to do with it. He could not wear it as a sign of his office, so he received it as a symbol of friendship with the Swedish church. It remained lying in a cabinet.

When Söderblom traveled to America, he was in the midst of preparing for the Stockholm Conference. He wanted to insure the participation of other Protestant churches since broad American support of the event was required for its success. While Anna remained in Rock Island, Söderblom alone made a long journey to Detroit, Pittsburgh, Baltimore, and Philadelphia. A meeting with the Federal Council, the American section of both Life and Work and the Church Peace Union, was fitted in between addresses concerning the essence of Lutheranism and academic lectures on the influence of India and China on European religious thought, on the temptations of Buddha and Jesus, and on evangelical catholicity. By this time he was well worn out, but he kept going at the same pace day after day. Everyone had to be satisfied. After having visited all the Swedish monuments in Delaware and also having preached at Holy Trinity in Wilmington — the oldest stone church on American soil — he was reunited with his family in Chicago. After an additional seven engagements in the Midwest, it was time to return to the East Coast. He lectured at Harvard, Clark, and Yale Universities. On the First Sunday in Advent, he had the chance one more time to reflect on his memories of student days. He visited James Reinholds who had come to Uppsala and invited him to the student conference of 1890. Reinholds was now a prominent lawyer who was taken up with coordinating criminal law codes in the American states. He still lived in his childhood home where Söderblom had spent several weeks. Memories swept over him. Massachusetts was culturally and intellectually a totally different world than the Midwest, turned as it was toward Europe and serving as a breeding ground for much of the ecumenical movement. Here, the confessional walls were low. A generation earlier he had written the prayer that he had prayed ever since: "Lord, give me humility and wisdom to serve the great cause of the free unity of Thy Church." It had all begun in that way. Now he would return to Uppsala to fulfill his ecumenical calling.

But how torn he was between the ecumenical and the confessional! He moved with ease among Methodists, Presbyterians, or Congregationalists and was often more highly regarded by them than by the Lutherans. Even in the Augustana Synod he was met with suspicion over both his talk of God's revelation in other religions and his ecumenical work. Yet he was part of the Lutheran tradition. It was his spiritual home, both theologically and emotionally. If he could not get the Lutherans to join him on his ecumenical journey, it was not worth much. Therefore, he put all his strength and diplomacy toward establishing strong support for the idea of unity among them. With his personal charisma and his international reputation he was able to convince many, but by no means all. Neither in Germany nor the United States would confessional fundamentalists support him.

Ecumenists on the American East Coast found it incomprehensible that he paid so much attention to the reluctant Lutheran churches. Charles Macfarland, who had supported all his plans since Oud Wassenaar, was unable to hide his dissatisfaction when he commented on Söderblom's American journey. The archbishop had had all too little contact with the leaders of the large communions who believed in the unity of the church. Instead, he had given his time to those who were unfavorably disposed toward cooperation. It was extremely unfortunate, wrote Macfarland, that Söderblom's hosts had forced him to reject the invitation of the Federal Council. "I had spoken of you as the great prophet of unity, but when you came you thought it best not only to reject that description but also to keep your distance from me," he wrote a little bitterly. Söderblom had given the impression that he stood for an exclusive pan-Lutheranism rather than for cooperation among all the churches. And it was true that Söderblom had difficulty in uniting his great ecumenical vision with his Lutheran loyalty. In his heart, he was both confessional and ecumenical in the same way that he was both conservative and radical, both deeply Swedish and international.

By Christmas, they were again at home in Uppsala after a journey that in all essential respects had been richly successful. Anna immediately began to write a travel description, *En Amerikabok* (*An America Book*), which at times has been compared to Fredrika Bremer's famous work of 1853, *Hemmen i Nya Världen* (*The Homes of a New World: Impressions of America*). So many official duties awaited him that Söderblom had to write his America book in small intervals. The coming Stockholm Conference cast its shadow over everything. During Söderblom's absence, Anders Sjöstedt had held the reins and at that he had not been lazy. Now there were only one-and-a-half years to go and there was still much to be done. Söderblom had to find donors and sponsors as well as host families for the delegates; schedule receptions, meals, and festival programs; plan the worship; and above all, see to it that the conference received proper organization and a program in line with its intentions. He must make certain that both Orthodox and Protestant church leaders who had a sincere ecumenical disposition came to Stockholm.

The Roman Catholic Church had declined. In 1921, Söderblom, together with the bishops in Copenhagen and Oslo, had sent a letter to the pope. It emphasized that cooperation between the churches in no way involved an encroachment on any church's faith, rites, or teachings; they appealed to all disciples of Christ to follow their Master in love and action in order to meet the needs of the world. Cardinal Gasparri had answered in a way that made it clear that the Vatican would not send representatives to Stockholm. The planning committee then decided not to pursue the matter further and the Vatican received no formal invitation to Stockholm. This perhaps also had something to do with the anti-Catholic wave that swept through Protestant Europe at the beginning of the 1920s, but in actuality, Söderblom never had real expectations that the Catholics would participate.

With the Orthodox it was otherwise. Söderblom had developed a good relationship with Constantinople through Metropolitan Germanos, and also through Johannes Kolmodin and Herman Neander. Since there was an attempt on the part of the Church of England to draw nearer to Rome, Söderblom took as his strategy bringing Uppsala closer to Constantinople and the other Eastern churches. But the situation in Turkey complicated matters. After the Great War, the Ottoman caliphate fell to pieces. In 1919, the Patriarchate broke with the Ottoman Empire and oriented itself toward Greece, but it had to find a *modus vivendi* in Kemal Atatürk's national state so that it could remain in its own part of Istanbul, the Phanar. Then the Patriarch Germanos V resigned. The election of his successor stretched out over time. Söderblom hoped against hope that Germanos Strenopoulos would be chosen, but that did not happen. In 1920, the hard-pressed Patriarchate published an encyclical that proposed the creation of a kind of ecclesial parallel to the League of Nations. This suggestion closely paralleled the plans of Life and Work and the doors were opened for Orthodox participation in Stockholm.

In his regular correspondence with Kolmodin, Söderblom showed a surprisingly positive attitude toward Muslims. Previously he had not paid Islam any special attention, but when the diplomat Kolmodin intimated at the possibility of an "entente" between Christianity and Islam on the basis of common ideas concerning revelation, Söderblom immediately embraced the idea. With a freedom from judgment that was extremely uncommon among archbishops, he answered: "Thanks for the good news and a magnificent and exact understanding of the affinity of the religions of revelation." He went further and wrote that Islam gives the impression of "holding our Lord's heritage in trust" in Constantinople at least as actively as Christianity. He himself wanted to regard the patriarch's presence as a foretaste of the day when the church and Islam would acknowledge each other as servants of the high God. No wonder that Kolmodin, who did not have the best of relations with the Swedish Foreign Ministry, would have liked to have his visiting cards inscribed, "Délégué spécial de Monsigneur l'Archevêque d'Upsala auprès de Sa Sainteté le Patriarche Ecuménique et Son Altesse le Sheikh-ul-Islam." Even if that kind of double representation was in line with Söderblom's understanding of Kolmodin's calling, such a possibility had to be seen only in the far-off future. Söderblom had to be satisfied with the Orthodox accepting the invitation to his Protestant-dominated movement; to widen his horizon to include other religions was beyond possibility, even if his horizon was wider than most.

To develop a mathematical formula for determining how many people should be invited from each church was no easy task, and the fact was that Söderblom himself intervened to identify those he wanted to come. The large church bodies were not to dominate; even small groups such as the Salvation Army, the Quakers, and the Armenian Church should receive places. The delegates also had to know English, German, or French since simultaneous translation could not be provided. The lectures were to be printed in advance in those three languages. As the conference neared, the small staff in Uppsala worked intensively sending out invitations, answering questions, and dealing with logistical matters. He himself took part in everything, not only to satisfy his need to control but because his personal knowledge of things was enormous. Throughout his life he had worked more than most people. His time was "stretchable" and his energy was inexhaustible, but he had never worked harder than he did during the year before the great conference. The nights were short and there was no talk of free days. In a letter to Friedrich Heiler he wrote what he had also said to others: "God's intention is that we should work ourselves to death in his service. But this should happen slowly and wisely so that we can do as much as possible with the gifts he has loaned to us." This is what he did. And when his conference was over, he was so worn out that he never again recovered his health.

In the midst of everything there were a few other matters that especially interested him. One was the design of a new bishop's cope, which would portray his view of Uppsala's place within Christianity and his own responsibility among the world's church leaders. He had a great interest in liturgy and his liturgical garments had often given rise to discussion. He had defended himself by pointing out that ecclesiastical vestments were a sign of continuity through time and that Sweden's first evangelical archbishop, Laurentius Petri, never rejected their use. Vestments were surely not necessary for salvation, but they both enhanced worship and signified the church's catholicity. Söderblom did not encourage the high church movement, but he was as eager as they to preserve a living tradition. The office of the bishop was indispensable and it should be clear from the cope's embroidery how he interpreted his ministry.

It was the textile artist Agnes Branting who suggested that a new cope be sewn. She was one of his old friends and many times she had helped him with textiles for the cathedral. Söderblom immediately began sketching out what the cope should look like. As he had done both with the renovation of Holy Trinity Church and the building of the Church of the Revelation at Saltsjöbaden, he translated his own theology into art. The basic color of the cope should be violet, the color of Lent and Penitential Sundays and also the traditional episcopal color. A festive cope was usually gold or white, but Söderblom was determined: it should be violet. In the middle of the breastplate he wanted a Luther rose, symbolizing Wittenberg and the Reformation. Above it would be St. Erik's apple with a cross and under it an open Bible and the keys of St. Peter. On the cope's right border he wanted a depiction of the cross that he had received at his consecration from the Archbishop of Canterbury; and on the left border the Order of the Savior, which he had been given by the Patriarch of Constantinople together with a seven-armed candelabra. A fortress and a ship were to complete the symbols. Bible verses concerning the call to unity should be embroidered on the cope's border in Latin, Greek, and Swedish. At the bottom he wanted St. George and the dragon on one side and Old Uppsala's mounds and church on the other. On the back shield a Hebrew verse from the Psalter should be embroidered, together with the star that the Ethiopian crown prince Ras Teferi had given him. These figures and texts were to signify the universal church: its birth, history, unity, prayer, and vigilance.

He had often talked of the See of Uppsala in relation to that of Canterbury, Rome, and Constantinople. The archbishopric of Sweden was placed in the particular context of the Reformation, symbolized by the Luther rose and the Bible. The Lutheran Church of Sweden was a historic continuation of the Roman Catholic tradition symbolized by the keys. The apple of the royal martyr, also found over the cathedral's west doorway, pointed to the entire Swedish context. Söderblom was to wear this magnificent cope many times. It identified him as the Archbishop of the Church of Sweden called by God to unify the Christian church.

Together with the poet Emil Liedgren he also prepared, in many languages, an ecumenical hymnal, *Communio in adorando et serviendo œkoumenica*. At the time — the summer of 1925 — only a few weeks before the conference was to begin, he developed a troublesome infection that required him to have a large bandage around his head. An old straw hat hid part of the gauze bandage and he went daily to the Academic Hospital to have it changed. The episode demonstrated the confidence with which he worked, caring little as to what others might think. To choose sixty hymns from different traditions was a process both delicate and lengthy and securing good translations of certain Swedish hymns was not easy. Söderblom persuaded Charles Wharton Stork, who was known for his fine rendering of Swedish poetry, to translate Natanael Beskow's "Ack saliga dag," "O Jubilee Day," into English. That hymn reflected Söderblom's own theology of the

Kingdom of God and became one of the most frequently sung hymns of the ecumenical movement:

> O jubilee day of the world's expectation
> When earth is God's Kingdom of blessed accord,
> When man's erring race finds the path of salvation
> And all shall acknowledge that Christ is the Lord,
> When sin has been banished and death slain forever
> And blessed redemption will part from us never.

Services of worship were to give the Stockholm Conference its collective heartbeat, and what would worship be if the congregation did not sing together? The Latin title given to the hymnal summarized the whole conference: communion in ecumenical adoration and service. The ecumenical movement was a spiritual pilgrimage with prayer and praise as its source of power. Söderblom conceived of the Stockholm Conference as a resting place with wide horizons and inner peace in the midst of a world filled with unresolved guilt and smoldering conflicts. In light of this conception, he devoted considerable time to the planning of worship and prayers.

To the very last, the preparations were filled with stark conflicts. At a meeting at Farnham Castle in Winchester just a few weeks prior to the conference, many problems still remained to be solved. Söderblom was able to prevent the English and Americans from changing the meeting's agenda and struggled hard to hold his own against the Reformed. He became somewhat discouraged, but was able to maneuver things so that most matters remained as he had planned. "It was absolutely necessary for me to come here," he wrote to Anna. He was the only one who had enough authority both to guide discussions and to safeguard Swedish and Lutheran perspectives so that the program maintained the balance he wished for. In London he met not only with Archbishop Davidson, but also with Patriarch Photios of Alexandria who agreed to come to Stockholm.

At the end of July the delegates were already beginning to arrive. At the ferry from Sassnitz to Trelleborg, they were met by Swedish volunteers who helped them on to Stockholm and kept the reception committee there informed by telegraph as to who was on the way. The World Alliance for International Friendship through the Churches first held its own conference, August 5–9, with 150 delegates. That was followed by a week-long session of the large conference preparatory committee, which immediately set about receiving reports from advance meetings that had been held in different countries. The committee was divided into small groups, which were quartered at the Sigtuna Foundation, folk high schools, and various country estates. They worked intensively at translating the chaotic material into working documents. Just two days before the conference opened, those documents were ready for printing and distribution. Nathan Söderblom could breathe more easily.

Meticulous practical preparations involving hundreds of people were required, but under the command of the high-ranking military officers O. B. Malm and Anders Sjöstedt, this major undertaking was successfully carried out. "The Ecumenical Office" with its subdivisions employed at most a hundred people. All of the delegates were guests of Sweden. Söderblom had made sure that more than half of the funding would come through large donations. The parishes of Stockholm earmarked a share of the funds and smaller gifts streamed in from various sources. It was not the Church of Sweden that stood behind the conference; it was, rather, completely Söderblom's own enterprise, financed by sponsors, and led by an international committee. The Swedish bishops were scarcely in evidence; actually, it was only Einar Billing who, at the side of Söderblom, made a meaningful contribution.

The conference, marked as it was by a spirit of hope, occurred between the Great War and the Great Depression. The wounds from World War I had not been healed. The fragile peace could not be relied on. In Sweden, one weak government succeeded another; at the time, Rickard Sandler was prime minister. The Nazi Putsch in the Bürgerbräukeller in Munich had already taken place. Mussolini led the Blackshirts marching in the streets of Rome. Hitler's *Mein Kampf* sat on the shelves of bookstores. The 1930s were in the wings. A new orientation in theology had been introduced in 1922 when Karl Barth published the second edition of his commentary on Romans. He rejected every attempt to associate God with culture and progress. In Sweden, Gustaf Aulén had come out, in 1923, with the first edition of *Den allmänneliga kristna tron* (*The Faith of the Christian Church*), heralding another way of doing theology and of understanding the church. Söderblom had been warned. Just before the conference, the Swiss ecumenist Adolf Keller wrote to Söderblom: "Already I have heard at the door the footsteps of those who will carry it (the conference) to the cemetery."

After ten years of hopes and miscalculations, fits and starts, the Stockholm Conference was finally about to begin. For weeks things had been changing in the capital city. All flags were raised. To a person, the residents of Stockholm had turned out to catch a glimpse of all the notables. No pains had been spared. The conference would be a magnificent feast. Concerts and banquets, sailboat outings and open air worship services would frame the program and the royal family would give splendor to everything. And the sun was shining.

30

Christianity's Conference

> What happened was not accomplished easily. On the contrary, it cost the greatest exertion of efforts. It was necessary to contribute every drop of will and blood and to strain the powers of soul and body and spirit to the uttermost.
>
> *Nathan Söderblom, 1925*

Nathan Söderblom has difficulty holding back tears when, in his black priest's cape, he takes his place in the procession. In cassocks, copes, and academic gowns, miters and strange caps, with ruffled collars and pectoral crosses, with croziers and staffs, bishops and professors from Wittenberg and Alexandria, Canterbury and Geneva, Berlin, Bombay, and Paris walk toward the altar of Storkyrkan, the Great Church of Stockholm. Orthodox metropolitans weighed down by tradition walk alongside smooth-shaven American church entrepreneurs. The centuries and cultures meet. Not since the Council of Nicaea sixteen hundred years earlier has there been so representative a gathering of church leaders. They will translate the creed into action in a world torn to shreds. For Söderblom, this is the moment of his life. His prayers are answered and his dreams are fulfilled. It is August 19, 1925.

* * *

In Stockholm, no one had ever before seen anything like it. The crowds of onlookers were tight. Nearly seven hundred delegates from thirty-seven countries were there. They had sailed for days and nights across the Atlantic, traveled by train through Europe and by steamboat across the Baltic. Sweden was an insignificant country on the periphery of the world map, without ruins or revolutions, yet prosperous and welcoming in the late, light summer. Many of Stockholm's citizens had opened their homes for the foreign guests; others had contributed to hotel costs. The Patriarch of

Alexandria was seen fishing for perch from the Djurgården bridge of the royal furrier Lindahl and four of the conference leaders with the Bishop of Peterborough at the helm were guests of Crown Prince Gustaf Adolf at Ulriksdal. The general and temperance leader O. B. Malm and the major and transportation director Anders Sjöstedt, together with Yngve Brilioth and a few other priests, managed the conference's nearly perfect organization. A swarm of volunteer workers, mostly students, saw to it that everything functioned well. The Academy of Music gave its building for administration and discussions. The official sessions took place in the Blasieholm Church, which seated three thousand people, and day after day was filled to overflowing. Listeners streamed to the church. One could see Father Gunnar Rosendal with his backwards collar and his jacket with striped trousers, hear Gustaf Aulén's cackling laughter, or meet Eivind Berggrav among the journalists. Those who could not gain entrance could read full reports in the conference newspaper, *Life and Work*, or in the Stockholm press where column after column was devoted to the event. Foreign correspondents made the conference known around the Christian world. Sweden showed its best side. With his charm and indomitable will, Söderblom had brought all of Sweden to its feet. The train system put on extra cars and lowered the ticket price for the delegates, a special telephone network was set up, the Royal Automobile Club passed out membership cards granting all privileges, and sponsors gave all sorts of gifts to the conference from fine crystal to the specially made clock that broke off long-winded speakers.

Later generations, who are familiar with international conferences concerning everything from nuclear disarmament to climate change and have reason to be disappointed over what are frequently meager results, have difficulty imagining what a breakthrough this ecumenical assembly was. Churches had been alien to each other for centuries and believed that differences in doctrine amounted to heresy. Now they gathered for the first time ever for authentic dialogue dealing with their common responsibility for peace and social justice. European church leaders did not attack each other. Protestants who were clearing the way for modernity embraced Orthodox Christians who lived in the conceptual world of the early church. It happened in Stockholm during one of the first great international conferences. Against the background of a homogeneous Swedish culture permeated by Lutheran views of both faith and society, the Eastern churches stood out as extremely exotic. For Swedes accustomed to worshiping in

Nathan Söderblom in August 1925 at the Universal Christian Conference on Life and Work, Stockholm and Uppsala.

medieval churches, the American and Asian communions stood out as modern. Those who attempted to speak with their guests used German or possibly French. English for most was an unknown language.

Nathan Söderblom was clearly the chief person at the conference, although he kept in the background and allowed others to lead the daily proceedings: Arthur J. Brown, Theodore Woods, and Metropolitan Germanos. He himself spoke at the opening, preached at the conclusion, and gave one of the many lectures. His lecture dealt with social problems caused by alcohol, a serious problem during the time of prohibition but scarcely a central ecumenical issue. He held all the threads of the conference in his own hands, mediated disagreements, encouraged and thanked the speakers, led the conference steering committee at its luncheon meetings, and conferred with individuals about various matters. He was constantly active behind the scenes, making adjustments and compromises. At times he had to tone down the prophetic ambitions of the conference in order to reach unity.

He had been through a significant number of international meetings: Northfield in 1890, Amsterdam in 1891, the evangelical socialist conference in Erfurt in 1896, the history of religions congress in Stockholm in 1897, conversations with the Church of England in 1909, the academic conference on religion and the World Student Christian Federation meeting in Constantinople in 1911, the conference of churches from neutral nations in Uppsala in 1917, the post-war meeting of the Alliance in Oud Wassenaar in 1919, the Geneva meeting in 1920, several Lutheran conferences in Germany, Birmingham in 1924, and a long list of preparatory meetings for Stockholm. He believed wholeheartedly in the conference as a working method, provided that it gave opportunity for personal meetings, contributed to lasting friendships, and tore down walls between churches and nations. This was precisely what the Stockholm conference aimed to do. Meals and receptions complemented each other and there were many opportunities to meet new people. Throughout, Söderblom could be observed in typical fashion seeking out individuals whom he would bring together.

The conference program was catastrophically overloaded. In nine days there were 115 lectures on different topics followed by 140 interventions. On top of that, there were 36 sermons, 40 talks on various occasions, and the reading of the conference message in different languages. This was too much of a good thing. Further, much of what was said did not make a lasting impression. Already on the first day, the pews began to empty. One of those who persevered longest was the crown prince, and not only because he was a personal friend of Söderblom's. He had taken part in the conference preparations and was genuinely interested in what was going on. He was one of the few who would see the Stockholm conference bear fruit forty-three years later when he visited the Fourth General Assembly of the World Council of Churches, held in Uppsala. That Söderblom had trusting and close contacts with the royal family was apparent to everyone. The Orthodox pointed out what a blessing it was for Sweden to still have a monarchy.

The chance to speak was given to as many people as possible. During a "Swedish evening," Prince Carl, Natanael Beskow, Selma Lagerlöf, and Elsa Brändström participated and Söderblom's brother-in-law, John Forsell, who was head of the Royal Opera, sang. Every day the speakers took up most of the time and not much was left over for plenary discussions. Some diplomats and lawyers helped to translate, but they were not familiar with theological terminology and soon gave up. At that point, the Swiss Alphons Koechlin stepped in and saved the conference. Day after day he stood at the rostrum and translated all the interventions. The people of Stockholm thought that the whole inner city buzzed like a beehive, but many of the visitors could not understand each other's language.

The delegates, with few exceptions, were named by churches and national and regional organizations. This was something new. Previous conferences mostly brought together self-appointed enthusiasts who themselves had the means to assume the costs. Söderblom had attempted to make sure that people in whom he had special confidence would come to Stockholm, but he had been rebuked for that by the strong-willed Lucy Gardner from England. He had to be content with delegations that were composed as they were. No fewer than forty-five delegates came from Germany. There were such intense tensions within the group that it could scarcely be held under control. One delegate left the conference in anger and the ecumenically influential and pacifistically inclined Friedrich Siegmund-Schultze refrained from speaking at all in order not to arouse protests from the other Germans. The question of war guilt was avoided. Söderblom made certain that even conservative voices were heard. He backed the involvement of the French in the discussions by designating the French language as official, even though Francophone participants were relatively few. The British delegates were the best prepared. Their conference in Birmingham the year before — on politics, economics, and citizenship — had produced twelve printed reports. Söderblom had to take care that the British, with all of their preparatory material, did not take over the conference. The Americans, with Arthur J. Brown and Charles

Macfarland in the lead, radiated the optimism that made the Stockholm Conference possible. Söderblom felt especially pleased that his journey to the United States resulted in having not only the Augustana Synod but also two other American Lutheran churches represented at Stockholm.

The Orthodox presence garnered the most attention. Patriarch Photios of Alexandria had just celebrated the sixteen-hundredth anniversary of the Council of Nicaea in Westminster Abbey. He came to Stockholm from that event together with a number of metropolitans. Söderblom had worked for a long time at winning the Orthodox churches to his cause. His ambassadors Johannes Kolmodin and Herman Neander had contributed, and the Anglicans and Old Catholics had helped. Several delegations had been sent to the Byzantine and Oriental churches to secure their participation. Söderblom's close friend Harald Bildt had kept him well informed from Cairo. In the tense situation that prevailed in Turkey, the Ecumenical Patriarch needed all the external support he could get. When Rome did not come forth with support, the patriarch had no other choice but to rely on the evangelical and Anglican churches. The Russian Orthodox Church had been totally cut off from the surrounding world and slowly ground down by the Soviet state. The Stockholm Conference showed its solidarity with the persecuted by holding a service of remembrance for the deceased Patriarch Tikhon of Moscow who had died as a martyr on April 7.

Söderblom had a clear vision of what he wanted to accomplish at the meeting. The conference should lay the groundwork for practical cooperation between the churches that would promote peace and social justice. There was a direct line from his social Christianity of the 1890s to Stockholm. His ecclesiology was built on the conviction that the church was both body and soul, institution and spirit. During the tension-filled 1920s, it had become clearer than ever that both society and the international organizations needed to be animated by the Christian spirit. Söderblom felt that the Life and Work movement could provide a soul for the League of Nations, for without soul, it was nothing more than "dead mechanics." The Stockholm Conference aimed at providing a contribution to a new world order.

There were two principles involved: First, that the inner life was of decisive importance. No matter how well institutions and organizations, laws and regulations function, they remain like shells without a core and like dead bodies without life if they are not inspired by prayer, faith, love, and hope. Only the transformation of the heart and the sovereignty of God can create genuine peace. Second, that Christian love is not an end in itself. It is to be directed outwards and it must conquer the world. If the richness of the inner life does not serve the well-being of other people, it will disappear like "the gold of a troll." Without putting one's life in the service of peace and love a human being cannot preserve the peace of the heart. Söderblom desired most of all that his conference would lead to spiritual renewal for a world devastated by war, greed, and nationalism. The ecumenical movement was to be a revival movement borne up by praise and intercession. The evangelical revival of the nineteenth century had dealt with the salvation of individuals. Now much more was at stake. The ecumenical movement was concerned with nothing less than saving Christian civilization and the entire world. And that required the visible unity of the Christians.

Nowhere is unity revealed more clearly than in common prayer and worship, and most of all when Christians from differing traditions share the Sacrament. The Church of Sweden invited the conference delegates to high mass in the newly built and impressive Engelbrekt Church on Sunday, August 23. For Söderblom himself, and for many of the delegates, this became the greatest experience of a conference that was filled throughout with services of worship. Hymns were sung in many languages. Arthur J. Brown preached and the Bishops of Lund and Vaxjö presided. Söderblom described his own feelings: "Was it a vision of heaven that opened, or only an earthly view? Multitudes came forward and knelt. Souls were lost in mystery, in the suffering Savior's secret, and praised God. I could not escape seeing and inwardly rejoicing at all the disciples from differing communions within evangelical catholic Christianity who were gathered there as brothers and sisters around their older brother, Christ." The eucharist, which had been so neglected in the Church of Sweden, was being restored, partly thanks to the agreement concerning eucharistic fellowship between the Churches of Sweden and of England and would have great influence, not only on Swedish church life. "This instant when Christians from all countries and all churches and all theological persuasions united in the fellowship of the love of Christ was without doubt the high point of the conference," wrote Söderblom. "We all felt that the Spirit and the love of Christ are far greater than the human practices which we with our limitations derive from loyalty only to our own spiritual legacies."

Even though theological issues in a more qualified sense were to be left to Faith and Order, the conference had barely begun before one of the era's sharpest theological controversies came to the fore: How are the biblical expressions concerning the kingdom of God to be understood? The issue had been debated for more than a quarter of a century. Söderblom himself had written a book about the issue in 1898. In his comprehensive report on the conference, he devoted a hundred pages to what, without even being on the agenda, came to be the "main question" of the Stockholm Conference. It had not been a matter discussed in advance and was not included in the six subject areas that were to be dealt with. But from the first day on, the kingdom of God, the kingdom of heaven, became a consistent theme. Bishop Woods of Winchester, who was an eloquent speaker and one of the conference leaders, preached at the opening service of worship. The text chosen was the word of Jesus: "Repent, for the kingdom of heaven has come near." For Woods, "conversion" meant to turn toward the future, contribute to the progress of civilization, and for the glory of God, build his kingdom on earth. This was the task of all Christians, no matter how utopian it seemed. "To establish God's kingdom in the complicated civilization of the twentieth century is a colossal task. It requires thought, talent, patience, wisdom. But in Christ we can accomplish the impossible," said the bishop.

His optimism subsequently received the support of an American who, with the help of statistics, sought to show that the United States was already well on the way to establishing the kingdom of heaven. He received applause but was soon opposed by the German bishop Ludwig Ihmels. On the basis of his Lutheran tradition, he asserted that nothing "was more mistaken or more disastrous" than to believe that the kingdom of God is to come here in time. God's kingdom is God's reign in human hearts. God's kingdom belongs to objective revelation and it is nothing that humans can bring about. God's kingdom is the new creation, which would appear at the end of time. Söderblom listened attentively to everyone who spoke. He heard voices from different traditions of piety; however, he did not interpret them as being in opposition to one another but rather as variations on the same theme. He himself stood closer to Woods than to Ihmels, but endeavored to bridge the gulf between them. Their opposing interpretations, which had their roots back in the Middle Ages, were to persist throughout the conference and would often appear in the ecumenical movement into the twenty-first century.

Much of what was delivered from the podium lost its sharpness and passion when it was boiled down to the dry prose of committees. This was above all true of the report on the churches and international politics, especially its section on war and peace. The Germans and French had reluctantly agreed to avoid the question of who started the war, although it continued to hang like a storm cloud over the conference. Many argued for disarmament and some took a pacifist position that was attractive to Söderblom. But the final message was watered down. The question of peace received only a few lines: "We summon the Churches to share with us our sense of the horror of war, and of its futility as a means of settling international disputes, and to pray and work for the fulfillment of the promise that under the scepter of the Prince of Peace, 'mercy and truth shall meet together, righteousness and peace shall kiss each other.'" It was not possible to reach unity on a common ethical position against armaments and war. Perhaps that should not have been expected, but there were many more than Söderblom who found the statement's pronouncement regarding the most important question of the conference altogether too feeble and vacuous. Some, therefore, abstained from agreeing to the entire message.

The conference dealt with practical Christianity and many questions were touched on, but no common or guiding ethical principles came from the discussions. Some problems that were burning at the time were unfairly treated, for example, racism. That issue was to occupy the ecumenical movement during the entire twentieth century. Colonialism was a similar case, but for most, the responsibility of the Christian world to "civilize" people was so apparent that colonialism was not questioned in a conference dominated by Western middle-class men. There were only some thirty women among the delegates, most from the United States, and youth were even fewer. Their questions were very much disregarded. In contrast, family, upbringing, and education were high on the agenda; to nurture Christian personalities was the responsibility not only of parents and schools but also of the churches. No one asked how youth themselves saw the question. The youngest of the delegates was Willem A. Visser 't Hooft. One day he requested the word and spoke briefly on behalf of all the absent youth. But he did gain a hearing when, thirteen years later, he became General Secretary of the World Council of Churches, which was then in the process of formation. Nevertheless, there were perhaps more people than the German Erich Stange who wanted to hear what young people thought. In the youth leaders' journal *Führerdienst*, he wrote: "Think if one of the fresh, blond young persons who in these days have so loyally helped us were simply placed in the midst of the solemn assembly. I wonder if in the eyes of youth things in many respects would seem quite different than we ourselves think." He could have been alluding to Dag Hammarskjöld or the Söderblom boys who helped with all sorts of things during the conference. For Hammarskjöld, Söderblom himself and the Stockholm Conference remained important sources of inspiration during his life in the service of the United Nations.

After eleven overcrowded days, when words threatened to drown the delegates and Gerda Rodling and others in the secretariat began to totter from fatigue, the conference message was adopted and Nathan Söderblom could bring the meeting to a close. He emphasized that trust had made the impossible possible, for the conference had demanded unprecedented effort. He had seen how human weakness, unclear motives, lack of unity, smallness, vanity, and self-centeredness had shown themselves both in the preparations and in the conference itself. But he had also seen how God could use humans in spite of their sin and miserable unwillingness to do his will. Prayers for direction by the Spirit had been answered. The conference had been a success, not thanks to human competence, but through God's Spirit.

In a warm and friendly atmosphere, the Swedish organization Pro Fide et Christianismo invited the conference to dinner at the Grand Hotel. But that was not the actual conclusion to the conference activities. At 9:33 on Sunday morning, a train with all delegates on board left for Uppsala. In the cathedral, a high mass was celebrated that would not soon be forgotten. The most lasting impression was of Patriarch Photios of Alexandria reading from the high altar the Nicene Creed in its original language. That an Orthodox patriarch proclaimed the sixteen-hundred-year-old confession of faith in an evangelical cathedral was a kind of prophecy that Christianity could be united even in teaching.

Nathan Söderblom preached on the text from Mark 7, "'Ephphatha,' that is, 'Be opened.'" The saints passed in review: the apostles in the upper room in Jerusalem, Augustine and Monica, Peter Waldo and the poor of Lyon, Francis of Assisi, Luther, Calvin, and John Wesley. He had invited all of Christianity to the conference, but some churches had declined to come. The Roman Catholic Church had shown no interest in a meeting in Lutheran Sweden. The most quoted words from Söderblom's sermon are his allusion to this absence: "Two men are here gathered together. John, the Apostle of tender love and contemplation who at the Savior's breast learned the rule: Brethren, love one another. Paul, the greatest disciple of the Savior who witnessed, 'I worked harder than any of them — though it was not I, but the grace of God that is with me.' His faith worked by love. The third man, Peter, the spokesman of the disciples, still tarries. Christendom stands out as divided, but Christ is one. Divisions do not reflect his mind." At that point, Söderblom could not have imagined that sixty-five years later, Pope John Paul II would pray at his grave.

The mighty congregation that filled every corner of the great cathedral — estimated at 4,000 people — was joined by everyone who listened to the radio transmission on crackling crystal receivers. With deep feeling they all sang, "Oh, blest communion, fellowship divine, we feebly struggle, they in glory shine," a hymn that Söderblom had learned in England and later translated into Swedish. The Our Father was prayed in Greek and, vested in his ecumenical cope, Söderblom blessed the diverse congregation before the boys' choir sang the sixteenth-century hymn by Felice Anerio, "Laudamus Dominum."

The university aula, which had a level floor for the day, was set for lunch: consommé, cold cheese, and Prague ham with vegetables, Napoleon pastry, and coffee. Light beer and lemonade were served. Söderblom's closest friends stood as hosts: the university rector and pro-rector, the provincial governor, the mayor. Söderblom had deeply wished that the entire conference could be held in Uppsala and not in Stockholm. Even long afterwards he would sigh, "If only it had happened in Uppsala." But now they were all there and he made the most of it. From his place he could look out over the nine hundred luncheon guests. There sat the Russian Nicolai Glubokovski who had found asylum in Bulgaria, and there sat Einar Billing who contributed more than the other Swedish bishops to the success of the conference. There he saw Bishop Jaako Gummerus from Tammerfors who led an unofficial Finnish delegation after Archbishop Gustaf Johansson completely refused to support the conference. Söderblom could catch a glimpse of Bishop Motoda from Tokyo, Metropolitan Mar Timotheos from India, and Gideon Cheng from China, the conference's few Asians. Dean George K. A. Bell prepared the final notes for the official conference report and the German deaconess Emma von Bunsen was relieved after having given a speech of thanks at the final session on Saturday. Now it was the turn of others to express thanks.

First to take the floor was Hjalmar Hammarskjöld, the former prime minister. Like the Rector Magnificus of the university, he spoke in French and then himself translated for the Swedish people. He saw the dawn of a new era that was to follow dark times of misunderstanding, hate, suffering, and unhappiness. He dwelt on the international order of justice that must be created and described the Stockholm conference as a new, beautiful chapter in the great and steadily growing book of faith, hope, and love inscribed *De fide, spes et caritas*. Before Patriarch Photios, Professor Deissman, Bishops Brent and Woods, and finally, Söderblom's old friend Wilfred Monod had spoken and the male chorus OD had sung, the entire afternoon was gone. Everyone took rapid leave and hurried to the station to catch the train back to Stockholm.

As soon as they had left, Söderblom gathered the continuation committee. At his suggestion, Bishop Woods was named chairperson and Dr. Atkinson general secretary. Immediately there was a discussion concerning seats on the working committee. As in all ecumenical groups since, there were disputes as to how a committee could be made as representative as possible. The conference, despite Söderblom's hopes, did not achieve unity about forming a permanent ecumenical council for advancing the cause of Christianity, but on Monday, August 31, 1925, the continuation committee, meeting in the plenary hall of Parliament's First Chamber, reached a conclusion that in time would lead to the formation of the World Council of Churches. It had taken Söderblom eleven years of enduring work and network building to arrive at this point. Leaders of very large portions of Christianity had finally assembled, acknowledged one another, worshiped together, and on the basis of their common faith, attempted together to contribute toward a world of justice and peace. After Stockholm, Christianity was no longer what it had been. It had received power and inspiration to go in the direction of unity, justice, and peace. Nathan Söderblom would always maintain that the Stockholm ecumenical meeting was the work of the Holy Spirit. Others would say that it also was his, for he had invited everyone to the conference and had led it. It was an expression, almost an extension of his personality. He was Stockholm 1925.

31

The Difficult Way Forward

> They belong to great kingdoms, families, associations, parties. I am just Nathan Söderblom, called to serve.
>
> *Nathan Söderblom, 1926*

ONE SEPTEMBER DAY IN 1927, *when the deep blue water of Lake Ladoga is surrounded by birch trees that are beginning to turn yellow, Nathan Söderblom arrives by the steamer* Pitkäranta *at the Valamo Monastery in Finnish Karelia. He visits the monastery's father confessor, the ascetic Efrem, who receives him with deep bows. After their conversation, they kneel beside one another in front of the royal doors of the iconostasis. In low voice they pray the Our Father together, the Orthodox monk in Russian, the Lutheran archbishop in Greek. They visit the small cell where the monk uses a casket with a skeleton drawn on the open lid for his bed. The walls are covered with pictures of holy men, the murdered Russian czar, the Finnish president. At the end of the sixteenth century, Swedish soldiers ravaged Valamo. Some eighty monks were killed. Now the ascetic and the archbishop separate with a kiss of peace and love. Both know that death will soon catch up with them. The monk prepares himself by leaving everything behind, the archbishop by using his time to the uttermost.*

* * *

On January 15, 1926, flags flew all over Uppsala. The archbishop was sixty. He had carried out his life's greatest task and was known all over the world like no other Swede of the time. The Stockholm Conference had been praised in every key. Journalists maintained that it was completely his accomplishment. He had put Sweden on the map. Without deserving it, the nation had gotten the name of Christian and the Swedes felt pride in their archbishop, even those who did not have much to do with the church. The criticism that surrounded his being named archbishop had long since disappeared and Söderblom was both admired and loved by the people. If anyone was to be honored it was he. The queue of those who would congratulate him on his birthday stretched out into the courtyard. From morning to late in the evening, one deputation after another filled the staircase up to the red salon where Söderblom received representatives of church commissions, learned academies, the Swedish-English Society, the Antiquities Association, and many other organizations he had had dealings with, as well as deans, professors, and politicians — all with the same warmth. The Telegraph Bureau had called in extra workers to expedite the thousand telegrams that came from all over the world. When the Gunilla bell up toward the castle chimed, student singers came with burning torches to sing for their old friend who "was an incarnation of the heart's and mind's youthfulness." This reminded him of how thirty years earlier he had himself given the jubilee speech to the poet, composer, and politician Gunnar Wennerberg and taken the student cap from a standard bearer and placed it on Wennerberg's head. "Stjärnorna tindra" ("The Stars Twinkle") and "Hör oss Svea" ("Hear Us, Sweden") were perhaps also sung on that occasion.

The bishops sent a message of congratulation handwritten on parchment by the famed calligrapher Berta Svensson-Pihl who also prepared the diplomas for the Nobel prizes. They gave thanks for what God "during times of suffering and division" had given to the evangelical Lutheran Church of Sweden and, indeed, to all of Christianity through the archbishop. After the Stockholm Conference even Bishop J. A. Eklund expressed admiration for him. Anders Sjöstedt, who was involved in the financing and organizing of the ecumenical conference, donated a large amount as a start-up grant for continuation work. The fund completely and without restrictions was to be controlled by Söderblom, and additional donations followed. Others also offered financial gifts since they knew that the archbishop was prone to spend more than he earned. A gold medal had been struck with his portrait on one side and the archbishop's palace on the other. Its Latin text read: "To the adornment of the fatherland and the church, the supporter of scholarship and art" and "He surrounds the world, the homeland, and the home with the same love in God." The provincial governor in Stockholm, Nils Edén — a liberal politician in whom Söderblom never had great confidence — expanded eloquently on the many-sidedness of the great archbishop and his ability to hold together science, art, and religion to the benefit of both church and state.

Some months had passed since the conclusion of the ecumenical conference. Söderblom was completely worn out. He needed rest, and he took that rest in the way in which he was accustomed: he worked at something else. He gave himself to parish visitations. He had neglected a number of these, so he set out traveling in the immediate time at hand. In twelve months he traveled to nineteen parishes to lead formal visitations, install rectors, rededicate churches, and deliver lectures. Even before all of the Stockholm delegates had traveled home, he was on the road again. Skepptuna was first on his list. There, while Adolf Deissmann was preaching in the imposing medieval church, Söderblom received word that Patriarch Photios had died in Zurich on his way back to Egypt. The reading of the Nicene Creed in the language of Plato and Paul in the Uppsala Cathedral had been his final official act. At that time, Söderblom in his inner eye had seen the whole history of the church come together in a living unity. Dogmas of the early church had met with difficult contemporary questions. Now the patriarch was dead. Söderblom was convinced that with his passing, God had sealed and sanctified the man's ecumenical work. When Photios spoke in Stockholm's Klara Church, he had turned toward the altar and prayed: "There is but one language: the love of Jesus. There is but one work: the love of Jesus. Take us into your love, Lord, that in that love we may work here in the world while it is still day, and at life's evening may we enter into your glory. Amen."

Skepptuna was the locale for the first memorial service. It was to be followed by many, for after the ecumenical conference it seemed that Photios belonged to all of Christianity. He certainly was not the most prominent of Orthodox patriarchs, but his presence at Stockholm had an enormous symbolic significance. Considering the reluctance of many Protestants to invite Orthodox and Catholics — and that would surely not have happened if Söderblom had not surprisingly brought Metropolitan Germanos into the picture — the twenty-two Orthodox delegates had a prominent place in the conference. This made it apparent that Life and Work from the very beginning had a genuine ecumenical character. This also made it possible for Anglicans and Old Catholics to participate without reservation. That the Roman Catholics chose to remain outside was regrettable but perhaps unavoidable.

In light of the later development of the ecumenical movement and how it marked the entirety of twentieth-century church history, one can understand the significance of the Stockholm Conference. From a short-term perspective it was more difficult to clearly see that significance, but many participants could agree with the words of Ludwig Ihmels: "We have looked into each other's hearts. Hereafter it can never again be as it was, before we learned to know each other." The American Presbyterian William Adams Brown spoke euphorically: "The most remarkable thing about the Stockholm conference was that it took place." Söderblom agreed, but he also felt a great need to understand what had actually happened. He immediately began to systematically review everything, analyzing the background to the event, characterizing the participants and their churches, gathering their comments, studying the many lectures, re-experiencing the worship, and thinking through everything that had occurred at the conference. He undertook this thorough evaluation so that both he and others would see how great and meaningful the event had been. The result was the most personal, lively, and far-reaching book he ever wrote. *Kristenhetens möte i Stockholm* (*Christianity's Conference in Stockholm*) was on the shelves of bookstores by 1926; the book was 964 pages long. In small snippets of time, between all his administrative responsibilities, university duties, travels, and family concerns, he organized the large body of material, made notes and reflections, and dictated it all. When a chapter was finished, he mailed it off immediately to the publisher so that type could be set in steps. It was a remarkable accomplishment. The book was selective in its content, subjective in its judgments, personal in its language, and written by the one who, more than any other person, was party to the enterprise. At least in Sweden, it carried more weight than the official report of the conference.

Söderblom asked himself if the conference had been only a dream or an optical illusion. He and all the others had experienced nothing less than a revelation of the church's inner unity in God. For a long time everything had seemed nearly impossible. Without his compelling sense of calling, his inventive diplomacy, and his unflagging will, the conference would never have taken place. He had, in spite of the objections of many and his own doubts, invested all of his strength in seeing that the meeting occurred. It was not just one of many projects; it was his life's work. Doors were opened, enemies became friends, the conversation began, and a church that transcended borders began to develop a concrete and stable structure. He himself was completely convinced that success could be reached only if the conference were gathered around the Savior where that unity could be found that relativized diversity and overcame divisions. In the final message of the conference were a few lines that Söderblom certainly drafted:

"Only as we become inwardly one shall we attain real unity of mind and spirit. The nearer we draw to the Crucified, the nearer we come to one another, in however varied colors the Light of the World may be reflected in our faith. Under the cross of Jesus Christ we reach out hands to one another. The Good Shepherd had to die in order that He might gather together the scattered children of God. In the Crucified and Risen Lord alone lies the hope of humanity."

This had been the consistent theme of the conference. Speaker after speaker had stopped at the cross as the place of reconciliation and the only possibility of salvation. It was like a revival meeting in childhood Hälsingland, but translated and applied to the entire shattered post-war world.

The Stockholm Conference was only a beginning. If it were to survive, ecumenism must take on institutional forms. Like every movement of revival, it needed a permanent organizational place of residence if it were not to dissipate. Söderblom had not called Christianity's leaders together only to share experiences with one another, but to build a permanent ecumenical council that could advance Christianity's cause in the world. That had been his goal ever since Oud Wassenaar. The question of such a council had been thrashed over in one of the commissions at Stockholm, but there had been no agreement. Some, like Söderblom, wanted to create a permanent structure; others were content with a continuation committee. The latter won the tussle, but that did not exclude the possibility of forming a council later. Söderblom was disappointed, but interpreted it, as he was accustomed to doing, all for the best. A representative committee was a good start. Yet again, he had to be patient. Instead of a council, he concentrated his efforts on creating an ecumenical institute for peace, social ethics, and labor laws.

Since the conference delegates had been appointed by their churches, the ecumenical movement had taken deep root and no longer consisted only of enthusiasts who appointed themselves and traveled from conference to conference at their own expense. Ecumenism had become a concern of the churches themselves. That Orthodox leaders had taken part changed the conference to something other and more than a gathering of like-minded people. In Stockholm, a spiritual and psychological climate was created that caused the participants to experience solidarity across confessional and national boundaries. Swedish hospitality and beautiful weather contributed to communication and understanding. On a couple of occasions, the conference came very close to treading on untouched minefields of French-German antagonism. Old doctrinal controversies also sprouted up. Nevertheless, the conference proceeded with no great crises. The fact that even conservative participants experienced it as a milestone in church history was a triumph for Söderblom. At times, some were reminded of the ecumenical council at Nicaea sixteen hundred years earlier, but that comparison was misleading since at Stockholm no ecumenical credo was formulated, nor were burning political conflicts solved. The king of Sweden, Gustaf V, stood wholeheartedly behind the conference but he was no Constantine the Great. The presence of the Swedish monarchy, which had been blessed by the church since the days of Archbishop Stefan but whose wings had been clipped by the farmers' march in 1914, was important symbolically, especially since the war had overturned so many other royal thrones. Crown Prince Gustaf Adolf was the one who made the most of the occasion. He spoke warmly of the churches' responsibility in the wounded world and took part day after day in everything that went on.

Criticism was not long in coming, however — not of the royal house's involvement, but that the conference confused religion and politics and was all too preoccupied with worldly questions. What did the German supreme court justice, the British foreign minister, or the American naval minister have to do with a conference of this kind? Why did so many heads of state and international organizations send telegrams wishing success and then follow closely all that was said? The Finnish Archbishop of Åbo, Gustav Johansson, was not alone in dismissing the conference as a violation of the church's faith and confession. His judgment was unforgivingly hard when he took his distance from Söderblom: "Our paths have parted so far from each other that they can no longer be united," he wrote. Criticism also came from liberal newspapers. One described the conference's content as "castrated socialism and watery gruel," another as a "harmless smörgåsbord." They had expected vociferous clashes of opinion and insoluble antagonism, but heard only modest thoughts and pious prayers.

The horizon of the conference really did not go beyond Europe and the United States. Only a handful of participants came from other continents. Leaders of the labor movement were not present, even though the life of workers and questions of social justice were high on the conference agenda. Issues of mission were left to the International Missionary Council, and questions of doctrine to Faith and Order. Nevertheless, the Stockholm Conference provided stimulation to the churches. If nineteenth-century church history was determined by evangelical awakenings, twentieth-century church history was to be characterized by the ecumenical movement and its social concerns.

After a year, the continuation committee met in Bern. It was so warm that the asphalt softened and heavy rainstorms forced people to take refuge under the arcades. Söderblom viewed multicultural Switzerland as a foretaste of a united Europe about which he had thought and spoken for so many years. Switzerland was also a stronghold for evangelical freedom, which the Counter Reformation had not succeeded in crushing. It was there that "the men from Stockholm" gathered. By this time, they knew each other well and many had become personal friends. Söderblom, using the money from his sixtieth birthday, generously invited all eighty participants to a great dinner and saw to it personally that the menu, placements, and other arrangements were the very best. In a trustful atmosphere, his guests shared memories of Stockholm with each other and evaluated their experiences. "Stockholm" was already a concept and it also became the name of the journal they started.

The committee approved the official reports, which, with small variations in content, were published in English, German, and French. From beginning to end, Söderblom had the meeting in his hands, but it deadlocked over the question of an ecumenical institute for social ethical questions. The debate over the purpose of such an institute was stormy. Should it give priority to formation of opinion, practical social work, or academic research? Where should it be located? Zurich, Geneva, or possibly Bern? Söderblom recommended the third alternative because of the fact that the Old Catholic Church had its theological center there. With its lively contacts with the Anglicans and Orthodox, that small church could be a significant bridge builder between differing traditions. The committee was reluctant; not until the next year in Winchester did they come to a decision. The institute was to be located in Geneva. It would, in spite of its financial fragility, become an embryo for the World Council of Churches. In 1930, the Ecumenical Council for Life and Work was formed. By that time it had been a decade since Söderblom had first made his proposal.

With Bishop George Bell of England at the helm, this Council navigated the storms of the 1930s and passed by the hidden rocks of Nazism. The culture-conditioned idealist and liberal theology that set the tone in Stockholm had been infiltrated by notions of racism and totalitarianism and thus no longer offered durable grounds for ecumenism. And Söderblom had left the scene.

The most serious challenge in Bern 1926 was *la Schuldfrage*, the question of guilt, which was avoided in Stockholm but had been referred to the continuation committee. That Germany was ascribed guilt for the Great War was still a bloody sore, but the issue had reached a new stage. The Pact of Locarno, October 1925, had brought a genuine relaxation of tensions. When it was agreed on, Söderblom, as the self-designated international politician he was, sent words of congratulation to the German and French foreign ministers. In Bern, a French–German working group was able, after all-night negotiations, to agree on a text that set aside the political aspects of the guilt question, concentrating instead on the border-transcending community of faith. When Wilfred Monod, tottering from exhaustion and emotion, made a proposal that the entire meeting supported, it was, according to Söderblom, "one of the finest hours in the history of our assembly." For seven years the question of guilt had cast its shadow over their work. Finally, it could be left behind. It was, as Söderblom put it, "heaved overboard."

Around the world, Söderblom was viewed at this time as the greatest Swedish European since St. Birgitta, Gustavus Adolphus, and Carl von Linné. He received one invitation after another to preach, lecture, and speak in academic and political contexts. When the League of Nations opened its annual session in Geneva on September 5, 1926, he preached in the Saint Pierre Cathedral. During the spring of that year a shameful and sad power game concerning seats on the League's council had taken place. In order for a place to be awarded to Germany, the Swedish foreign minister Östen Undén, who was among Söderblom's personal friends, declared Sweden's seat available. Söderblom was in favor of that but he did not look forward to preaching to a congregation that had been taken hostage by national interests and that he himself had called a "fallen angel." If only the League of Nations could stand for common and genuinely acknowledged truth! The international order of justice was a prolongation of God's order of creation and could not be compromised. He preached on "Le sel et la paix," "Salt and Peace." The salt of justification should not only provide taste, but also prevent rotting. He beat around the bush for a while before he dealt with the sensitive question of the struggle between member states. No selfish calculations, no matter how wise, could create peace, he said. Something else was required: the truth must gain recognition. Peace demanded incredible efforts. It was not possible to put together "egos" and think that it would become anything other than egoism. "Zero plus zero plus zero finally is nothing other than zero." He posed the question of whether or not the League of Nations was a corporation in which those who had shares sought only to satisfy their own demand for profit, or if the League was something new and higher and where the members acted as "servants of a common, generally acknowledged authority of truth and justice."

The sermon was transmitted by radio and received broad reactions. And Söderblom's perennial critic Torgny Segerstedt, now a journalist in Gothenburg, threw himself into it. He had written off the Stockholm Conference, which he regarded as lacking the nerve and conviction of Christianity. Now he rejected Söderblom's sermon as tame and completely harmless. Söderblom had, according to Segerstedt, said nothing more than was expected of him; no one had been wounded and everyone could agree. Perhaps there was something to Segerstedt's judgment. Söderblom had not been clear enough to make an impression on seasoned politicians. After the miserable spring session with all its bickering Segerstedt wished for a regular sermon of judgment that punished the League of Nations. He poured sarcasm over his old friend and irony over Sweden's naïve actions: "We are more honorable than other parties believe and more stupid than any of them have dreamed."

Söderblom most often was tolerant toward those who criticized him, but this time it was too much. He wrote a friendly letter to Segerstedt and asked him what he would have said if he had preached in Geneva. Would he have spoken in a way that would have resulted in his being stoned outside the cathedral or expelled from the country? He had many critics, he wrote, but "among those who readily and preferably in a poisonous way reject what I do and say, you come first because you are superior to all the others combined." But Söderblom did not feel sorry for himself. He had received many great and unmerited tributes of honor, but he also had to withstand more criticism than any other church leader. Since he had neither money nor power, he could be dealt with in any way. The only thing he could defend himself with was the truth as he understood it and as he could express it. The letter concluded with, "In unchanging friendship, yours sincerely Nathan." As detached as he was from Segerstedt's spiteful remarks, his own good will was equally genuine. Segerstedt understood that, for in his depths their friendship was still there. He wrote back, "Your letter genuinely moved me, and I am not one to be easily moved. It was kind of you, and by 'kind' I mean something very good. Here I sit in my reviewer's seat and watch the drama that is passing by on the stage. If I were free to decide for myself, I would certainly button my lips and quietly await the greater silence. But one must have something on hand. The work that is my diversion perhaps one-sidedly trains the critical faculty and creates an empty space around its practitioner. I get along well there but I also know that it feels warm and good when an open hand reaches out to me through the empty space." The nihilist in him could not really grasp the archbishop's certainty of belief and the critic in him was irritated that Söderblom remained so generous. He thus continued condescendingly and at a safe distance to criticize him for whatever he did. This hurt Anna. She never gave up her hope for a reconciliation between the two old friends.

Despite the fact that his vascular cramps were getting worse, Söderblom continued to travel at the same furious pace in both the archdiocese and on the continent, his two arenas. Even in purely secular contexts, he always had his clerical garb on and wherever he went he was prepared to give a sermon. Europe had become his parish. The children had to fend for themselves — "Putte," the youngest, was twelve during the summer of 1926. Anna traveled on as many of his trips as she could. With her elegant, somewhat reserved style and her linguistic gifts, she made a deep impression on those she encountered. She had become the ecumenical movement's "first lady" and in public circumstances she always spoke of her husband in the third person. When in December 1926 they spent eleven days together in Paris, the city of their youth, in order to visit the Swedish congregation and help celebrate its three hundredth jubilee, Söderblom lectured at the Sorbonne, met with the leadership of the French Academy, had discussions with the Protestant leaders, and visited both Alfred Loisy and Wilfred Monod in their homes. With the former foreign minister of Sweden Albert Ehrensvärd as their host, the Söderbloms had unforgettable days of theater, art, and music. The opposition of the Swedish bishops to the occupation of the Ruhr was forgotten, friendships were restored, and Söderblom with his French *esprit* stood at the center of things.

In 1927, Faith and Order held its first conference. It took place in Switzerland at the University of Lausanne, and with 394 delegates from 108 church bodies, it was to be compared to Stockholm, even though it was not marked by the same splendid hospitality. For many of the participants, it was the first time they had met Christians who had totally different views than theirs on matters such as the authority of the Bible, the basic confession of faith, and the nature of the church. The conference was disposed to misunderstanding and heated discussions, and it was nearly impossible to come to any common conclusions.

Söderblom participated loyally even as the founder of Faith and Order, the American Episcopal bishop Charles Brent, had in Stockholm. In practice there were at this point in time four parallel ecumenical movements: the International Missionary Council, the World Alliance for Promoting International Friendship through the Churches, Life and Work, and Faith and Order, not counting the YMCA, the YWCA, and the World Student Christian Federation. The movements overlapped and it was often the same people who participated in their meetings and conferences. Söderblom was not only a famed historian of religion, but also a knowledgeable and broadly interested though not systematic theologian. Long-drawn-out theological debates were not for him. He was too much a man of action to spend his time waiting for agreement on theological matters. Given the situation of the world, there was a need for haste in getting something practical accomplished. The theologians who came to Lausanne did not all think in that same way. Life and Work and Faith and Order, however, were mutually dependent on each other and Söderblom saw to it that that was included in one of the reports. After Lausanne he went even further, stating of the movements that "the question of their coming union, yes merger, not only in the intimate fellowship of the Spirit but also in external forms of work ought only to be a matter of time." He was correct. In 1937, the two movements decided together to form the World Council of Churches.

Söderblom had seen to it that the Swedish delegation to Lausanne was highly qualified. Three promising younger theologians — Gustaf Aulén, Yngve Brilioth, and Anders Nygren — were there, and also two theologians from the older generation, Otto Norberg and Magnus Pfannenstill. In addition, he had brought his most faithful coworkers: Herman Neander, who had invaluable contacts among the Orthodox, Harald Bildt, who was ambassador in Cairo and who steadily reported on the church situation in the Middle East, the always helpful Major Anders Sjöstedt, and Paul Sandegren who, after his missionary service in India, had become Söderblom's secretary. Söderblom probably hoped that Sweden could keep the initiative in the entire ecumenical movement, but Lausanne defied his efforts and in the end, turned out as a failure for him.

The conference was tense and difficult to manage. The purpose of the event had never been made completely clear. Some of the Americans expected agreement on a plan for a united church, something others absolutely could not conceive of. Indians and Chinese, who hoped that the missionaries would display unity, were impatient and disappointed. Old-fashioned Orthodox bishops and self-confident Lutheran professors put the brakes on things. Söderblom did not really know what positions he should take. His distinction between institution and spirit did not elicit much response, and his loose references to "evangelical catholicity" were questioned by those who read into the concept a relativization of apostolic succession. Toward the end of the conference, one church family after another made its own independent statement. That showed how deeply divided the churches were.

Söderblom preached at the opening service of worship and also led the section that dealt with "The unity of Christendom and the Relation thereto of Existing Churches." If there was uncertainty as to what the conference should achieve, he did not clarify matters with his actions. He gave a long address on how concrete unity could be realized, but disregarded his text, which had been distributed and on which many were dependent, and spoke extemporaneously. At length and retrospectively, he reviewed the Reformation history of the Church of Sweden and how it maintained an unbroken succession of consecration "which was stronger and more faithful in its continuity with the medieval church than any other non-Roman part of Western Christianity." He referred to Stockholm and declared that Christian unity above all could be realized in works of love and devotion of the heart and not in the churches' doctrine or organization. Unity in its depths was spiritual, invisible, and independent of external orders, rites, teachings, and confessions. The outer "body" was simply a means for unity in faith. Thus, there was no sense in speculating on how a united church should be organized before there was mutual sharing of the eucharist.

These words were an implicit criticism of those who had not participated in the Reformed service of Communion that took place the previous day.

Some may have interpreted Söderblom as calling into question the entire work of Faith and Order. For it was the relationship among the church's faith, its external order, and unity which was Faith and Order's thoroughgoing concern. For a long time Söderblom had consistently built his view of the church on a distinction between the church's body and soul. At Lausanne, he offered three different ways of seeing these relationships. One could emphasize the institutional. The Roman Catholic Church, the more dogmatic Lutherans, and the high church Anglicans were positive about this, but it was something that the Churches of Sweden and England had relegated to the background with their agreement concerning eucharistic fellowship five years earlier. One could also go in the opposite direction and give preeminence to the inner life and deny the value of the institution as such. Communions that went this way lost both consistency and continuity and were at the mercy of the leadership of the moment. But if Söderblom were forced to choose between these two views, he would have, in spite of everything, preferred the second. His own position, which he held to be genuinely Lutheran, was a third view. It was based on the understanding that faith was central but that the institution was indispensable for faith to mature and bear fruit. For the true unity of the church, no other conditions were necessary than that the gospel is purely proclaimed and the sacraments rightly administered. This view, which was based on the Augsburg Confession, left space for the high regard for the ministry and liturgy that characterized the Church of Sweden, but rejected the idea that external orders were necessary for salvation; such ideas were all created by humans. Unity must be a unity in diversity. To demand uniformity was tantamount to limiting the freedom of the Spirit and to oppressing humans. This had always been Söderblom's line.

When he defended each church's freedom "in regard to interpretations about sacramental grace and ministerial order and authority" the socially engaged, intellectually gifted, and high church English bishop Charles Gore mounted a counterattack and the report from Söderblom's working group was entirely repudiated. Things were at a stalemate. The Swedish theologians worked day and night to find acceptable formulations that could save face for Söderblom. It was not simply that his formulations in the report gave rise to opposition. He had also gathered the Lutheran delegates around an independent statement that opposed premature adoption of any position concerning the form of a future united church. The intent was to prevent the Lutheran delegation from being run over roughshod by the Anglo-Saxon majority. The result was virtual chaos. Finally, the matter was dealt with in a way not uncommon in ecumenical contexts: the conference chose to "receive" the report on Christian unity in order to return to it at a later occasion. By then Söderblom had left for home.

He was noticeably tired and more than a little resigned. Problems piled up. Life and Work could not find its form, the ecumenical institute did not receive the financial support it needed, the paper *Stockholm* had to be discontinued after a few editions, the Americans began to lose interest in European questions, and Faith and Order proved to be as sluggish and dominated by American Episcopalians as he had feared. And he had no more than arrived home before Pope Pius XI, with unexpected force, struck hard against everything the ecumenical movement stood for.

32

The Pope in Conflict with the Swedish Archbishop

> To the same degree that a genuine sense of communion is growing in Christianity, it becomes disastrous for Rome to stand outside. It is coming more evidently to stand out as a "sect" beyond the others.
>
> *Nathan Söderblom, 1925*

On his way home from the Orient, Herman Neander stops in Rome where a Jubilee Year is being celebrated. To his astonishment, Pope Pius XI receives him in a private audience and questions him closely about his meetings with Orthodox church leaders. Neander willingly shares his knowledge, but he is not especially impressed with the Holy Father. The meeting gives rise to the rumor that the Swedish priest, who stands so close to Söderblom, intends to convert. On December 9, 1925, he is called to the archbishop. Söderblom points to a Bavarian newspaper where there is a detailed discussion of the Swedish pastor's intentions and the potential consequences of his crossing over to the Catholic Church. "What do you say about that?" asks the archbishop, a bit irritated. "Yes, what shall I say?" answers the bewildered Neander. "You will not allow me to become a Bolshevik, nor a Roman Catholic," he says. The archbishop responds with a gleam in his eye, "You may be a Bolshevik, but not a Roman Catholic."

* * *

Ever since he lived in Paris, Nathan Söderblom had followed developments in the Roman Catholic Church. It was not only a religion, but a world view with clear political goals. It stood in sharp contrast to the liberal ideology on which modern society was built and was in principle antidemocratic. Söderblom's picture of Catholicism had been formed by its unrelenting battle against modernism. His contacts with "ordinary" Catholics were limited, but he was careful to distinguish between the Roman Church's unacceptable hierarchical structure and what was in many ways the exemplary piety of ordinary Catholics. He had done what he could to have Catholics participate in his planned peace conference in 1918, but the Vatican Secretary of State Cardinal Pietro Gasparri had rejected the invitation. Yet things were not entirely hopeless. A delegation from the American Episcopal Church was warmly received by the pope in 1919, and in England Catholics had taken part in preparations for the 1924 ecumenical conference in Birmingham, although they ultimately withdrew. Söderblom hoped against hope that the Roman Catholic Church would send delegates to Stockholm in 1925, but no one came, nor did they come to the Faith and Order conference in Lausanne. Relations between the Catholic Church and other Christian communions were, for all intents and purposes, completely frozen. At the same time, the Protestants also felt exposed to an orchestrated mission offensive on the part of the Catholics.

A discussion of this Catholic campaign surged in the Swedish press. But the fears of "catholicizing tendencies" within the Church of Sweden itself were greater than any dread of Catholic breakthroughs. Debates about the use of vestments, the sign of the cross, kneeling, and processions seemed never to go away. Priests whose behavior was "too catholic" were reported to Diocesan Chapters, something that was reported by the local press. Theologians such as Gustaf Aulén and Yngve Brilioth attempted to tone down the anti-Catholic atmosphere. Both were sympathetic — but not uncritically — to the British high church movement and both were of the view that the Church of Sweden was threatened more by its own spiritual weakness than by Catholicism. The Swedish Association of Priests, with Sam Stadener in the lead, campaigned for a confessionalistic Lutheranism and against all efforts toward a eucharistic-centered liturgical renewal. Every positive evaluation of the Roman Catholic Church was excluded. The debate reached its culmination in 1923 when Cardinal Willem Marinus van Rossum visited the Catholic outposts in the North. He was responsible for the missionary work of Propaganda Fide in the Western world and entertained exaggerated hopes that the Nordic Lutherans would return to the mother church. His aggressive and triumphal appearances were provocative and his reports on the ecclesiastical situation contained so much misinformation that the Lutheran clergy were forced to protest. Söderblom shared Aulén's and Brilioth's judgments and urged the evangelical church to see to its own house rather than indulge in polemics. He did not expect Rome to acknowledge either his definition of catholicity or that he was a "proper" bishop. In two letters to Prince Carl he gave vent to his feelings. In 1926, he wrote: "One should never expect accommodation from Rome. If Rome or its leaders is questioned about something, one must always expect a negative reply. As soon as the possibility appears for Rome to fulfill its expectations, it consistently makes the most of the situation." A year later, he wrote: "I admire and respect many Catholics. But, unfortunately, we must here in the land of Gustavus Adolphus as well as throughout the world keep our eyes open for the action now being organized by Rome; its like has not been seen since the days of the Thirty Years War."

The encyclical of Pius XI, *De vera religionis unitate fovenda*, or "On Fostering True Religious Union," was promulgated on Epiphany 1928. As is common, it was given a shorter name following its introductory words, *Mortalium animos*. The encyclical was obviously directed against the World Alliance for Promoting International Friendship through the Churches, Life and Work, and Faith and Order. Söderblom was engaged in all three of these movements and thus was clearly one of the encyclical's foremost addressees. It was aimed at those who seek a "fraternal agreement on certain points of doctrine which will form a common basis of the spiritual life." With that intention, a number of large conferences and meetings had taken place to which all without distinction were welcome — faithful of all sorts, but also people who denied Christ and his divinity. This could not be approved by the Roman Catholic Church. The encyclical offered no compromise. The view that all religions in their various forms of expression were acceptable was not only misleading. It distorted the truth of Christianity and led step-by-step to naturalism and atheism. The pope judged everyone alike: interchurch conferences and various interreligious initiatives, which were frequent at the time. To encourage ecumenical and interreligious activities was tantamount to rejecting the religion revealed by God. But it was easy to be blinded by the good intentions of the ecumenical movement. Was it not proper that those who called on the name of Christ also show unity and love and abstain from mutual accusations? Certainly, but not at the cost of the Catholic faith.

The encyclical repeated the claim of the Roman Catholic Church to be the one true church. Since Protestant communions viewed it as one church among others, it was surely obvious that the Holy See could not participate in their conferences. No Catholic could encourage or support such enterprises. That would be to establish a false Christianity, totally alien to the church of Christ. It was essential to hold to established dogmas since they were based on the authority of Christ, as exercised by his earthly deputy. The dogma of the immaculate conception should be embraced with the same sincerity as the mystery of the Holy Trinity, and the teaching of papal infallibility was comparable to that of the incarnation. If Protestants wish to further the cause of Christian unity there is only one way: to return to the one true church of Christ from which they once fell away. Therefore the straying were encouraged to come home again. The encyclical concluded with a passionate exhortation to call on the blessed Virgin Mary, the divine mother of grace who overcomes all errors, and a prayer that the day might soon come when all humans are united by the Spirit in the bond of peace.

Christians outside the Catholic Church had long understood that they could not expect anything else, but the reactions were filled with disappointment and bitterness. The leaders of both Life and Work and Faith and Order reflected over the possibility of defending their movements but chose to keep silent. Yet a number of individual evangelical church leaders did speak, Söderblom receiving the most attention. Within six weeks he wrote no fewer than seven critical articles in *Svenska Dagbladet, Stockholms-Tidningen, Nya Daglig Allehanda,* and *Vår Lösen.* They were distributed widely, translated into a number of languages, and published in German in a booklet of over one hundred pages, *Christliche Einheit!* (*Christian Unity!*). Söderblom viewed the encyclical as being a caricature of the ecumenical movement and was astounded that it did not distinguish between faith as assent to doctrine and trust, nor did it clarify the relationship between truth and love. Even if there are differences in church teaching, the churches should not be prevented from working together for the betterment of humanity.

What Söderblom thus described was the "hierarchy of truths," which was first established at the Second Vatican Council in the 1960s. Pius XI did not distinguish between the great and the small. For him, the entire Roman system was like an ingenious mechanism in which not a single bolt or pin could be removed without everything being thrown out of order. If one screw came loose, the entire apparatus was in danger. Söderblom described this as an essential difference between "catholic" and "evangelical." The issue concerned a quantitative or qualitative interpretation of faith, a distinction between primary and secondary. To stubbornly equate the dogma of papal infallibility with the teaching of salvation through Christ was completely unacceptable. To pit Stockholm against Rome and claim that the encyclical was the most important document sent by the pope to the church in decades was remarkable and could be explained only by the apprehension within the Roman Church over the fact that the thought of Christian unity was asserting itself even within its own ranks. Söderblom did not give high marks to the pope's encyclical. "It is an embarrassing obligation to scrutinize what he has to say to his own people about us. It is a comfort to pass over to an agenda of positive work," he concluded in an article in *Vår Lösen.*

That comfort did not last long. In 1929, a Catholic professor in Munich, the Jesuit Max Pribilla, published *Um kirchliche Einheit. Stockholm–Lausanne–Freiburg* (*On Church Unity. Stockholm–Lausanne–Freiburg*). This was a commentary on the encyclical, milder in tone and more detailed, but following the same line as the pope. Pribilla was well informed. He was one of the editors of the influential journal *Stimmen der Zeit* and had taken seriously what had happened in Stockholm and Lausanne through contact with none other than Herman Neander. Pribilla had read of the papal audience in the same Bavarian newspaper as Söderblom and turned directly to Neander. After correspondence, they met at a Benedictine monastery in the Black Forest and had many conversations regarding Söderblom. Pribilla had heard of a lecture that Söderblom had once given in Munich, which garnered attention because of its penetrating analysis of the founder of the Jesuit Order, Ignatius Loyola. Now he had the opportunity to learn, from a Swedish rector who was both close to Söderblom and had had personal experience working with Catholic priests in Russian prison camps, all he wanted to know about the Swedish archbishop and his attitude toward the Roman Catholic Church. Neander and Pribilla had contact with each other for many years, but it is uncertain how much Söderblom knew of this.

It was not surprising that Pribilla was so well informed. He had especially noticed the apparent contradiction in that Söderblom judged the power position of the pope symbolized by the tiara even as he himself loved the miter and crozier. Even if Pribilla had not fully grasped the substance of "evangelical catholicity," Söderblom took seriously the Jesuit father's sharp criticism and seized the opportunity to defend himself.

In 1931, he published a one hundred page *apologia* for ecumenical work, *Pater Max Pribilla und die ökumenische Erweckung* (*Father Max Pribilla and the Ecumenical Awakening*). Pribilla replied, but by then Söderblom had already died.

When *Mortalium animos* was promulgated, nearly two decades had passed since Söderblom had observed Holy Week in Rome. He had been deeply impressed by what was serious in Roman Catholic piety and since then had always made a distinction between the Roman Church's monarchical structure and its genuine religious devotion. Söderblom carried home many of his experiences and translated them to worship during Holy Week in the Uppsala Cathedral, worship that was quite unique in Sweden. For him, Good Friday was the highest day in the church year while Easter occupied a more subdued place. Year after year, he himself led Good Friday worship, preaching on the history of Christ's suffering. He gathered his meditative sermons and published them in 1928 as an exposition of the entire passion history. *Kristi pinas historia* (*The History of Christ's Suffering*) was part of his spiritual testament. Simultaneous to his involvement in disputes with the Catholic Church and especially with the pope, he devoted himself to editing a large collection of texts for the inner life for which he had received great inspiration in Rome.

The cross was central to Söderblom's spirituality and theology. It is not difficult to see the line from the gentle pietism of his childhood and his conversion in 1889. Every year he had read of Jesus's suffering as it was described in the four Gospels. In *Kristi pinas historia* he wove together the different versions of the Synoptic Gospels with that of John. The attentive reader cannot avoid seeing that he valued John's Gospel more highly than the others. He reworked the course of events up to Jesus's crucifixion as an ancient drama in six acts. The *peripeteia* — the turning point — came when Jesus was interrogated and events then led inexorably to the cross. Söderblom wrote a tight, coherent text, commented on events, and inserted here and there his own memories and experiences. In a few places he offered comparisons from the history of religions, especially in connection with the long narrative concerning the eucharist, which he compared with ancient mystery meals. He had, as all theologians before him, a difficult time finding an adequate concept for explaining the presence of Christ in the eucharist; instead, he chose pastorally to guide doubtful people, encouraging them to freely take part in the sacrament even if they did not understand everything. "Fortunately a soul in need can be helped by the Savior without having to be capable of understanding the mysteries of the Savior's person and his work of salvation," he wrote in consolation both to himself and others. He had been impressed by Yngve Brilioth's great book of 1926, which in 1930 appeared in English in a somewhat revised form, *Eucharistic Faith and Practice Evangelical and Catholic*, but in Söderblom's own exposition, the elements of praise and thanksgiving in the sacrament — which were to become characteristic of eucharistic theology even in Sweden — were nearly completely missing. For him, Holy Communion was a meal of remembrance and fellowship that was still only occasionally celebrated. It symbolized God's communion with humanity and was an active sign that brought about participation in the forgiveness of sins. Virtually never did Söderblom use sacramental language for this. For him, the eucharist was finally nothing more than a support for weak faith and an act of worship, an encounter with the love that seeks out humans.

Every section of *Kristi pinas historia* concluded with a hymn. When he wrote of the woman in Bethany who anointed Jesus's feet with expensive nard and the disciples said that the money should be used to aid the poor, Söderblom found no suitable hymn. When the book was published, it included an anonymous verse that Söderblom himself had written:

> The vessel burst and fragrant oil is pouring!
> Its scent is reaching to the ends of earth.
> Your soul of heavenly perfume now surrounded
> Is blest and lifted up from dust and dirt.
>
> May vessels burst, with costly perfume streaming!
> Don't hesitate. Prepare your soul for feast.
> What joyous splendor! May your love be giving
> Its greatest gift to Him, your honored guest.

This was, according to Emil Liedgren, authentically existential poetry. Söderblom's life had been "distilled to one solitary and clear drop of balm, fragrant with the blessedness of self-sacrifice" and was caught in the words "what joyous splendor!"

Söderblom constantly deepened himself in the drama of the passion, a drama that concretely, with rich details, and inscrutable depth, illuminated humanity's condition in an unsurpassed way. The passion history had various meanings and was interpreted in different ways. After having studied every aspect of the narrative academically and preaching over every element in it, Söderblom concluded that music interpreted the breadth and intensity of the history of the passion better than words could. Bach, in the *St. Matthew Passion* and the *B-Minor Mass*, peered like no one else into the mystery of suffering and reconciliation. But he was not the only one. Söderblom loved to sing the Good Friday "Reproaches" (Latin, *Improperia*). If, during the church year, the liturgy stood on ordinary Sundays as a protection against subjective preaching, so faith's most fragile confession was protected on Good Friday by these Reproaches. They were poetry that had its origin with the prophet Micah and then grew through the centuries. The Reproaches struck hard with the question: "O my people, what have I done to you? In what have I wearied you? Answer me!" In the Orthodox Trisagion, everything hidden in the life of humans is brought forth to God in changing triplets with an even rhythm: "Holy God, Holy and strong, Holy and immortal, have mercy upon us!" Söderblom saw to it that these words in elemental musical form were incorporated into the Good Friday liturgy. He himself sang, articulately, nearly speaking, so that the message would reach the congregation. The music of the church was for the sake of the word, not the word for the sake of the music. That "my people" in this text referred to all humanity, to the Roman Empire and to every individual person was for him self-evident; to think that it was an accusation against the Jews never occurred to him.

In *Kristi pinas historia,* he inserted a brief additional section, 18 of the 465 pages. It dealt with the resurrection of Christ. If the crucifixion had occurred on "the world's public square," so the resurrection had only a few chosen witnesses. What they were witnesses to was not a concrete external event but rather a revelation of Christ similar to what Paul experienced on the Damascus Road. One must, like Paul, understand that the resurrection was not physical but spiritual. But even though the resurrection belonged to the categories of faith, he spoke of it as a fact of world history. He did this not because anyone knew how the resurrection happened, but because the disciples' experience of encounter with the Risen One had such immeasurable historic consequences. For an event to be counted as an historic fact, it must discernibly have affected the course of history. Nothing in human history has done that more than the resurrection of Christ. Söderblom did not refer to the empty tomb as an argument for the truth of the resurrection and he rejected all theories of a stolen body, exchange of bodies, or apparent death. Faith in the resurrection is built solely on the experience of the disciples. They had met the Resurrected One in a spiritual form and it had changed their hearts. "That which lives, that is the spirit. God is spirit. In him our spirit lives, if it really is alive" was Söderblom's summation.

The book was widely circulated as a devotional book and it went through several editions, most recently in 1965. It touched on aspects of Söderblom's Christology, his view of the eucharist, and his understanding of salvation, but it was not a systematic overview of his theology. For his old adversary in Åbo, Gustav Johansson, however, the short additional section concerning the resurrection provided more than enough evidence to show that Söderblom denied the bodily resurrection of Christ and was thus a heretic. Söderblom was explicitly asked not to participate when the cathedral in Åbo celebrated its seven hundredth jubilee in 1929. Johansson wrote to him: "It was natural for the Archbishop of Uppsala to be invited. But Brother's conduct makes that impossible. Several among Brother's actions have grieved us." Söderblom had planned to call together the Nordic bishops' conference in connection with the jubilee, but under the circumstances, the celebration became an exclusively Finnish affair. Since Johansson wanted nothing to do with him, he instead sent congratulatory telegrams to the president of Finland and to the city of Åbo. When Johansson died the next year, Söderblom nevertheless in a telegram of condolence expressed his gratitude "for the venerable archbishop's blessedly long, convinced, zealous, and mentally animated and richly blessed work in his office."

The history of Christ's suffering was enacted in Jerusalem. Söderblom described with considerable precision the streets and alleys, the steep way through the Kidron valley up to Gethsemane, the Antonia Fortress, and Golgotha. But he himself had never visited the place. While he was working on his book, the International Missionary Council, the third and oldest branch of the ecumenical movement, planned a world conference in Jerusalem. Söderblom, who was not only the grand old man of ecumenism but also chairperson of the Church of Sweden Mission, was naturally invited to participate and he looked forward to that. He carefully prepared his lecture in advance. Ambassador Harald Bildt in Cairo attempted to convince him not to be in such a rush this time. In "the home of leisure and meditation" one could not accomplish anything new if one did not take time. Bildt informed the Swedes who had settled in Jerusalem that the archbishop was perhaps on the way and he hoped very much that his journey would include

Cairo. Already in the fall of 1926 he had attempted to entice Söderblom to the Middle East by inviting him on a six-week trip and promising to be his personal guide. At that point there was not enough time for such a journey, but now the possibilities were more encouraging. Johannes Kolmodin took it upon himself to plan Söderblom's trip down to the most minute detail. It should — in five days — bring him by train from Istanbul through Anatolia and Iconium to Aleppo and further on to Tripoli, Haifa, and Jerusalem. But even though this was an attractive adventure, Söderblom was forced to remain at home. His heart problems had become worse and his doctor warned him strongly against strenuous travels. How sick he was is evident from an uncommonly self-revealing set of cryptic notes: "Heart bathes in agony. It struggles to reach the firm shore. Convulsive swings of the will's tired arms. But that which seemed to be shore was a misty zone, mercifully inclined to hide the stretch of anxiety from the eye. Will the anxiety drown me? Will I sink to the bottom without having sensed God's terra firma beneath me? Perhaps it is intended that we should be kept afloat. Only when this is past do we reach the shore. But the agony in my fluttering mind gives me no rest to see. I make out a floating buoy. My swimming comes to an end. I may rest in the confidence of prayer, a buoy. It holds me up over 8,000 fathoms of water. Anxiety's ocean. Look up to the stars."

33

In Weakness, Strong

A supranational order of justice is being built. Binding treaties between states, which are committed to mediation or arbitration rather than warring over mutual disputes, constitute the first steps in constructing an edifice of greater justice. What we commend is obedience to Christ and the apostles' rule of subjection to the authorities. But we do not limit the horizon to our own nation.

Nathan Söderblom, 1930

AFTER THIRTY-THREE YEARS, *the remains of the North Pole explorers Salomon August Andrée, Nils Strindberg, and Knut Frænkel were found on the nearly inaccessible White Island in the Barents Sea, 80.15° N., 32.59° E. On St. Michael's day, October 5, 1930, their catafalques are carried through Stockholm on horse-drawn wagons in pouring rain. The funeral service is held in Storkyrkan. Nathan Söderblom speaks: "You do not utter words, but in the document you left behind, the condition in which you were found, you speak silently but clearly to the world: We have struggled and endured to the end. Our calculations burst asunder. Our hopes came to nothing. But we did not give in to mute complaint. We did what we could, we continued our exploration. We remained faithful to our calling to the end." The nineteenth century sense of manly adventure is hailed. It is as though he speaks to himself. He concludes his funeral address: "When our turning globe after millions of years perhaps silently reports the frozen saga of humanity to speechless worlds, shall then the ending of the last humans be as honorable as yours? All that is mortal is but a parable. From the parable reality comes forth. The veil falls. The Spirit lives. Jesus said: For God all are alive."*

* * *

Those who report on Nathan Söderblom easily forget the common for the uncommon. His days, like everyone's, were filled with routine tasks, normal business, and, not seldom, difficult family worries. Hardest of all was the news in 1929 of his oldest son Helge's becoming hopelessly ill in Paris. The pain and sadness broke out in a talk at a rector's installation in Gamla Uppsala on Midsummer Day: "Is there any meaning in it all, or is life mere chance, or a hard, unavoidable necessity emanating from dead causes? The one who experiences life's distress can simply greet decay as liberation. It can be a comfort to hope for the end, when the drama with its grimness and meaninglessness come to an end. Ah, believe me, life — that is hard, but it is good to die. Bitterness at life's brevity and death's certainty, bitterness in suffering and grief lies not in death which threatens, but in sin which accuses: What have we left undone? What have we done wrong?" Helge died two years later.

Söderblom felt that time had begun to run out on him. His illness was painful and it became more difficult to undertake all that he wanted to and all that he had to do. He thought of his relations in Hälsingland where his ancestors had been buried ever since the Iron Age, and his father was especially often in his thoughts. But there was so much else that laid claim to him. One year it was the dedication of a statue of Gustav II Adolf at the university in Tartu, another the homecoming from the Ukraine of residents of the Swedish village there, a third year it was the burial of the Queen of Sweden, Victoria. In the summer of 1929, his doctor forbade him to remain in Uppsala where so much was expected of him. He required complete rest and so he took refuge with his friends Wera and Fredrik von Essen at Salsta, their castle in Vattholma about twenty miles north of Uppsala. They had many times urged him to take a breather from his daily labors and they now received him with open arms.

In 1930, it had been eleven hundred years since the Benedictine monk Ansgar came to the marketplace of Birka on the island of Björkö in Lake Mäleren, sent by the Frankish King Louis the Pious and welcomed by the King of the Swedes Björn Ironside. On Midsummer Day, Nathan Söderblom dedicated the Ansgar Chapel on Björkö. A commander in the Salvation Army in 1919 had suggested that it be built. Söderblom raised the funds and with the help of a famous architect and well-known artists, it was built. The long procession from the shore to the chapel included King Gustaf V and all of the Nordic bishops followed by hundreds of pilgrims. The archbishop knocked on the copper doors with his crozier. The bell-shaped space opened in toward the high choir and out toward the island's low hills. Once again Söderblom in stone and art had made manifest that the church was universal and open to the entire world. The gospel belonged to everyone. Christianity was the soul of the Royal Kingdom of Sweden. More than forty years earlier, Söderblom had published his first article. It dealt with Ansgar. The circle was beginning to close.

The previous autumn, in 1929, the bishops made a common attempt to change the relation of the church to the state. After Arthur Engberg's

Dedication of the Ansgar Chapel on Björkö, Midsummer Day 1930. Sweden's two best-known people, representing the earthly and spiritual realms, King Gustaf V and Archbishop Nathan Söderblom, meet under God's heaven.

political maneuver in 1918 and the debate that followed, the question smoldered. Engberg had proposed that the General Synod should be abolished and the church's property be taken over by the state. If that happened, the state church would be an accomplished fact and the state alone would be in a position to determine its demise. The bishops regarded the threat of a totally controlled state church as worse than a divorce with self-governance and property retained. They were supported by strong popular opinion when they argued for greater freedom for the church. That required that the church be modernized and that whoever wished could freely leave the church. Yngve Brilioth, who was then a professor at Åbo, had good knowledge of how the Finnish church was organized; it had greater freedom than the Church of Sweden. He conferred with Söderblom about the matter and proposed that the bishops together should move in the General Synod for a higher degree of self-governance. When the question came up in the Bishops' Assembly, the groundwork was already prepared. The archbishop instructed the indecisive Billing, together with Edvard Rodhe and Sam Stadener, to prepare a draft of such a motion. The bishops were not totally united, but Söderblom forced the issue. He also wanted the General Church Assembly to take action in the same direction, but Billing would not cooperate and some of the other bishops stayed away from the meeting, protesting that Söderblom was using the Assembly for the building of church political opinion. Arthur Engberg, of course, was totally against the right of people to freely give up church membership; that would be to acknowledge the independence of the church. Most politicians viewed the church more as an element in the apparatus of the state than as a Christian community of faith, but among church people, there were not many who opposed free resignation from church membership. Since the requirement of church burial had been given up in 1925, all compulsions in regard to ritual had come to an end. To be consistent, membership in the church should be a matter of free choice.

The three bishops grappled with the preparation of a motion. Fortunately, they came to an agreement and in spite of tensions in the bishops' collegium the others also came along. As things were, everyone saw both that the traditional division of labor between church and state no longer functioned and that the church must adapt to modern times. For Söderblom this meant that the Boström idea that the church was a dimension of the state's life had to be given up once and for all. The basic question was whether the Church of Sweden was to be a Christian church in a more qualified sense or a general religious institution supported by taxation and regulated by the state. In light of the tumult of the war and the Russian Revolution and after his encounter with the American churches, Söderblom had begun to lose his belief in the excellence of the Swedish state church model. The common responsibility of the churches for a more secure world required them to be lords in their own houses.

The motion was formulated on the basis of a long discussion concerning the folk church being rooted in the gospel and how the folk church could best take part in the ongoing construction of a welfare state. The bishops insisted that the Synod should clarify its fundamental understanding of the "religiously motivated folk church" as the starting point for necessary reform. This implied strengthening the church as a community of faith and removing whatever concealed the gospel as a free gift. The church must become more of a popular movement and less authoritarian, but it should continue to be financed by taxation and regulated by law. Otherwise it ran the risk of being reduced to an association for the religiously like-minded.

The General Synod, which was still made up of a group of older and, for the most part, very conservative men from rural areas, surprisingly passed the bishops' motion without change. It was Einar Billing's ecclesiology that permeated the motion, although Söderblom had seen that it was written, presented, and approved. By then he had not only won greater authority in the Synod, he had also learned how to create opinion in the media society that was then being born. He had nearly undivided support for whatever he undertook in the leading newspapers, *Svenska Dagbladet*, *Dagens Nyheter*, and *Stockholms-Tidningen*. National broadcasting, which began with a New Year's Day service of worship in 1925, sent out programs for a few hours every evening and a half-hour at midday. Söderblom's voice was well known in that new medium. The other bishops were completely overshadowed by him. When he had made up his mind about something, things as a rule went as he desired. Now, after thirty years, the Young Church Movement's heirs had their understanding of the church confirmed by the Synod. It involved a synthesis between church and culture but was set free of its nationalistic ballast. The Synod, however, could not act to change the church's organization; only the Parliament and government could do that. When Bishop Sam Stadener, who had become one of Söderblom's adversaries, was appointed Minister of Ecclesiastical Affairs in 1930, he chose to ignore the bishops' program at all points save one: the church's right to its own property. Thus, the bishops' motion became no more than an empty gesture. Not until the latter part of the 1990s were large elements of the bishops' motion of 1929 carried out.

When Söderblom became archbishop in 1914, nearly all Protestant and Orthodox churches in Europe were still national state churches. The exception was France where a divorce had taken place under dramatic circumstances in 1905. In countries like Spain and Italy, the Roman Catholic Church had a strong grip on the population and still had control over both moral and civil law. The war and revolutions turned things upside down; only the Nordic and Anglican churches remained intact. To mobilize the churches, which were so interlaced with national interests, to common efforts for peace had proven to be well-nigh impossible. The distinction between their "body," which was determined by culture and history, and their "soul," which was determined by the common Christian tradition, had been a presupposition for Söderblom's ecumenical work. Only if the churches gave priority to their "soul" and allowed themselves to be guided by the gospel and not by the interests of national states could they be agents for peace. If the state church system were broken up, the ecumenical presuppositions would be changed and the churches would be freer to shape their own positions and act independently.

The theological presuppositions had also begun to change. On the continent, Karl Barth had considerable impact with his sharp distinction between culture and gospel. In Sweden, the Lund theologians Gustaf Aulén and Anders Nygren, using the method of "motif research," emphasized the "genuine" Christianity, which orthodox, pietistic, and liberal theologies had compromised. When Aulén gave the Olaus Petri Lectures in Uppsala in 1930 under the title "The Christian Idea of the Atonement," he did not emphasize the cross and vicarious suffering as Söderblom always did, but rather, he emphasized the resurrection and Christ's victory over destructive powers. The lectures were published in English under the title *Christus Victor*. They set a line of division between culture-conditioned Protestantism and the opposition to foreign ideologies characteristic of the 1930s.

Söderblom read the signs of the times. It was the occasion to make the Christian alternative more distinct. It was not, however, an easy thing to get the other Swedish bishops on his side. Many of them were stuck with their old valuations and were irritated at his working style, especially at his way of creating public opinion, which in the old state church would be viewed as populism. When he again brought up the question of peace and, moreover, sharpened his tone, they refused to follow along.

Ever since he sent out his appeal for peace in 1914 it had been his great concern that peace be based on an international order of justice and maintained by arbitration. In autumn 1925, Germany, Belgium, France, Great Britain, and Italy, through the Locarno Pact, pledged mutually to guarantee peace in Europe. That set in motion a number of nongovernmental initiatives to strengthen peace and make war unlawful. In Sweden, many groups, especially within the Social Democratic Party, began to propagate for unilateral and total disarmament. When the Stockholm Conference continuation committee reached agreement regarding the question of war guilt in 1926, international ecumenical leaders again took up the peace issue with renewed energy. They felt that they had the ears of many political leaders.

The World Alliance met in Prague in 1928. Söderblom was there. The same week, in Paris, the Kellogg-Briand Pact was signed, in which a long list of countries bound themselves to solve conflicts by arbitration and not to use force against each other. In one stroke, that changed the political climate in Europe and it became easy to unite the conference in Prague around a reduction of armed forces and the creation of a system of peaceful and just methods for the resolution of conflicts.

Söderblom's presence in Prague was significant. His status on the continent had never been stronger. The president of Czechoslovakia, Tomáš Masaryk, spent his vacation in Topolčianky in the Slovak mountains. Söderblom regarded this philosopher and champion of freedom as being among the world's great statesmen and had tried to get him to Stockholm as a leader of the ecumenical conference. Now he was invited to the president's summer castle, a rebuilt old cloister. The two had much to talk about in front of the evening fireplace. Soon the conversation dealt with God. Masaryk was a humanist and rationalist, critical of both idealism and Marxism. He had been a Catholic, but in protest against the dogma of papal infallibility he chose to be a nonpracticing Unitarian Protestant. He knew well Söderblom's criticism of the encyclical *Mortalium animos*. Each showed the other great mutual respect, but it was late in life's days for both of them and no significant collaboration came about. Nevertheless, Söderblom came to believe that this dinner with the seasoned father of his people contributed to changing the world for the better.

From Prague it was not far to Eisenach. When the Life and Work committee met there in September 1929, it would take a position regarding a resolution that Bishop George Bell of Chichester had prepared at Söderblom's suggestion. He was seconded by Wilfred Monod and Walter Simons, who had served as president of the German *Reichsgericht*, Supreme Court. Bell's proposal led to one of the most far-reaching and controversial decisions made by the ecumenical movement during the period between the two World Wars. The churches should not only fully support the Kellogg Pact, but should go a step further in their own application of it. If necessary, they should advise people to refuse to bear arms. Söderblom himself was not at Eisenach. His heart condition had forced him to stay at home, but he had given explicit instructions to Herman Neander and Paul Sandegren as to how they should represent him. Among the meeting's participants there was great concern for Söderblom's health. Even though he was not present, he influenced the committee to unanimously stand behind Bell's proposal.

One of the four points in the resolution urged responsible leaders in all Christian churches not to acknowledge or to give support in any way even to their own governments if they refused to accept an offer for mediation or arbitration. Around this issue there was considerable discussion. The original text included these words: "We earnestly appeal to the respective authorities of all Christian communions to declare in unmistakable terms that they will not countenance, nor assist in any way in, any war with regard to which the Government of their country has refused a bona fide offer to submit the dispute to arbitration." This meant, in clear language, that the churches called into question the unconditional obligation of defense and that under certain conditions, they would recommend disobedience to their own governments even during war. After the Life and Work committee came to its decision, the World Alliance followed suit at its meeting in Avignon a few weeks later. The resolution was then sent to the churches for their response and action. In England, it was approved unanimously by the Lambeth Conference, 307 bishops from the entire British Empire and the United States. In Denmark, 1,000 priests signed the document, although six bishops abstained.

The resolution became generally known in Sweden at the end of 1930. Then Söderblom had made his own translation, which was rather free but reflected the spirit of the text. The Swedish version was somewhat sharper than the original text, recommending active opposition in word and deed if the government does not go along with an implementation of arbitration. Söderblom gave the controversial paragraph the following form: "The legal system is God's work, and it is the church's duty to stress its sanctity and work for its strengthening even across national borders. If a state in relation to another state or many states has taken upon itself a general responsibility to submit forthcoming disputes to reconciliation, arbitration, or legal decisions, the church in such a situation should under all circumstances firmly uphold the unconditional character of such an agreement, and also, if in a given case a nation's government sets aside this obligation and refuses to submit disputes to such procedures, the church should express its condemnation of every war that arises and in word and deed take its distance from such war."

The Eisenach resolution was the fruit of many years' cooperation across national and confessional boundaries and it contained an action that was a concrete moral alternative to violence. It was also adopted by the newly formed ecumenical council in Chexbres in September 1930. That was the last large ecumenical conference in which Söderblom took part. When the resolution was passed, he summed up: "Perhaps this, for which I have endured unbelievable pain, could become a blessing." His vision of an ecumenical council had been realized and its first action dealt with his great question: peace in Europe and the world.

On November 11, Söderblom made the resolution public in Sweden. As was often the case when he was taking up an urgent question, he did it from the pulpit in the Engelbrekt Church in Stockholm. It was the same evening that the Swedish Peace and Arbitration Society held a peace rally in Stockholm's Auditorium. Present and participating there were the mayor of Stockholm, Carl Lindhagen, who was to compete with Söderblom for the Nobel Prize, and the member of Parliament Arthur Engberg. The question of arbitration as an instrument for peace was also high on the agenda of the League of Nations where it was supported not least by Hjalmar Branting. Söderblom was far from being the only peace activist in the country, but he was internationally the most well known and he expressed himself on the matter in terms of his Christian faith. In the fully packed church and for radio listeners throughout the land he was to answer the question, "Is the idea of peace an illusion?" He described in detail what had been agreed on in Eisenach. After he read the recommendation of civil disobedience in certain situations, he put some rhetorical questions that caused his listeners to sharpen their ears: "What? Betray the fatherland when it goes to war? Abandon it in its fateful hour? Oppose the nation's lawful government?" With this he drew attention to the resolution's most delicate point, which ought to have given rise to protests. But most of the press was positive toward what they correctly saw as a new and more resolute line from the side of the church. Söderblom's lecture was printed and distributed throughout the church. Thereafter, he took every opportunity that arose to speak of the issue of peace within the framework of international justice.

Two weeks after his appearance in the Engelbrekt Church, it was announced that he was to be awarded the Nobel Peace Prize. Sixty members of the Swedish Parliament had proposed Söderblom. Karl Gustaf Westman, who sixteen years earlier had successfully worked for his being named archbishop, took the initiative. Behind the proposal were representatives of all political lines, from Fabian Månsson of the labor movement to Hjalmar von Sydow of the Swedish Employers Confederation. Söderblom was scarcely surprised when he was awarded the prize. His name had been proposed several times and there is a letter that infers that he may have, when it became a serious possibility, acted on his own behalf. The money — approximately 4.7 million Swedish crowns in 2010 valuation — would come to be well used in continuing ecumenical work for peace. When the word came, he did not hold back his happiness, but he pointed out with becoming modesty that it was not he who should be honored but the entire ecumenical movement. The prize was "an acknowledgment of the Christian aspiration for unity, in which to the best of my ability I have taken part, and I find from this perspective joy in the certainty that the more Christian unity is realized, the more certainly it becomes a bulwark for peace in the world." That Christian solidarity was deepened and that the churches upheld the sanctity of the order of justice benefited peace. In an interview, Söderblom confirmed that he received his first impulses to work for Christian unity in the United States in 1890 and that the prayer he composed then was the first expression of that calling.

When he received the prize in Oslo, at the banquet he spoke of Alfred Nobel's view of peace. He had believed that the destructive potential of dynamite would render war impossible. Söderblom especially noted Nobel's comments concerning arbitration between nations. Since Söderblom was the only Nobel Prize recipient at the time who had known Nobel personally, his memories of the great philanthropist awakened considerable attention. They had met at a banquet held by the Swedish–Norwegian Society in Paris in observance of King Oscar's Day in 1896 and had a lively conversation. Shortly afterwards, Söderblom was called to Nobel's deathbed in San Remo. Toward the end of his life, the eccentric man had worked on a manuscript, which he asked Anna Söderblom to proofread. In light of the manuscript's contents, however, Nathan and Anna advised against publication. In his public Nobel Lecture in Oslo, however, Söderblom cited some words from it: "Silence, you who stand before the altar of death! Life here and life hereafter is an eternal mystery; but its final spark awakens us to holy prayer and silences every voice save that of religion. Eternity has the word." These were words that Söderblom had also used at the Memorial Service held in Nobel's villa, Mio Nido, in San Remo thirty-four years earlier.

He was tired and suffering from a cold when he delivered his Nobel Lecture in the university aula in Oslo and a bit subdued as he reviewed

Work, illness, and difficult family issues took their toll on the archbishop, even as his self-confidence increased. To the left is Söderblom shortly before being named archbishop and to the right as he appeared when he received the Nobel Prize sixteen years later.

the ecumenical movement's development. Nevertheless, he succeeded in captivating his audience to the extent that Frank B. Kellogg, the American Secretary of State, who at the same occasion had received the 1929 prize, nearly faded away at his side. Söderblom gave special words of praise to the Norwegians who from the beginning had been part of the ecumenical movement. He emphasized the significance of the Eisenach resolution, arguing strongly for binding international legislation. The possibility of peace lay in a generally accepted practice of arbitration. He reported enthusiastically on the ecumenical council that had just been formed in Chexbres in Canton Vaud in Switzerland and how it was organized. Perhaps the day would come when even the Roman Catholic Church would be represented in the council. He concluded the lecture in an extremely personal way by citing "a friend" in San Francisco who had written down his thoughts at the end of the war. The friend was none other than his son Sven who had fought on the Western Front. Time goes, he wrote. The shattered cannons, which remain in the bushes of the battlefield, frighten no longer. Perhaps young people sit on the gun carriage and speak of their dreams, loves, and the future. The death rattles are heard no longer; the dead sleep under the earth. But, he continued, one can hear hoofbeats, drums, and signals from shining trumpets. Men are marching — but not those who are between thirty-five and forty — they have no such wish. But those who are growing up, the youths who hold out for new gods, new ideas, new dreams, new tasks — young people who will build a new world? Pity the world!

Honored and more famous than ever, Söderblom returned to his daily duties. On his way home from Oslo he made it to committee meetings both in Stockholm and in Sigtuna. But when he finally arrived at the railroad station in Uppsala, the whole city was on its feet. He left his doctor's hat in its box and put on the old floppy cap that he used to wear before he met the theological faculty, which came into the train compartment in order to pay its respects, and then the student body gathered with torches and banners and with song and speech to greet the Nobel Prize winner. Söderblom gave a charming response, the crowd cheered and he joined with the students who marched up to the brightly lit archbishop's residence. As the happiest among the happy students he joined the procession, although without his heart medicine he would not have had the strength to do so. In front of the residence there were more songs and additional speeches. As he stood on the steps of the house in the December chill with thousands of people pressing forward to see and hear him, he knew that he had reached his goal: the ecumenical movement had received its recognition. It was worth all his labor.

His work for peace had intensified and become more radical during the last years, but he never became a pacifist. Every nation had the right to self-defense. Accordingly, defense forces were necessary, although they should be reduced in size. He concentrated on strengthening the international order of justice and hoped that the churches would stand together in this task and thus confirm the authority of the ecumenical movement. He knew that he did not have a long time to live. Before it became too late, he wanted to firmly establish the Eisenach resolution in Sweden. It offered the guiding principles that the church should follow in the event of an acute threat of war. The handling of the dispute between Finland and Sweden over the future of the Åland islands had shown that arbitration was a constructive alternative to war. But it was no easy thing to get a Lutheran church, which for centuries had distinguished between spiritual life and public affairs and which at its root was both conservative and nationalist, to commit itself to an order of justice that transcended its own nation.

None of the other bishops stood close to Söderblom. Only in exceptional cases had they cooperated in his international activities and they were often uneasy about his various initiatives. Even if they felt a reluctant admiration for his ability to solve problems and followed his international achievements with respect, they were constantly uneasy that he would go too far and "go completely astray," as Einar Billing wrote to Manfred Björkquist. Nevertheless, it was precisely Billing who stood closest to Söderblom. He was theologically the most penetrating among the bishops and had worked with Söderblom for three decades. When the Bishops' Assembly, at the end of January 1931, could not agree to support the Eisenach resolution, Billing was given the task of reformulating the controversial paragraph so they could stand behind it. The new version had basically the same content, but Billing's writing was significantly milder than Söderblom's. It was approved by the Bishops' Assembly, which Söderblom accepted.

But the newspapers were merciless. They wrote that the bishops had repudiated the archbishop and "left not only Nathan Söderblom but even God the Father in the lurch." By mutilating the resolution they had "deprived it of all juice and marrow." Söderblom was criticized for having repudiated his own address in the Engelbrekt Church. He answered that he held firmly to his own formulation and, in spite of what the bishops were united on, was free to defend his own position. He maintained that the statement of the Bishops' Assembly should be understood only as preparatory material for the General Church Assembly to be held in April where the matter would be dealt with.

It was remarkable that the archbishop could be treated by his brother bishops in this way. Again, he intended to use the General Church Assembly, which had no formal status or legislative role, for his own ends. The Assembly was given a choice between two versions, his own and that of the other bishops. He argued heatedly for his own version, pointing out that the bishops did not equally stress the duty of civil disobedience if an internationally binding rule of law was violated. It was a vigorous debate that went on all day. Söderblom was pale and tense, visibly ill. His introductory address was met with silence and he felt completely deserted on the podium. No one else in the church leadership was prepared to support so uncompromising a politics for peace. Most likely, a majority of the priests in the hall were against him as he confronted deeply rooted nationalism and ingrained obedience to authority.

Many who had once supported Manfred Björkquist in his fund-raising for a naval ship sat in the pews. They wanted no resolution at all. Manfred Björkquist was seconded by the conservative chairman of the General Union of Clergy and some of the most influential church leaders. Other delegates supported Söderblom, but the atmosphere became so unpleasant that a countess from Södermanland attempted to divert everything by introducing a motion of general support for Söderblom's peace work. He declined such support. Finally, the tension was dissolved when John Cullberg, who later succeeded Billing as Bishop of Västerås, proposed an amendment that would satisfy the advocates of a strong national defense force and clearly indicate that Söderblom's proposal did not deal with either pacifism or disarmament. The amendment was needed for the Assembly to accept Söderblom's proposal. He agreed to it with reluctance. For him, the decisive issue was that the church took a position regarding the principle of the matter. In the daily press he received strong support from Social Democrat sources, especially from Arthur Engberg in *Social-Demokraten*, while right-wing papers objected that the church involved itself in political questions. On Sweden's West Coast, every paper came out against him. Torgny Segerstedt looked for "the vigorous old Lutheran piety in our church." According to him, only remnants of that were left; the church gave the picture of advanced dissolution.

This was the last time that Söderblom took part in a public event of this kind. His final controversy dealt with achieving peace through legal proceedings. The bishops wanted to put the brakes on him. Björkquist planned a church political counteraction. In spite of the fact that Söderblom had just received the Nobel Prize for his indefatigable work for peace, he did not have the leadership of his own church with him. But he had sufficient support among the laity to have his way. Three months later, he died. Then the question of the divine order of justice implemented through an international rule of law and the Christian responsibility for peace vanished into thin air until Arvid Runestam and Gustaf Aulén again actualized the issue in the mid-1930s. By then, the Nazis had taken the law into their own hands and in the homeland of the Reformation, the church's freedom was lost.

34
The Death of a Saint

> Every hour of our life is an ending and at the same time a new beginning. In every hour we can experience eternal life if we turn ourselves over to God.
>
> *Nathan Söderblom, 1930*

NATHAN SÖDERBLOM COMES TO SPARREHOLM in Södermanland where the Anglo-Scandinavian theology conference is taking place under the leadership of Professor Gustaf Aulén. A few decades have passed since Söderblom laid the groundwork for communion with the Anglican Church. At that white castle on the shore of Lake Båven, the fellowship is affirmed in grandiose forms that remind him of what he had just experienced in Scotland. The host at the castle, Chamberlain Emil Dickson, is of Scottish descent and maintains lively contacts with the west. Aulén is the last ever to call on Söderblom in an ecumenical conference: "The Chair has decided to give the word to His Grace the Archbishop of Sweden." The following morning Söderblom takes the train back to Uppsala in order, as usual, to dictate letters, receive visitors, and plan everything that lies ahead. It is his last working day.

* * *

Shortly after the General Synod, which was so trying for him, Söderblom came in May 1931 to Scotland in order to give the Gifford Lectures at the University of Edinburgh. Behind these lectures lay a large donation to the Scottish universities from Lord Adam Gifford for a strictly academic and totally free discussion of natural theology and the knowledge of God in the widest sense. This had developed into an extremely prestigious series of lectures. For the study of religion, the Gifford Lectures were comparable to the Nobel Peace Prize in the world of politics. The invited lecturers could belong to any religion, be skeptics, agnostics, or freethinkers, but they must be known as serious seekers of truth. Among previous lecturers were C. P. Tiele, William James, Henri Bergson, James Frazer, and Alfred North Whitehead.

Söderblom had taken a few months to prepare for this. It was not possible for him to work out ten entirely new lectures, so he chose some lectures that he had given on other occasions, updated them, and compiled them into a series. After considerable editing, they were published by the Oxford University Press — Söderblom's self-taught English was good but far from perfect. Having been overburdened by other tasks for seventeen years, he now had the opportunity to return to his studies in the history of religion and also the possibility to complete his trilogy of fundamental academic works: *La vie future* in French, *Das Werden des Gottesglaubens* in German, and now *The Living God: Basal Forms of Personal Religion* in English. Before his time ran out, he summarized a whole lifetime's academic work by bringing to the fore that which had occupied him most in his research on the religions of the world.

The lectures were public. He took his auditors on a long journey through the worlds of "primitive" religions, Hinduism, Buddhism, Zoroastrian, Hellenism, Judaism, and Christianity. He went from "lower" to "higher" forms of personal religious experience, but not in a simplistic evolutionary sense. Higher forms of religion were not necessarily developments from lower forms but rather hard-won and more complete answers to revelation. The risk of regression in the world of religion could not be excluded.

From the start, Söderblom clarified his basic point of view. He would speak of characteristic differences between various forms of religion, not of superficial and misleading similarities. For him, all religion was personal and individual before it was social. He approached the religions from a historical and theological perspective; he was not a sociologist. He wanted to uncover the actual encounter with the living God and was not content to stop with religions' various social and ritual forms of expression. The encounter with God could not be brought about through spiritual exercises or mental activities. It could occur only if God revealed himself. In lecture after lecture, when he dealt with the attempts of other religions to reach unity with the divine by various means, he returned to the Christian's unconditional dependence on God's initiative and the cross of Christ. His final lecture — the last of his life — was a reiteration of what he had written already in 1911 concerning continuing revelation. This, the principle theme of his three decades of academic study of religion, also rounded out his theological work. His testament became the oft-repeated words: When God's self-communication penetrates a person's heart and life so that the divine life and justification become determinative for it, one can speak of sainthood. "Saints are such as show clearly and plainly in their lives and deeds and in their very being that God lives."

As the celebrity he was, Söderblom was received by the King's Governor at Holyrood Castle. In clerical garb adorned with medals and orders conferred upon him, he approached the impressive throne hall in firm steps and with his head held high. At his side was Anna, dressed in white "as the moon beside the sun." When the bagpipes sounded and he recalled the romance, tragedy, heroism, and cheerfulness in Scottish history, he had a hard time holding back tears. He was fond of Scotland with its culture and Calvinist tradition. There he had met some of the times' most prominent scholars of religion, and there he had also found some of his most loyal colleagues in the ecumenical movement.

They were guests at the thirteenth-century Culzean Castle on the craggy coast. Lady and Lord Ailsa — leaders of Clan Kennedy — invited the Söderbloms for a weekend filled with memorable experiences: worship in the local church, the view over the ocean and the Isle of Arran, a picnic interrupted by a heavy rainstorm, and conversations at the library fireplace. Anna and Nathan gave lively accounts of their time in Paris when they were young and discussed with their cultivated hosts how an old truth could age and then take on new form as a higher truth.

Söderblom enjoyed these early summer weeks when he was able to return to an academic milieu marked by free intellectual conversation, leaving far behind the narrow-minded Swedish church politics. Edinburgh reminded him of his "happy professor's time" and he had already begun to prepare for his second series of Gifford Lectures. He intended to concentrate on Christian spirituality and to summarize everything with discussions of the practice of mysticism and sanctity, the interplay of human and divine activity, the essence of prayer, and "the living God."

On the way home to Uppsala he stopped in Lund where he baptized his youngest grandchild in the cathedral. Then he continued, as usual, to all that awaited him in the archdiocese. On July 4, he spoke to a large group of young people in his beloved home province Hälsingland. While his car waited, they gathered on the highway to bid farewell. With them, Söderblom sang a summer hymn written by Paul Gerhardt in 1653, "Go forth, my heart, and seek delight." Söderblom himself had composed a melody, which had become one of the most beloved hymns in Sweden. When he died, the young people would especially remember which of the original fourteen verses he chose:

> Oh, were I there! Oh that I now,
> dear God, before Thy throne could bow,
> and bear my heavenly palm!
> Then like the angels would I raise
> my voice and sing Thy endless praise
> in many a sweet-toned psalm.

Death came suddenly but not unexpectedly. Söderblom had been sick off and on for half of his adult life. After ten years of relatively good health, in 1922 he began to have heart problems. They increased with the years and after the Stockholm Conference, which demanded inhuman effort, he never recovered his full strength. He was required to lessen his working pace and periodically refrain from all public engagements. He became more and more convinced that his life would be short. Accordingly, he attempted to make the most of every day. On Wednesday, July 8, he became acutely ill, was taken to the Academic Hospital, and operated on for ileitis. On the following Sunday afternoon, July 12, he suffered a number of heart attacks and at 6:40 P.M. he died. He was sixty-five years old.

The news spread quickly. The next morning it filled the front pages of the nation's newspapers. The doctors had kept the journalists well informed concerning his condition, giving them daily reports. For public figures, death was also public. He was highly respected and immensely popular, a model of energy and goodness. Even though his death was not the result of an accident or a crime, the whole nation was paralyzed by sorrow and dismay. Everyone felt related to him. Even his sharpest adversaries laid their criticisms aside. Black headlines announced: ARCHBISHOP SÖDERBLOM DECEASED; A GREAT MAN OF THE SPIRIT DEPARTS THIS LIFE; ALL THE WORLD'S CHRISTENDOM SHARES SORROW FOR HIM. Page after page was filled with words of remembrance. Heads of state, bishops, scholars, politicians, authors, and composers all wanted to express their sorrow. The debate over riots and fatal shootings in the north of Sweden ceased for some time. The German monetary crisis, which rocked the world's stock markets and made international emergency loans necessary, ended up in the shadows at the death of the Swedish archbishop.

The reports on Söderblom's last days quickly took on the character found in "the legends of the saint." He died as he had lived, working to the end. He had endured his pain by expressing gratitude and love. His final words had been a confession to the truth of the living God and to the truth of eternal life. Early on, Söderblom was aware that his end was approaching and he thought through how he would meet death. When the story of his death spread, it became an edifying and consoling message that touched an entire nation.

As late as Wednesday, when Söderblom returned home from Sparreholm, the young priest Sven Hellqvist visited him in the residence in order to discuss his work in Poland. There were many who waited to meet with the archbishop: a French journalist, an old lady, and two other priests. When it was Hellqvist's turn, the archbishop began to give way to pain and he had to lie down on a sofa, but he continued the conversation. When the pain became too much to bear, he asked Hellqvist to come back an hour later. Sweating and weak, but clear and concise, he discussed the Polish situation and blessed the young priest from the sofa. "Go with God and be fearless!"

A number of years later, the surgeon who operated on him published an essay on what actually happened. He was substituting for the chief surgeon who was on summer leave. When Söderblom was brought in with severe abdominal pain he at first suspected kidney stones, but quickly discovered intestinal failure — ileitis that required immediate surgery. While preparations were being made, the archbishop had prayers with his family. When he woke from the anesthesia he said to the doctor, "The chief thing in human life is that a person can come to a decision and stand by his acts. It seems to me that you, doctor, are such a person. I congratulate you." He soon felt a little better and began to dictate letters to his secretary. One was to Manfred Björkquist with suggestions for the delegation to a conference with the Swedish free churches. He did not mention a word concerning his illness. He also planned the program for the English theologians who were coming to Uppsala from Sparreholm with a reminder that they should be served mead when they visited Gamla Uppsala, Old Uppsala. He requested his son-in-law Yngve Brilioth to read his sermon in the cathedral on Sunday and he received daily greetings from the crown prince.

Sunday was a sunny and beautiful day. Just then, his heart began to fail, as his doctor had feared. He was surrounded by Anna and five of his children, his three sons-in-law, a couple of friends, two doctors, and a nurse. He asked how long he had to live and he understood that it was a matter of a few hours. Söderblom left three instructions: his library should not be sold but should go to the theologians in the family; the family should hold together and not quarrel; and his book with the lectures given at Edinburgh should be called *The Living God*. Then in a loud voice he said, "I thank God that I have been a priest in the Church of Sweden." He took each person by the hand and said an encouraging word to them. They prayed the Our Father together and he recited some Bible passages: "Those who believe in me, even though they die, will live, and everyone who lives and believes in me will never die" and "If we live, we live to the Lord, and if we die, we die to the Lord; so then, whether we live or whether we die, we are the Lord's." He read two hymns and in his usual lively way he explained that the body certainly ceases to exist, but the spirit continues to live even if in forms that humans cannot foresee. Then he said, "There is a God who lives, I can prove it through the history of religion." Anna repeated the words, "Blessed are the pure in heart, for they shall see God," and he said — he could hardly be heard — "This is eternity," or perhaps it was "This is life." Then he passed away.

Soon the flag at the Archbishop's Palace was flying at half-staff and all Uppsala knew what had happened. The body was brought to his study where the family kept watch. *Dagens Nyheter*, with the help of its foreign correspondents, was able by Monday to gather more than twenty personal reactions from Protestant, Orthodox, and Catholic church leaders from around the world. It was obvious that Söderblom was an archbishop of all Christianity, or — as it said in the headlines of one paper — "Pope of Protestantism."

On Wednesday evening, many thousands filled the Uppsala Cathedral. The high altar and the organ gallery were draped in black and the open grave was surrounded by candelabra with burning lights, but the bells were silent. Algot Anderberg, who was the husband of the youngest of the three daughters, led the Memorial Service of Prayer. He reported thoroughly concerning Söderblom's death and concluded: "We have seen God revealed. We have through this death been placed before the living God. Even though our hearts are bleeding, we thank God for what he has given us through this revelation, this death, which has become a powerful seal on a life lived in faith, hope, and love. We thank God for the spiritual testament this dear and honorable shepherd, father, and friend has given to us through his departure — it is a firm word, the word of the living God."

The burial took place on Saturday. The Diocesan Chapter had had only a short time for the necessary preparations. The government had with no delay decided that Söderblom should be buried beneath the cathedral's high altar, close to his predecessor and model, Laurentius Petri, but it proved difficult to open the grave since unknown masonry was discovered and the antiquarian authorities had to give approval. Guests from far distances came to Uppsala and the entire royal house was present. When the cathedral's great bells rang out over the city twelve times at noontime, everything was ready for one of the most memorable burial services ever held in the national sanctuary. Four thousand people were in attendance, with fifteen thousand observers outside. Not only in Uppsala but also in Stockholm, the flags flew at half-staff and from all the churches in the capital city bells rang in thanksgiving. In Uppsala, offices and stores were closed. Throughout the whole country, people gathered around crackling radios in order to participate.

In the Archbishop's Palace, where Söderblom lay in a flower-bedecked casket dressed in an alb with lace that had been given to him by Estonian women, King Gustaf V and the entire royal family filed past while Wilhelm Kempff played subdued music. The simple oak casket was closed and carried to the cathedral by eight students as the student choir sang the pilgrim's hymn, "Dejlig er jorden," "Fairest Lord Jesus," in the original Danish. Through the crowded mass of people and between rows of students, the long procession passed slowly, led by flowered standards. The family, the royal house, the cabinet, all of the nation's bishops, the diplomatic corps, international church leaders, professors, representatives of archdiocesan parishes, and a long line of organizations together formed a procession of several hundred people.

In the cathedral, the high altar was draped in black. Bach's Fantasia and Fugue in C Minor was played and the congregation sang "Go forth my heart, and seek delight" to the melody composed by Söderblom. Yngve Brilioth presided at the burial. Just as Söderblom himself used to do during his later years, he delivered no funeral meditation, but read a number of Bible passages and some sections from Söderblom's own writings. Many recognized the words from an often-repeated sermon: "The inner guest is my friend. Before him my soul is still. Oh, let me always have access to that refuge." Söderblom's name was never mentioned.

The cathedral choir sang "Pie Jesu" and "Agnus Dei" from Cherubini's *Requiem*. The altar service was led by three priests from the diocese. After the benediction, the casket was lowered into the grave while the boys' choir sang Schütz's "Venite ad me" with his friend from Paris, Sven Kjellström, accompanying on the violin. A hundred wreaths were laid before the postlude was played and everyone filed by the open grave as the great bells again rang out over Uppsala.

What resembled a state funeral was over. Everyone was speaking of Söderblom. He had left no one unmoved. Arthur Engberg's remembrance in *Social-Demokraten* aroused considerable attention:

> With Nathan Söderblom a remarkable personality has left time, dazzling, rich, and puzzling. Even those who in essential matters thought otherwise than he are filled with sorrow, pain, and dismay as they stand before the suddenly and unexpectedly opened grave. He was like no other. He fell completely outside the frame of the ordinary. Light, charm, and warmth radiated from his being. Dogma, theses, and systems were against his nature. His life and work were like an emanation from the creative development, the évolution créatrice in which Bergson chose to see the principle of existence. The rhythm, style, and character of his personality were those of an authentic genius. He was a learned man. But above his learnedness was not the dust of books, but rather life's fresh and sparkling dew.

Thus wrote one of the foremost critics of the archbishop who had stood on the public stage for nearly seventeen years. When the tombstone was put in place, an audible silence arose both in the church and in culture.

Tor Andrae succeeded him in the Swedish Academy. He had known Söderblom extremely well, was his doctoral student, and now served as professor of the history of religion. In his introductory address to the Academy on December 21, 1932, he spoke of Söderblom as a genius of fellowship. In his modest and intimate daily life, one caught a glimpse of saintliness in his being, but Andrae warned against idealizing him and "distorting this genuine, light-hearted, free, convincing humanity with its light and shadows, its strength and its weakness into a traditional Christian image for school and home."

One after another applied Söderblom's own definition of a saint to the man. Surely he, if anyone, had shown with his life, his speech, and his actions that God lived. The memory of his strong personality made a lasting impression and pictures of him were like icons in many homes and churches. But what became of his work? What remained when the memory of his charisma faded and his undivided presence was no more? "It is an ungrateful fate," Andrae pointed out, "that awaits artists of living words and melodies — worshiped more than others — to be forgotten more rapidly than others. When the great actor completes his final presentation, when the final tone of the virtuoso's stroke fades away, then also the best in his art is lost."

When Söderblom's splendid performance, which his critics sometimes called theatrical, was ended and the applause had become silent, then happened just what Andrae had said would happen. The Church of Sweden chose a new archbishop. Three people were on the slate: Söderblom's loyal partner Knut B. Westman, who had extensive international experience and a great knowledge of languages; Tor Andrae, who was Söderblom's foremost student as a historian of religion; and Erling Eidem, an unobtrusive New Testament scholar who never moved in Söderblom's circles. Sam Stadener, who was then Minister of Ecclesiastical Affairs and who would rather have seen himself as archbishop but did not receive enough votes, saw to it that Eidem was named. He remained in his position until 1950 and, retiring and uncertain and with great caution, he led the church through the difficult times of the 1930s and the Second World War. He merited respect, but the brightness of the archbishop's ministry faded. Stadener had consciously broken the continuity. He did not belong among the ecumenists. Now the time had come to put an end to their adventurous undertakings.

Söderblom was spared the experience of knowing how the bishops' common attempt to strengthen the folk church's integrity was betrayed when Stadener preserved the church's ownership of land and forests at the price of political parties keeping a tight grip on church affairs. Söderblom was not there when Communists, Fascists, and Nazis occupied Europe, trampled on the freedom of the individual, and in country after country nearly crushed the Christian church. He knew how fragile the Peace of Versailles was. He felt that the time between the wars was only an interlude before war would break out again with an even greater devastation of the spiritual and material values of Western civilization. A new tyranny rumbled in the darkness. But that it should go as far as the Holocaust he could not have imagined, even if his Jewish friends often looked for his support during his last years.

The ecumenical network he had helped to create was immature and vulnerable, but it survived the Second World War as a kind of resistance movement. Söderblom had wanted to integrate church and culture. After his death, a polarization came about between "authentic" Christianity and foreign ideologies, which did not leave much space for his brand of Christian humanism. The European scene was completely transformed. Yet again the churches became entangled in national and ideological loyalties and had great difficulty expressing their boundary-transcending communion in practice. The church's "body" in many countries became the state's hostage and the church's "soul" had its wings clipped by ideologies that were contemptuous of humanity. When culture-conditioned Protestantism and liberal theology capitulated to Nazism's call, the theological initiative on the continent went to Karl Barth and in Sweden to the theologians at Lund. Together with the enduring Anglo-Saxon churches, this saved the ecumenical movement, but it took on a new shape.

Even scholarship in the history of religion took a different direction. When the first generation of Söderblom's disciples left the universities and the atheistic professor of philosophy Ingemar Hedenius declared that Söderblom's reasoning concerning the place of logic in theology was "muddle-headed to the point of incomprehensibility," the beleaguered theologians took refuge in the security of historical research and empiricism. Söderblom's attempt to keep theology and the history of religion together, and his defense of Christianity as the highest rung of the ladder of religious evolution, had had its day.

Söderblom's Life and Work initiative lived on in spite of the fact that he had not been able to create a stable structure for it. Nor did he have many heirs who could carry his work further. The most prominent Swedish ecumenists, Gustaf Aulén and Yngve Brilioth, chose to make their contributions in Faith and Order. Söderblom's legacy, which centered on peace and social justice, was best carried on by the English bishops George Bell and William Temple. When World War II was over, the World Council of Churches was established and that became the stable organization that Söderblom dreamt of but was never able to carry into effect. During this

There are innumerable portraits, sculptures, and photographic representations of Söderblom. Here a bust is being cast.

period, a confessional and self-sufficient Lutheranism also got wind in its sails. The tension between Lutheranism and ecumenism, which Söderblom struggled with, lived on in organized form. But many Lutherans had learned that Luther's teaching concerning justification had universal validity and therefore they could openly and constructively participate in greater ecumenical work.

When Söderblom passed on, Eurocentrism and colonialism were still unshaken, but social optimism was fractured, civil society was threatened to death, and trust in individual personalities was becoming increasingly problematic. He had broken the provincialism of the Church of Sweden and given it a new self-image with his emphasis on evangelical catholicity, universality, and an historically conditioned responsibility for unity and peace. He had liberated the church from much of Lutheran orthodoxy's oppressive dogmatism and pietism's narrow moralism. Moreover, he had strengthened the place of music in the church and created the conditions for a liturgical renewal. From all of this there was no turning back.

Söderblom's ten children were spread all over the world. Brita, Lucie, and Yvonne were married to men who would become bishops. Helge died shortly after his father. Sven lived in the United States. Staffan was a diplomat, Jon Olof worked in the government secretariat, Carl migrated to Argentina, Lag was a teacher, and Gustaf was an officer. He later became a priest.

Anna lived in Uppsala for twenty-four more years in an apartment in "Domtrapphuset," at the foot of steps to the cathedral. She lived with her memories among paintings, sculptures, books, and documents. While Nathan Söderblom's splendid days were being overshadowed by totalitarian ideologies, violence against international law, and devastating war, she put his archives in order, helped scholars and students, traveled to ecumenical conferences, and saw to it that his intentions were not forgotten. She died in 1955, a death that was the symbolic completion of his work. On his gravestone, where each day Anna set fresh flowers, words are carved that he often, very often, had cited:

SO LIKEWISE YE,
WHEN YE SHALL HAVE DONE
ALL THOSE THINGS WHICH ARE COMMANDED YOU,
SAY, WE ARE UNPROFITABLE SERVANTS:
WE HAVE DONE THAT WHICH WAS OUR DUTY TO DO.
LUKE 17:10

Afterword

Source material concerning Nathan Söderblom is extensive. The Söderblom collection available at the library of Uppsala University amounts to shelves of boxes measuring forty-three meters, including some 38,000 letters, 130 notebooks, and 2,800 manuscripts. A bibliography of Söderblom's printed writings was compiled as early as 1931 by Sven Ågren. It listed 669 titles and has been expanded a number of times. To complete the picture of Söderblom, a nearly limitless number of clippings from both the Swedish and foreign press, a rich photo collection, and archives of radio recordings and films must be added to the printed texts. Additionally, a large number of photographs, paintings, and sculptured portraits are available. Statues are to be found in Uppsala, Eisenach, Söderhamn, and Trönö. His large academic library has been collected and catalogued and can be found in the Archbishop's Palace in Uppsala.

Within four months of his death, two biographies were published in Swedish, a penetrating one by Tor Andrae and a more popular one by Olle Nystedt. Both of these books appeared in many editions. In Norway, Eivind Berggrav published a short psychological portrait of his life. Together, these three books described the contours of Söderblom's life and work and have subsequently determined the public's picture of him. They were written shortly after his death and have a strongly hagiographic character. That applied to an even higher degree to several memorial volumes, each including many photographs, which were soon published. The same year that Söderblom died *Nathan Söderblom: In Memoriam*, edited by Nils Karlström, appeared, a volume of 460 pages with detailed and carefully prepared articles by Tor Andrae, Gustaf Aulén, Einar Billing, Manfred Björkquist, Yngve Brilioth, Gunnar Dahlquist, Bengt Jonzon, Emil Liedgren, and Gustaf Lizell, all of whom in various ways had worked closely with the archbishop. This book is richly knowledgeable, but with its short perspective, all of the authors present Söderblom nearly without shadows or nuance. Worth paying attention to is Yngve Brilioth's balanced and elegant biography of his father-in-law found in the English edition of Söderblom's Gifford Lectures, *The Living God* (1933). During the period 1931–1934, Sven Thulin produced many volumes of "Recollections and Impressions," which contained no fewer than 138 contributions by Swedish and international authors, comprising 1,100 pages. If one adds to these sources all of the recorded memories in both the Swedish and international press, there appears an undividedly positive, yet richly nuanced and frequently anecdotal, personal portrait of a man who above all was remembered for his trustworthiness, capacity for work, knowledge of people, endurance, and unfailing friendship.

In this large body of material there is very little that deals with his close personal relationships; in accordance with his family's wishes, the family archives are not available for research. Immediately after Söderblom's death, an almost inviolable biographical image arose that was protected by his widow and family members who raised ethical objections to any intrusion into the most private aspects of his life. A biography that does not deal with a person's private family life is incomplete, but can be defended if the emphasis is directed to the public *persona*. For Söderblom, his social and public life increasingly became his real self. He was modeled by the function he performed and to a great extent he was known for the character he projected to an audience. His life became a performance played out in the public arena, dependent on its reception and recognition. His real self was difficult to disentangle from this performed public life.

Anna, Söderblom's wife, outlived him by twenty-four years. She organized his intellectual inheritance and complemented the collections by requesting many of his correspondents to return his letters either as originals or copies. She can also be credited with collecting and publishing posthumously many of his essays, addresses, and sermons. Among those books were *Ett år: Ord för varje dag* (*One Year: A Word for Every Day*), the partially autobiographical *Sommarminnen* (*Summer Memories*), and a collection of his writings, *Svenskars fromhet* (*The Piety of Swedes*). Anna Söderblom also published her own memoirs, which had the characteristic title *På livets trottoir* (*On the Sidewalk of Life*), and a book on the 1923 journey to the United States, *En Amerikabok*.

No one can fail to notice the mighty and many-voiced chorus of praise directed toward Söderblom after his death. Everyone who studies his work must exercise source criticism regarding his one-sided and positive posthumous reputation. Even a most attentive treatment of sources would not be able to completely remove this blanket of hagiography. An accurate picture of Söderblom requires both depth and nuance and a number of academic dissertations have contributed to this. An authoritative study of Söderblom's ecumenical activity was published in Swedish by Nils Karlström in 1947 and is largely included in Ruth Rouse and Stephen Neill, eds., *A History of the Ecumenical Movement*, Vol. 1 (1954). Folke Holmström published a valuable study of Söderblom's theology of revelation and mysticism in 1937 and J. M. van Veen released, in German, a study of his theology of world religions in 1940. This was followed by Sigfrid Estborn's study of Söderblom's preaching (1944). Erland Ehnmark dealt with the problem of religion in 1949. At that point, the use of personal biographical studies as a genre in academic historical study almost completely disappeared. In research influenced by Marxism, the individual's role in history was no longer interesting. This virtually rendered as antiquated Söderblom's personalistic view of history.

Nevertheless, studies of Nathan Söderblom and his work continued to appear. In 1933, a translation of *Uppenbarelsereligion* was issued in the United Kingdom. That translation reappeared in 1966 in the United States with an extensive introduction to Söderblom by Edgar M. Carlson. Also in the United States, Charles J. Curtis published two volumes: *Nathan Söderblom: Theologian of Revelation*, which portrayed Söderblom in relation to Alfred North Whitehead (1966), and *Nathan Söderblom: Ecumenical Pioneer* (1966). Söderblom's theology was also studied carefully in *The Reinterpretation of Luther* by Edgar Carlson (1948) and *Swedish Contributions to Modern Theology* by Nels F. S. Ferré (1967).

In 1968, Bengt Sundkler's literarily brilliant and extremely thorough *Nathan Söderblom: His Life and Work* appeared. This work, which appeared only in English, was also a contribution to preparations for the General Assembly of the World Council of Churches held in Uppsala the same year. It built largely on the most thorough examination of Söderblom's correspondence yet undertaken. Seven years later, in 1975, Sundkler published *Nathan Söderblom och hans möten* (*Nathan Söderblom and His Conference*), which provided a lively picture of Söderblom as well as his wife and many of his closest colleagues.

The ice was broken and Söderblom again became the object of serious academic work. Hans Åkerberg published a psychological study of Söderblom's religious development (1975), Sven-Erik Brodd placed Söderblom's position on evangelical catholicity in a wider context (1982), and Eric Sharpe wrote on Söderblom and the academic study of religion (1990). Sara Gehlin analyzed his use of the concepts of peace and ecumenism (2008) and Anders Mogård dealt with his interpretation of Luther (2014). Each of these publications has an English summary.

In the extensive research on the church history and the history of theology of twentieth-century Sweden, Söderblom is correctly given a prominent place, but more detailed studies are relatively few. Two, however, are worthy of special mention. Staffan Runestam, who through his cataloguing of the Söderblom archives at Uppsala University gained both an overview and detailed knowledge like no one else, has written a number of meticulous and well-documented studies, with English summaries, concerning various aspects of Söderblom's activities during the time when he was archbishop. *Söderblomsstudier* (2004) and *I kärlekens tjänst* (*In the Service of Love*, 2013) are invaluable sources for those who wish to approach Söderblom. The German professor of systematic theology at Göttingen Dietz Lange in 2011 completed *Nathan Söderblom und seine Zeit* (*Nathan Söderblom and His Time*), a volume that has been translated into Swedish but not into English. It is a wide-ranging and extremely thorough intellectual biography, the most profound and comprehensive of all.

I have made use of primary sources in the Söderblom archives, but above all, I have made use of published sources and the research of others. Since I am not offering much new knowledge, I have chosen not to make use of footnotes. Citations in my text come nearly exclusively from Söderblom's letters and writings. I have endeavored to capture something of a life that was like an "exuberant fountain" but has now begun to be forgotten. My narrative makes no claim to be complete. It is a tentative construction of a significant person's life in a time so different from our own. It should be regarded as a contribution to general knowledge rather than to research.

Sources and Literature

For a more complete bibliography, including many books and articles in Swedish, the reader is advised to consult the original Swedish edition of this book. There one will also find references to sources for each individual chapter.

For the most complete available bibliography regarding Nathan Söderblom, see Nils Karlström, ed., *Nathan Söderblom in Memoriam.* Stockholm, 1931, pp. 391-451.

Archives

The Royal Library, Stockholm (KB): films.
The Nordic Museum, Stockholm (NM): photos.
The Sigtunastiftelsen Archives, Sigtuna (SSt): letters and clippings.
Church of Sweden Archives, Uppsala (SvK): minutes and protocols.
The Uppsala University Library (UUB), Uppsala: Nathan Söderbloms Samling: photos.

Books and Articles

ÅKERBERG, HANS

1975 *Omvändelse och kamp: En empirisk religionspsykologisk undersökning av den unge Nathan Söderbloms religiösa utveckling 1866-1894,* Lund.

ANDRAE, TOR

1931 "Nathan Söderblom som religionshistoriker," Karlström, 1931, 25-62.

1931 *Nathan Söderblom*, Uppsala.

AULÉN, GUSTAF

1922 *Evangeliskt och romerskt,* Stockholm.

1931a "Den teologiska gärningen," Karlström, 1931, 63-104.

1931b "Nathan Söderblom såsom teolog," *Svensk Teologisk Kvartalskrift*, 7, 211-235.

1953 *Hundra års svensk kyrkodebatt, Drama i tre akter*, Stockholm.

BELL, G. K. A.

1926 *The Stockholm Conference, 1925*, London.

BERGGRAV, EIVIND

1931 *Nathan Söderblom: Geni og karakter*, Oslo.

BLÜCKERT, KJELL

2000 *The Church as Nation: A Study in Ecclesiology and Nationhood*, Frankfurt am Main.

BRÅKENHIELM, CARL REINHOLD, AND WINQVIST HOLLMAN, GUNHILD, EDS.

2002 *The Relevance of Theology: Nathan Söderblom and the Development of an Academic Discipline*, Uppsala.

BRILIOTH, YNGVE

1931 "Den ekumeniska gärningen," Karlström, 1931a, 273-347.

1933 "A Biographical Introduction," Söderblom, 1933a, xi-xxiv.

BRODD, SVEN-ERIK

1982 *Evangelisk katolictet: Ett studium av innehåll och funktion under 1800 och 1900-talen*, Lund (English summary).

CARLSON, EDGAR M.

1948 *The Reinterpretation of Luther*, Philadelphia.

CURTIS, CHARLES J.

1966 *Nathan Söderblom: Theologian of Revelation*, Chicago.

1967 *Nathan Söderblom: Ecumenical Pioneer*, Minneapolis.

DAHLGREN, SAM, ED.

1993 *Nathan Söderblom as a European*, Uppsala, *Tro och Tanke*, 1993:7.

DAHLQUIST, GUNNAR

1931 "Ärkebiskop Söderblom och missionen," Karlström, 1931, 235-272.

DRĂGOI, MACARIE, ED.

2014 *Artisan of Christian Unity between North and East: Nathan Söderblom. His Correspondence with Orthodox Personalities* (1896-1931), Stockholm.

DUFFY, EAMON

1997 *Saints and Sinners — A History of the Popes,* New Haven and London.

EHNMARK, ERLAND

1949 *Religionsproblemet hos Nathan Söderblom*, Lund.

EHRENSTRÖM, NILS

1954 "Movements for International Friendship and Life and Work, 1925-1948," Rouse and Neill, 1954, 545-596.

ERLING, MARIA AND GRANQUIST, MARK

2008 *The Augustana Story: Shaping Lutheran Identity in North America*, Minneapolis.

ESTBORN, SIGFRID

1944 *Under Guds grepp: En studie i Nathan Söderbloms forkunnelse,* Stockholm.

FERRÉ, NELS F. S.

1967 *Swedish Contributions to Modern Theology*, New York.

FRANZÉN, RUTH

2008 *Ruth Rouse among Students: Global, Missiological and Ecumenical Perspectives,* Uppsala.

FURBERG, TORE

2004 *Ett ekumeniskt tecken: Svenska kyrkans biskopsämbete i mission och ekumenik under första hälften av 1900-talet,* Uppsala (English summary).

GEHLIN, SARA

2008 "Nathan Söderblom, freden och ekumeniken," *Kyrkohistorisk Årsskrift,* 59-90 (English summary).

GRÖNQVIST, VIVI-ANN, ED.

2012 *Siri Dahlquist: Psalmförfattere, prästfru och teolog,* Skellefteå (English summary).

HANSSON, KLAS

2012 "Nathan Söderblom's ecumenical cope," *Studia Theologica — Nordic Journal of Theology,* 66:1, 62-79.

2014 *Svenska kyrkans primas: Ärkebiskopsämbetet i förändring 1914-1990,* Uppsala (English Summary).

HASTINGS, ADRIAN

1986 *A History of English Christianity 1920-1985*, London.

HENSON, HERBERT HENSLEY

1939 *Retrospect of an Unimportant Life*. Volume 2, 1920-1939, Oxford.

HOLMSTRÖM, FOLKE

1935 "Nathan Söderbloms självbiografiska uttalanden om ungdomsårens avgörande kriser," *Svensk Teologisk Kvartalskrift*, 321-329.

1937a *Uppenbarelsereligion och mystic: En undersökning av Nathan Söderbloms teologi*, Stockholm.

1937b "Bidrag till Nathan Söderbloms bibliografi: Teologiska prolegomena till metodisk Söderblomsforskning," *Svensk Teologisk Kvartalskrift*, 251-273.

JOHNSON, PAUL

1997 *The Papacy*, London.

JONSON, JONAS

2011 *Gustaf Aulén: Biskop och motståndsman*, Skellefteå.

2013 *Wounded Visions: Unity, Justice, and Peace in the World Church after 1968*, Grand Rapids.

KARLSTRÖM, NILS

1931a *Nathan Söderblom: In Memoriam*, Stockholm.

1931b "Rom und die Stockholmer Bewegung: Ein chronologischer Beitrag," *Kyrkohistorisk Årskrkift*, 100-112.

1947 *Kristna samförståndssträvanden under världskriget 1914-1918. Med särskild hänsyn till Nathan Söderbloms insats*, Stockholm.

1954 "Movements for International Friendship and Life and Work." Rouse and Neill, 507-542.

KUNTER, KATARINA, AND SCHJØRRING, JENS HOLGER, EDS.

2011 *European and Global Christianity: Challenges and Transformations in the Twentieth Century*, Göttingen.

LANGE, DIETZ

2011 *Nathan Söderblom und seine Zeit*, Göttingen.

LIEDGREN, EMIL

1931 "En Kristen människas frihet," Karlström, 1931a, 348-390.

LIPSEY, ROGER

2013 *Hammarskjöld: A Life*, Ann Arbor.

MALM, O. B.

1925 *Bilder och blad från ekumeniska motet i Stockholm 1925*, Stockholm.

MOGÅRD, ANDERS

2012 *Förtröstans hermeneutic: Nathan Söderbloms Lutheranvändning och traditionsbearbetnings problematic*, Skellefteå (English summary).

NEANDER, HERMAN

1912 "Den ortodoxa kyrkan i Grekland," *Kyrkohistorisk Årskrift*.

1932 *Med Nathan Söderblom: Krigsfångevård och ekumenisk gärning*, Stockholm.

NYSTEDT, OLLE

1931 *Nathan Söderblom: Kort levnadsteckning*, Stockholm.

OLSSON, SUSANNE, ED.

2013 *Sällskapet: Tro och vetande i 1900-talets Sverige*, Stockholm.

ÖSTERLIN, LARS, ED.

1995 *Churches of Northern Europe in Profile: A Thousand Years of Anglo-Nordic Relations*, Norwich.

PRIBILLA, PATER MAX

1931 "Drei Grundfragen der ökumenische Bewegung," *Kyrkohistorisk Årsskrift*, 113-127.

RENGMYR, BIRGITTA

1982 *Personlighetens sakrament: Lydia Wahlströms författarskap och tänkande i religiösa och kyrkliga frågor 1900-1925*, Uppsala.

ROUSE, RUTH

1954 "Voluntary Movements and the Changing Ecumenical Climate." Rouse and Neill, 307-349.

ROUSE, RUTH, AND NEILL, STEPHEN, EDS.

1954 *A History of the Ecumenical Movement 1517-1948*, Philadelphia and London.

RUNESTAM, STAFFAN

2004 *Söderblomsstudier*, Uppsala (English summaries).

2008 "Kyrkans uppgift: Ur Nathan Söderbloms efterkrigsprogram 1918-1919," *Kyrkohistorisk Årsskrift*, 91-97, Uppsala (English summary).

2013 *I kärlikens tjänst: Från Nathan och Anna Söderbloms humanitära verksamhet*, Uppsala.

SHARPE, ERIC J.

1984 *Karl Ludvig Reichelt: Missionary, Scholar, and Pilgrim*, Hong Kong.

1990 *Nathan Söderblom and the Study of Religion*, Chapel Hill.

1995 "Nathan Söderblom, 1866-1931." Bria, Ion, and Heller, Dagmar, *Ecumenical Pilgrims: Profiles of Pioneers in Christian Reconciliation*, 221-225, Geneva.

2014 *The Quest for the Kingdom of God: A Study in the History of a Vision*, Sydney.

SHARPE, ERIC J., AND HULTGÅRD, ANDERS, EDS.

1984 *Nathan Söderblom and His Contribution to the Study of Religion*, Uppsala.

SIEGMUND-SCHULTZE, FRIEDRICH

1966 *Nathan Söderblom: Briefe und Botschaften an einen deutschen Mitarbeiter. Gedächtnisschrift zum hundertsten Geburtstag des schwedischen Ertzbischofs*, Marburg/Lahn.

SJÖHOLM, ÖYVIND

1972 *Samvetets politik: Natanael Beskow och hans omvärld intill 1921*, Uppsala (English summary).

SÖDERBLOM, ANNA

1925 *En Amerikabok*, Stockholm.

1949 *På livets trottoir* 1, Lund.

1956 *På livets trottoir* 2, Lund.

SÖDERBLOM, NATHAN

1908 *Sveriges kyrka*, Stockholm.

1909 *Canterbury och Uppsala*, Stockholm.

1910a *Religionsproblemet inom katolicism och protestantism*, Stockholm.

1910b "Helgon" (*När stunderna växla och skrida*, II).

1911 *Tre heliga veckor*, Uppsala.

1914a "Ärkebiskop Stefans invigning i katedralen i Sens 1164," *Kyrkohistorisk Årskrift*, Uppsala.

1914b *Herdabref till prästerskapet och församlingarna i Uppsala ärkestift*, Uppsala.

1916 *Svenska kyrkans kropp och själ*, Stockholm.

1918a *Religionen och staten*, Stockholm.

1918b *Vaksamhet*, Stockholm.

1919 *Humor och melankoli och andra Lutherstudier*, Stockholm.

1922 *De kristnas enhet: Kyrkan och de frireligiösa i vårt land*, Stockholm.

1923a "Tidens tecken," *Kirke og kultur*, Årgång XXX, 193-209.

1923b *Christian Fellowship or the United Life and Work of Christendom*, Chicago.

1924a *Från Upsala till Rock Island: En predikofärd in nya världen*, Stockholm.

1924b "Evangelical Catholicity," *The Lutheran Church Review*, 43, 1-10.

1926 *Kristenhetens mote i Stockholm*, Stockholm.

1928 *Kristi pinas historia: En passionsbok*, Stockholm.

1929-30 *Tal och Skrifter* 1-6, Malmö.

(1930, 1963) *Uppenbarelsereligion: Förord av Erland Ehnmark*, Stockholm.

1931 "Pater Max Pribilla und die ökumenische Erweckung: Einige Randbemerkungen," *Kyrkohistorisk Årsskrift*, 1-99, Uppsala.

1933a *The Living God: Basal Forms of Personal Religion*. The Gifford Lectures, London.

1933b *Ett år: Ord för varje dag*. Samlade av Anna Söderblom, Stockholm.

1935 *När stunderna växla och skrida*, II, Stockholm.

1941a *Sommarminnen*. Utg. Anna Söderblom, Uppsala.

1941b *Svenskars fromhet: Ny följd*. Bearb. Anna Söderblom, Stockholm.

1966 *The Nature of Religion* (1903, 1930, 1963). Introduction by Edgar M. Carlson, Philadelphia.

1974 *Tal och essayer: Inledning och urval av Sven Stolpe*, Stockholm.

SÖDLING, MARIA

2010 *Oreda I skapelsen: Kvinnligt och manligt i Svenska kyrkan under 1920-och 30-talen*, Uppsala.

SUNDEEN, JOHAN

2008 *Andelivets agitator: J. A. Eklund, kristendomen och kulturen*, Lund (English summary).

SUNDÉN, HJALMAR

1959 *Religionen och rollerna: Ett psykologiskt stadium av fromheten*, Stockholm.

1969 *Älgskyttar, helgon och exegeter: Några religionspsykologiska uppsatser*, Stockholm.

SUNDKLER, BENGT

1968 *Nathan Söderblom: His Life and Work*, Lund.

1975 *Nathan Söderblom och hans möten*, Stockholm.

1984 "Nathan Söderblom — A Complex Personality," Sharpe and Hultgård, 6-16.

1993 "The Paris Years and Their Role on Nathan Söderblom's Ecumenical Life-Work," Dahlgren, 9-14.

TATLOW, TISSINGTON

1954 "The World Conference on Faith and Order," Rouse and Neill, 403-441.

TERGEL, ALF

1969 *Ungkyrkomännen, arbetarfrågen och nationalismen 1901-1911*, Stockholm.

THELIN, BENGT

2001 *Dag Hammarskjöld. Barnet. Skolpojken. Studenten,* Stockholm.

THIDEVALL, SVEN

2000 *Kampen om folkkyrkan: Ett folkkyrkligt reformprograms öden 1928-1932*, Stockholm.

THULIN, SVEN

1931-34 *Hågkomster och livsintryck av svenska män och kvinnor,* XII, XIV, XV, Uppsala.

TJEDER, DAVID

2008 "Det manliggörande tvivlet," Werner, 2008, 93-118.

TOMKINS, OLIVER STRATFORD

1954 "The Roman Catholic Church and the Ecumenical Movement 1910-1948," Rouse and Neill, 677-693.

TSETSIS, GEORGES

1992 "Nathan Söderblom and the Orthodox Church," Dahlgren, 89-102.

VISSER 'T HOOFT, W. A.

1980 *Memoirs*, Geneva.

WAHLSTRÖM, LYDIA

1949 *Trotsig och försagd: Mitt livs minnen*, Stockholm.

WEISSE, WOLFRAM

1993 "Irenic Mediator for Unity — Partisan Advocate for Truth: Nathan Söderblom's Initiatives for Peace and Justice," Dahlgren, 15-42.

WERNER, YVONNE MARIA

1996 *Världsvid men främmande: Den katolska kyrkan i Sverige 1873-1929*, Uppsala.

2008 *Kristen manlighet: Ideal och verklighet 1830-1940*, Lund.

Index of Selected Names

(This index does not include the names of biblical figures, well-known historical persons, nor names mentioned only in passing or authors found in "Sources and Literature.")

Åberg, Axeline, Anna's mother, 59
Abrahamson, Lars G., American, editor of "Augustana," 191, 195, 350
Ahnfelt, Oscar, composer of revival songs, 60, 117
Ailsa, Lady, Scottish clan leader, 416
Ailsa, Lord, Scottish clan leader, 416
Åkerberg, Hans, Swedish theologian, 430
Alfvén, Hugo, director of music at Uppsala University, 77, 190, 196, 290
Almkvist, Herman, professor of Semitic languages, 27, 33, 103
Ammundsen, Valdemar, Danish church historian, bishop, 220, 311
Anderberg, Algot, bishop of Visby, son-in-law, 419
Andersson, Axel, leader of Mission Covenant Church, 249
Andersson, Gunnar, explorer and paleontologist, 304
Andreæ, Tor, bishop of Linköping, 103, 185, 241, 295, 421f., 427
Ansgar, missionary bishop to Sweden (801–865), 25, 174, 228, 400
Atkinson, Henry, American ecumenist, 344, 350, 374
Aulén, Gustaf, theologian, bishop of Strängnäs, 101, 105, 132, 138, 145, 148, 198, 324, 337, 341, 361, 364, 385, 390, 404, 413, 414, 423

Bach, Johann Sebastian, German composer and organist, 112, 117, 125, 178, 210, 225, 235, 396, 420
Bahr, Sally von, philanthropist, 237, 255
Barth, Karl, Swiss theologian, 361, 404, 423
Beethoven, Ludwig van, German composer, 112, 117, 210
Bell, George K. A., bishop of Chichester, 373, 382, 406, 423
Benedict XV, pope (1914–1922), 189, 214, 221
Berg, Fridtjuv, minister of ecclesiastical affairs, 243
Berggrav, Eivind, journalist and later bishop of Oslo, 220, 223, 292, 311, 315, 364, 427
Bergson, Henri, French philosopher and Nobel laureate, 297, 415
Bernadotte, Carl, prince, chairman of Swedish Red Cross, 190, 262, 367, 391
Bernadotte, Oscar, prince, chairman of Swedish YMCA, 147

Bernhard, E. R., canon of Salisbury, 195
Beskow, Natanael, social reformer, artist, poet, 18, 24, 37, 291, 298, 359, 367
Bildt, Harald, diplomat, 129, 157, 199, 342, 367, 386, 397
Billing, Einar, bishop of Västerås, 37, 138, 144, 146ff., 150, 184, 273, 276, 324, 361, 373, 403, 411
Billing, Gottfrid, bishop of Lund, 54, 62, 63, 70, 146, 161, 180, 181, 182, 186f., 190ff., 242, 276, 290, 294, 298, 312, 347, 402
Birgitta, Swedish saint, 14th cent., 170, 174, 228, 382
Bismarck, Otto von, Prussian statesman, 83, 169
Björck, Albert, Swedenborgian minister, 89
Björkquist, Manfred, bishop of Stockholm, 125, 146, 148, 182ff., 251, 252, 260, 311, 312, 314, 411ff., 413, 418
Bjørnson, Bjørnstjerne, Norwegian writer, Nobel laureate, 32
Blume, Laurentius, physician, father-in-law of Nathan, 8, 12
Boberg, Ferdinand, architect, 172, 174
Bohlin, Torsten, bishop of Härnösand, 247
Boström, Christopher Jacob, philosopher, 17, 18, 20, 21, 28, 402
Brandelle, Gustaf, president of Augustana Synod, 354
Brändström, Elsa, nurse and philanthropist, 261, 367
Branting, Agnes, textile artist, 358
Branting, Hjalmar, first Social Democratic prime minister, 1, 90, 123, 183, 218, 254, 282, 407
Bremer, Fredrika, 19th-cent. Swedish writer and feminist, 356
Brent, Charles, Episcopalian bishop, founder of Faith and Order, 265, 341, 345, 374, 385
Brilioth, Yngve, archbishop, son-in-law, 136, 208, 216, 232, 256, 265, 268, 337, 385, 390, 395, 402, 418, 420, 423, 428
Bring, J. C., pastor, Stockholm, 70
Brodd, Sven-Erik, Swedish theologian, 430
Brown, Arthur J., American ecumenist, 339, 366ff., 369
Brown, William Adams, American theologian, 378
Brun, Lyder, Norwegian theologian, 220
Bunsen, Emma von, German deaconess, 373
Burge, Hubert, bishop of Oxford, 343, 345

Carlson, Edgar M., American theologian, 429
Cheng, Gideon, Chinese ecumenist, 373
Colliander, Immanuel, bishop of Mikkeli (Finland), 314
Coolidge, Calvin, American president, 349
Cullberg, John, theologian, bishop of Västerås, 412
Curtis, Charles J., biographer, 429

Dahlquist, Siri, poet and hymnist, 290, 326
Danell, Hjalmar, bishop of Skara, 51, 103, 182, 184f., 194, 251, 276, 302f.
Danielsson, Anders, missionary to India, linguist, 167
Darboy, Georges, archbishop of Paris, 84
Darmesteter, James, French Orientalist, 68

Darwin, Charles, English naturalist, 15, 159, 331
Davidson, Randall, archbishop of Canterbury, 135f., 137, 188, 195, 257, 263, 268f., 273, 360
Deissmann, Adolf, German theologian, 216, 287, 344, 374, 377
Delitzsch, Friedrich, German Assyriologist, 106
Dreyfus, Alfred, French artillery officer, 71f., 84
DuBois, Henri, Swiss professor, 222
Duchesne, Louis, French priest and philologist, 162

Eck, Johannes, Roman Catholic opponent of Luther, 279
Ede, Moore, dean of Worcester cathedral, 344
Edén, Nils, Liberal prime minister, 250, 376
Ehnmark, Erland, Swedish theologian, 429
Ehrensvärd, Albert, former foreign minister, 384
Eidem, Erling, successor archbishop, 422
Eklund, J. A., bishop of Karlstad, 18, 27, 37, 94f., 98f., 125, 145f., 148, 150, 182, 184ff., 190, 194, 196, 244, 246, 247f., 251, 290f., 298, 324, 376
Eklund, Pehr, professor in Lund, 50, 103, 105, 136
Ekman, Johan August, archbishop (1900–1913), 28, 62, 65, 91, 94, 117, 135, 138, 147, 180, 181, 195, 227
Ekman, Oscar, landowner, philanthropist, 129, 161, 208, 260, 346
Eldh, Carl, sculptor, 77, 122
Engberg, Arthur, leading Social Democrat, 245ff., 251ff., 292, 401f., 407, 412, 421
Engels, Friedrich, German philosopher, 82
Engström, Albert, member of Swedish Academy, 289
Eriksson, Christian, Swedish sculptor, 77
Eriksson, John, Swedish-American inventor, 124
Esbjörn, Lars Paul, leader in the Augustana Synod, 228
Eskil, archbishop of Lund, 12th cent., 193
Estborn, Sigfrid, theologian, 429
Eucken, Rudolf, German philosopher, Nobel laureate, 136, 216

Fagerlin, Anna, wife of Sam Fries, 31, 61
Fehr, Fredrik, pastor primarius at Storkyrkan, Stockholm, 50, 55, 59, 63, 66, 70, 80
Ferré, Nels F. S., Swedish-American theologian, 429
Fogelklou, Emilia, theologian, writer, mystic, 131, 162
Fogelqvist, Torsten, journalist, member of Swedish Academy, 204, 247
Folke, Erik, missionary to China, 23, 304
Forsell, Carl-August, sea captain, Anna's father, 59
Forsell, John, director of the Royal Opera, Anna's brother, 59, 77, 137
Frazer, James, Scottish anthropologist, 133, 415
Fries, Karl, YMCA secretary, 24, 31, 44, 47, 163, 184, 208, 337
Fröding, Gustaf, poet, 26, 143, 292

Gabrielsson, Samuel, priest and hymnist, 131ff., 290
Gandhi, Mahatma, Indian leader, 322, 325

Gardiner, Robert, Episcopalian lay ecumenist, 341, 345
Gardner, Lucy, British Quaker ecumenist, 341, 345, 367
Gasparri, Cardinal Pietro, Vatican secretary of state, 356, 390
Gehlin, Sara, Swedish theologian, 430
Geijer, Erik Gustaf, philosopher and historian (1783–1847), 17, 21, 103, 109, 122, 143, 174
Germanos V, partriarch of Constantinople, 257
Germanos Strenopoulos, archbishop of Thyateira and Great Britain, 357
Giampiccoli, Ernesto, moderator of the Waldensian Church, 339
Gifford, Adam, Scottish lord, philanthropist, 414
Glubokovski, Nikolai, Russian theologian, 228, 259, 373
Göransson, Nils Johan, professor of dogmatics, 31, 32, 49, 60f., 82, 85, 182
Gore, Charles, Anglican bishop and theologian, 341, 387
Gummerus, Jaako, bishop of Borgå (Porvoo) in Finland, 314, 317, 373
Gustaf V, king of Sweden (1907–1950), 248, 311, 380, 400, 401, 420
Gustaf Adolf, crown prince, king of Sweden (1950–1973), 305, 344, 364, 380
Gustavus Adolphus (Gustav II Adolf), Swedish king (d. 1632), 56, 62, 76f., 124, 126, 137, 152, 168f., 178, 193, 228, 284, 288, 317, 382

Hägerström, Axel, Swedish philosopher, 246
Haile Selassie (Ras Teferi), Ethiopian royalty, 302, 332-35
Hallén, Harald, priest, Social Democrat, 246, 249, 254, 324
Hammarskjöld, Agnes, mother of Dag, 209
Hammarskjöld, Dag, United Nations general secretary, 183, 209, 372
Hammarskjöld, Gustaf, American Episcopalian priest, 138f.
Hammarskjöld, Hjalmar, prime minister, father of Dag, 183, 186, 189f., 197, 289, 294, 315, 374
Hansson, Per Albin, Social Democrat, prime minister, 245, 350
Harding, Warren, American president, 347
Hårleman, Carl, architect, 18th cent., 17
Harnack, Adolf von, German professor, 71, 80, 86, 159, 176, 216, 285
Hauck, Albert, German professor, 177
Hecker, Isaac, American Roman Catholic priest, 158
Hedin, Sven, explorer of central Asia, 1, 125, 147
Heidenstam, Verner von, poet, novelist, Nobel laureate, 26, 30, 33, 125, 289, 293f.
Heiler, Friedrich, German convert to Lutheranism, 322, 323ff., 327, 358
Hellerström, Albert, rector of Swedish church in London, 268, 342
Hellqvist, Sven, priest of the Church of Sweden, 418
Henson, Herbert Hensley, bishop of Durham, 228, 273ff., 343
Hermann, Wilhelm, German professor, 83, 86, 216
Herold, Otto, Swiss ecumenical leader, 268, 337
Heuman, Ernst, missionary to India, bishop, 23, 303
Hjärne, Harald, professor of history, 1, 25, 27, 55, 62, 67, 95, 103, 142, 167f., 170, 186, 213, 215, 257, 294

Holmåsen, Jenny, teacher, hymnist, 290
Holmgren, Fritz, early missionary to China, 304
Holmquist, Hjalmar, professor of church history, 95
Holmström, Folke, Swedish theologian, 429
Holmström, Otto, artist, 77
Hoover, Herbert, American president, 349
Hügel, Friedrich von, Austrian-English Catholic mystic, 158

Ibsen, Henrik, Norwegian playwright, 32, 97
Ihmels, Ludwig, German systematic theologian, 177, 217, 287, 370, 378
Irbe, Kãrlis, Latvian bishop, 318f.

James, William, American psychologist, 415
Jansson, Erik, sect leader, founder of Bishop's Hill, 9
Jaurès, Jean, French socialist, 83f., 212
Joachim III, patriarch of Constantinople, 164
Johansson, Gustav, bishop of Åbo, 312ff., 373, 380, 397
Johansson, Martin, bishop of Härnösand, 26

Kaftan, Julius, German theologian, 34, 71
Kant, Immanuel, German philosopher, 95, 159
Kapler, Hermann, German ecumenist, 345
Karlfeldt, Erik Axel, poet, member of Swedish Academy, 95, 125, 290, 294f., 296f.
Karlström, Nils, biographer, 427
Keller, Adolf, Swiss ecumenist, 361
Kellogg, Frank B., American secretary of state, 410
Kempff, Georg, German organist, priest in Church of Sweden, 225, 236, 323
Kempff, Wilhelm, violinist, 420
Kesküla, Alexander, Estonian nationalist, 317
Key, Ellen, feminist, author, 125
Kierkegaard, Søren, Danish philosopher, 15, 28, 32, 97, 111, 160, 172, 295
Kittel, Rudolf, German professor, 177
Kjellström, Sven, violinist, 126, 137, 421
Klefbeck, Ernst, priest, Social Democrat, 254
Klein, Gottlieb, Jewish rabbi, Stockholm, 33, 72, 89, 98
Koch, Martin, author, Social Democrat, 251
Koechlin, Alphons, Swiss ecumenist, 367
Kolmodin, Adolf, New Testament professor, 103, 144, 184, 257, 327
Kolmodin, Johannes, representative in Constantinople, 257, 335, 342, 356f., 368
Kræpelin, Emil, German psychiatrist, 119
Kukk, Jacob, bishop of Estonia, 317f.
Kulenkampff-Post, Georg, German violinist, 323

Lagercrantz, Herman, industrialist, 305
Lagerfelt, Greta, philanthropist, 331
Lagerlöf, Selma, novelist, Nobel laureate, 1, 26, 105, 296, 298, 367
Lamprecht, Karl, rector of Leipzig University, 177
Lang, Andrew, Scottish anthropologist, 167

Lange, Dietz, German theologian, 430
Larsson, Carl, artist, 126
Larsson, Hans, philosopher, 298
Lasse Lucidor (Lars Johansson), 17th-cent. poet, 292
Lehman, Edvard, Danish scholar of religion, 132, 177
Lemire, J. A., French Catholic priest, 84
Leo XIII, pope (1878–1903), 84, 132, 154f.
Lie, Jonas, Norwegian author, 74, 77
Liedgren, Emil, hymnist, 95, 185, 290, 291, 359, 395
Lind, Jenny, Swedish singer, 170
Lindblad, Anna, mystic, donor, 130f.
Linderholm, Emanuel, church historian, 250, 276
Lindhagen, Carl, mayor of Stockholm, 407
Linné, Carl von, botanist (d. 1778), 16, 124, 382
Løchen, Sigurd, Norwegian businessman, 98
Loisy, Albert, French Catholic modernist, 131f., 158, 384
Lövgren, Nils, bishop of Västerås, 184, 231
Lundström, Herman, professor, 138, 182, 190
Lunn, Henry, English ecumenist, 336
Luther, Martin, church reformer, 52ff., 58, 87f., 92, 117f., 160, 169, 174, 177, 178, 193, 196, 204, 205, 234, 251, 270, 277-84, 304, 372, 424
Lynch, Frederick, American ecumenist, 337, 338, 340, 349
Lysander, Albert, leader of Swedish high church movement, 337

Macay, William Paton, English revivalist, 35f.
Macfarland, Charles, American churchman, 219, 268, 337, 340, 349, 355, 367f.
Magni, Petrus, 16th-cent. bishop of Västerås, 199
Malm, O. B., Swedish military officer, 361, 364
Mannerheim, Carl Gustaf, president of Finland, 314
Månsson, Fabian, Christian Social Democrat, 251f., 254, 408
Marx, Karl, philosopher, 15, 82
Masaryk, Tomáš, president of Czechoslovakia, 405
Mason, Arthur, canon of Canterbury, 140, 195
Meillet, Alfred, professor, Paris, 64
Mellander, Fredrik, Uppsala cathedral choir master, 237
Merry del Val, Rafael, cardinal, 162
Milles, Carl, sculptor, 77, 173
Mogård, Anders, Swedish theologian, 430
Möller, Gustav, Social Democrat, 245
Monod, Wilfred, French Reformed pastor, 45f., 83, 267, 348, 374, 382, 384, 406
Moody, Dwight L., American revivalist, 36, 39, 42ff., 46, 80
Motoda, S., bishop from Tokyo, 373
Mott, John R., American ecumenical pioneer, 39, 45, 147, 163, 165, 261, 303-4
Myrberg, Otto, New Testament professor, 28

Nathorst, Ruth, missionary to China, 304, 308
Naumann, Friedrich, German pastor and politician, 86
Neander, Herman, Greek- and Russian-speaking priest, 131, 261f.,

324, 339, 342, 356, 368, 385, 389, 393, 406
Newman, John Henry, British convert and cardinal, 158
Nietzsche, Friedrich, German philosopher, 67, 124, 143
Nobel, Alfred, inventor, founder of the Nobel Prize, 77, 408f.
Nordenskjöld, Adolf, explorer, 125
Nordling, Gustav, Swedish consul general in Paris, 92
Nordström, N. J., leader of Baptist Church, 249
Noreen, Adolf, professor of Nordic languages, 25, 103, 294
Nygren, Anders, theologian, later bishop of Lund, 385, 404
Nystedt, Olle, biographer, 427
Nyström, Erik, geologist in China, 304f.

Olofsdotter, Margta, grandparent, 7
Olsson, Jon, grandparent, 7
Olsson, Olof, minister of ecclesiastical affairs, 244, 246
Oscar II, king of Sweden (1872–1905), 89f., 123, 137, 283
Ostenfeld, Harald, bishop of Copenhagen, 220, 221f., 255
Österlin, Gustaf, China missionary, 306f.
Otto, Rudolf, German scholar of comparative religion, 95

Papadopoulos, Chrysostomos, archbishop of Athens, 339
Petri, Laurentius, Swedish reformer, 199, 205, 275, 420
Petri, Olaus, Swedish reformer, 174, 234
Pfannenstill, Magnus, theologian, 385
Pfleiderer, Otto, German professor, 71
Photios, patriarch of Alexandria, 360, 363f., 368, 372, 374, 377
Pius IX, pope (1846–1878), 155
Pius X, pope (1903–1914), 85, 154f., 162, 189, 214
Pius XI, pope (1922–1939), 388, 389, 391f.
Platon, Orthodox bishop, martyr in Estonia, 318
Poelchau, P. H., German bishop in Latvia, 318
Poincaré, Raymond, premier of France, 348
Pribilla, Max, German Jesuit theologian, 393

Quirelle, Barbie de, French journalist and translator, 92

Rastamji Edulji, Parsi high priest, 116
Reichelt, Karl Ludvig, Norwegian missionary to China, 307ff.
Reinholds, James, American civil servant, 39, 41, 354
Reuterdahl, Henrik, archbishop (1856–1870), 105
Ribbing, Gustaf, district judge, 136, 196, 315
Richards, Timothy, Welsh university-founder in China, 304
Ritschl, Albrecht, German theologian, 49ff., 65, 80, 109, 204, 210
Rodhe, Edvard, bishop of Lund, 402
Rodhe, Edvard H., bishop of Gothenburg, 190
Rodling, Gerda, personal secretary to Söderblom, 208, 260, 372
Rompolla, Mariano, Italian cardinal, 162
Roosevelt, Theodore, American president, 136
Rosendal, Gunnar, leader of Swedish high church movement, 364

Rosenius, C. O., 19th-cent. evangelical revivalist, 9, 204
Rossum, Cardinal Willem Marinus van, Vatican official, 390
Rudin, Waldemar, New Testament professor, mystic, 24, 28, 33, 42, 80, 89, 116, 210, 292, 295
Rundgren, Viktor, bishop of Visby, 276
Runestam, Arvid, bishop of Karlstad, son-in-law, 413
Runestam, Staffan, librarian, grandson, 430
Rydberg, Viktor, novelist, poet, 20, 28, 31, 55, 67, 96, 295
Rydén, Vrner, minister of ecclesiastical affairs, 244, 249
Ryle, Herbert, bishop of Winchester, 128, 136f., 139

Sabatier, Auguste, professor in Paris, 79f., 89, 93, 95, 98, 101, 120, 152, 159
Sagnier, Marc, French politician, 85
Sahlin, Carl Yngve, rector magnificus, Uppsala University, 18
Sandegren, Paul, missionary to South India, 192, 301, 342, 386, 406
Sankey, Ira D., American gospel songwriter, 36, 39, 351
Schartau, Henrik, priest and influential preacher, 143, 284
Schéele, K. H. G. von, bishop of Visby, 17, 89, 190, 192, 242, 283
Schleiermacher, Friedrich, German theologian (d. 1834), 50, 105, 159
Schück, Henrik, professor of literature, rector magnificus, 103, 143, 192
Schweitzer, Albert, mission doctor, theologian, organist, 228, 302, 329-32
Segerstedt, Torgny, outstanding anti-Nazi publicist, 103f., 136, 247, 383f., 412
Seydel, Rudolf, German philosopher, 95
Sharpe, Eric, Australian theologian, 430
Siegmund-Schultze, Friedrich, German theologian, 219, 267, 287, 367
Sigfrid, 11th-cent. missionary bishop to Sweden, 25
Simons, Walter, German foreign minister, 337, 406
Singh, Sadhu Sundar, Indian Sikh, convert to Christianity, 325, 326-29
Sjöblom, P. H., Social Democratic leader, 252, 254
Sjögren, Emil, composer, 77
Sjöstedt, Anders, military official, philanthropist, 337, 340, 346, 356, 364, 376, 386
Sköld, Per Edvin, Social Democratic leader, 245
Skrefsrud, Lars, Norwegian missionary to India, 22, 23, 302
Smyth, Newman, New England ecumenist, 41
Söderblom, Anna, *nee* Forsell, 55, 57f., 60f., 63, 67ff., 71ff., 80, 98f., 118, 157, 180f., 184f., 187f., 194, 207, 209, 250, 255, 292, 320, 324, 346, 348, 350-56, 360, 384, 409, 416, 419, 425, 428
Söderblom, Brita, daughter, 79, 85, 187, 216
Söderblom, Bror Carl, son, 132
Söderblom, Elsa, sister of Nathan, 12, 58, 199
Söderblom, Hanna, sister of Nathan, 12, 63, 70, 199
Söderblom, Helge, son, 79, 85, 177, 187, 400
Söderblom, Ingrid, daughter, 79

Söderblom, Johan, brother of Nathan, 12, 199
Söderblom, Jon Olof, son, 209, 310, 348, 350
Söderblom, Jonas, father of Nathan, 5ff., 10f., 14f., 70, 80, 98, 120
Söderblom, Lucie, daughter, 118
Söderblom, Sophia, mother of Nathan, 5, 10, 12f., 35, 59
Söderblom, Staffan, son, 79
Söderblom, Svante, younger brother of Nathan, 5, 12, 35, 199
Söderblom, Sven, son, 79, 177, 221, 352, 410
Söderblom, Yvonne, daughter, 210
Sommar, Magnus, first Lutheran bishop of Strängnäs, 201
Sörensen-Ringi, Harald, Swedish sculptor, 77, 122
Soulier, Edouard, French pastor, 259
Spencer, Herbert, English philosopher and anthropologist, 108
Spiecker, F. A., German industrialist and ecumenist, 287
Staaff, Karl, Liberal prime minister, 26, 182f., 186, 190
Stadener, Sam, bishop and government minister, 284, 390, 402, 403f., 422
Stange, Erich, German theologian, 371
Stefan, first archbishop of Uppsala, consecrated 1164, 191ff., 194, 380
Stoecker, Adolf, German pastor, 86
Stork, Charles Wharton, American translator, 359
Strauss, David Friedrich, German theologian, 83
Strenopoulos, Germanos, metropolitan of Thyateira, 163ff., 274, 276, 339, 356, 366, 377
Strindberg, August, playwright, novelist, painter, 1, 33, 74f., 125, 143, 292ff.
Strömstedt, August, Methodist leader, 249
Sundberg, Anton Niklas, archbishop (1870–1900), 14, 18, 28, 64, 68, 79, 90, 99, 136, 180
Sundkler, Bengt, biographer of Söderblom, 181, 208, 429
Svensson-Pihl, Berta, calligrapher, 376
Swedenborg, Emanuel, Swedish philosopher (d. 1772), 76, 327
Sydow, Hjalmar von, leader of Swedish employers, 408

Tagore, Rabindranath, Indian poet, Nobel laureate, 322, 325
Talbot, Edward, bishop of Winchester, 267
Tandberg, Jens Frølich, bishop of Oslo, 221f., 256
Taylor, Hudson, founder of China Inland Mission, 35
Tegnér, Esaias, poet, bishop of Växjö, 143
Temple, William, archbishop of Canterbury, 343, 423
Tiele, C. P., Dutch scholar of world religions, 105, 323, 415
Tikhon, patriarch of Moscow, 368
Timotheos, Mar, metropolitan of Mar Thoma Church, 373
Tolstoy, Leo, Russian author, 79, 87f., 97
Torén, Carl Axel, professor and dean, 106
Tottie, Henry William, bishop of Kalmar, 68, 135, 138f.
Tutu, Desmond, South African bishop, 352
Tyrell, George, Irish Jesuit priest, 158

Ullman, Uddo Lechard, bishop of Strängnäs, 190
Ulvsson, Jakob, archbishop (d. 1521), 77
Undén, Östen, foreign minister, 382

Vannutelli, Vincent, Italian cardinal, 133, 161
Victoria, queen of Sweden (d. 1930), 288, 400
Victoria, queen of the United Kingdom (d. 1901), 68, 161
Visser 't Hooft, Willem, Dutch ecumenist, 371
Vivikananda, Swami, Indian neo-Hindu, 325
Vodskov, Hans Sofus, Danish scholar of religion, 66

Wachtmeister, Axel, Swedish count and philanthropist, 312
Wahlström, Lydia, teacher, feminist, 58, 67, 250
Waldenström, P. P., founder, Swedish Mission Covenant Church, 9, 14
Wallenberg, Knut, banker, minister of foreign affairs, 172, 186, 199
Wallin, Johan Olof, hymnist, archbishop, 97, 174, 290f., 298
Wang Chenting, Chinese minister of foreign affairs, 164f.
Weiss, Johannes, German theologian, 88
Wellhausen, Julius, German biblical scholar, 33, 37, 159
Wennerberg, Gunnar, composer, governor, 60, 117, 376
Westin, Gunnar, church historian, Baptist leader, 249
Westman, Knut B., China missionary, professor, 147, 186, 215, 219, 223, 256, 302, 306f., 344, 347, 422
Whitehead, Alfred North, English philosopher, 415, 429
Wiberg, Anders, founder, Swedish Baptist Church, 9
Wicksell, Knut, economist, 27
Widner, Nils, pastor primarius in Stockholm, 220, 311, 346
Widor, Charles-Marie, French organist, 329
Wijk, Hjalmar, 157
Wikander, Ingeborg, China missionary, 147, 303
Wikner, Pontus, philosopher, 16
Wilhelm II, German emperor until 1918, 68, 83, 86, 283, 285
Williams, Gershom Mott, Episcopalian bishop, 138f.
Wilson, Woodrow, American president, 221, 263
Winnington-Ingram, Arthur, bishop of London, 136f.
Wolde-Selassie, Blata Hiruy, Ethiopian statesman, 334
Woods, Frank Theodore, bishop of Peterborough, Winchester, 273ff., 343, 364, 366, 370, 374
Wordsworth, John, bishop of Salisbury, 136ff., 170
Wrangel, Herman, Swedish ambassador, 134

Zettervall, Helgo, architect, 17
Ziegenbalg, Bartholomew, Danish missionary to India, 299
Zinzendorf, Nicolaus, German pietist, 127
Zorn, Anders, Swedish artist, portrait painter, 75, 125f., 278, 296f.